SAP Data Services 4.x Cookbook

Delve into the SAP Data Services environment to efficiently prepare, implement, and develop ETL processes

Ivan Shomnikov

[PACKT] enterprise
PUBLISHING professional expertise distilled

BIRMINGHAM - MUMBAI

SAP Data Services 4.x Cookbook

First published: November 2015

Production reference: 1261115

Published by Packt Publishing Ltd.
Livery Place
35 Livery Street
Birmingham B3 2PB, UK.

ISBN 978-1-78217-656-5

www.packtpub.com

Credits

Author

Ivan Shomnikov

Reviewers

Andrés Aguado Aranda

Dick Groenhof

Bernard Timbal Duclaux de Martin

Sridhar Sunkaraneni

Meenakshi Verma

Commissioning Editor

Vinay Argekar

Acquisition Editors

Shaon Basu

Kevin Colaco

Content Development Editor

Merint Mathew

Technical Editor

Humera Shaikh

Copy Editors

Brandt D'mello

Shruti Iyer

Karuna Narayanan

Sameen Siddiqui

Project Coordinator

Francina Pinto

Proofreader

Safis Editing

Indexer

Monica Ajmera Mehta

Production Coordinator

Nilesh Mohite

Cover Work

Nilesh Mohite

About the Author

Ivan Shomnikov is an SAP analytics consultant specializing in the area of Extract, Transform, and Load (ETL). He has in-depth knowledge of the data warehouse life cycle processes (DWH design and ETL development) and extensive hands-on experience with both the SAP Enterprise Information Management (Data Services) technology stack and the SAP BusinessObjects reporting products stack (Web Intelligence, Designer, Dashboards).

Ivan has been involved in the implementation of complex BI solutions on the SAP BusinessObjects Enterprise platform in major New Zealand companies across different industries. He also has a strong background as an Oracle database administrator and developer.

This is my first experience of writing a book, and I would like to thank my partner and my son for their patience and support.

About the Reviewers

Andrés Aguado Aranda is a 26-year-old computer engineer from Spain. His experience has given him a really technical background in databases, data warehouse, and business intelligence.

Andrés has worked in different business sectors, such as banking, public administrations, and energy, since 2012 in data-related positions.

> This book is my first stint as a reviewer, and it has been really interesting and valuable to me, both personally and professionally.
>
> I would like to thank my family and friends for always being willing to help me when I needed. Also, I would like to thank to my former coworker and currently friend, Antonio Martín-Cobos, a BI reporting analyst who really helped me get this opportunity.

Dick Groenhof started his professional career in 1990 after finishing his studies in business information science at Vrije Universiteit Amsterdam. Having worked as a software developer and service management consultant for the first part of his career, he became active as a consultant in the business intelligence arena since 2005.

Dick has been a lead consultant on numerous SAP BI projects, designing and implementing successful solutions for his customers, who regard him as a trusted advisor. His core competences include both frontend (such as Web Intelligence, Crystal Reports, and SAP Design Studio) and backend tools (such as SAP Data Services and Information Steward). Dick is an early adopter of the SAP HANA platform, creating innovative solutions using HANA Information Views, Predictive Analysis Library, and SQLScript.

He is a Certified Application Associate in SAP HANA and SAP BusinessObjects Web Intelligence 4.1. Currently, Dick works as senior HANA and big data consultant for a highly respected and innovative SAP partner in the Netherlands.

He is a strong believer in sharing his knowledge with regard to SAP HANA and SAP Data Services by writing blogs (at http://www.dickgroenhof.com and http://www.thenextview.nl/blog) and speaking at seminars.

Dick is happily married to Emma and is a very proud father of his son, Christiaan, and daughter, Myrthe.

Bernard Timbal Duclaux de Martin is a business intelligence architect and technical expert with more than 15 years of experience. He has been involved in several large business intelligence system deployments and administration in banking and insurance companies. In addition, Bernard has skills in modeling, data extraction, transformation, loading, and reporting design. He has authored four books, including two regarding SAP BusinessObjects Enterprise administration.

Meenakshi Verma has been a part of the IT industry since 1998. She is an experienced business systems specialist having the CBAP and TOGAF certifications. Meenakshi is well-versed with a variety of tools and techniques used for business analysis, such as SAP BI, SAP BusinessObjects, Java/J2EE technologies, and others. She is currently based in Toronto, Canada, and works with a leading utility company.

Meenakshi has helped technically review many books published by Packt Publishing across various enterprise solutions. Her earlier works include *JasperReports for Java Developers, Java EE 5 Development using GlassFish Application Server, Practical Data Analysis and Reporting with BIRT, EJB 3 Developer Guide, Learning Dojo,* and *IBM WebSphere Application Server 8.0 Administration Guide.*

I'd like to thank my father, Mr. Bhopal Singh, and mother, Mrs. Raj Bala, for laying a strong foundation in me and giving me their unconditional love and support. I also owe thanks and gratitude to my husband, Atul Verma, for his encouragement and support throughout the reviewing of this book and many others; my ten-year-old son, Prieyaansh Verma, for giving me the warmth of his love despite my hectic schedules; and my brother, Sachin Singh, for always being there for me.

www.PacktPub.com

Support files, eBooks, discount offers, and more

For support files and downloads related to your book, please visit www.PacktPub.com.

Did you know that Packt offers eBook versions of every book published, with PDF and ePub files available? You can upgrade to the eBook version at www.PacktPub.com and as a print book customer, you are entitled to a discount on the eBook copy. Get in touch with us at service@packtpub.com for more details.

At www.PacktPub.com, you can also read a collection of free technical articles, sign up for a range of free newsletters and receive exclusive discounts and offers on Packt books and eBooks.

https://www2.packtpub.com/books/subscription/packtlib

Do you need instant solutions to your IT questions? PacktLib is Packt's online digital book library. Here, you can search, access, and read Packt's entire library of books.

Why subscribe?

- ▶ Fully searchable across every book published by Packt
- ▶ Copy and paste, print, and bookmark content
- ▶ On demand and accessible via a web browser

Free access for Packt account holders

If you have an account with Packt at www.PacktPub.com, you can use this to access PacktLib today and view 9 entirely free books. Simply use your login credentials for immediate access.

Instant updates on new Packt books

Get notified! Find out when new books are published by following @PacktEnterprise on Twitter or the *Packt Enterprise* Facebook page.

Table of Contents

Preface

SAP Data Services delivers an enterprise-class solution to build data integration processes as well as perform data quality and data profiling tasks, allowing you to govern your data in a highly-efficient way.

Some of the tasks that Data Services helps accomplish include: migration of the data between databases or applications, extracting data from various source systems into flat files, data cleansing, data transformation using either common database-like functions or complex custom-built functions that are created using an internal scripting language, and of course, loading data into your data warehouse or external systems. SAP Data Services has an intuitive user-friendly graphical interface, allowing you to access all its powerful Extract, Transform, and Load (ETL) capabilities from the single Designer tool. However, getting started with SAP Data Services can be difficult, especially for people who have little or no experience in ETL development. The goal of this book is to guide you through easy-to-understand examples of building your own ETL architecture. The book can also be used as a reference to perform specific tasks as it provides real-world examples of using the tool to solve data integration problems.

What this book covers

Chapter 1, Introduction to ETL Development, explains what Extract, Transform, and Load (ETL) processes are, and what role Data Services plays in ETL development. It includes the steps to configure the database environment used in recipes of the book.

Chapter 2, Configuring the Data Services Environment, explains how to install and configure all Data Services components and applications. It introduces the Data Services development GUI—the Designer tool—with the simple example of "Hello World" ETL code.

Chapter 3, Data Services Basics – Data Types, Scripting Language, and Functions, introduces the reader to Data Services internal scripting language. It explains various categories of functions that are available in Data Services, and gives the reader an example of how scripting language can be used to create custom functions.

Chapter 4, Dataflow – Extract, Transform, and Load, introduces the most important processing unit in Data Service, dataflow object, and the most useful types of transformations that can be performed inside a dataflow. It gives the reader examples of extracting data from source systems and loading data into target data structures.

Chapter 5, Workflow – Controlling Execution Order, introduces another Data Services object, workflow, which is used to group other workflows, dataflows, and script objects into execution units. It explains the conditional and loop structures available in Data Services.

Chapter 6, Job – Building the ETL Architecture, brings the reader to the job object level and reviews the steps used in the development process to make a successful and robust ETL solution. It covers the monitoring and debugging functionality available in Data Services and embedded audit features.

Chapter 7, Validating and Cleansing Data, introduces the concepts of validating methods, which can be applied to the data passing through the ETL processes in order to cleanse and conform it according to the defined Data Quality standards.

Chapter 8, Optimizing ETL Performance, is one of the first advanced chapters, which starts explaining complex ETL development techniques. This particular chapter helps the user understand how the existing processes can be optimized further in Data Services in order to make sure that they run quickly and efficiently, consuming as less computer resources as possible with the least amount of execution time.

Chapter 9, Advanced Design Techniques, guides the reader through advanced data transformation techniques. It introduces concepts of Change Data Capture methods that are available in Data Services, pivoting transformations, and automatic recovery concepts.

Chapter 10, Developing Real-time Jobs, introduces the concept of nested structures and the transforms that work with nested structures. It covers the mains aspects of how they can be created and used in Data Services real-time jobs. It also introduces new a Data Services component—Access Server.

Chapter 11, Working with SAP Applications, is dedicated to the topic of reading and loading data from SAP systems with the example of the SAP ERP system. It presents the real-life use case of loading data into the SAP ERP system module.

Chapter 12, Introduction to Information Steward, covers another SAP product, Information Steward, which accompanies Data Services and provides a comprehensive view of the organization's data, and helps validate and cleanse it by applying Data Quality methods.

What you need for this book

To use the examples given in this book, you will need to download and make sure that you are licensed to use the following software products:

- SQL Server Express 2012
- SAP Data Services 4.2 SP4 or higher
- SAP Information Steward 4.2 SP4 or higher
- SAP ERP (ECC)
- SoapUI—5.2.0

Who this book is for

The book will be useful to application developers and database administrators who want to get familiar with ETL development using SAP Data Services. It can also be useful to ETL developers or consultants who want to improve and extend their knowledge of this tool. The book can also be useful to data and business analysts who want to take a peek at the backend of BI development. The only requirement of this book is that you are familiar with the SQL language and general database concepts. Knowledge of any kind of programming language will be a benefit as well.

Sections

In this book, you will find several headings that appear frequently (Getting ready, How to do it, How it works, There's more, and See also).

To give clear instructions on how to complete a recipe, we use these sections as follows:

Getting ready

This section tells you what to expect in the recipe, and describes how to set up any software or any preliminary settings required for the recipe.

How to do it...

This section contains the steps required to follow the recipe.

How it works...

This section usually consists of a detailed explanation of what happened in the previous section.

There's more...

This section consists of additional information about the recipe in order to make the reader more knowledgeable about the recipe.

See also

This section provides helpful links to other useful information for the recipe.

Conventions

In this book, you will find a number of text styles that distinguish between different kinds of information. Here are some examples of these styles and an explanation of their meaning.

Code words in text, database table names, folder names, filenames, file extensions, pathnames, dummy URLs, user input, and Twitter handles are shown as follows: "We can include other contexts through the use of the `include` directive."

A block of code is set as follows:

```
select *
from dbo.al_langtext txt
  JOIN dbo.al_parent_child pc
  on txt.parent_objid = pc.descen_obj_key
where
  pc.descen_obj = 'WF_continuous';
```

When we wish to draw your attention to a particular part of a code block, the relevant lines or items are set in bold:

```
AlGUIComment ("ActaName_1" = 'RSavedAfterCheckOut', "ActaName_2" =
  'RDate_created', "ActaName_3" = 'RDate_modified', "ActaValue_1"
  = 'YES', "ActaValue_2" = 'Sat Jul 04 16:52:33 2015',
  "ActaValue_3" = 'Sun Jul 05 11:18:02 2015', "x" = '-1', "y" = '-
  1')
CREATE PLAN WF_continuous::'7bb26cd4-3e0c-412a-81f3-b5fdd687f507'(
  )
DECLARE
  $1_Directory VARCHAR(255) ;
  $1_File VARCHAR(255) ;
BEGIN
  AlGUIComment ("UI_DATA_XML" = '<UIDATA><MAINICON><LOCATION><X>
  0</X><Y>0</Y></LOCATION><SIZE><CX>216</CX><CY>-
  179</CY></SIZE></MAINICON><DESCRIPTION><LOCATION><X>0</X><Y>-
  190</Y></LOCATION><SIZE><CX>200</CX><CY>200
  </CY></SIZE><VISIBLE>0</VISIBLE></DESCRIPTION></U
```

```
IDATA>', "ui_display_name" = 'script', "ui_script_text" =
  '$1_Directory = \'C:\\\\AW\\\\Files\\\\\';
$1_File = \'flag.txt\';

$g_count = $g_count + 1;

print(\'Execution #\'||$g_count);
print(\'Starting  \'||workflow_name()||\' ...\');
sleep(10000);
print(\'Finishing \'||workflow_name()||\' ...\');', "x" = '116',
  "y" = '-175')
BEGIN_SCRIPT
$1_Directory = 'C:\\AW\\Files\\';$1_File = 'flag.txt';$g_count =
  ($g_count + 1);print(('Execution #' ||
  $g_count));print((('Starting  ' || workflow_name()) || '
  ...'));sleep(10000);print((('Finishing ' || workflow_name()) ||
  ' ...'));END
END
  SET ("loop_exit" = 'fn_check_flag($1_Directory, $1_File)',
  "loop_exit
_option" = 'yes', "restart_condition" = 'no', "restart_count" =
  '10', "restart_count_option" = 'yes', "workflow_type" =
  'Continuous')
```

Any command-line input or output is written as follows:

```
setup.exe SERVERINSTALL=Yes
```

New terms and **important words** are shown in bold. Words that you see on the screen, for example, in menus or dialog boxes, appear in the text like this: "Open the workflow properties again to edit the continuous options using the **Continuous Options** tab."

> Warnings or important notes appear in a box like this.

> Tips and tricks appear like this.

Reader feedback

Feedback from our readers is always welcome. Let us know what you think about this book—what you liked or disliked. Reader feedback is important for us as it helps us develop titles that you will really get the most out of.

To send us general feedback, simply e-mail `feedback@packtpub.com`, and mention the book's title in the subject of your message.

If there is a topic that you have expertise in and you are interested in either writing or contributing to a book, see our author guide at `www.packtpub.com/authors`.

Customer support

Now that you are the proud owner of a Packt book, we have a number of things to help you to get the most from your purchase.

Downloading the example code

You can download the example code files from your account at `http://www.packtpub.com` for all the Packt Publishing books you have purchased. If you purchased this book elsewhere, you can visit `http://www.packtpub.com/support` and register to have the files e-mailed directly to you.

Downloading the color images of this book

We also provide you with a PDF file that has color images of the screenshots/diagrams used in this book. The color images will help you better understand the changes in the output. You can download this file from: `https://www.packtpub.com/sites/default/files/downloads/6565EN_Graphics.pdf`.

Errata

Although we have taken every care to ensure the accuracy of our content, mistakes do happen. If you find a mistake in one of our books—maybe a mistake in the text or the code—we would be grateful if you could report this to us. By doing so, you can save other readers from frustration and help us improve subsequent versions of this book. If you find any errata, please report them by visiting `http://www.packtpub.com/submit-errata`, selecting your book, clicking on the **Errata Submission Form** link, and entering the details of your errata. Once your errata are verified, your submission will be accepted and the errata will be uploaded to our website or added to any list of existing errata under the Errata section of that title.

To view the previously submitted errata, go to `https://www.packtpub.com/books/content/support` and enter the name of the book in the search field. The required information will appear under the **Errata** section.

Piracy

Piracy of copyrighted material on the Internet is an ongoing problem across all media. At Packt, we take the protection of our copyright and licenses very seriously. If you come across any illegal copies of our works in any form on the Internet, please provide us with the location address or website name immediately so that we can pursue a remedy.

Please contact us at `copyright@packtpub.com` with a link to the suspected pirated material.

We appreciate your help in protecting our authors and our ability to bring you valuable content.

Questions

If you have a problem with any aspect of this book, you can contact us at `questions@packtpub.com`, and we will do our best to address the problem.

1
Introduction to ETL Development

In this chapter, we will cover:

- ▶ Preparing a database environment
- ▶ Creating a source system database
- ▶ Defining and creating staging area structures
- ▶ Creating a target data warehouse

Introduction

Simply put, **Extract-Transform-Load** (**ETL**) is an engine of any data warehouse. The nature of the ETL system is straightforward:

- ▶ Extract data from operational databases/systems
- ▶ Transform data according to the requirements of your data warehouse so that the different pieces of data can be used together
- ▶ Apply data quality transformation methods in order to cleanse data and ensure that it is reliable before it gets loaded into a data warehouse

> ▸ Load conformed data into a data warehouse so that end users can access it via reporting tools, using client applications directly, or with the help of SQL-based query tools

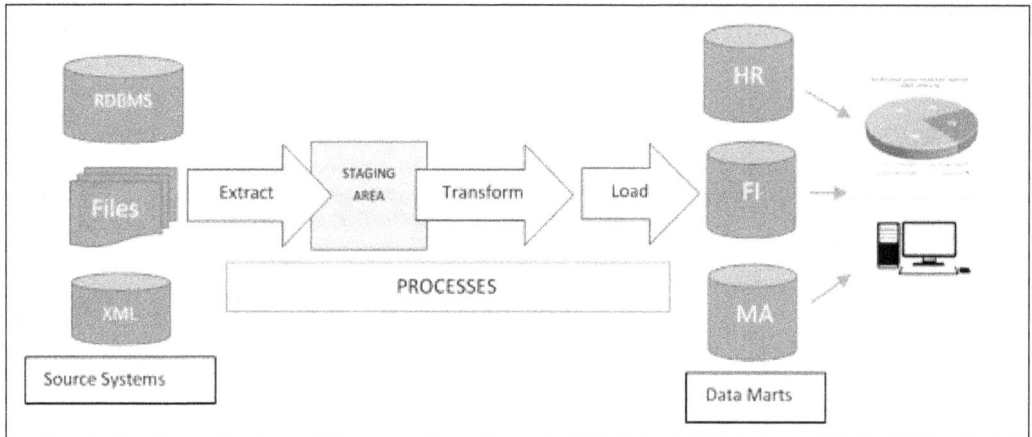

While your data warehouse delivery structures or data marts represent the frontend or, in other words, what users see when they access the data, the ETL system itself is a backbone backend solution that does all the work of moving data and getting it ready in time for users to use. Building the ETL system can be a really challenging task, and though it is not part of the data warehouse data structures, it is definitely the key factor in defining the success of the data warehouse solution as a whole. In the end, who wants to use a data warehouse where the data is unreliable, corrupted, or sometimes even missing? This is exactly what ETL is responsible for getting right.

The following data structure types most often used in ETL development to move data between sources and targets are flat files, XML datasets, and DBMS tables, both in normalized schemas and dimensional data models. When choosing an ETL solution, you might face two simple choices: building a handcoded ETL solution or using a commercial one.

The following are some advantages of a handcoded ETL solution:

> ▸ A programming language allows you to build your own sophisticated transformations
>
> ▸ You are more flexible in building the ETL architecture as you are not limited by the vendor's ETL abilities
>
> ▸ Sometimes, it can be a cheap way of building a few simplistic ETL processes, whereas buying an ETL solution from a vendor can be overkill
>
> ▸ You do not have to spend time learning the commercial ETL solution's architecture and functionality

Here are some advantages of a commercial ETL solution:

▶ This is more often a simpler, faster, and cheaper development option as a variety of existing tools allow you to build a very sophisticated ETL architecture quickly

▶ You do not have to be a professional programmer to use the tool

▶ It automatically manages ETL metadata by collecting, storing, and presenting it to the ETL developer, which is another important aspect of any ETL solution

▶ It has a huge range of additional ready-to-use functionality, from built-in schedulers to various connectors to existing systems, built-in data lineages, impact analysis reports, and many others

In the majority of DWH projects, the commercial ETL solution from a specific vendor, in spite of the higher immediate cost, eventually saves you a significant amount of money on the development and maintenance of ETL code.

SAP Data Services is an ETL solution provided by SAP and is part of the Enterprise Information Management product stack, which also includes SAP Information Steward; we will review this in one of the last chapters of this book.

Preparing a database environment

This recipe will lead you through the further steps of preparing the working environment, such as preparing a database environment to be utilized by ETL processes as a source and staging and targeting systems for the migrated and transformed data.

Getting ready

To start the ETL development, we need to think about three things: the system that we will source the data from, our staging area (for initial extracts and as a preliminary storage for data during subsequent transformation steps), and finally, the data warehouse itself, to which the data will be eventually delivered.

How to do it...

Throughout the book, we will use a 64-bit environment, so ensure that you download and install the 64-bit versions of software components. Perform the following steps:

1. Let's start by preparing our source system. For quick deployment, we will choose the Microsoft SQL Server 2012 Express database, which is available for download at `http://www.microsoft.com/en-nz/download/details.aspx?id=29062`.

2. Click on the **Download** button and select the **SQLEXPRWT_x64_ENU.exe** file in the list of files that are available for download. This package contains everything required for the installation and configuration of the database server: the SQL Server Express database engine and the SQL Server Management Studio tool.

3. After the download is complete, run the executable file and follow the instructions on the screen. The installation of SQL Server 2012 Express is extremely straightforward, and all options can be set to their default values. There is no need to create any default databases during or after the installation as we will do it a bit later.

How it works...

After you have completed the installation, you should be able to run the SQL Server Management Studio application and connect to your database engine using the settings provided during the installation process.

If you have done everything correctly, you should see the "green" state of your Database Engine connection in the Object Explorer window of SQL Server Management Studio, as shown in the following screenshot:

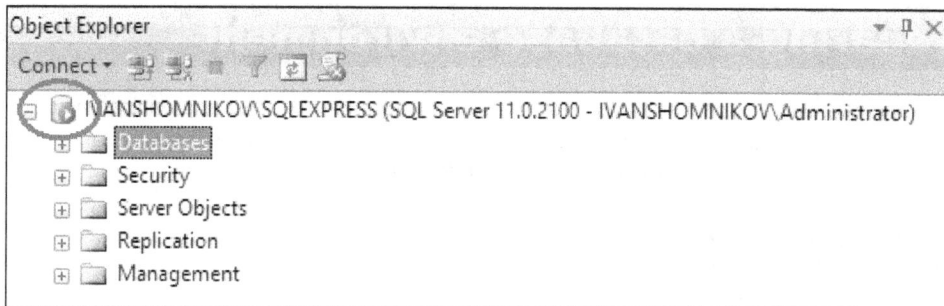

We need an "empty" installation of MS SQL Server 2012 Express because we will create all the databases we need manually in the next steps of this chapter. This database engine installation will host all our source, stage, and target relational data structures. This option allows us to easily build a test environment that is perfect for learning purposes in order to become familiar with ETL development using SAP Data Services.

In a real-life scenario, your source databases, staging area database, and DWH database/appliance will most likely reside on separate server hosts, and they may sometimes be from different vendors. So, the role of SAP Data Services is to link them together in order to migrate data from one system to another.

Creating a source system database

In this section, we will create our source database, which will play the role of an operational database that we will pull data from with the help of Data Services in order to transform the data and deliver it to a data warehouse.

How to do it...

Luckily for us, there are plenty of different flavors of ready-to-use databases on the Web nowadays. Let's pick one of the most popular ones: Adventure Works OLTP for SQL Server 2012, which is available for download on the CodePlex website. Perform the following steps:

1. Use the following link to see the list of the files available for download:

    ```
    https://msftdbprodsamples.codeplex.com/releases/view/55330
    ```

2. Click on the **AdventureWorks2012 Data File** link, which should download the `AdventureWorks2012_Data.mdf` data file.

3. When the download is complete, copy the file into the `C:\AdventureWorks\` directory (create it before copying if necessary).

The next step is to map this database file to our database engine, which will create our source database. To do this, perform the following steps:

1. Start SQL Server Management Studio.

2. Click on the **New Query** button, which will open a new session connection to a **master** database.

3. In the SQL Query window, type the following command and press *F5* to execute it:

    ```
    CREATE DATABASE AdventureWorks_OLTP ON
    (FILENAME = 'C:\AdventureWorks\AdventureWorks2012_Data.mdf')
    FOR ATTACH_REBUILD_LOG;
    ```

4. After a successful command execution and upon refreshing the database list (using *F5*), you should be able to see the `AdventureWorks_OLTP` database in the list of the available databases in the Object Explorer window of SQL Server Management Studio.

> **Downloading the example code**
>
> You can download the example code files for all Packt books you have purchased from your account at `http://www.packtpub.com`. If you purchased this book elsewhere, you can visit `http://www.packtpub.com/support` and register to have the files e-mailed directly to you.

How it works...

In a typical scenario, every SQL Server database consists of two data files: a database file and a transaction log file. A database file contains actual data structures and data, while a transaction log file keeps the transactional changes applied to the data.

As we only downloaded the data file, we had to execute the CREATE DATABASE command with a special ATTACH_REBUILD_LOG clause, which automatically creates a missing transaction log file so that the database could be successfully deployed and opened.

Now, our source database is ready to be used by Data Services in order to access, browse, and extract data from it.

There's more...

There are different ways to deploy test databases. This mainly depends on which RDBMS system you use. Sometimes, you may find a package of SQL scripts that contains the commands required to create all the database structures and commands used to insert data into these structures. This option may be useful if you have problems with attaching the downloaded mdf data file to your database engine or, for example, if you find the SQL scripts created for SQL Server RDBMS but have to apply them to the Oracle DB. With slight modifications to the command, you can run them in order to create an Oracle database.

Explaining RDBMS technologies lies beyond the scope of this book. So, if you are looking for more information regarding how a specific RDBMS system works, refer to the official documentation.

What has to be said here is that from the perspective of using Data Services, it does not matter which source system or target systems you use. Data Services not only supports the majority of them, but it also creates its own representation of the source and target objects; this way, they all look the same to Data Services users and abide by the same rules within the Data Services environment. So, you really do not have to be a DBA or database developer to easily connect to any RDBMS from Data Services. All that is required is a knowledge of the SQL language to understand the principle of methods that Data Services uses when extracting and loading data or creating database objects for you.

Defining and creating staging area structures

In this recipe, we will talk about ETL data structures that will be used in this book. Staging structures are important storage areas where extracted data is kept before it gets transformed or stored between the transformation steps. The staging area in general can be used to create backup copies of data or to run analytical queries on the data in order to validate the transformations made or the extract processes. Staging data structures can be quite different, as you will see. Which one to use depends on the tasks you are trying to accomplish, your project requirements, and the architecture of the environment used.

How to do it...

The most popular data structures that could be used in the staging area are flat files and RDBMS tables.

Flat files

One of the perks of using Data Services against the handcoded ETL solution is that Data Services allows you to easily read from and write information to a flat file.

Create the C:\AW\ folder, which will be used throughout this book to store flat files.

> Inserting data into a flat file is faster than inserting data into an RDBMS table. So, during ETL development, flat files are often used to reach two goals simultaneously: creating a backup copy of the data snapshot and providing you with the storage location for your preliminary data before you apply the next set of transformation rules.

Another common use of flat files is the ability to exchange data between systems that cannot communicate with each other in any other way.

Lastly, it is very cost-effective to store flat files (OS disk storage space is cheaper than DB storage space).

The main disadvantage of the flat files storage method is that the modification of data in a flat file can sometimes be a real pain, not to mention that it is much slower than modifying data in a relational DB table.

RDBMS tables

These ETL data structures will be used more often than others to stage the data that is going through the ETL transformation process.

Let's create two separate databases for relational tables, which will play the role of the ETL staging area in our future examples:

1. Open SQL Server Management Studio.
2. Right-click on the **Databases** icon and select the **New Database...** option.

3. On the next screen, input ODS as the database name, and specify 100 MB as the initial size value of the database file and 10 MB as that of the transactional log file:

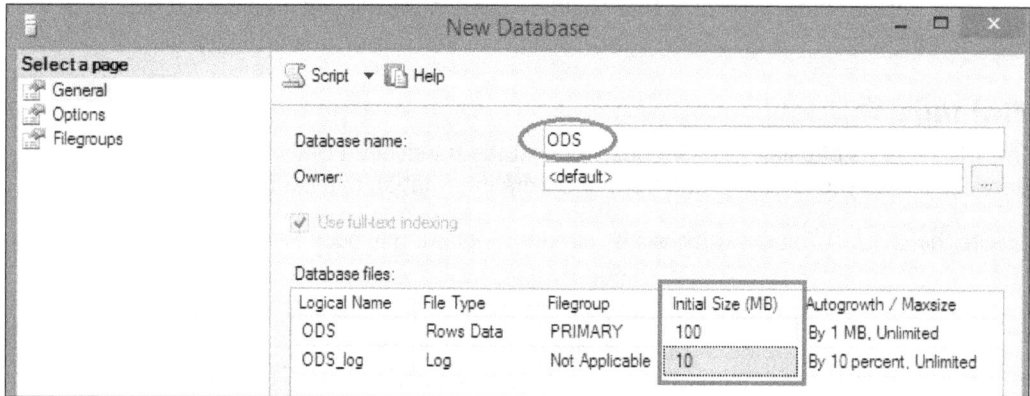

4. Repeat the last two steps to create another dataset called STAGE.

How it works...

Let's recap. The ETL staging area is a location to store the preliminary results of our ETL transformations and also a landing zone for the extracts from the source system.

Yes, Data Services allows you to extract data and perform all transformations in the memory before loading to the target system. However, as you will see in later chapters, the ETL process, which does everything in one "go", can be complex and difficult to maintain. Plus, if something goes wrong along the way, all the changes that the process has already performed will be lost and you may have to start the extraction/transformation process again. This obviously creates extra workload on a source system because you have to query it again in order to get the data. Finally, big does not mean effective. We will show you how splitting your ETL process into smaller pieces helps you to create a well-performing sequence of dataflow.

The ODS database will be used as a landing zone for the data coming from source systems. The structure of the tables here will be identical to the structure of the source system tables.

The STAGE database will hold the relational tables used to store data between the data transformation steps.

We will also store some data extracted from a source database in a flat file format to demonstrate the ability of Data Services to work with them and show the convenience of this data storage method in the ETL system.

Creating a target data warehouse

Finally, this is the time to create our target data warehouse system. The data warehouse structures and tables will be used by end users with the help of various reporting tools to make sense of the data and analyze it. As a result, it should help business users to make strategic decisions, which will hopefully lead to business growth.

We should not forget that the main purpose of a data warehouse, and hence that of our ETL system, is to serve business needs.

Getting ready

The data warehouse created in this recipe will be used as a target database populated by the ETL processes developed in SAP Data Services. This is where the data modified and cleansed by ETL processes will be inserted in the end. Plus, this is the database that will mainly be accessed by business users and reporting tools.

How to do it...

Perform the following steps:

1. `AdventureWorks` comes to the rescue again. Use another link to download the `AdventureWorks` data warehouse data file, which will be mapped in the same manner to our SQL Server Express database engine in order to create a local data warehouse for our own learning purposes. Go to the following URL and click on the **AdventureWorksDW for SQL Server 2012** link:

   `https://msftdbprodsamples.codeplex.com/releases/view/105902`

2. After you have successfully downloaded the `AdventureWorksDW2012.zip` file, unpack its contents into the same directory as the previous file:

   `C:\AdventureWorks\`

3. There should be two files in the archive:

   ❑ `AdventureWorksDW2012_Data.mdf`—the database data file

   ❑ `AdventureWorksDW2012_Log.ldf`—the database transaction log file

4. Open SQL Server Management Studio and click on the **New Query...** button in the uppermost tool bar.

5. Enter and execute the following command in the SQL Query window:

```
CREATE DATABASE AdventureWorks_DWH ON
(FILENAME = 'C:\AdventureWorks\AdventureWorksDW2012_Data.mdf'),
(FILENAME = 'C:\AdventureWorks\AdventureWorksDW2012_Log.ldf') FOR
ATTACH;
```

6. After a successful command execution, right-click on the **Databases** icon and choose the **Refresh** option in the opened menu list. This should refresh the contents of your object library, and you should see the following list of databases:

   ❑ ODS

   ❑ STAGE

   ❑ AdventureWorks_OLTP

   ❑ AdventureWorks_DWH

How it works...

Get yourself familiar with the tables of the created data warehouse. Throughout the whole book, you will be using them in order to insert, update, and delete data using Data Services.

There are also some diagrams available that could help you see the visual data warehouse structure. To get access to them, open SQL Server Management Studio, expand the Databases list in the Object Explorer window, then expand the AdventureWorks_DWH database object list, and finally open the Diagrams tree. Double-clicking on any diagram in the list opens a new window within Management Studio with the graphical presentation of tables, key columns, and links between the tables, which shows you the relationships between them.

There's more...

In the next recipe, we will have an overview of the knowledge resources that exist on the Web. We highly recommend that you get familiar with them in order to improve your data warehousing skills, learn about the data warehouse life cycle, and understand what makes a successful data warehouse project. In the meantime, feel free to open **New Query** in SQL Server Management Studio and start running the SELECT commands to explore the contents of the tables in your AdventureWorks_DWH database.

> The most important asset of any DWH architect or ETL developer is not the knowledge of a programming language or the available tools but the ability to understand the data that is, or will be, populating the data warehouse and the business needs and requirements for this data.

2

Configuring the Data Services Environment

In this chapter, we will install and configure all components required for SAP Data Services. In this chapter, we will cover the following topics:

- ▶ Creating IPS and Data Services repositories
- ▶ Installing and configuring Information Platform Services
- ▶ Installing and configuring Data Services
- ▶ Configuring user access
- ▶ Starting and stopping services
- ▶ Administering tasks
- ▶ Understanding the Designer tool

Introduction

The same thing that makes SAP Data Services a great ETL development environment makes it quite not a trivial one to install and configure. Here though, you have to remember that Data Services is an enterprise class ETL solution that is able to solve the most complex ETL tasks.

See the following image for a very high-level Data Services architecture view. Data Services has two basic groups of components: **client tools** and **server-based** components:

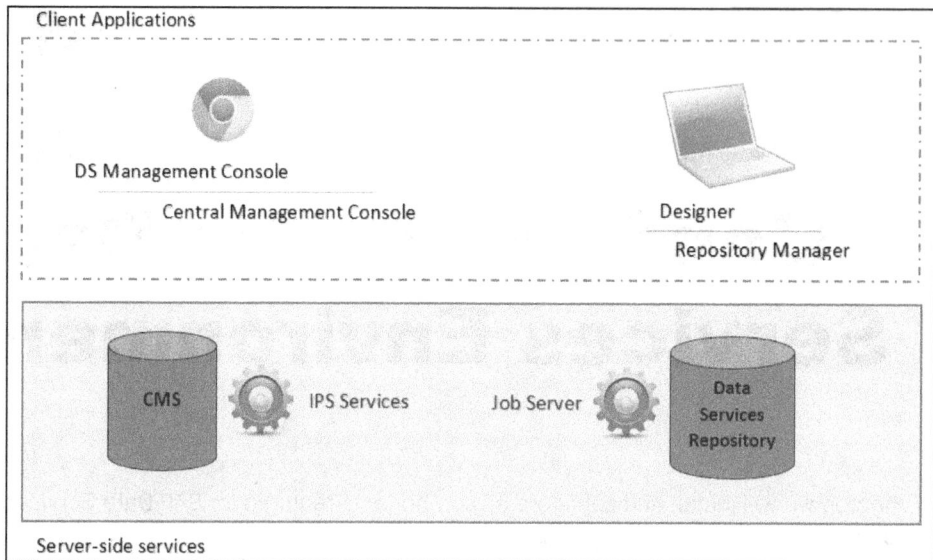

Client tools include the following (there are more, but we mention the ones most often used):

▸ **The Designer tool**: This is the client-based main GUI application for ETL development

▸ **Repository Manager**: This is a client-based GUI application for Data Services to create, configure, and upgrade Data Services repositories

The main server-based components include the following ones:

▸ **IPS Services**: This is used for user authentication, system configuration storage, and internal metadata management

▸ **Job Server**: This is a core engine service that executes ETL code

▸ **Access server**: This is a real-time request-reply message broker, which implements real-time services in the Data Services environment

▸ **Web application server**: This provides access to some Data Services administration and reporting tasks via the **DS Management Console** and **Central Management Console** web-based applications

In the course of the next few recipes, we will install, configure, and access all the components required to perform the majority of ETL development tasks. You will learn about their purposes and some useful tips that will help you effectively work in the Data Services environment throughout the book and in your future work.

Data Services installation supports all major OS and database environments. For learning purposes, we have chosen the Windows OS as it involves the least configuration on the user part. Both client tools and server components will be installed on the same Windows host.

Creating IPS and Data Services repositories

The IPS repository is a storage for environment and user configuration information and metadata collected by various services of IPS and Data Services. It has another name: the CMS database. This name should be quite familiar to those who have used SAP Business Intelligence software. Basically, IPS is a light version of SAP BI product package. You will always use only one IPS repository per Data Services installation and most likely will deal with it only once: when configuring the environment at the very beginning. Most of the time, Data Services will be communicating with IPS services and the CMS database in the background, without you even noticing.

The Data Services repository is a different story. It is much closer to an ETL developer as it is a database that stores your developed code. In a multiuser development environment, every ETL developer usually has its own repository. They can be of two types: central and local. They serve different purposes in the ETL lifecycle, and I will explain this in more detail in the upcoming chapters. Meanwhile, let's create our first local Data Services repository.

Getting ready...

Both repositories will be stored in the same SQL Server Express RDBMS ((local) \ SQLEXPRESS) that we used to create our source OLTP database, ETL staging databases, and target data warehouse. So, at this point, you only need to have access to SQL Server Management Studio and your SQL Server Express services need to start.

How to do it...

This will consist of two major tasks:

1. **Creating a database**:
    1. Log in to SQL Server Management Studio and create two databases: IPS_CMS and DS_LOCAL_REPO.

2. Right now, your database list should look like this:

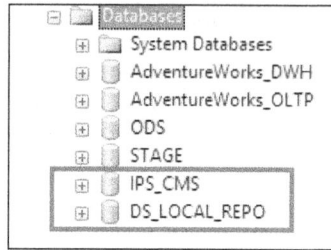

2. **Configuring the ODBC layer**: Installation requires that you create the ODBC data source for the `IPS_CMS` database.

    1. Go to **Control Panel | Administrative Tools | ODBC Data Sources (64-bit)**.

    2. Open the **System DSN** tab and click on the **Add...** button.

    3. Choose the name of the data source: `SQL_IPS`, the description SQL Server Express, and the SQL Server you want to connect to through this ODBC data source: `(local)\SQLEXPRESS`. Then, click on **Next**.

    4. Choose **SQL Server authentication** and select the checkbox **Connect to SQL** to obtain the default settings. Enter the login ID (`sa` user) and password. Click on **Next**.

    5. Select the checkbox and change the default database to `IPS_CMS`. Click on **Next**.

    6. Skip the next screen by clicking on **Next**.

    7. The final screen of the ODBC configuration should look like the following screenshot. Then, clicking on the **Test Data Source** button should give you the message, **TESTS COMPLETED SUCCESSFULLY!**

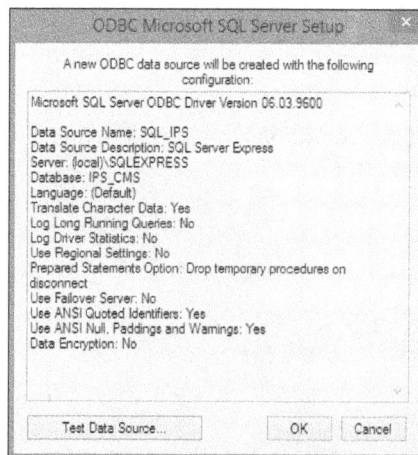

How it works...

These two empty databases will be used by Data Services tools during installation and post-installation configuration tasks. All structures inside them will be created and populated automatically.

Usually, they are not built for users to access them directly, but in the upcoming chapters, I will show you a few tricks on how to extract valuable information from them in order to troubleshoot potential problems, do a little bit of ETL metadata reporting, or use an extended search for ETL objects, which is not possible in the GUI of the Designer tool.

The ODBC layer configured for the `IPS_CMS` database allows you to access it from the IPS installation. When we install both IPS and Data Services, you will be able to connect to the databases directly from the Data Services applications, as it has native drivers for various types of databases and also allows you to connect through ODBC layers if you want.

See also

References to a future chapter containing techniques mentioned in the preceding paragraph.

Installing and configuring Information Platform Services

The **Information Platform Services** (**IPS**) product package was added as a component into the Data Services bundle starting from the Data Services 4.x version. The reason for this was to make the Data Services architecture flexible and robust and introduce some extra functionality, that is, a user management layer to the existing SAP Data Services solution. As we mentioned before, IPS is a light version of SAP BI core services and has a lot of similar functionality.

In this recipe, we will perform the installation and basic configuration of IPS, which is a mandatory component for future Data Services installations.

> As an option, you could always use the existing full enterprise SAP BI solution if you have it installed in your environment. However, this is generally considered a bad practice. Imagine that it is like storing all eggs in one basket. Whenever you need to plan downtime for your BI system, you should keep in mind that it will affect your ETL environment as well, and you will not be able to run any Data Services jobs during this period. That is why, IPS is installed to be used only by Data Services as a safer and more convenient option in terms of support and maintenance.

Getting ready...

Download the Information Platform Services installation package from the SAP support portal and unzip it to the location of your choice. The main requirement for installing IPS as well as Data Services in the next recipe is that your OS should have a 64-bit architecture.

How to do it...

1. Create an EIM folder in your C drive to store your installation in one place.

2. Launch the IPS installer by executing InstallIPS.exe.

3. Make sure that all your critical prerequisites have the **Succeeded** status on the **Check Prerequisites** screen. Continue to the next screen.

4. Choose C:\EIM\ as the installation destination folder. Continue to the next screen.

5. Choose the **Full** installation type. Continue to the next screen.

6. On **Select Default or Existing Database**, choose **Configure an existing database** and continue to the next screen.

7. Select **Microsoft SQL Server using ODBC** as the existing CMS database type.

8. Select **No auditing database** on the next screen and continue.

9. Choose **Install the default Tomcat Java Web Application Server and automatically deploy web applications**. Continue to the next screen.

10. For version management, choose **Do not configure a version control system at this time**.

11. On the next screen, specify the SIA name in the **Node name** field as IPS and **SIA port** as 6410.

12. Do not change the default CMS port, 6400.

13. On the **CMS account configuration** screen, input passwords for the administrator user account and the CMS cluster key (they can be the same if you want). Continue further.

14. Use the following settings from the following screenshot to configure the CMS Repository Database:

Configure CMS Repository Database - SQL Server (ODBC)

Specify information about the existing database to use for the CMS repository

System DSN	Description
SQL_IPS	SQL Server Express

Data Source: SQL_IPS

Server: (local)\SQLEXPRESS

User Name: sa

Password: *************

Database: IPS_CMS

☐ Use Trusted Connection
☐ Show system database
☑ Reset existing database
☐ Consume DSN created under WOW64

[Refresh]   Back   Next   Cancel

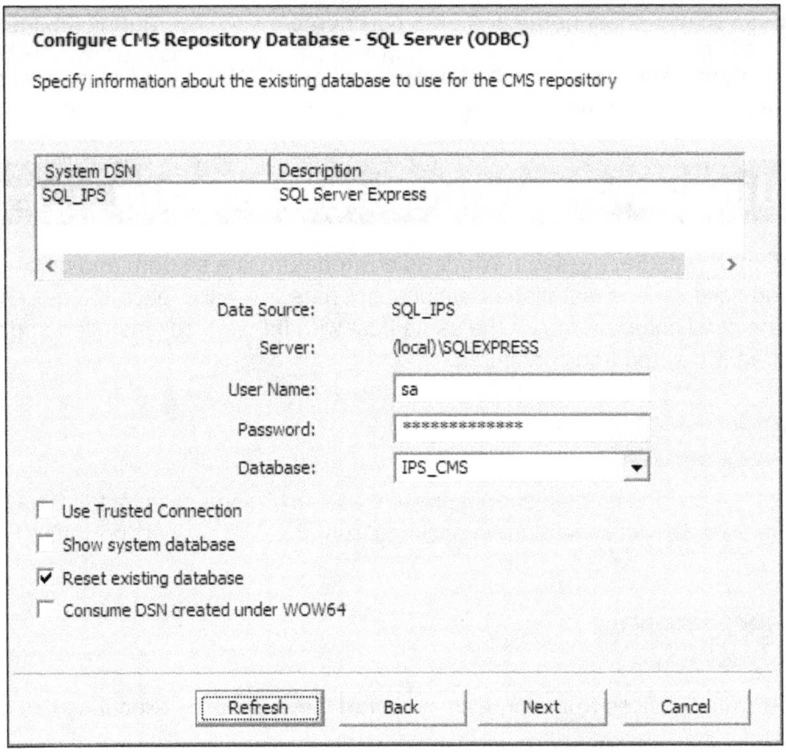

15. Leave the default values for Tomcat ports on the next screen and click on **Next**. Remember the **Connection Port** setting (default is 8080) as you will require it to connect to the IPS and Data Services web applications.

16. Do not configure connectivity to SMD Agent.

17. Do not configure connectivity to Introscope Enterprise Manager.

18. Finally, the installation will begin. It should take approximately 5–15 minutes, depending on your hardware.

How it works...

Now, by installing IPS, we prepared the base layers, on top of which we will install the Data Services installation package itself.

To check that your IPS installation was successful, start the Central Management Console web application using the `http://localhost:8080/BOE/CMC` URL and use the administrator account that you set up during IPS installation to log in. In the system field, use `localhost:6400` (your host name and CMS port number specified during IPS installation).

Check out the **Core Services** tree in the **Servers** section of CMC. All services listed should have the **Running** and **Enabled** statuses.

Installing and configuring Data Services

The installation of Data Services in a Windows environment is a smooth and quick process. Of course, you have various installation options, but here, we will choose the easiest path: the full installation of all components on the same host with IPS services installed and the local repository already created and configured.

Getting ready...

Completion of the previous recipe should prepare your environment to install Data Services. Download the Data Services installation package from the SAP support portal and unzip it to a local folder.

How to do it...

1. Start Data Services from Windows **command line** (**cmd**) by executing this command:

   `setup.exe SERVERINSTALL=Yes`

2. Make sure that all your critical prerequisites have the **Succeeded** status on the **Check Prerequisites** screen.

3. Choose the destination folder as `C:\EIM\` if required.

4. On the CMS connection information step, specify the connection details to your previously installed CMS (part of IPS) installation. The system is `localhost:6400`, and the user is `Administrator`. Click on **Next**.

5. In the **CMS Service Stop/Start** pop-up window, agree to restart SIA servers.

6. Choose **Install with default configuration** on the **Installation Type** selection screen.

7. Make sure that you select all features by selecting all the checkboxes on the next feature selection screen and click on **Next**.

8. Specify **Microsoft_SQL_Server** as a database type for a local repository.

9. Use the following details as a reference to configuring your local repository database connection on the next screen:

Option	Value
Registration name for CMS	`DS4_REPO`
Database Type	`Microsoft_SQL_Server`
Database server name	`(local)\SQLEXPRESS`
Database port	`50664`
Database name	`DS_LOCAL_REPO`
User Name	`sa`
Password	`<sa user password>`

10. For login information, choose the account recommended by installation.
11. The installation should be completed in 5–10 minutes, depending on your environment.

How it works...

After finishing this recipe, you will have all the Data Services servers and client components installed on the same Windows host. Also, your Data Services installation is integrated with IPS services.

To check that the installation and integration were successful, log in to CMC and see that in the main menu, there is a new section called **Data Services** (see the **Organize** column). Go to this section and see whether your **DS4_REPO** exists in the list of local repositories.

Configuring user access

In this recipe, I will show you how to configure your access as a fresh ETL developer in a Data Services environment. We will create a user account, assign all the required functional privileges, and assign owner privileges for our local Data Services repository. In a multiuser development environment, you would require to perform this step for every newly created user.

Getting ready...

Choose the username and password for your ETL developer user account. We will log in to the CMC application to create a user account and grant it the required set of privileges.

How to do it...

1. Launch the **Central Management Console** web application.

2. Go to **Users and Groups**.

3. Click on **Create a user** button (see the following screenshot):

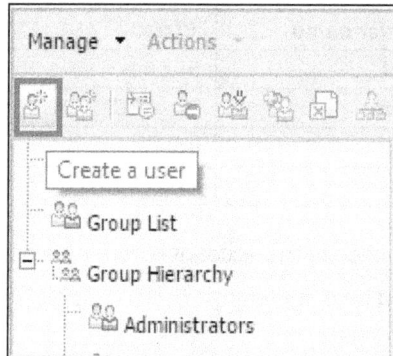

4. In the opened window, choose a username (we picked et1) and password. Also, select the **Password never expires** option and unselect **User must change password at next logon**. Choose **Concurrent User** as the connection type.

5. Now, we should add our newly created account to two pre-existing user groups. Right-click on the user and choose the **Member Of** option in the right-click menu.

6. Click on the **Join Group** button in the newly opened window and add two groups from the group list to the right window panel: **Data Services Administrator Users** and **Data Services Designer Users**. Click on **OK**.

7. From the left-side instrument panel, click on the **CMC Home** button to return to the main CMC screen.

8. Now, we have to grant our user extra privileges on the local repository. For this, open the Data Services section, right-click on **DS4_REPO**, and choose **User Security** from the context menu.

9. Click on the **Add principals** button, move the et1 user to the right panel and click on the **Add and Assign Security** button at the bottom of the screen.

10. On the next screen, assign the *full control (owner)* access level on the **Access Levels** tab and go to the **Advanced** tab.

11. Click on the **Add/Remove Rights** link and set the following two options that appear to **Granted** for the **Data Services Repository** application (see the following screenshot):

Add/Remove Rights					
Object: DS4_REPO	▾Specific Rights for Data Services Repository		Implicit Value	⊘	⊗ ?
Principal: etl	Allow user to retrieve repository password		Not Specified	⊛	○ ○
▾General	Allow user to retrieve repository password that user owns		Not Specified	⊛	○ ○
General		Override General			
▾Application	▾General Rights for Data Services Repository	Global	Implicit Value	⊘	⊗ ?
Data Services Repository	Add objects to folders that the user owns	▣	Not Specified	○	○ ⊛
	Add objects to the folder	▣	Not Specified	○	○ ⊛

12. Click on **OK** in the **Assign Security** window to confirm your configuration.

13. As a test, log out of the CMC and log in using a newly created user account.

How it works...

In a complex enterprise environment, you can create multiple groups for different categories of users. You have full flexibility in order to provide users with various kinds of permissions, depending on their needs.

Some users might require administration privileges to start/stop services and to manage repositories without the need to develop ETL and access Designer.

The ETL developer role might require only permissions for the Designer tool to develop ETL code.

In our case, we have created a single user account that has both administration and developer privileges.

Starting and stopping services

In this recipe, I will explain how you can restart the services of all the main components in your Data Services environment.

How to do it...

This relates to the three different services:

▸ **Web application server**:

  ❑ The Tomcat application server configured in our environment can be configured from two places:

    Computer Management | **Services and Applications** | **Services** where it exists as a standard Windows service BOEXI40Tomcat

Central Configuration Management tool installed as a part of IPS product package:

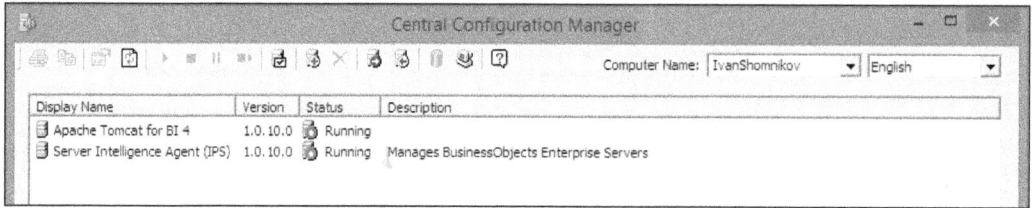

Using this tool, you can:

1. Start/stop services.
2. Back up and restore system configuration.
3. Specify the Windows user who starts and stops the underlying services.

▶ **Data Services Job Server**:

❑ To manage Data Services Job Server in the Windows environment, SAP created a separate GUI application called Data Services Server Manager.

❑ Using this tool, you can perform the following tasks:

1. Restart Job Server.
2. Create and configure Job Servers.
3. Create and configure Access Servers.
4. Perform SSL configuration.
5. Set up a pageable cache directory.
6. Perform SMTP configuration for the `smpt_to()` Data Services function.

▶ **Information Platform Services**:

❑ To manipulate these services, you have two options:

Central Management Console (to stop/start and configure services parameters)

Central Configuration Management (to stop/start services)

In most cases, you will be using the CMC option, as it is a quick and convenient way to access all services included in the IPS package. It also allows you to see much more service-related information.

The second option is useful if you have the application server stopped for some reason (CMC as a web-based application will not be working, of course), and you still need to access IPS services to perform basic administration tasks such as restarting them, for example.

How it works...

Sometimes, things turn sour, and restarting services is the quickest and easiest option to return them to a normal state. In this recipe, I mentioned all the main server components and points of access to perform such a task.

The last thing you should keep in mind regarding this is the recommended startup/shutdown sequences of those components.

1. The first thing that should start after Windows starts is your database server, as it hosts the CMS database required for the IPS services and Data Services local repository.

2. Second, you should start IPS services (the main one is the CMS service) as an underlying level for Data Services.

3. Then, it is the turn of the Data Services Job Server.

4. Finally, it goes to Tomcat (web application server) that provides users with access to web-based applications.

See also

▶ I definitely recommend that you get familiar with the *SAP Data Services Administrators Guide* to understand the details regarding IPS and Data Services component management and configuration.

▶ Knowledge sourced and documentation links from *Chapter 1, Introduction to ETL Development*.

Administering tasks

The previous recipe is part of the basic administration tasks too, of course. I separated it from the current one as I wanted to put an accent on Data Services architecture details by explaining the main Data Services components in relation to the methods and tools you can use to manipulate them.

How to do it...

Here, we will look at some of the most important administrative tasks.

1. **Using Repository Manager:**

   As you can probably remember, there are two types of repositories in Data Services: the local repository and central repository. They serve different purposes but can be created in quite a similar way: with the help of the Data Services Repository Manager tool.

This is a GUI-based tool available on your Windows machine and installed with other client tools.

As we already have one repository created and configured automatically during the Data Services installation, let's check its version using the Repository Manager tool.

Launch Repository Manager and enter the following values for the corresponding options:

Field	Value
Repository type	Local
Database Type	Microsoft SQL Server
Database server name	(local)\SQLEXPRESS
Database name	DS_LOCAL_REPO
User Name	sa
Password	*******

After entering these details, you have several options:

Create: This option creates repository objects in the defined database. As we already have a repository in DS_LOCAL_REPO, the application will ask us whether we want to reset the existing repository. Sometimes, this can be useful, but keep in mind that it will cleanse the repository of all objects, and if not careful, all your ETL that resides in the repository can be lost.

Upgrade: This option upgrades the repository to the version of the Repository Manager tool. It is useful during software upgrades. After installing the new version of IPS and Data Services, you have to upgrade your repository contents as well. This is when you launch the Repository Manager tool (which has already been updated) and upgrade your repository to the current version.

Get version: This is the safest option of them all. It just returns the string containing the repository version number. In our case, it returned: **BODI-320030: The local repository version: <14.2.4.0>**.

2. **Using Server Manager and CMC to register the new repository**:

After you create the new repository with Repository Manager, you have to register it in IPS and link it to the existing Job Server.

To register a new repository in IPS, use the following steps:

1. Launch **Central Management Console**.
2. Open the **Data Services** section from the CMC home page.
3. Go to **Manage | Configure Repository**.
4. Enter database details of your newly created repository and click on **Save**.

5. To assign users a required set of privileges, use **User Security** when right-clicking on the repository in the list. For details, see the *Configuring user access* recipe.

To link a new repository to the Job Server, perform these steps:

1. Launch the **Data Services Server Manager** tool.

2. Choose the **Job Server** tab.

3. Press on the **Configuration Editor...** button.

4. Select **Job Server** and press the **Edit...** button.

5. In the **Associated Repositories** panel, press the **Add...** button and fill in database-related information of the new repository in the correspondent fields on the right-hand side.

6. Use the **Close and Restart** button in the **Data Services Server Management** tool to apply the changes done to a Job Server.

3. **Using License Manager**:

1. License Manager exists only in a command-line mode.

2. Use the following syntax to run License Manager:

```
LicenseManager [-v | -a <keycode> | -r <keycode> [-l <location>]]
```

3. Use the -v option to view existing license keys, -a to add a new license key, and -r to remove the existing license key from the -l location specified.

This tool is available at C:\EIM\Data Services\bin\.

How it works...

Creating and configuring a new local repository is usually required when you set up an environment for a new ETL developer or want to use an extra repository to migrate your ETL for ETL testing purposes or to test a repository upgrade.

After creating a new local repository, you should always link it to an existing Job Server. This link ensures that Job Server is aware of the repository and can execute jobs from it.

Finally, License Manager can be used to see the license key used in your installations and to add new extra ones if required.

See also

You can practice with your Data Services admin skills by creating a new database and new local Data Services repository. Do not forget that you do not just have to create it, but also register it with IPS services and Data Services Job Server so that you can successfully run jobs from it.

Some other administrative tasks can be found in the following chapters:

▸ The *Starting and stopping services* recipe from this chapter

▸ The *Configure ODBC layer* point from the *How to do it...* section of the *Creating IPS and Data Services repositories* recipe of this chapter

Understanding the Designer tool

Now that we have reviewed all the important server and client components of our new Data Services installation, it is time to get familiar with the most usable and most important tool in the Data Services product package. It will be our main focus in the following chapters, and of course, I am talking about our development GUI: the Designer tool.

Every object you create in Designer is stored in a local object library, which is a logical storage unit part of the physical local repository database. In this recipe, we will log in to a local repository via Designer, set up a couple of settings, and write our first "Hello World" program.

Getting ready...

Your Data Services ETL development environment is fully deployed and configured, so go ahead and start the Designer application.

How to do it...

First, let's change some default options to make our development life a little bit easier and to see how options windows in Data Services looks:

1. When you launch your Designer application, you see quite a sophisticated login screen. Enter the `etl` username we created in one of the previous recipes and its password to see the list of repositories available in the system.

2. At this point, you should see only one local repository, `DS4_REPO`, that was created by default during the Data Services installation. Double-click on it.

3. You should see your Designer application started.

4. Go to **Tools | Options**.

5. In the opened window, expand the **Designer** tree and choose **General**.

6. Set the **Number of characters in workspace icon name** option to 50 and select the **Automatically calculate column mappings** checkbox.

7. Click on **OK** to close the options window.

Before we create our first "Hello World" program, let's quickly take a look at Designer's user interface.

In this recipe, you will be required to work with only two areas: **Local Object Library** and the main development area. The biggest window on the right-hand side with the **Start Page** tab will open by default.

Local Object Library contains tabs with lists of objects you can create or use during your ETL development. These objects include **Projects**, **Jobs**, **Work Flows**, **Data Flows**, **Transforms**, **Datastores**, **Formats**, and **Custom Functions**:

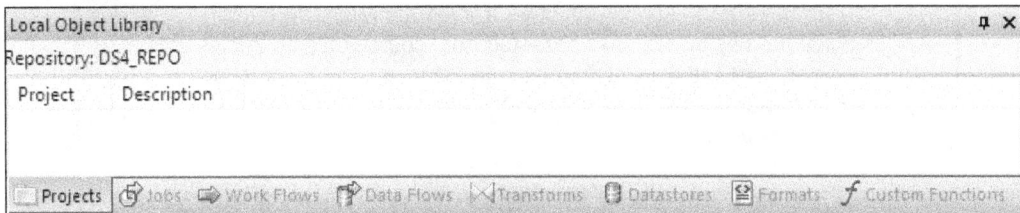

Local Object Library	🔲 ✕
Repository: DS4_REPO	

Project	Description

Projects   🔁 Jobs   ➡ Work Flows   🔁 Data Flows   📐 Transforms   🗐 Datastores   📑 Formats   *f* Custom Functions

All tabs are empty, as you have not created any objects of any kind yet, except for the **Transforms** tab. This tab contains a predefined set of transforms available for you to use for ETL development. Data Services does not allow you to create your own transforms (there is an exception that we will discuss in the upcoming chapters). So, everything you see on this tab is basically everything that is available for you to manipulate your data with.

Now, let's create our first "Hello World" program. As ETL development in Data Services is not quite the usual experience of developing with a programming language, we should agree on what our first program should do. In almost any programming language related book, this kind of program just performs an output of a "Hello World" string onto your screen. In our case, we will generate a "Hello World" string and output it in a table that will be automatically created by Data Services in our target database.

In the Designer application, go to the **Local Object Library** window, choose the **Jobs** tab, right-click on the **Batch Jobs** tree, and select **New** from the list of options that appears.

1. Choose the name for a new job Job_HelloWorld and enter it. After the job is created, double-click on it.

2. You will enter the job design window (see **Job_HelloWorld – Job** at the bottom of the application), and now, you can add objects to your job and set up its variables and parameters.

3. In the design window of the **Job_HelloWorld – Job** tab, create a dataflow. To do this, from the right tool panel, choose Data Flow object and left-click on a main design window to create it. Name it DF_HelloWorld.

4. Double-click on a newly created dataflow (or just click once on its title) to open the **Data Flow** design window. It appears as another tab in the main design window area.

5. Now, when we are designing the processing unit or dataflow, we can choose the transforms from the **Transforms** tab of the **Local Object Library** window to perform manipulation with the data. Click on the **Transforms** tab.

6. Here, select the **Platform** transforms tree and drag and drop the **Row_Generation** transform from it to the **Data Flow** design window.

> As we are generating a new "Hello World!" string, we should use the **Row_Generation** transform. It is a very useful way of generating rows in Data Services. All other transforms are performing operations on the rows extracted from source objects (tables or files) that are passing from source to target within a dataflow. In this example, we do not have a source table. Hence, we have to generate a record.

7. By default, the **Row_Generation** transform generates only one row with the ID as 0. Now, we have to create our string and present it as a field in a future target table. For this, we need to use the **Query** transform. Select it from the right tool panel or drag and drop it from **Transforms** to **Platform**. The icon of the **Query** transforms looks like this:

8. In the **Data Flow** design window, link **Row_Generation** to **Query**, as shown here, and double-click on the **Query** transform to open the **Query Editor** tab:

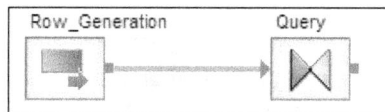

> In the next chapter, we will explain the details of the **Query** transform. In the meantime, let's just say that this is one of the most used transforms in Data Services. It allows you to join flows of your data and modify the dataset by adding/removing columns in the row, changing data types, and performing grouping operations. On the left-hand side of the **Query Editor**, you will see an incoming set of columns, and on the right-hand side, you will see the output. This is where you will define all your transformation functions for specific fields or assign hard-coded values. We are not interested in the incoming ID generated by the **Row_Generation** transform. For us, it served the purpose of creating a row that will hold our "Hello World!" value and will be inserted in a table.

9. In the right panel of **Query Editor**, right-click on **Query** and choose **New Output Column...**:

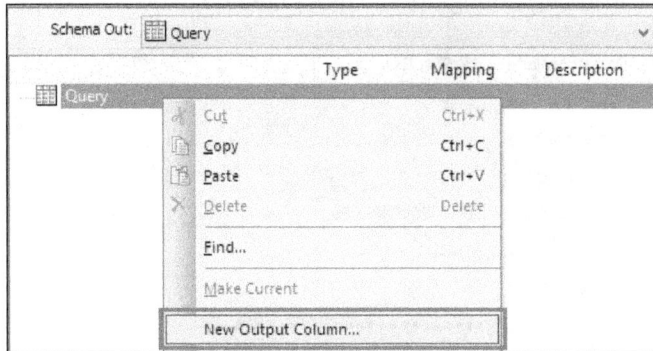

10. Select the following settings in the opened **Column Properties** window to define the properties of our newly created column and click on **OK**:

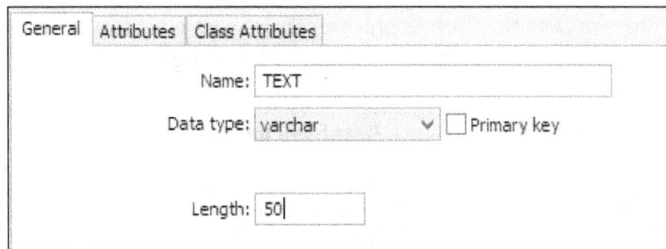

11. Now, when our generated row has one column, we have to populate it with value. For this, we have to use the **Mapping** tab in **Query Editor**. Select our output field TEXT and enter the "Hello World!" value in the mapping tab window. Do not forget single quotes, which mean a string in DS. Then, close **Query Editor** either with the tab cross in the top-right corner (do not confuse it with the Designer application cross that is located dangerously close to it) or just use the **Back** button (*Alt + Left*), a green arrow icon in the top instrument panel.

At this point, we have a source in our dataflow. We also have a transformation object (the **Query** transform), which defines our text column and assigns a value to it. What is missing is a target object we will insert our row to.

As we will use a table as a target object, we have to create a reference to a database within Data Services. We will use this reference to create a target table. Those database references are called datastores and are used as a presentation of the database layer. In the next step, we will create a reference to our STAGE database created in the previous chapter.

12. Go to the **Datastores** tab of **Local Object Library**. Then, right-click on the empty window and select **New** to open the **Create New Datastore** window.

13. Choose the following settings for the newly created datastore object:

Datastore Name:	DS_STAGE
Datastore Type:	Database
Database Type:	Microsoft SQL Server — No CDC
Database Version:	Microsoft SQL Server 2012
Database server name:	(local)\SQLEXPRESS
Database name:	STAGE
User Name:	sa
Password:	••••••••••••••••••••••••
	☑ Enable Automatic Data Transfer

14. Repeat steps 12 and 13 to create the rest of datastore objects connected to the databases we created in the previous recipes. Use the same database server name and user credentials and change only the **Datastore Name** and **Database name** fields when creating new datastores. See the following table for reference:

Datastore Name	Database name
DS_ODS	ODS
DWH	AdventureWorks_DWH
OLTP	AdventureWorks_OLTP

Now, you should have four datastores created, referencing all databases created in the SQL server: DS_STAGE, DS_ODS, DWH, and OLTP.

15. Now, we can use the DS_STAGE datastore to create our target table. Go back to the DF_HelloWorld in the **Data Flow** tab of the design window and select **Template Table** on the right tool panel. Put it on the right-hand side of the **Query** transform and choose **HELLO_WORLD** as the table name in the DS_STAGE datastore.

16. Our final dataflow should look like this now:

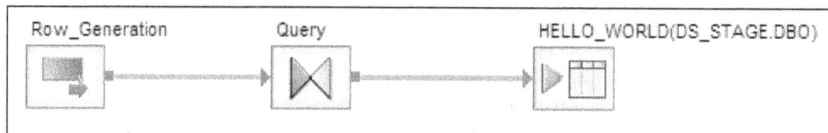

17. Go back to the **Job_HelloWorld – Job** tab and click on the **Validate All** button in the top instrument panel. You should get the following message in the output window of **Designer** on the left-hand side of your screen: **Validate: No Errors Found (BODI-1270017)**.

18. Now, we are ready to execute our first job. For this, use the **Execute...** (*F8*) button from the top instrument panel. Agree to save the current objects and click on **OK** on the following screen.

19. See that the log screen that shows you the execution steps contains no execution errors. Then, go to your SQL Server Management Studio, open the STAGE database, and check the contents of the appeared HELLO_WORLD table. It has just one column, TEXT, with only one value, "Hello World!".

How it works...

"Hello World!" is a small example that introduces a lot of general and even sophisticated concepts. In the following sections, we will quickly review the most important ones. They will help you get familiar with the development environment in Data Services Designer. Keep in mind that we will return to all these subjects again throughout the book, discussing them in more detail.

Executing ETL code in Data Services

To execute any ETL code developed in the Data Services Designer tool, you have to create a job object. In Data Services, the only executable object is job. Everything else goes inside the job.

ETL code is organized as a hierarchy of objects inside the job object. To modify any new object by placing another object in it, you have to open the edited object in the main workspace design area and then drag and drop the required object inside it, placing them in the workspace area. In our recipe, we created a job object and placed the dataflow object in it. We then opened the dataflow object in the workspace area and placed transform objects inside it. As you can see in the following screenshot, workspace areas opened previously could be accessible through the tabs at the bottom of the workspace area:

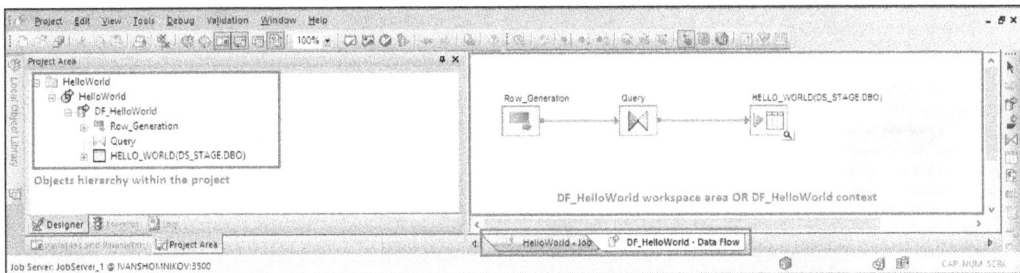

The **Project Area** panel can display the hierarchy of objects in the form of a tree. To see it, you have to assign your newly created job to a specific project and open the project in **Project Area** by double-clicking on the project object in **Local Object Library**.

Executable ETL code contains one job object and can contain script, dataflow, and workflow objects combined in various ways inside the job.

As you saw from the recipe steps, you can create a new job by going to **Local Object Library | Jobs**.

Although you can combine all types of objects by placing them in the job directly, some objects, for example, transform objects, can be placed only into dataflow objects as dataflow is the only type of object that can process and actually migrate data (on a row-by-row basis). Hence, all transformations should happen only inside the dataflow. In the same way, you can only place datastore objects, such as tables and views, directly in dataflows as source and target objects for data to be moved from source to target and transformed along the way. When a dataflow object is executed within the job, it reads data row by row from the source and moves the row from left to right to the next transform object inside the dataflow until it reaches the end and is sent to the target object, which usually is a database table.

Throughout this book, you will learn the purpose of each object type and how and when it can be used.

For now, remember that all objects inside the job are executed in the sequential order from left to right if they are connected and simultaneously if they are not. Another important rule is that the parent object starts executing first and then all objects inside it. The parent object completes its execution only after all child objects have completed successfully.

Validating ETL code

To avoid job execution failures due to incorrect ETL syntax, you can validate the job and all its objects with the **Validate Current** or **Validate All** button on the top instrument panel inside the Designer tool:

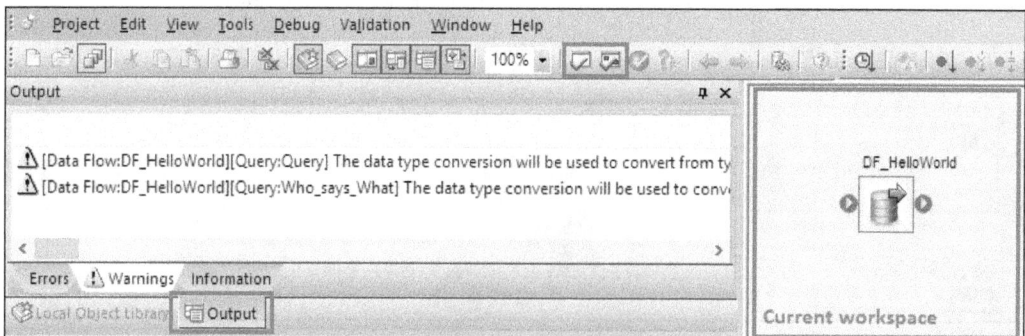

Validate Current validates only the current object opened in the workspace design area and script objects in it and does not validate the underlying child object such as dataflows and workflows. In the preceding example, the object opened in the workspace is a job object that has one child dataflow object called `DF_HelloWorld` inside it. Only one job object will be validated and not `DF_HelloWorld`.

Validate All validates the current and all underlying objects. So, both are currently opened in the workspace object, and all objects you see in the workspace are validated. The same applies to the objects nested inside them, down to the very end of the object hierarchy.

So, to validate the whole job and its objects, you have to go to the job level by opening the job object in the workspace area and clicking on **Validate All button** on the top instrument panel.

Validation results are displayed in the **Output** panel. Warning messages do not affect the execution of the job and often indicate possible ETL design problems or show data type conversions performed by Data Services automatically. Error messages in the **Output | Errors** tab mean syntax or critical design errors made in ETL. Whenever you try to run the job after seeing "red" error validation messages, the job will fail with exactly the same errors that you saw at the beginning of execution, as every job is implicitly validated when executed.

Always validate your job manually before executing it to avoid job failures due to incorrect syntax or incorrect ETL design.

Template tables

This is a convenient way to specify the target table that does not yet exist in the database and send data to it. When a dataflow object where the template target table object is placed is executed, it runs two DDL commands, `DROP TABLE <template table name>` and `CREATE TABLE <template table name>`, using the output schema (set of columns) of the last object inside the dataflow before the target template table. Only after that, the dataflow processes all the data from the source, passing rows from left to right through all transformations, and finally inserts data into the freshly created target table.

> Note that tables are not created on the database level from template tables until the ETL code (dataflow object) is executed within Data Services. Simply placing the template table object inside a dataflow and creating it in a datastore structure is not enough for the actual physical table to be created in the database. You have to run your code.

They are displayed under different categories in the datastore. They appear separately from normal table objects:

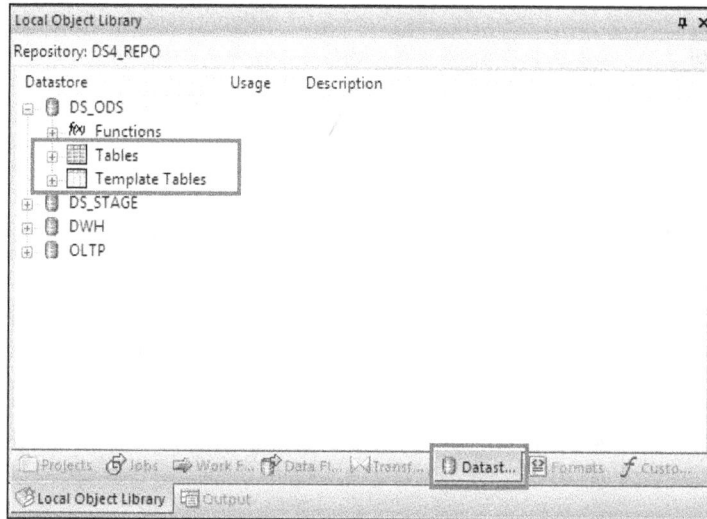

The usage of template table is extremely useful during ETL development and testing. It enables you to not think about going to the database level and changing the structure of the tables by altering, deleting, or creating them manually if the ETL code that inserts the data in the table changes. Every time dataflow runs, it will be deleting and recreating the database table defined through the template table object, with the currently required table structure defined by your current ETL code.

Template table objects are easily converted to normal table objects using the "Import" command on them. This command is available from the object's context menu in the dataflow workspace or in the datastores tab in **Local Object Library**.

Query transform basics

Query transform is one of the most important and most often used transform objects in Data Services. Its main purpose is to read data from left object(s) (input schema(s)) and send data to the output schema (object to the right of the Query transform). You can join multiple datasets with the help of the **Query** transform using syntax rules of the SQL language.

Additionally, you can specify the mapping rules for the output schema columns inside the Query transform by applying various functions to the mapped fields. You can also specify hard-coded values or even create additional output schema columns, like we did in our HelloWorld example.

The example in the next screenshot is not from our `HelloWorld` example. However, it demonstrates how the row extracted previously from the source object (input schema) can be augmented with extra columns or can get its columns renamed or its values transformed by functions applied to the columns:

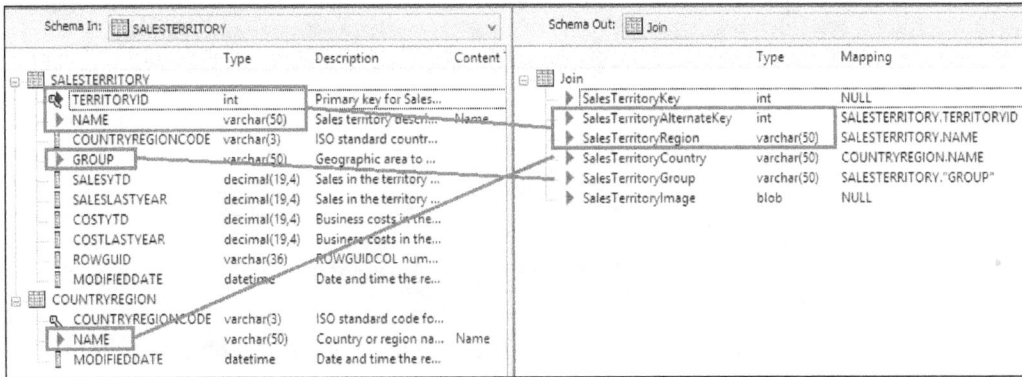

See how columns from two different tables are combined in a single dataset in the output schema, with columns renamed according to new standards and new columns created with NULL values in them.

The HelloWorld example

You have just created the simplest dataflow processing unit and executed it within your first job.

The dataflow object in our example has the **Row_Generation** transform, which generates rows with only one field. We generated one row with the help of this transform and added an extra field to the row with the help of the Query transform. We then inserted our final row into the `HELLO_WORLD` table created automatically by Data Services in the **STAGE** database.

You also have configured a couple of Designer properties and created a Datastore object that represents the Data Services view of the underlying database level. Not all database objects (tables and views) are visible within your datastore by default. You have to import only those you are going to work with. In our `HelloWorld` example, we did not import the table in the datastore, as we used the template table. To import the table that exists in the database into your datastore so that it can be used in ETL development, you can perform the following steps:

1. Go to **Local Object Library | Datastores**.
2. Expand the datastore object you want to import the table in.

3. Double-click on the **Tables** section to open the list of database tables available for import:

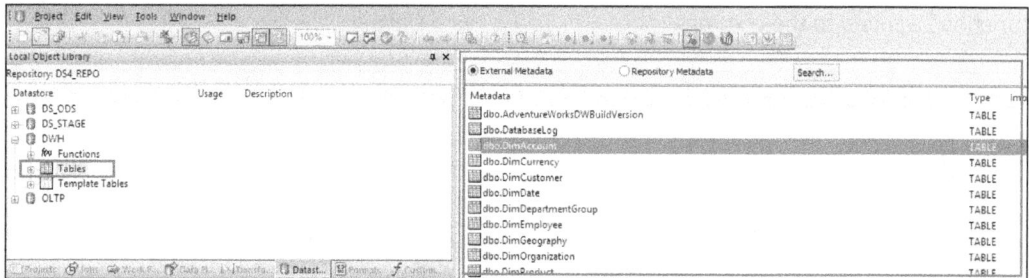

4. Right-click on the specific table in the **External Metadata** list and choose **Import** from the table context menu.

5. The table object will now appear in the **Tables** section of the chosen datastore. As it has not yet been placed in any dataflow object, the **Usage** column shows a 0 value:

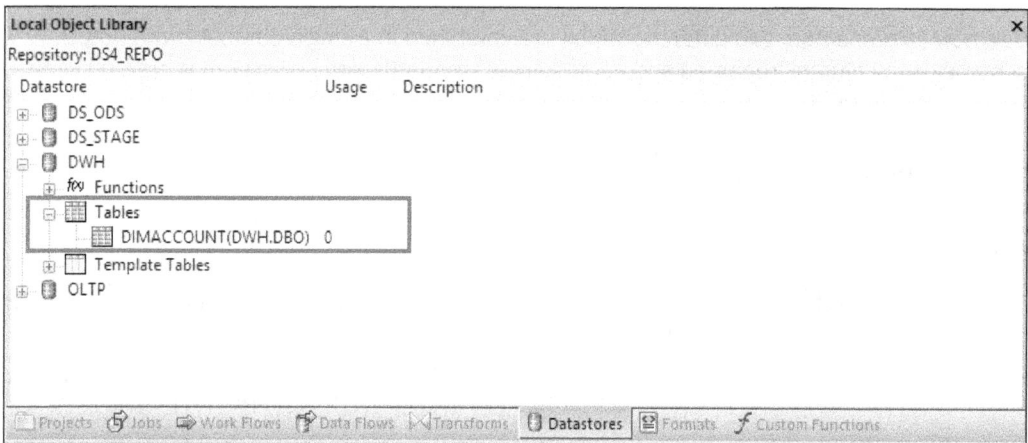

Creating different datastores for the same database could also be a flexible and convenient way of categorizing your source and target systems.

There is also a concept of configurations when you can create multiple configurations of the same datastore with different parameters and switch between them. This is very useful when you are working in a complex development environment with development, test, and production databases. However, this is a topic for future discussion in the upcoming chapters.

3

Data Services Basics – Data Types, Scripting Language, and Functions

In this chapter, I will introduce you to scripting language in Data Services. In this chapter, we will cover the following topics:

- ▶ Creating variables and parameters
- ▶ Creating a script
- ▶ Using string functions
- ▶ Using date functions
- ▶ Using conversion functions
- ▶ Using database functions
- ▶ Using aggregate functions
- ▶ Using math functions
- ▶ Using miscellaneous functions
- ▶ Creating custom functions

Introduction

It is easy to underestimate the importance of the scripting language in Data Services, but you should not fall for this pitfall. In simple words, scripting language is a glue that allows you to build smart and reliable ETL and unite all processing units of work (which are dataflow objects) together.

The scripting language in Data Services is mainly used to create custom functions and script objects. Script objects rarely perform data movement and data transformation. They are used to assist the dataflow object (main data migration and transformation processes). They are usually placed before and after them to assist with execution logic and calculate the execution parameter values for the processes that extract, transform, and load the data.

The scripting language in Data Services is armed with powerful functions that allow you to query databases, execute database stored procedures, and perform sophisticated calculations and data validations. It even supports regular expressions matching techniques, and, of course, it allows you to build your own custom functions. These functions can be used not just in the scripts but also in the mapping of Query transforms inside dataflows.

Without further delay, let's get to learning scripting language.

Creating variables and parameters

In this recipe, we will extend the functionality of our Hello World dataflow (see the *Understanding the Designer tool* recipe from *Chapter 2, Configuring the Data Services Environment*). Along with the first row saying "Hello World!", we will generate the second row, providing you with the name of the Data Services job that generated the greetings.

This example will not just allow us to get familiar with how variables and parameters are created but also introduce us to one of the Data Services functions.

Getting ready

Launch your **Designer** tool and open the `Job_HelloWorld` job created in the previous chapter.

How to do it...

We will parameterize our dataflow so that it can receive the external value of the job name where it is being executed, and create the second row accordingly.

We will also require an extra object in our job, in the form of a script that will be executed before the dataflow and that will initialize our variables before passing their values to the dataflow parameters.

1. Using the script button (🗎) from the right instrument panel, create a script object. Name it `scr_init`, and place it to the left of your dataflow. Do not forget to link them, as shown in the following screenshot:

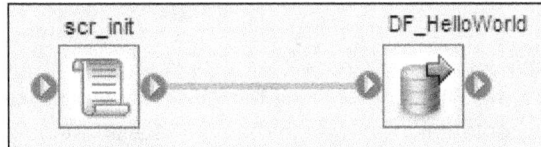

2. To create dataflow parameters, click on the dataflow object to open it in the main workspace window.

3. Open the **Variables and Parameters** panel. All panels in **Designer** can be enabled/displayed with help the of the buttons located in the top instrument panel, as in the following screenshot:

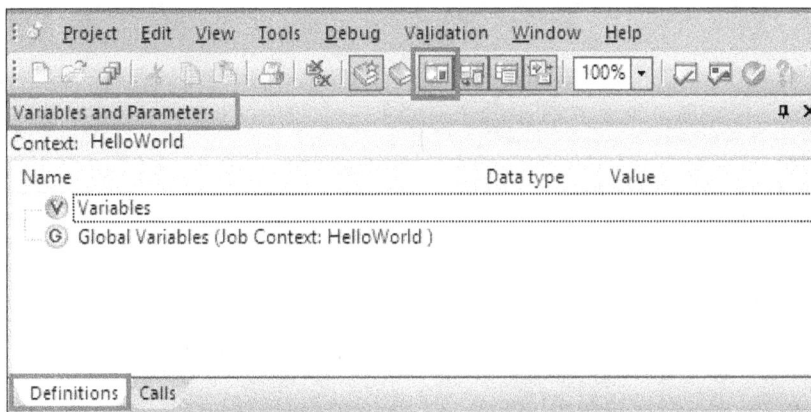

4. If they are not displayed on your screen, click on the **Variables** button on the top instrument panel (🗔). Then, right-click on **Parameters** and choose **Insert** from the context menu. Specify the following values for the new input parameter:

> Note that the $ sign is very important when you reference a variable or parameter, as it defines the parameter in Data Services and is required so that the compiler can parse it correctly. Otherwise, it will be interpreted by Data Services as a text string. Data Services automatically puts the dollar sign in when you create a new variable or parameter from the panel menus. However, you should not forget to use it when you are referencing the parameter or variable in your script or in the **Calls** section of the dataflow.

5. Now, let's create a job variable that we will use to pass the value defined in the script to the dataflow parameter. For this, use the **Back** (*Alt + Left*) button to go to the job level (so that its content is displayed in the main design window). Then, right-click on **Variables** in the **Variables and Parameters** panel and choose **Insert** from the context menu to insert a new variable. Name it `$1_JobName` and assign the `varchar(100)` data type to it, which is the same as the dataflow parameter created earlier.

6. To pass variable values from the job to the input parameter of the dataflow, go to the **Calls** tab of the **Variables and Parameters** panel on the job design level. Here, you should see the input dataflow `$p_JobName` parameter with an empty value.

7. Double-click on the `$p_JobName` parameter and reference the `$1_JobName` variable in the **Value** field of the **Parameter Value** window. Click on **OK**:

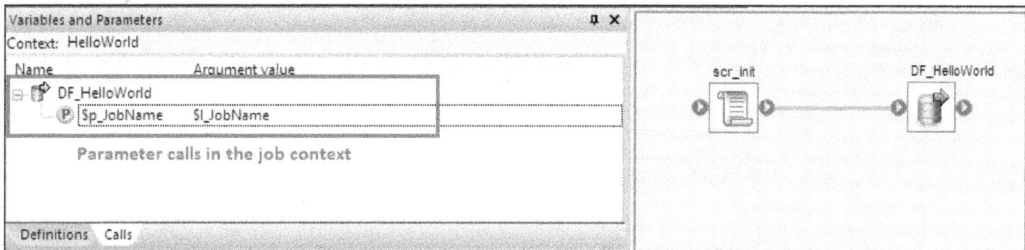

8. Assign a value to a job variable in the previously created script object. To do this, open the script in the main design window and insert the following code in it:

```
$1_JobName = 'Job_HelloWorld';
```

9. Finally, let's modify the dataflow to generate a new column in the target table. For this, open the dataflow in the main design window.

10. Open the Query transform and right-click on the `TEXT` column to go to **New Output Column... | Insert Below**.

11. In the opened **Column Properties** window, specify `JOB_NAME` as the name of the new column and assign it the same data type, `varchar(100)`.

12. In the **Mapping** tab of the Query transform for the `JOB_NAME` column, specify the `'Created by '||$p_JobName` string.

13. Go back to the job context and create a new global variable, $g_JobName, by right-clicking on the **Global Variables** section and selecting **Insert** from the context menu.

14. Your final Query output should look like this:

15. Now, go back to the job level and execute it. You will be asked to save your work and choose the execution parameters. At this point, we are not interested in modifying them, so just continue with the default ones.

16. After executing the job in **Designer**, go to **Management Studio** and query the HELLO_WORLD table to see that a new column has appeared with the 'Created by Job_HelloWorld' value.

How it works...

All main objects in Data Services (dataflow, workflow, and job) can have local variables or parameters defined. the difference between an object variable and an object parameter is very subtle. Parameters are created and used to accept the values from other objects (input parameters) or pass them outside of the object (output parameters). Otherwise, parameters can behave in the same way as local variables—you can use them in the local functions or use them to store and pass the values to other variables or parameters. Dataflow objects can only have parameters defined but not local variables. See the following screenshot of the earlier example:

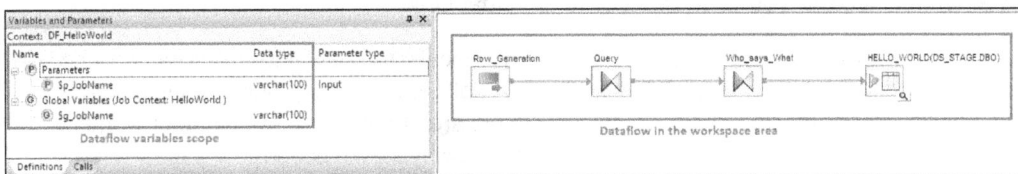

Workflow and job objects, on the other hand, can only have local variables defined but not parameters. Local variables are used to store the values locally within the object to perform various operations on them. As you have seen, they can be passed to the objects that are "calling" for them (go to **Variables and Parameters | Calls**).

There is another type of variable called a global variable. These variables are defined at the job level and shared among all objects that were placed in the job structure.

What you have done in this chapter is a common practice in Data Services ETL development: passing variable values from the parent object (job in our example) to the child object (dataflow) parameters.

To keep things simple, you can specify hard-coded values for the input dataflow parameters, but this is usually considered bad practice.

What we could also do in our example is pass global variable values to dataflow parameters. Global variables are created at a very top job level and are shared by all nested objects, not just with immediate job child objects. That is why they are called global. They can be created only in the job context, as shown here:

Also, note that in Data Services, you cannot reference parent object variables directly into child objects. You always have to create input child object parameters and map them on the parent level (using the **Calls** tab of the **Variables and Parameters** panel) to local parent variables. Only after doing this, you can go in your child object and map its parameters to the local child object's variables.

Now, you can see that parameters are not the same thing as variables, and they carry an extra function of bridging variable scope between parent and child. In fact, you do not have to map them to a local variable inside a child object if you are not going to modify them. You can use parameters directly in your calculations/column mapping.

Last thing to say here is that dataflows do not have local variables at all. They can only accept values from the parents and use them in function calls/column mapping. That is because you do not write scripts inside a dataflow object. Scripts are only created at the job or workflow level or inside the custom functions that have their own variable scope.

Data types available in Data Services are similar to common programming language data types. For a more detailed description, reference the official Data Services documentation.

> The **blob** and **long** data types can only be used by structures created inside a dataflow or, in other words, columns. You cannot create script variables and dataflow / workflow parameters of blob or long data types.

There's more...

Try to modify your `Job_HelloWorld` job to pass global variable values to dataflow parameters directly. To do this, use the previously created global variable `$g_JobName`, specify a hard-coded value for it (or assign it a value inside a script, as we did with the local variable) and map it to the input dataflow parameter on the **Calls** tab of the **Variables and Parameters** panel in the job context. Do not forget to run the job and see the result.

Creating a script

Yes, technically we created our first script in the previous recipe, but let's be honest—this is not the most advanced script in the world, and it does not provide us with much knowledge regarding scripting language capabilities in Data Services. Finally, although simplicity is usually a virtue, it would be nice to create a script that would have more than one row in it.

In the following recipe, we will create a script that would do some data manipulation and a little bit of text processing before passing a value to a dataflow input parameter.

How to do it...

Clear the contents of your `scr_init` script objects and add the following lines. Note that every command or function call should end with a semicolon:

```
# Script which determines name of the job and
# prepares it for data flow input parameter

print('INFO: scr_init script has started...');

while ($l_JobName IS NULL)
  begin
    if ($g_JobName IS NOT NULL)
    begin
      print('INFO: assigning $g_JobName value'
      ||' of {$g_JobName} to a $l_JobName variable...');
      $l_JobName = $g_JobName;
    end
    else
      print('INFO: global variable $g_JobName is empty,'
      ||' calculating value for $l_JobName'
      ||' using Data Services function...');
      $l_JobName = job_name();
      print('INFO: new value assigned to a local '
```

```
            ||'variable: $1_JobName = {$1_JobName}!');
    end


    print('INFO: scr_init script has successfully completed!');
```

Try to run a job now and confirm that the row inserted into the target HELLO_WORLD table has a proper job name in the second column.

How it works...

We introduced a couple of new elements of scripting language syntax. The # sign defines the comment section in Data Services scripts.

Note that we also referenced variable values in the text string using curly brackets {$1_JobName}. If you skip them, the Data Services compiler will not recognize variables marked with the $ sign and will use the variable name and dollar sign as part of the string.

> You can also use square brackets [] instead of curly brackets to reference variable/parameter values within a text string. The difference between them is that if you use curly brackets, the compiler will put the variable value in the quoted string `value` instead of using it as it is used in the text string.

Scripting language in Data Services is easy to learn as it does not have much variety in terms of conditional constructs. It has a simple syntax, and all its powers come from functions.

In this particular example, you can see one while loop and one conditional construct. The while loop is the only type of loop supported in the Data Services scripting language and the only conditional supported as well. This is really all you need in most cases.

The while (<condition>) loop expression should include a block of code starting with begin and ending with end. The condition check happens at the beginning of each iteration (even the very first one), so keep it in mind as even your very first loop iteration can be skipped. In our example, the loop runs while the $1_JobName local variable is empty.

The syntax of the if conditional element is the same—each conditional block should be wrapped in begin/end. It supports else if, and you can include multiple conditional statements separated by AND or OR. We can use the conditional to check whether the global variable from which we will be sourcing value for the local variable is empty or not. If it is not empty, we would assign it to a local variable, and if it's empty, we should generate a job name using the job_name() function that returns the name of the job it is executed in.

The print() function is a main logging function in the Data Services scripting language. It allows you to print out messages in the trace log file. Look at the following screenshot. It shows an excerpt from the trace log file displayed in one of the tabs in the main design window after you execute the job.

When you execute the job, Data Services generates three log files: trace log, monitor log, and error log. We will explain these logs in detail in the upcoming recipes and chapters. For now, use the trace log button to see the result of your job execution.

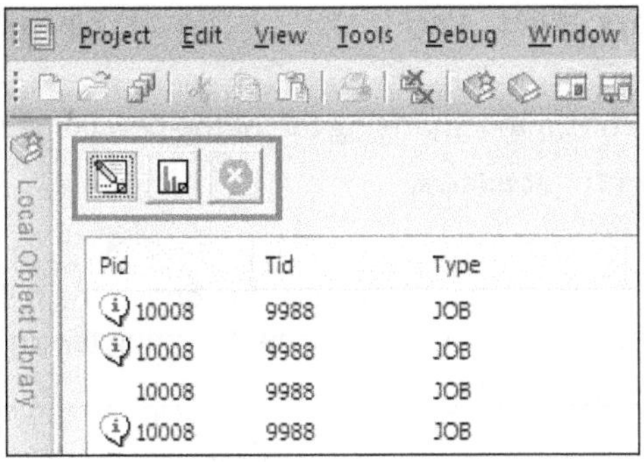

Pid	Tid	Type
ⓘ 10008	9988	JOB
ⓘ 10008	9988	JOB
10008	9988	JOB
ⓘ 10008	9988	JOB

Messages generated by the `print()` function are marked in the trace log as **PRINTFN** (see the following screenshot). You can also add your own formatting in the `print()` function to make the messages more distinguishable from the rest of the log messages (see the **INFO** word added in the example here):

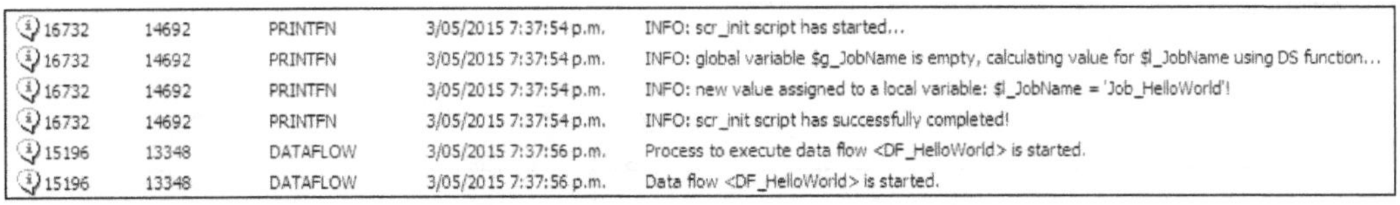

ⓘ 16732	14692	PRINTFN	3/05/2015 7:37:54 p.m.	INFO: scr_init script has started...
ⓘ 16732	14692	PRINTFN	3/05/2015 7:37:54 p.m.	INFO: global variable $g_JobName is empty, calculating value for $l_JobName using DS function...
ⓘ 16732	14692	PRINTFN	3/05/2015 7:37:54 p.m.	INFO: new value assigned to a local variable: $l_JobName = 'Job_HelloWorld'!
ⓘ 16732	14692	PRINTFN	3/05/2015 7:37:54 p.m.	INFO: scr_init script has successfully completed!
ⓘ 15196	13348	DATAFLOW	3/05/2015 7:37:56 p.m.	Process to execute data flow <DF_HelloWorld> is started.
ⓘ 15196	13348	DATAFLOW	3/05/2015 7:37:56 p.m.	Data flow <DF_HelloWorld> is started.

Using string functions

Here, we will explore a few useful string functions by updating our `HelloWorld` code to include some extra functionality. There is only one data type in Data Services used to store character strings, and that is `varchar`. It keeps things pretty simple for string-related and conversion operations.

How to do it...

Here, you will see two examples: applying string functions transformation within a dataflow and using string functions in the script object.

Follow these steps to use string functions in Data Services using the example of the `replace_substr()` function, which substitutes part of the string with another substring:

1. Open the `DF_HelloWorld` dataflow in the workspace window and add a new Query transform named **Who_says_What**. Put it after the Query transform and before the target template table.

2. Open the **Who_says_What** Query transform and add a new `WHO_SAYS_WHAT` output column of the `varchar(100)` type.

3. Add the following code into a mapping tab of the new column:

   ```
   replace_substr($p_JobName,'_',' ') || ' says ' ||
       word(Query.TEXT,1)
   ```

4. Your new Query transform should look like the one in the following screenshot. Note that you should use single quotes to define the string text in mapping or script:

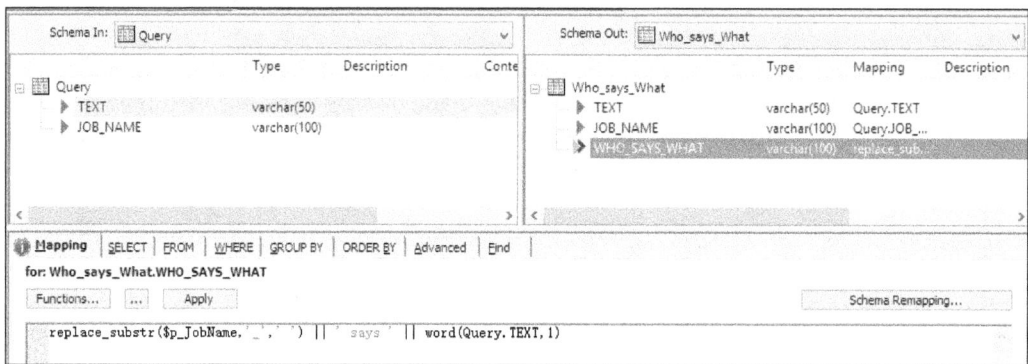

5. The final version of the dataflow should look like this:

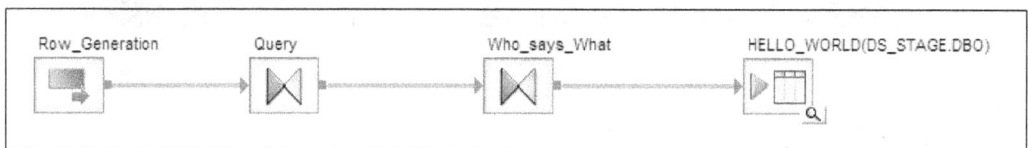

Save your work and execute the job. Go to **Management Studio** to see the contents of the `dbo.HELLO_WORLD` table. The table now has a new column with the `"Job HelloWorld"` says Hello string.

Using string functions in the script

We are not quite happy with the `Who_says_What` string. Obviously, only `HelloWorld` should be put in double quotes (they do not affect the behavior of string text in Data Services). Also, we will use the `init_cap()` function to make sure that only the first letter of our job name is capitalized.

Change the mapping of `WHO_SAYS_WHAT` to the following code:

```
'Job "' || init_cap(ltrim(lower($p_JobName),'job_')) ||
  '"' || ' says ' || word(Query.TEXT,1)
```

According to this logic, we are expecting the job name to start with the `Job_` prefix. In this case, we have to add an extra logic to the script logic running before the dataflow to make sure that we have this prefix in our job name. The following code will add it if the job name is not valid according to our naming standards. Add the following code before the last `print()` function call:

```
# Check that job is named according to the naming standards
if (match_regex($1_JobName,'^(job_).*$',
    'CASE_INSENSITIVE') = 1)
  begin
    print('INFO: the job name is correct!'');
  end
else
  begin
    print('WARNING: job has not been named according '
    || 'to the standards. '
    || 'Changing the name of {$1_JobName}...');
    $1_JobName = 'Job_'||$1_JobName;
    print('INFO: new job name is '||$1_JobName);
  end
```

As the final step, save the job and execute it. Now, the string in your third column should be `Job "Helloworld" says Hello`. Now, even if you rename your job and remove the `Job_` prefix, your script should see this and add the prefix to your job name.

How it works...

As you can see in the preceding example, we used common string manipulation functions similar to the other programming languages.

In the first part of the recipe, we transformed the mapping of the `WHO_SAYS_WHAT` column to strip out the `Job_` prefix from the parameter value. This allows us to correctly wrap the rest of the job name into double quotes for better presentation.

The `init_cap()` function capitalizes the first character of the input string.

The `lower()` function transforms the input string to lowercase.

The `ltrim()` function trims the specified characters on the left-hand side of the input string. Usually, it is used to quickly remove leading blank characters in strings. The `rtrim()` function does the same thing but for trailing characters.

The `word()` function is extremely useful in parsing the input string to extract "words" or parts of a string separated by space characters. There is an extended version of the `word_ext()` function. It accepts a specified separator as the third parameter. As the second parameter in both these versions, you will specify the word number to be extracted from the string.

You probably have already guessed that `||` is used as a string concatenation operator.

The second part of the changes implemented in this recipe in the script object contained the very interesting and powerful `match_regex()` function. It is one of the few functions that represents regular expression support within Data Services. If you are not familiar with regular expression concept, you can find many sources on the Internet explaining it in detail. Regular expressions are supported in almost all major programming languages and allow you to specify matching patterns in a very short form. This makes them very effective to parse a string and find a matching substring or pattern for it.

In the Data Services `match_regex()` function, if you specify a regular expression pattern string as a second input parameter, it will return `1` if it finds the match of the pattern in the input string. It will return `0` if it does not find the match. It is a very effective way to validate the format of the text string or look for specific characters or patterns in the string.

Here, we checked whether our job has the prefix `Job_` in its name. If not, we should add it to the beginning of the job name before passing the value to a dataflow.

There's more...

Feel free to explore the existing string functions available in Data Services. There are some extended versions of the functions we already used in the preceding recipe. You can take a look at them. For example, the `ltrim_blanks()` function allows you to quickly remove blank characters without specifying extra parameters. Its extended version, the `ltrim_blanks_ext()`, `substr()` function returns part of the string from another string. The `replace_substr()` function is used to substitute part of the string with another string.

We will definitely use some of them in our future recipes throughout the book.

Using date functions

Correctly dealing with dates and time is critically important in data warehouses. In the end, you should understand that this is one of the most important attributes in a majority of fact tables in your DWH, which defines the "position" of your data records. Lots of reports are filtering data by date-time fields before performing data aggregation. This is probably why Data Services has a decent amount of date functions, allowing a variety of operations on date-time variables and table columns.

Data Services supports the following date data types: `date`, `datetime`, `time`, and `timestamp`. They define what part of time units are stored in the field:

- `date`: This stores the calendar date
- `datetime`: This stores the calendar date and the time of the day
- `time`: This stores only the time of the day without the calendar date
- `timestamp`: This stores the time of the day in subseconds

How to do it...

Generating current date and time

Here is a script that can be included in your current script object in the HelloWorld job to display the generated date values in the job trace log.

To test this script, create a new job called `Job_Date_Functions` and a new script within it called `SCR_Date_Functions`. Also, create four local variables in the job: `$l_date` of the `date` data type, `$l_datetime` of the `datetime` data type, `$l_time` of the `time` data type, and `$l_timestamp` of the `timestamp` data type.

Print out date function examples to the trace log:

```
$l_date = sysdate();
print('$l_date = [$l_date]');

$l_datetime = sysdate();
print('$l_datetime = [$l_datetime]');

$l_time = systime();
print('$l_time = [$l_time]');

$l_timestamp = systime();
print('$l_timestamp = [$l_timestamp]');

$l_timestamp = sysdate();
print('$l_timestamp = [$l_timestamp]');
```

The trace logfile displays the following information:

```
$l_date = 2015.05.05
$l_datetime = 2015.05.05 18:47:27
$l_time = 18:47:27
$l_timestamp = 1900.01.01 18:47:27.030000000
$l_timestamp = 2015.05.05 18:15:21.472000000
```

As you can see, different data types are able to store different amounts of data. Also, you see that the `systime()` function does not generate date-related data (days, months, and years), and `1900.01.01` that you see in the first `timestamp` variable output is a dummy default `date` value. The second output shows that we used the `sysdate()` function to get this information.

Extracting parts from dates

Here are some useful operations you can perform to extract parts from data type values. Note that all of them return integer values. You can append these commands to the script object already created in order to test how they work:

```
$l_datetime = sysdate();
print('$l_datetime = [$l_datetime]');

# Extract Year from date field
print('Year = '|| date_part($l_datetime,'YY'));

# Extract Day from date field
print('Day = '|| date_part($l_datetime,'DD'));

# Extract Month from date field
print('Month = '|| date_part($l_datetime,'MM'));


# Display day in month for the input date
print('Day in Month = '|| day_in_month($l_datetime));

# Display day in week for the input date
print('Day in Week = '|| day_in_week($l_datetime));

# Display day in year for the input date
print('Day in Year = '|| day_in_year($l_datetime));

# Display number of week in year
print('Week in Year = '|| week_in_year($l_datetime));
```

```
# Display number of week in month
print('Week in Month = '|| week_in_month($1_datetime));

# Display last day of the current month in the provided input date
print('Last date of the date month = '|| last_date($1_datetime));
```

The output in a trace log should be similar to this:

```
$1_datetime = 2015.05.05 15:55:09
Year = 2015
Day = 5
Month = 5
Day in Month = 5
Day in Week = 2
Day in Year = 125
Week in Year = 18
Week in Month = 1
Last date of the date month = 2015.05.31 15:55:09
```

How it works...

Some functions use the extra formatting parameter, for example, date_part() does. You can also use 'HH', 'MI', 'SS' to extract hours, minutes, and seconds respectively.

There are also shorter versions of the date_part() function that allow you to extract year, month, or quarter without specifying any extra formatting parameters. For this, you can use the year(), month(), and quarter() functions.

An interesting function is the isweekend() function. It returns 1 if the specified date value is a weekend, and 0 if it's not.

There's more...

You can access the full list of functions available in Data Services from different places in **Designer**. One option is to open the script object. There is a **Functions...** button at the top of the main design window. Click it to open the **Select Function** window. All functions are categorized and have a short description explaining how they work and what they require as input parameters. Look at this screenshot:

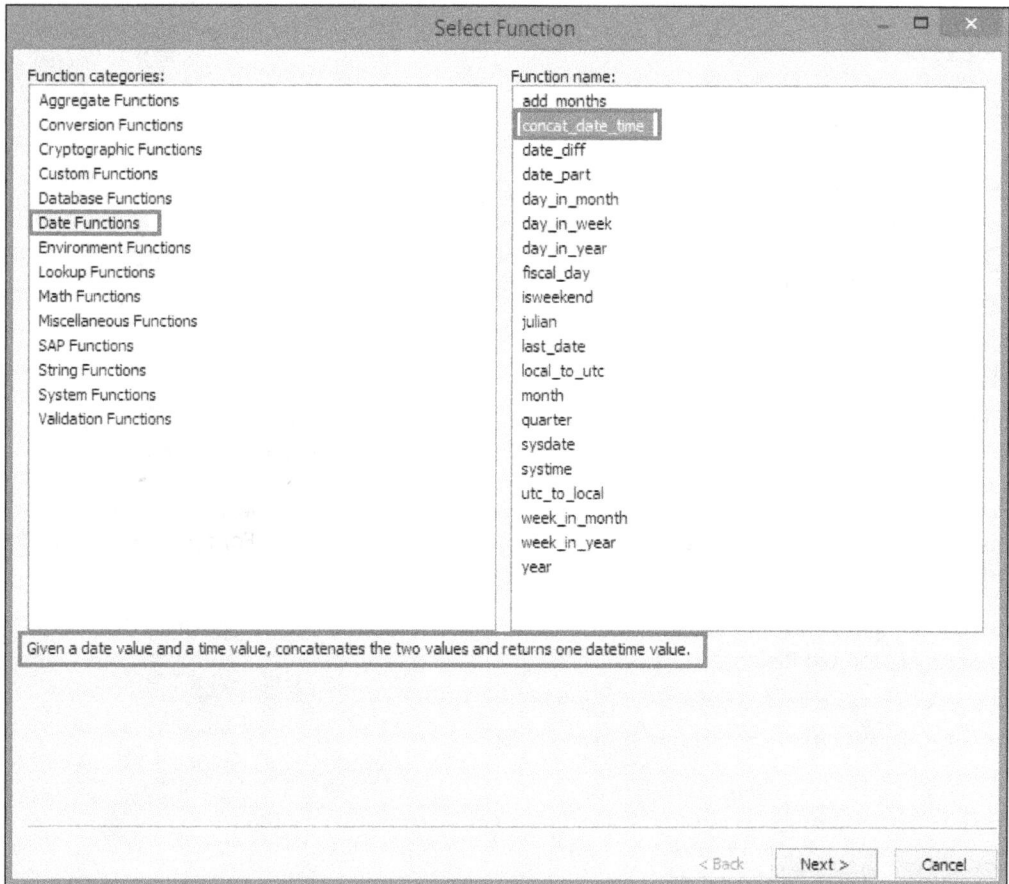

The same button is also available on the **Mapping** tab of the Query transform inside a dataflow, so you can access it if you are trying to create a transformation rule for one of the columns.

This list is also available in **Smart Editor**, but we will discuss it in detail in one of the next recipes. Of course, you can always reference the Data Services documentation to see all functions available in Data Services, and some examples of their usage.

Using conversion functions

Conversion functions allow you to change the data type of the variable or column data type in the Query transform from one to another. This is very handy, for example, when you receive date values as string characters and want to convert them to internal date data types to apply date functions or perform arithmetic operations on them.

How to do it...

One of the most used functions to convert from one data type to another is the `cast()` function. Look at the examples here. As usual, create a new job with an empty script object and type this code in it. Create a `$1_varchar` job local variable of the `varchar(10)` data type:

```
$1_varchar = '20150507';

# Casting varchar to integer
print( cast($1_varchar,'integer') );

# Casting varchar to decimal
print( cast($1_varchar,'decimal(10,0)') );

# Casting integer value to varchar
print( cast(987654321,'varchar'(10)') );

# Casting integer to a double
print( cast($1_varchar,'double') );
```

The output is shown here:

6932	8036	JOB	20/10/2015 2:37:36 p.m.	Job <Job_Conversion_functions> of runid <201510201437366932 8036> is initiated
6932	8036	JOB	20/10/2015 2:37:36 p.m.	Processing job <Job_Conversion_functions>.
6932	8036	JOB	20/10/2015 2:37:37 p.m.	Optimizing job <Job_Conversion_functions>.
6932	8036	JOB	20/10/2015 2:37:37 p.m.	Job <Job_Conversion_functions> is started.
6932	8036	PRINTFN	20/10/2015 2:37:37 p.m.	20150507
6932	8036	PRINTFN	20/10/2015 2:37:37 p.m.	20150507
6932	8036	PRINTFN	20/10/2015 2:37:37 p.m.	987654321
6932	8036	PRINTFN	20/10/2015 2:37:37 p.m.	20150507.000000

Remember that the `print()` function automatically converts the input to `varchar` in order to display it in a trace file. Note how casting to a `double` data type changed the appearance of the number.

Casting is helpful in order to make sure that you are sending values of the correct data type to the column of a specific data type or function that expects the data of the particular data type required for it to work correctly. Automatic conversions performed by Data Services when the value of one data type is assigned to a variable or column of a different data type could produce unexpected results and lead to errors.

However, the most useful conversion functions are functions used to convert a string to a date and vice versa. Add the following lines to your script and run the job:

```
$1_varchar = '20150507';

# Casting varchar to a date
print( to_date($1_varchar,'YYYYMMDD') );

# Converting changing format of the input date
# from ''YYYYMMDD' to 'DD.MM.YYYY'
print(
to_char(to_date($1_varchar,'YYYYMMDD'),'DD.MM.YYYY')
);
```

When converting text string to a date, you have to specify the format of the string so that the Data Services compiler can interpret and convert the values correctly. The full table of possible formats available in these two functions is available in the *Data Services Reference Guide* available for download at `http://help.sap.com`. Refer to it for more details. Here are some more examples of the `to_char()` function conversions of a `date` variable:

```
$1_date = sysdate();

print( to_char($1_date,'DD MON YYYY') );

print( to_char($1_date,'MONTH-DD-YYYY') );
```

The trace log should be similar to the following one:

```
07 MAY 2015
MAY-07-2015
```

Let's get familiar with another interesting data type: `interval`. It helps you perform arithmetic operations on dates. The script here performs arithmetic operations on a date stored in the $1_date variable by first adding 5 days to it, then calculating the first date of the next month, and finally subtracting 1 second from the date-time value stored in the $1_datetime variable.

See the example here:

```
$1_date = to_date('01/05/2015','DD/MM/YYYY');
print('Date = '|| $1_date );
```

```
# Add 5 days to the $l_date value
print('{$l_date} + 5 days = '|| $l_date + num_to_interval(5,'D')
   );

# Calculate first day of next month
print('Firs day of next month = '|| last_date($l_date) +
   num_to_interval(1,'D') );

# Subtract 1 second out of the datetime
$l_datetime = to_date('01/05/2015 00:00:00','DD/MM/YYYY
   HH24:MI:SS');
print('{$l_datetime} minus 1 second = '|| $l_datetime -
   num_to_interval(1,'S') );
```

How it works...

You probably have not noticed, but you have already seen the results of implicit data type conversion made automatically by Data Services in the previous recipes. For example, date extract functions returned `integer` values that were converted automatically to `varchar` so that they could be concatenated with the string part and displayed using the `print()` function, which, by the way, can accept only `varchar` as an input parameter.

Data Services does data type conversions automatically whenever you assign a value of one data type to a variable or column of a different data type. The only potential pitfall here is that if you rely on automatic conversion you are leaving some guessing work to Data Services and can get unexpected results in the end. So, understanding how and when conversion happens automatically to implement manual checks instead could be critical. Many bugs in ETL code are related to incorrect data type conversion, so you should be extra careful.

There's more...

Try to experiment with automatic conversion. For example, when adding integer numbers to date variables: `sysdate() + 10` to see how Data Services behaves and which default parameters it uses for formatting automatically converted value.

Using database functions

There is no great variety of functions in this area. Data Services encourages you to communicate with database objects and control the flow of data within a dataflow.

How to do it...

You will learn a little more about the functions here.

key_generation()

First, let's look at the `key_generation()` function. This is the function the can be called only from the dataflow (when used in column mapping), so we are not interested in it at this point as we cannot use it in the Data Services scripts.

This function is actually similar to the **Key_Generation** transform object that can be used as part of a dataflow as well, and it is used to lookup the highest key value from a table column and generate the next one. This is often used to populate the key column of the new record with the unique values before inserting this record to a target table. We will take a closer look at the **Key_Generation** transform in the upcoming chapters.

total_rows()

This function is used to calculate the total number of rows in the database table. The easiest and quickest way to check in the script whether the table is empty or not before running a dataflow populating this table is to run this function. Then, according to the results, you can make further decisions, that is, truncate the table directly from a script before running the next dataflow. Alternatively, you can use conditionals to skip the next portion of ETL code entirely.

See the example of how this function is used. As usual, you can create a new job with a script object inside it. Type the following code and run the job:

```
print(
total_rows('DWH.DBO.DIMACCOUNT')
);
```

Do not forget to import the table into your DWH datastore as you can reference only tables that have been imported in your Data Services repository. Look at this screenshot:

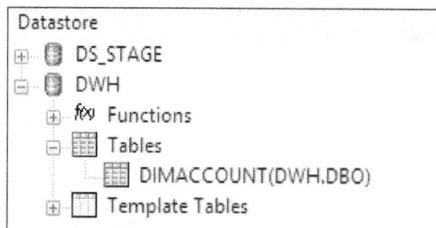

sql()

The `sql()` function is a universal function that allows you to perform SQL calls to any database for which you created a datastore object. You can run DDL and DML statements, `SELECT` queries, and even call stored procedures and database functions.

> You should be using the `sql()` function very carefully in your scripts, and we do not recommend that you use it at all in column mappings inside a dataflow. This function should only be used to return one record with as few fields as possible. So, always test the statement you place inside the `sql()` function directly in the database first to make sure it behaves as expected.

For example, to calculate the total number of rows in the `DimAccount` table with the `sql()` function, you can use the following code:

```
print('Total number of rows in DBO.DIMACCOUNT table is : '||
   sql('DWH','SELECT COUNT(*) FROM DBO.DIMACCOUNT')
);
```

How it works...

The `sql()` function is very convenient for doing stored procedures executions, truncating, and creating database objects and doing lookups for aggregated values when the query returns only one row or even one value. If you try to return the dataset of multiple rows, you will get only the value of the first field from the first row. It is still possible to query multiple fields, but it will require that you modify the query itself and add extra code to parse the returned string (see the example here):

```
# returning multiple fields from a database table
$1_row = sql('DWH','SELECT CONVERT(VARCHAR(10),ACCOUNTKEY) '||
   ' +\',\'+ CONVERT(VARCHAR(50),ACCOUNTDESCRIPTION) '||
   'FROM DBO.DIMACCOUNT');

$1_AccountKey = word_ext($1_row,1,',');
$1_AccountDescription = word_ext($1_row,2,',');

print('AccountKey = {$1_AccountKey}');
print('AccountDescription = {$1_AccountDescription}');
```

As you can see, this is a lot of code for such a simple procedure. If you want to extract and parse a multiple rows in the Data Services script, you will have to create a row-counting mechanism and loop through the rows by doing multiple query executions within a loop. However, you can try to do this yourself as an exercise to practice a little bit of Data Services scripting language.

> Note that you do not have to import the table you want to reference in the `sql ()` function into a datastore.

Using aggregate functions

Aggregate functions are used in dataflow Query transforms to perform aggregation on the grouped dataset.

You should be familiar with these functions as they are the same ones used in the SQL language: `avg ()`, `min ()`, `max ()`, `count ()`, `count_distinct ()`, and `sum ()`.

How to do it...

To demonstrate the use of aggregate functions, we will perform a simple analysis of one of our tables. Import the `DimGeography` table into the DWH datastore and create a new job with a single dataflow inside it using these steps:

1. Your dataflow should include the `DimGeography` source table and the `DimGeography` target template table in a `STAGE` database to send the output to:

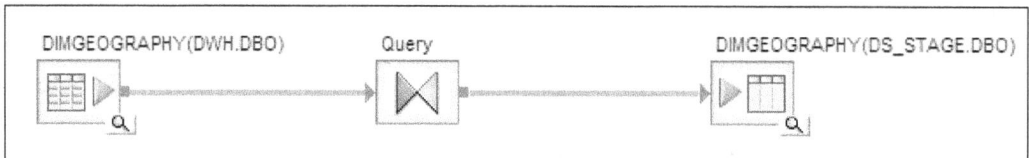

DIMGEOGRAPHY(DWH.DBO) Query DIMGEOGRAPHY(DS_STAGE.DBO)

2. Open the Query transform and create the following output structure:

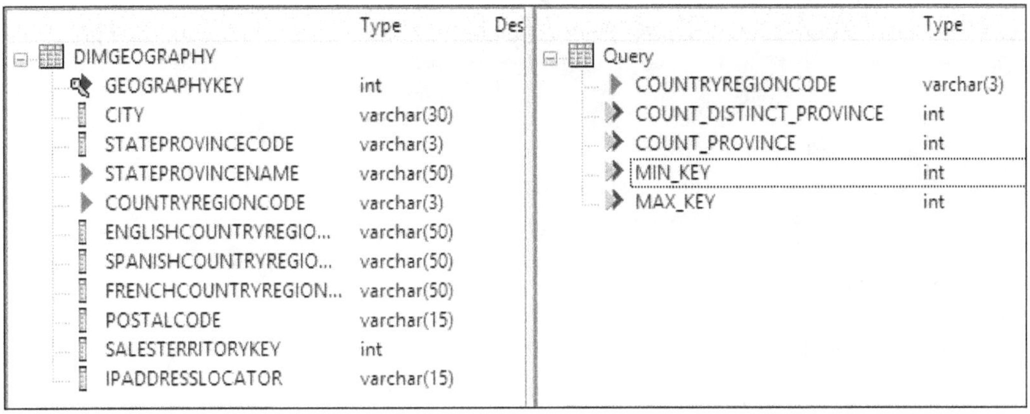

	Type	Des		Type
DIMGEOGRAPHY			Query	
GEOGRAPHYKEY	int		COUNTRYREGIONCODE	varchar(3)
CITY	varchar(30)		COUNT_DISTINCT_PROVINCE	int
STATEPROVINCECODE	varchar(3)		COUNT_PROVINCE	int
STATEPROVINCENAME	varchar(50)		MIN_KEY	int
COUNTRYREGIONCODE	varchar(3)		MAX_KEY	int
ENGLISHCOUNTRYREGIO...	varchar(50)			
SPANISHCOUNTRYREGIO...	varchar(50)			
FRENCHCOUNTRYREGION...	varchar(50)			
POSTALCODE	varchar(15)			
SALESTERRITORYKEY	int			
IPADDRESSLOCATOR	varchar(15)			

The COUNTRYREGIONCODE column contains country code values and will be the column on which we perform the grouping of the dataset. It is mapped from the input dataset to the output. Also, drag and drop it to the GROUP BY tab of the Query transform from the input dataset to specify it as a grouping column. Other columns are created as **New Output Column...** (choose this option from the context menu of the COUNTRYREGIONCODE column) and contain the following mappings (see the table here):

Output column name	Mapping expression
COUNT_DISTINCT_PROVINCE	count_distinct(DIMGEOGRAPHY.STATEPROVINCENAME)
COUNT_PROVINCE	count(DIMGEOGRAPHY.STATEPROVINCENAME)
MIN_KEY	min(DIMGEOGRAPHY.GEOGRAPHYKEY)
MAX_KEY	max(DIMGEOGRAPHY.GEOGRAPHYKEY)

3. Save the changes and run the job. Now, go to **Management Studio** and query the contents of the newly created DimGeography table in the STAGE database. You should get the results as shown in this screenshot:

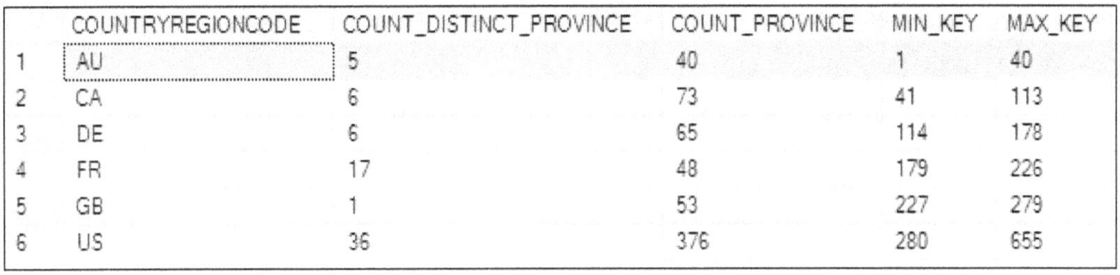

	COUNTRYREGIONCODE	COUNT_DISTINCT_PROVINCE	COUNT_PROVINCE	MIN_KEY	MAX_KEY
1	AU	5	40	1	40
2	CA	6	73	41	113
3	DE	6	65	114	178
4	FR	17	48	179	226
5	GB	1	53	227	279
6	US	36	376	280	655

How it works...

What we have just built in the dataflow in the Query transform can be done with the following SQL statement:

```
select
    CountryRegionCode,
    COUNT(DISTINCT StateProvinceName),
    COUNT(StateProvinceName),
    MIN(GeographyKey),
    MAX(GeographyKey)
from
    dbo.DimGeography
group by
    CountryRegionCode;
```

First, the `count_distinct()` function calculates the number of distinct provinces within each country, `count()` calculates the total number of rows for each country, and `min()` and `max()` show the lowest and highest `GeographyKey` values within each country group, respectively.

> You cannot use these functions directly in the scripting language but only in the Query transform. If you need to extract the aggregated values from the database tables within Data Services script, you can use `sql()` containing the `SELECT` statement with aggregated database functions.

Using math functions

Data Services has a standard set of functions available to perform mathematical operations. In this recipe, we will use the most popular of them to show you what operations can be performed on numeric data types.

How to do it...

1. Create a new job and name it `Job_Math_Functions`.
2. Inside this job, create a single dataflow called `DF_Math_Functions`.
3. Import the `FactResellerSales` table in your DHW datastore and add it to the dataflow as a source object.

4. Add the first Query transform after the source table and link them together. Then, open it and drag two columns to the output schema: PRODUCTKEY and SALESAMOUNT. Specify the FACTRESELLERSALES.PRODUCTKEY = 354 filtering condition in the **WHERE** tab:

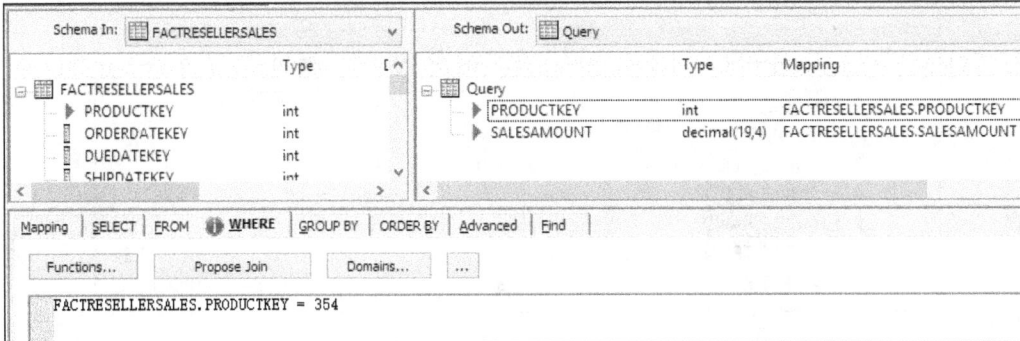

Schema In: ⊞ FACTRESELLERSALES ∨		[∧	Schema Out: ⊞ Query		
	Type			Type	Mapping
⊟ ⊞ FACTRESELLERSALES			⊟ ⊞ Query		
▶ PRODUCTKEY	int		▶ PRODUCTKEY	int	FACTRESELLERSALES.PRODUCTKEY
ORDERDATEKEY	int		▶ SALESAMOUNT	decimal(19,4)	FACTRESELLERSALES.SALESAMOUNT
DUEDATEKEY	int				
SHIPDATEKEY	int	∨			

Mapping | SELECT | FROM | ⓘ **WHERE** | GROUP BY | ORDER BY | Advanced | Find

Functions... | Propose Join | Domains... | ...

```
FACTRESELLERSALES.PRODUCTKEY = 354
```

5. Add the second Query transform and rename it Group. Here, we will perform a grouping operation on the product key we selected in the previous transform. To do this, add the PRODUCTKEY column in the **GROUP BY** tab and apply the sum() aggregate function on SALESAMOUNT in the **Mapping** tab:

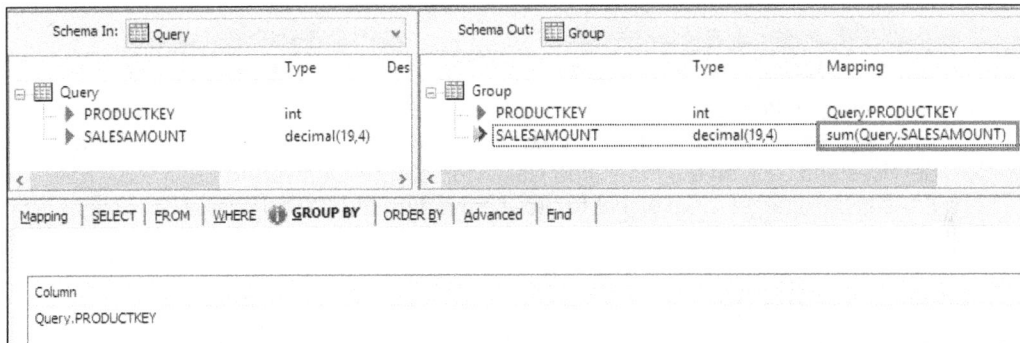

Schema In: ⊞ Query ∨		Des	Schema Out: ⊞ Group		
	Type			Type	Mapping
⊟ ⊞ Query			⊟ ⊞ Group		
▶ PRODUCTKEY	int		▶ PRODUCTKEY	int	Query.PRODUCTKEY
▶ SALESAMOUNT	decimal(19,4)		▶ SALESAMOUNT	decimal(19,4)	sum(Query.SALESAMOUNT)

Mapping | SELECT | FROM | WHERE | ⓘ **GROUP BY** | ORDER BY | Advanced | Find

Column

Query.PRODUCTKEY

6. Finally, add the last Query transform called `Math` and link it to the previous one. Inside it, drag all columns from the source to the target schema and add the new ones using **New Output Column...**. Specify mapping expressions, as in the following screenshot:

Schema Out: ⊞ Math	Type	Mapping
⊟ ⊞ Math		
▸ PRODUCTKEY	int	"Group".PRODUCTKEY
▸ SALESAMOUNT	decimal(19,4)	"Group".SALESAMOUNT
▸ EXAMPLE_CEIL	decimal(19,4)	ceil("Group".SALESAMOUNT)
▸ EXAMPLE_FLOOR	decimal(19,4)	floor("Group".SALESAMOUNT)
▸ EXAMPLE_RAND	decimal(19,4)	round(10 * rand_ext(),0)
▸ EXAMPLE_TRUNC	decimal(19,4)	trunc("Group".SALESAMOUNT,2)
▸ EXAMPLE_ROUND	decimal(19,4)	round("Group".SALESAMOUNT,2)

7. As the last step, add a new template table located in the `STAGE` database owned by the `dbo` user. This template is called `FACTRESELLERSALES`. Your dataflow should look like this now:

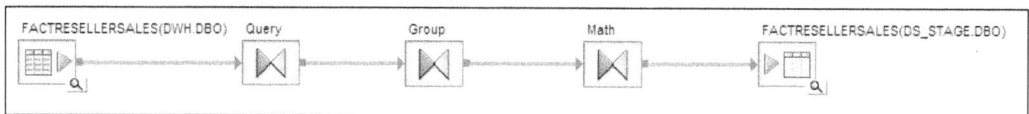

8. Save and run the job. Then, to check the result dataset, either query the new table from **SQL Server Management Studio**. Alternatively, open your dataflow in Data Services and click on the magnified glass icon of your FACTRESELLERSALES (DS_STAGE.DBO) target table object to browse the data directly from Data Services.

How it works...

The result you see here very well explains the effect of the math functions applied to your SALESAMOUNT column value:

PRODUCTKEY	SALESAMOUNT	EXAMPLE_CEIL	EXAMPLE_FLOOR	EXAMPLE_RAND	EXAMPLE_TRUNC	EXAMPLE_ROUND
354	1175932.5161	1175933.0000	1175932.0000	8.0000	1175932.5100	1175932.5200

The `ceil()` function returns the smallest integer value (automatically converted to an input column data type; that is why, you see trailing zeroes) equal to or greater than the specified input number.

The `floor()` function returns the highest integer value equal to or less than the input number.

The `rand_ext()` function returns a random real number from 0 to 1. In Data Services, you do not have much control over the behavior of the functions that generate random numbers. So, you have to apply extra mathematical operations to define the range of the generated random numbers and their types. In the example earlier, we generated random integer numbers from 0 to 10 inclusively.

The `trunc()` and `round()` functions perform rounding operations similar to `ceil()` and `floor()`, but `trunc()` just truncates the number to the length specified in the second parameter and shows you the result as is. On the other hand, the `round()` function rounds the number according to the precision specified.

There's more...

As an exercise, try the other Data Services mathematical functions. Modify the created dataflow to include examples of their usage. To see the full list of mathematical functions available, use the **Functions...** button in the script object or column mapping field and choose the **Math Functions** category in the **Select Function** window:

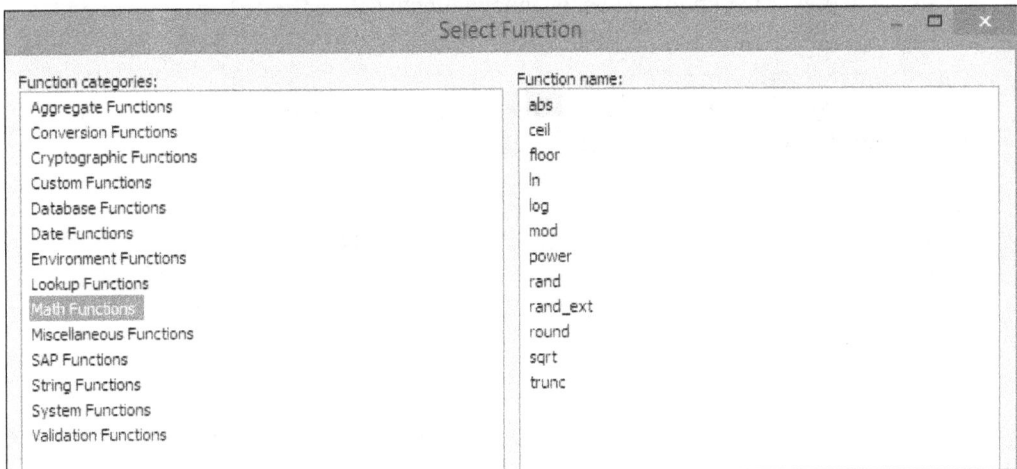

Function categories:	Function name:
Aggregate Functions	abs
Conversion Functions	ceil
Cryptographic Functions	floor
Custom Functions	ln
Database Functions	log
Date Functions	mod
Environment Functions	power
Lookup Functions	rand
Math Functions	rand_ext
Miscellaneous Functions	round
SAP Functions	sqrt
String Functions	trunc
System Functions	
Validation Functions	

Select Function

Using miscellaneous functions

Actually, miscellaneous groups include almost all types of functions that cannot easily be categorized. Among miscellaneous functions, there are functions that allow you to extract useful information from the Data Services repository, for example, name of the job, the workflow or dataflow it is executed from, functions that allow you to perform advanced string searches, functions similar to other standard SQL functions, and many others. Throughout the book, we will very often use Data Services miscellaneous functions. So, in this recipe, we will take a look at some of those that are usually used in the scripts and help you query the Data Services repository.

How to do it...

At this point, you should be pretty comfortable creating new jobs, script objects, and dataflow objects. So, I will not explain the steps in detail every time we need to create a new test job object. If you forgot how to do it, refer to the previous recipes in the book.

1. Create a new job and add a script object in it.

2. Open the script and populate it with the following code. This code shows you an example of how to use three miscellaneous functions: `ifthenelse()`, `decode()`, and `nvl()`:

```
# Conditional functions
$l_string = 'Length of that string is 38 characters';
$l_result = ifthenelse(length($l_string) = 8,print('TRUE'),print('
FALSE'));

$l_string = 'Length of that string is 38 characters';
$l_result = decode(
  length($l_string) = 10, print('TRUE'),
  length($l_string) = 12, print('TRUE'),
  length($l_string) = 38, print('TRUE'),
  print('FALSE')
);

$l_string = NULL;
$l_string = nvl($l_string,'Empty string');
print($l_string);
```

3. For this script to work, you should also make sure that you have local variables created at the job level— $l_string and $l_result of the `varchar(255)` data type.

How it works...

Most of the miscellaneous functions are functions that require advanced knowledge of Data Services. In this book, you will see a lot of examples of how they can be used in complex dataflows and Data Services scripts.

In this recipe, we can see three conditional functions: `ifthenelse()`, `decode()`, and `nvl()`. They allow you to evaluate the result of an expression and execute other expressions, depending on the result of the initial evaluation.

After executing the earlier script, you can see the following trace log records:

```
8172   12468   PRINTFN   18/05/2015 8:12:34 p.m.   FALSE
8172   12468   PRINTFN   18/05/2015 8:12:34 p.m.   TRUE
8172   12468   PRINTFN   18/05/2015 8:12:34 p.m.   Empty string
```

The `ifthenelse()` function accepts one input parameter: a comparison expression, which returns either TRUE or FALSE. If TRUE, then the second parameter of `ifthenelse()` is executed (if it is an expression) or just returned as the result of the function. The third parameter is executed (or returned) if the comparison expression returns FALSE.

The `decode()` function does the same thing as the `ifthenelse()` function, except that it allows you to evaluate multiple expressions. Its parameters go in pairs, as you can see in the example. The first parameter in a pair is a comparison expression and the second parameter is what is returned by the function if the comparison expression is TRUE. If it returns FALSE, then `decode()` moves to the next pair and then the next one until it reaches the last pair. If none of the expressions returned TRUE, then the last parameter of the `decode()` is returned as a default value.

> Bear in mind that the `decode()` function first returns TRUE without evaluating the rest of the conditions. So, be careful with the order of conditional expressions in the `decode()` function.

Finally, the last function in the example is the common SQL function `nvl()`. It returns the value specified in the second parameter if the first parameter is NULL. This function is very useful in dataflows. Usually, it is used as a mapping expression in the Query transform to prevent NULL values from coming through for a specific column. All NULL values will be converted to the value you define in the `nvl()` function.

Creating custom functions

In this recipe, we will get familiar with a **Smart Editor** tool available in **Designer** to help you write your scripts or functions in a convenient way.

We will create a new function that can be executed either within a script or within a dataflow. This function accepts two parameters: date value and number of days. It then adds the number of days to the input date and returns the result date.

How to do it...

1. Open **Designer** and go to **Tools | Custom Functions...** from the top level menu:

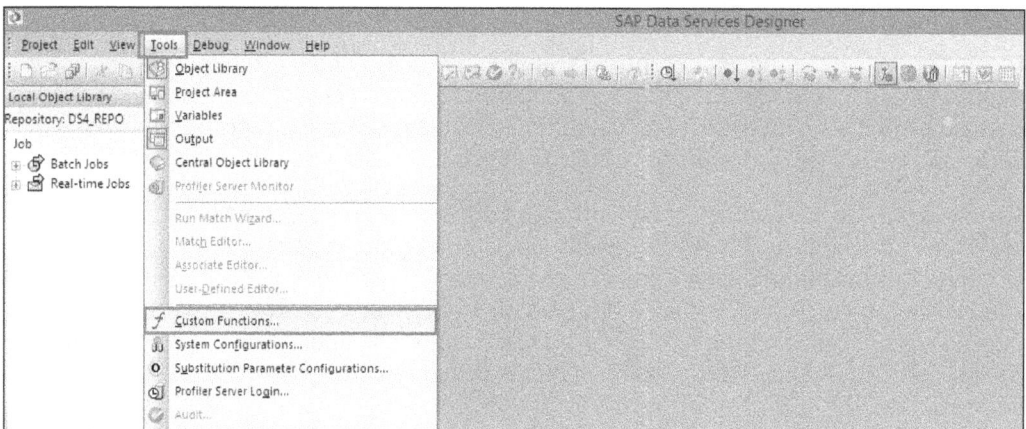

2. In the opened window, right-click in the area with the list of functions and choose **New....**

3. Choose the name of the new `fn_add_days` function and populate the description section, as shown in this screenshot:

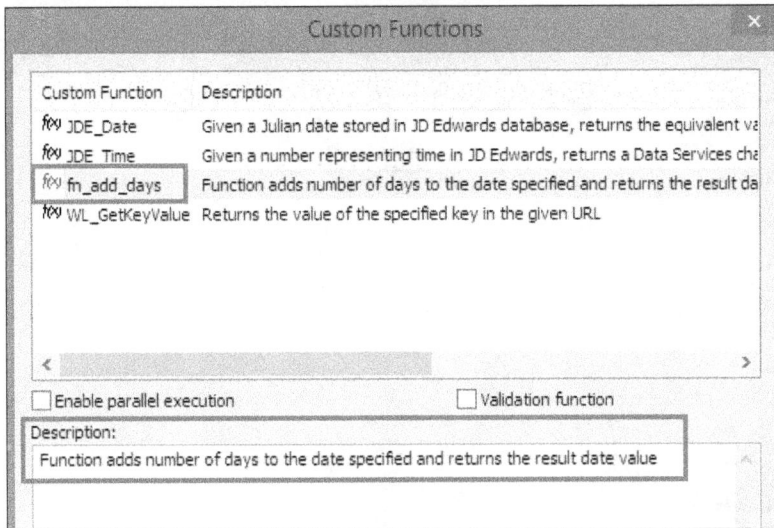

4. Then, click on **Next** to open a **Smart Editor** window and input the following code:

```
try
  begin
    $1_Date = to_date($p_InputDate,'DD/MM/YYYY');
    $1_Days = num_to_interval($p_InputDays,'D');
  end
catch ( all )
  begin
    print('fn_add_days() FAILED : check input
      parameters');
    raise_exception('fn_add_days() FAILED : check input
      parameters: '||
    ' Date format DD/MM/YYYY and number of days should be
      an integer value');
  end

$1_Result = $1_Date + $1_Days;

Return $1_Result;
```

5. For it to work, you have to create a set of required input/output parameters and local variables for this custom function. Your function in the **Smart Editor** should look like the one shown in this screenshot:

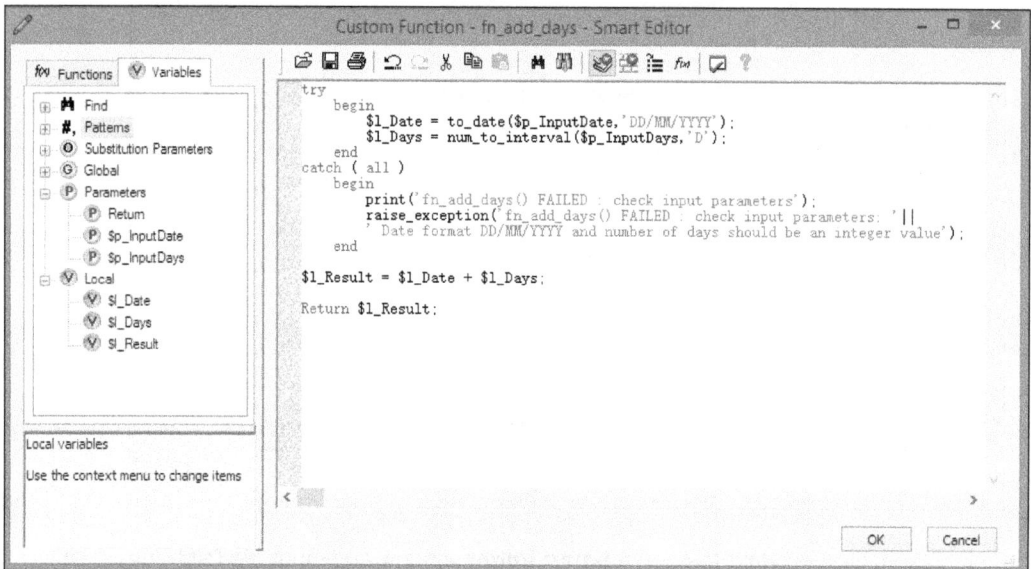

6. Create the following input parameters: $p_InputDate of the varchar data type and $p_InputDays of the integer data type. Use the left panel **Variables** inside the **Custom Function** window.

7. These local variables will be used only within a function and will not be accessible from outside of the function. Create $1_Date of the date data type, $1_Days of the interval data type, and $1_Result of the date data type.

8. Now, it is time to click on **OK** to create our first custom function and use it in the job. For this, you can create a simple job with one script object inside it using the following code:

```
print( to_char(fn_add_days('10/10/2015',12),'DD-MM-YYYY')
  );
```

How it works...

We made the input parameters of the varchar and integer data types for the convenience of calling the function. It will itself perform the conversion to the correct date and interval data types before returning the result of the date sum operation.

Even though we have not used the `num_to_interval()` function to convert integer values to intervals, Data Services will still perform the correct sum operation. This is because it does an automatic conversion of the numeric data type into intervals of days when it is used in arithmetic operation with dates. That is why, `print(sysdate() + 1)` will return you tomorrow's date.

In the code mentioned earlier, you can also see the error-handling mechanism that can be used in Data Services scripts: the `try-catch` block. Everything executed between `try` and `catch` if failed will never fail the parent object execution. It is very useful if you do not want to fail your job because of the non-critical piece of code failing somewhere inside it. In case of a failed execution, it is passed to the second `begin-end` block of the `try-catch`. Here, you can write extra log messages to the trace logfile and still fail the job execution with the `raise_exception()` function if you want to. We will discuss it in more detail in *Chapter 5, Workflow – Controlling Execution Order*, and *Chapter 9, Advanced Design Techniques*.

There's more...

The scripting language in Data Services is a very important tool extensively used in simple or complex jobs. In this chapter, we established a good base regarding building Data Services script language skills. You will find a lot more examples throughout this book.

4
Dataflow – Extract, Transform, and Load

In this chapter we will take a look at examples of the most important processing unit in Data Services—the dataflow object—and the most useful types of transformations you can use inside them. We will cover:

- ▶ Creating a source data object
- ▶ Creating a target data object
- ▶ Loading data into a flat file
- ▶ Loading data from a flat file
- ▶ Loading data from table to table – lookups and joins
- ▶ Using the Map_Operation transform
- ▶ Using the Table_Comparison transform
- ▶ Exploring the Auto correct load option
- ▶ Splitting the flow of data with the Case transform
- ▶ Monitoring and analyzing dataflow execution

Introduction

In this chapter we move to the most important component of the ETL design in Data Services: the dataflow object. The dataflow object is the container that holds all transformations that can be performed on data.

The structure of the dataflow object is simple: one or many source objects are placed, on the left-hand side (which we extract the data from), then source objects are linked to the series of transform objects (which perform manipulation on the data extracted), and finally, the transform objects are linked to one or many target table objects (telling Data Services where the transformed data should be inserted). During the transformation of the dataset inside the dataflow, you can split the dataset into multiple dataset flows, or conversely, merge multiple separately transformed dataflows together.

Manipulations performed on data inside dataflows are done on a row-by-row basis. The rows extracted from the source go from left to right through all objects placed inside the dataflow.

We will review all major aspects of dataflow design in Data Services, from creating source and target objects to the usage of complex transformations available as part of the Data Services functionality.

Creating a source data object

In a couple of previous recipes, you have already become familiar with data sources, importing tables, and using imported tables inside dataflows as source and target objects. In this recipe, we will create the rest of the datastore objects linking all our existing databases to a Data Services repository and will spend more time explaining this process.

How to do it...

In the *Understanding the Designer tool* recipe in *Chapter 2, Configuring the Data Services Environment*, we already created our first datastore object, STAGE, for the "Hello World" example.

So, why do you need a datastore object and what is it exactly? Datastore objects are containers representing the connections to specific databases and storing imported database structures that can be used in your Data Services ETL code. In reality, datastore objects do not store the database objects themselves but rather the metadata for the objects belonging to the application system or database that the datastore object connects to. These objects most commonly include tables, views, database functions, and stored procedures.

If you have not followed the steps in the "Hello World" example presented in *Chapter 2, Configuring the Data Services Environment,* you can find here the steps to create all datastore objects that will be used in the book explained in better detail. With these steps, we will create datastore objects referencing all databases we have created previously in SQL Server in the first two chapters:

1. Open the **Datastores** tab in **Local Object Library**.

2. Right-click on any empty space in the window and choose **New** from the context menu:

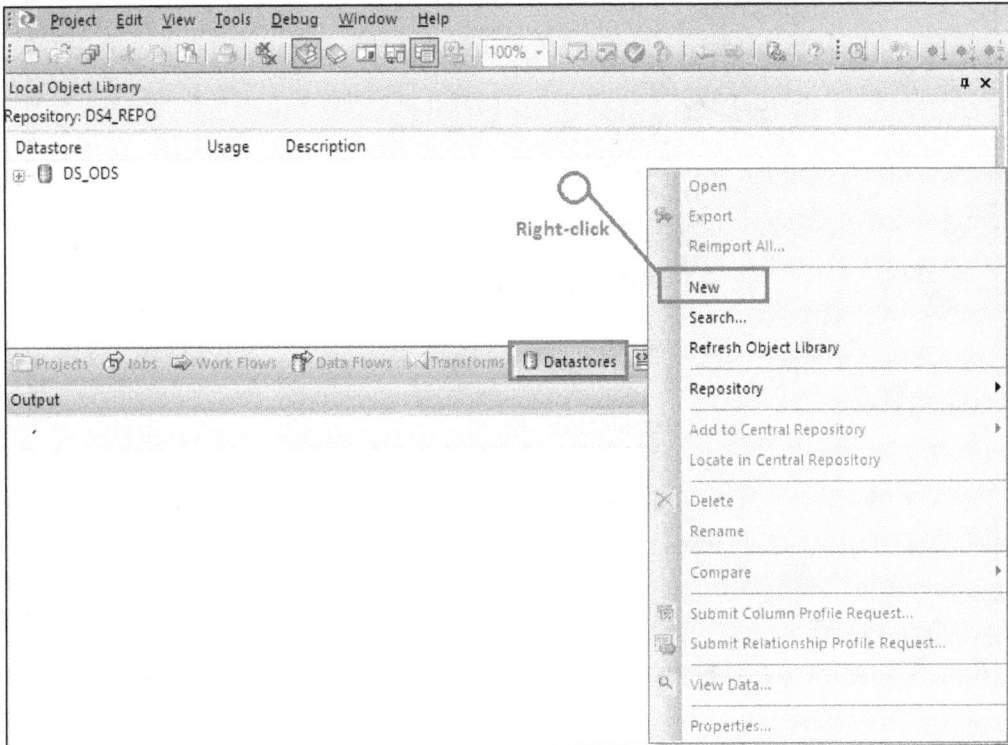

3. First specify **Datastore Type** for the datastore object. The datastore type defines the connectivity type and datastore configuration options that will be used by Data Services to communicate with referenced source/target system objects lying behind this datastore connection. In this book, we will mainly be working with datastores of the Database type. See that as soon as the datastore type **Database** is selected, a second **Database Type** option appears with a list of available databases:

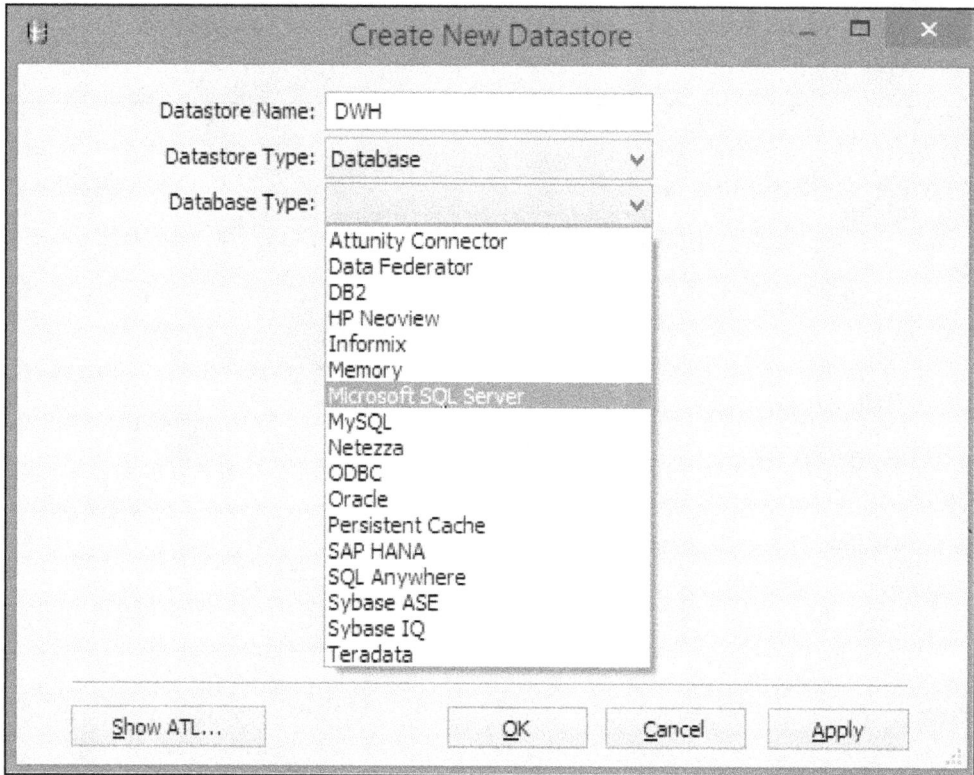

4. The **Create New Datastore** window, with all options expanding after you choose **Datastore Type** and **Database Type,** looks like this screenshot:

5. Leave all advanced options at their default values and configure only the mandatory options in the top window panel: the database connectivity details and user credentials, which will be used by Data Services to access the database and read/ insert the data.

6. Using the previous steps, create another datastore named ODS.

7. Altogether, you should have the following list of datastore objects created for all our local test databases. If you do not have all of them, please create the missing ones using the same steps just mentioned:

    ❏ DS_ODS: This is the datastore linking to the ODS database

    ❏ DS_STAGE: This is the datastore linking to the STAGE database

    ❏ DWH: This is the datastore linking to the AdventureWorks_DWH database

    ❏ OLTP: This is the datastore linking to the AdventureWorks_OLTP database

8. To create a reference to a database table in the datastore OLTP, expand the **OLTP** datastore in the **Local Object Library** tab and double-click on the **Tables** list.

9. The **Database Explorer** window opens in a workspace Designer section, showing you all the table and view objects in the OLTP database.

10. Find the HumanResources.Employee table in the **External Metadata** list, right-click on it, and choose the **Import** option from the context menu:

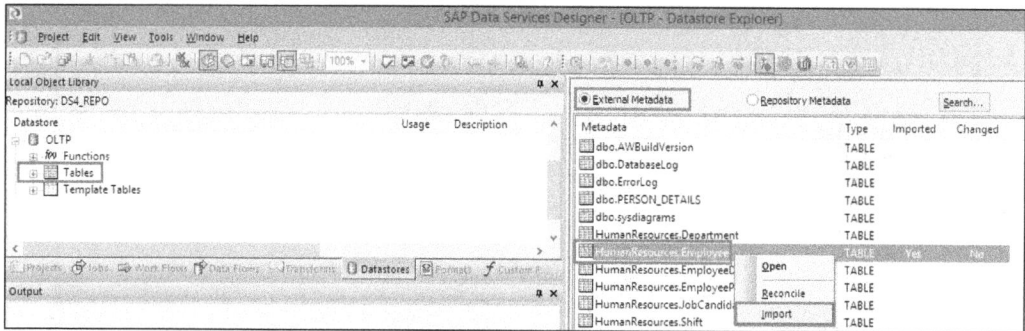

11. You can see how the table status has changed in **Database Explorer** to **Yes** under **Imported** and **No** under **Changed**.

12. Also, you can see the table references appear in the datastore OLTP table list. As it is not used anywhere in ETL code, the **Usage** column in the **Local Object Library** shows 0 for that table.

13. Now, close the **Database Explorer** window and double-click on the imported table name in the **Local Object Library** window. The **Table Metadata** window opens showing your table attributes and even allowing you to view the contents of the table:

Schema: EMPLOYEE(OLTP.HUMANRESOURCES)

	Type	Description
EMPLOYEE(OLTP.HUMANRESOURCES)		Employee information such as salary, department, and title.
BUSINESSENTITYID	int	Primary key for Employee records. Foreign key to BusinessEntity.BusinessEntityID.
NATIONALIDNUMBER	varchar(15)	Unique national identification number such as a social security number.
LOGINID	varchar(256)	Network login.
ORGANIZATIONLEVEL	int	The depth of the employee in the corporate hierarchy.

General | Attributes | Class Attributes | Indexes | Partitions | View Data

BUSINESSENTITYID	NATIONALIDNUMBER	LOGINID	ORGANIZATIONLEVEL	JOBTITLE	BIRTHDATE	MARITALSTATUS	GENDER
1	295847284	adventure-works\ken0	0	Chief Executive Officer	1963.03.02	S	M
2	245797967	adventure-works\terri0	1	Vice President of Engineering	1965.09.01	S	F
3	509647174	adventure-works\roberto0	2	Engineering Manager	1968.12.13	M	M
4	112457891	adventure-works\rob0	3	Senior Tool Designer	1969.01.23	S	M

> This **Table Metadata** window is extremely useful for performing a source system analysis when you have to learn the source data to understand it before starting to develop your ETL code and applying transformation rules on it.

14. The **View Data** tab has three subtabs within it: the **Data**, **Profile**, and **Column profile** tabs. Choose the **Column profile** tab and select the GENDER column in the drop-down list.

15. Click on the **Update** button to see the column profile data:

General | Attributes | Class Attributes | Indexes | Partitions | View Data

Top: 10 | GENDER | Update

Value	Total	Percentage, %
M	206	71.03%
F	84	28.97%
Other	0	0.00%

Column profiling data shows that there are **206** male employees (**71.03%**) against **84 (28.97%)** female ones.

How it works...

The most important thing you should understand about datastore objects is that when you import a database object into a datastore, all you do is you create a reference to the database object. You are not creating a physical copy of the table in your Data Services datastore when you import a table. Hence, when you use View data in the **Table Metadata** window for that table, Data Services executes the **SELECT** query in the background to extract this data for you.

Looking at the browsing external metadata screen again, you can see that there are two other options available in the table context menu: **Open** and **Reconcile**:

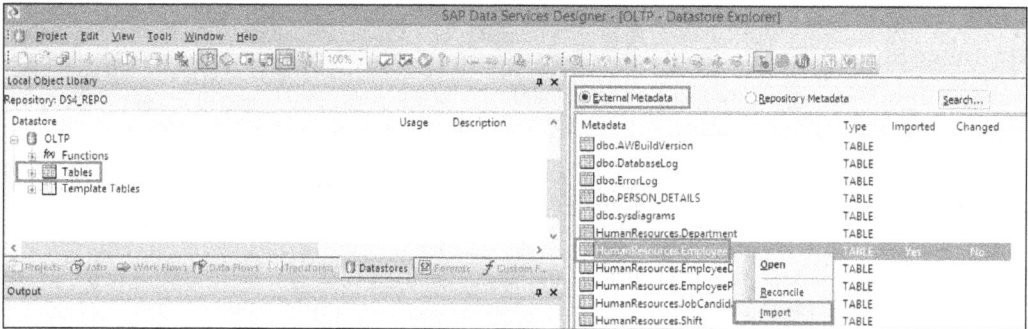

The **Open** option allows you to open an external table metadata window which can display table definition information, partitions, indices, table attributes, and other useful information.

The **Reconcile** option simply updates the two columns, **Imported** and **Changed**, in the **External Metadata** list. It is useful when you want to check whether the table object has been imported into a datastore already and whether it has changed in the database since the last time it was imported into a datastore.

> It is the ETL developer's responsibility to reimport the table objects in the datastore if their definition or structure has been changed on the database level. Data Services does not automatically perform this operation. The most common problem with table object synchronization is when the column populated by ETL gets removed from the table in the database. To reflect this change, the developer has to reimport the table object in the datastore to update table object structure in Data Services and then update ETL code to make sure that a non-existing column is not referenced as the target column anymore.

Views as source objects behave exactly as tables. They can be imported in the datastore in the same **Tables** section along with other table objects. The only difference is that you cannot specify the imported view as a target object in your dataflow.

You may also wonder that, if the datastore object represents the connection to a specific database, why do you not see all the database objects straight away after creating it. The answer is simple: you import only those database objects you will be using in your ETL code. If the database has a few hundred tables, it would be extremely time- and resource-intensive for Data Services to automatically synchronize all datastore object references with actual database objects each time you open a Designer application. It is also easier for the developer to be able to see only the tables used in ETL development. Plus, with the **datastore configurations** feature, you can use the same datastore object to connect to different physical databases, that might have different versions of the tables with the same names, so the synchronization of objects imported in the datastore is solely your responsibility and has to be done manually. We will discuss **configurations** in the future chapters.

The profiling functionality of Data Services that we used in this recipe allows you to look into the data without the need for going to SQL Server Management Studio and manually querying the tables. It is easy and convenient to use during ETL development.

There's more...

It is quite difficult to cover all the information about all datastore settings in one chapter, as Data Services is able to connect to so many different databases and application systems. As the datastore options are database specific, the number of options and their behavior vary depending on which database or system you are trying to connect to.

Creating a target data object

A target data object is the object to which we send the data within a dataflow. There are a few different types of target data objects, but the two main ones are tables and flat files. In this recipe, we will take a look at a target table object.

> Views imported into a datastore cannot be target objects within a dataflow. They can only be a source of data.

Getting ready

To prepare for this recipe, we need to create a table in our STAGE database. To do that, please connect to SQL Server Management Studio and create the Person table in the STAGE database using the following command:

```
CREATE TABLE dbo.Person
(
  FirstName varchar(50),
  LastName varchar(50),
  Age integer
);
```

This table will be used as a target table, which we will load data into by using Data Services. We will use the data stored in the `Person` table from the OLTP database as the source data to be loaded.

How to do it...

1. Open the Data Services Designer application.

2. In the `DS_STAGE` datastore, right-click on **Tables** and choose the option **Import By Name...** (another quick method to import a table definition into Data Services without opening Database Explorer). Of course, in order to do that, you should know the exact table name and schema it was created in.

3. In the opened window, enter the required details, as in the following screenshot:

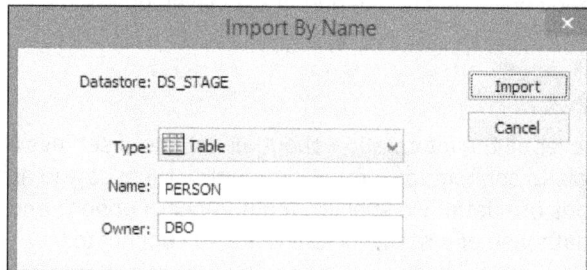

4. Click on the **Import** button to finish.

5. Also in the OLTP datastore, import a new table `Person` from the `Person` schema inside the `AdventureWorks_OLTP` database. We will use this table as a source of data.

> In the example of using SQL Server as an underlying database, the owner is synonymous with the database schema. When importing a table by name in the datastore or creating template tables, the **Owner** field defines the schema where the table will be imported from/created in the database. So, keep in mind that you have to use existing schema created previously.

6. Create a new job with a new dataflow object, open the dataflow, and drag the `Person` table from the OLTP datastore into this dataflow as a source. Then, drag the `Person` table from the `DS_STAGE` datastore as a target.

7. Create a new **Query** transform between them and link it to both source and target tables:

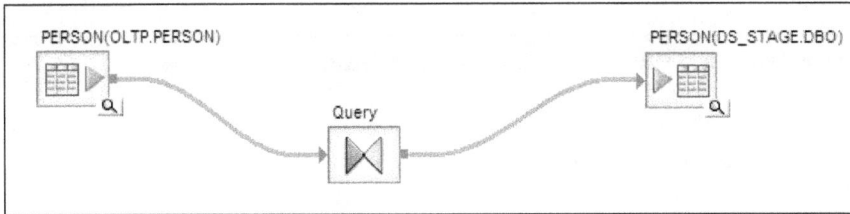

8. As soon as you open the **Query** transform, you will see that both input and output structures were created for you. All column names and data types were imported from the source and target objects you linked the **Query** transform to, and all you have to do is to map the column values from the source to pass to the columns in the target you want to pass them to.

9. Map the source `FIRSTNAME` column to the target `FIRSTNAME` column and perform the same mapping for `LASTNAME`. As there is no `AGE` column in the source, put `NULL` as the value for the mapping expression for the `AGE` target column in the **Query** transform. This can be done by dragging and dropping from the input to the output schema or by typing the mapping manually:

10. Each target object within a dataflow has a set of options that is available in the **Target Table Editor** window. To open it, double-click on a target table object in the dataflow workspace:

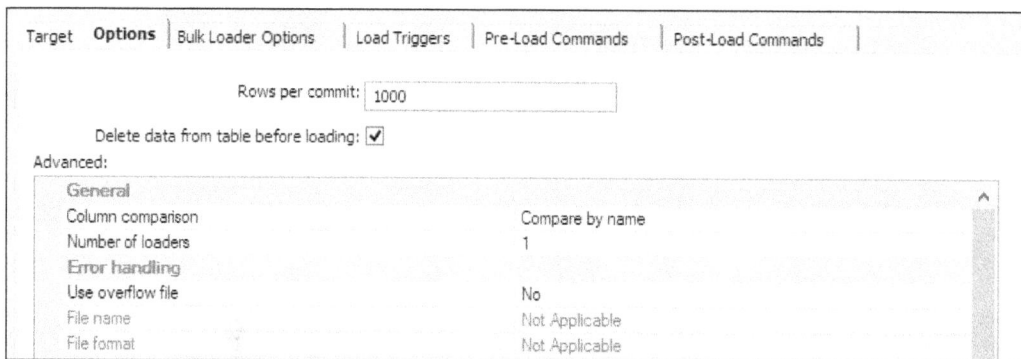

Target	**Options**	Bulk Loader Options	Load Triggers	Pre-Load Commands	Post-Load Commands	

Rows per commit: `1000`

Delete data from table before loading: ☑

Advanced:

General	∧
Column comparison	Compare by name
Number of loaders	1
Error handling	
Use overflow file	No
File name	Not Applicable
File format	Not Applicable

11. For now, let's just select the **Delete data from table before loading** checkbox. This option makes sure that each time the dataflow runs, all target table records are deleted by Data Services before populating the target table with data from a source object.

12. Validate the dataflow by clicking on the **Validate Current** button when the dataflow is opened in the main workspace to make sure that you have not made any design errors.

13. Now execute the job and click on the **View Data** button in the bottom-right corner of the target table icon within a dataflow to see the data loaded into the target table.

How it works...

You can see that the target table object has a lot of options. Data Services can perform different types of loading of the same dataset, and all those types are configured in the target table object tabs. Some of them are used if the inserted data set is voluminous, while some of them allow you to insert data without duplicating it. We will discuss all of this in detail in a later chapters.

When Data Services selects data from source tables, all it does is execute the `SELECT` statement in the background. But when Data Services inserts the data, there are risks such as incompatible data types/values, duplicate data (which violates referential integrity in the target table), slow performance, and so on. Do not forget that you insert data after transforming it, so it is your responsibility to understand the target database object requirements and specifics of the data you are inserting.

That is why the loading mechanism in Data Services has many more settings to configure and is much more flexible than the mechanism of getting source data inside a dataflow.

There's more...

As you might remember from the "Hello World" example in *Chapter 2, Configuring the Data Services Environment,* there is a great and simple way to create target table objects in a dataflow without the necessity to create a physical table in the database first and import it into the DS datastore. We used this type of target table before, and I am talking about **template** tables. Objects that we used in the previous recipes when we wanted Data Services to create a physical target table for us from the mappings we defined in a Query transform inside our ETL code in a dataflow.

> Note that the template target table has an extra target table option; **Drop and re-create table**. By default, it is ticked and gets physically dropped and recreated each time the dataflow runs. Data Services generates a table definition from the output schema of the last transform object in the dataflow linked to the target table object.

As you can see in the following figure, you can specify multiple target tables. They get populated with the same data set coming from the source table, and as they get populated from the same output schema of the Query transform, they have the same table definition format:

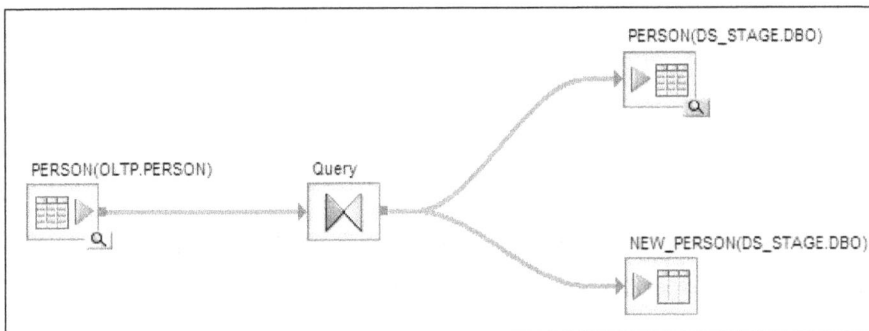

To create a template table, you use the right-hand side tool menu in the Designer and the template table icon shown in the following screenshot:

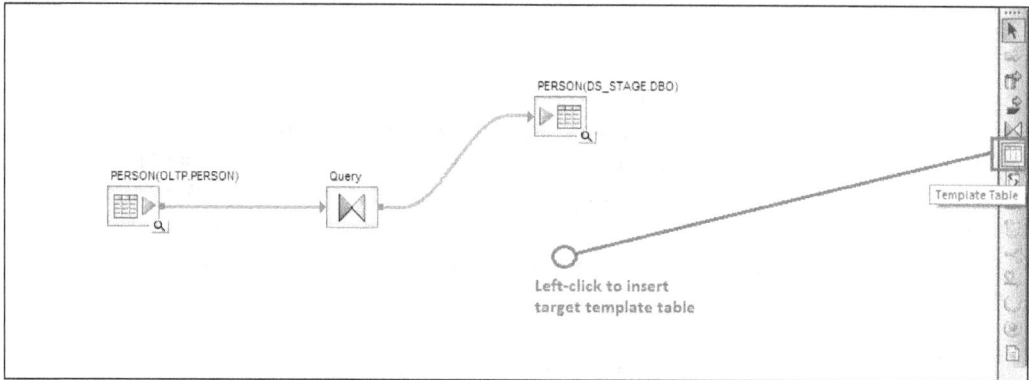

Click on the template table button in the tool menu and then on the empty space in the dataflow workspace to place it as a target table object.

Specify the template table name, the Data Services datastore where it should be created, and the database owner (schema) name where the table gets created physically when the dataflow is executed:

Loading data into a flat file

This recipe will teach you how to export information from a table into a flat file using Data Services.

Flat files are a popular choice when you need to store data externally for backup purposes or in order to transfer and feed it into another system or even send to another company.

The simplest file format usually describes a list of columns in specific order and a delimiter used to separate field values. In most cases, it's all you need. As you will see a bit later, Data Services has many extra configuration options available in the File Format object, allowing you to load the contents of the flat files into a database or export the data from a database table to a delimited text file.

How to do it...

1. Create a new dataflow and use the EMPLOYEE table from the OLTP datastore imported earlier as a source object.

2. Link the source table with a **Query** transform and drag - and - drop all source columns to the output schema for mapping configuration.

3. In the **Query** transform, right-click on the parent *Query* item, which includes all output mapping columns, and choose the **Create File Format...** option at the bottom of the opened context menu:

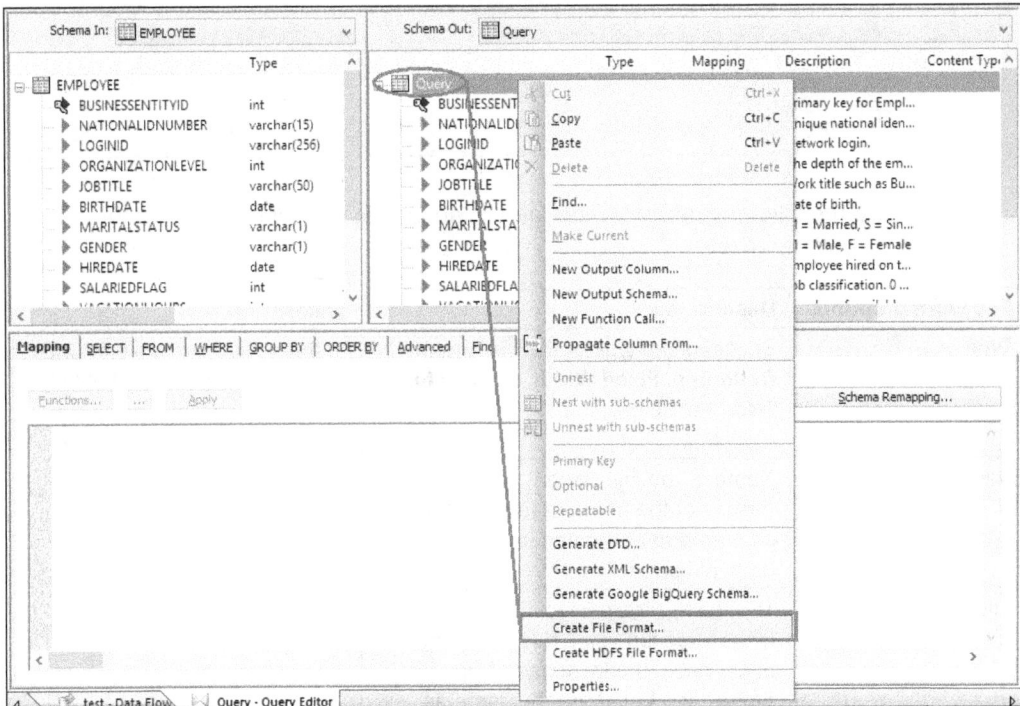

4. The main **File Format Editor** window opens:

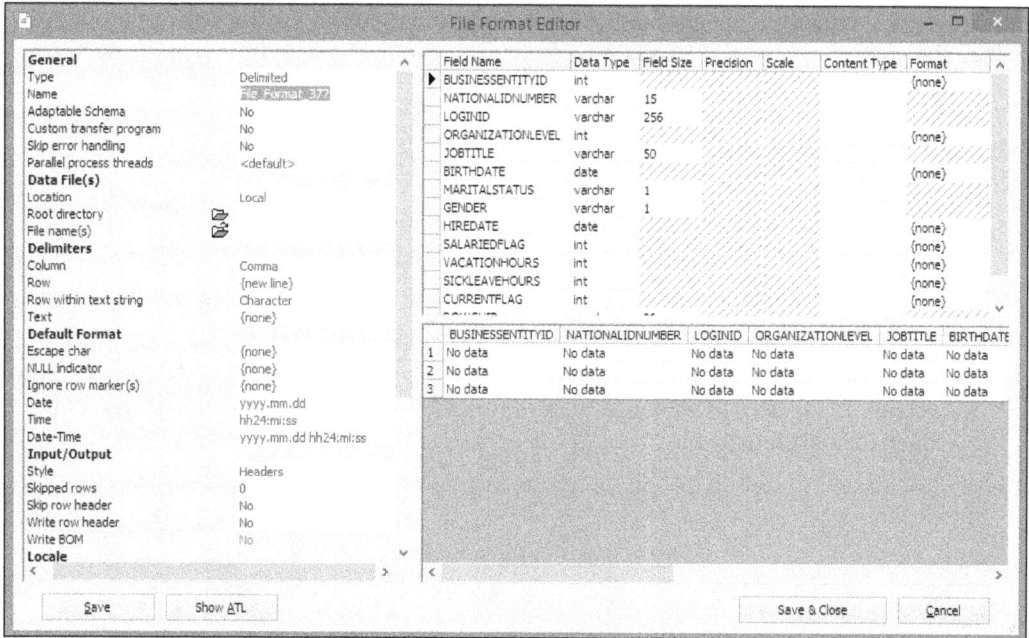

5. Refer to the following table for more details about File Format options and their corresponding values:

File Format options	Description	Value
Type	Specifies the type of the file format: **Delimited**, **Fixed Width**, **Unstructured Text**, and so on.	In this recipe, we are creating plain text file with row fields separated by a comma. Choose the **Delimited** option.
Name	Name of the File Format. Note that this is not the name of the file that will be created but the general name of the File Format.	Type F_EMPLOYEE.
Location	This is the physical location of the file referenced using this file format. In our case, the locations of **Job Server** and **Local** are the same as Data Services installed on the same machine where we executed our Designer application.	Choose **Job Server**.
Root directory	Directory path to the file. Make sure that this directory exists.	Type C:\AW\Files.

File Format options	Description	Value
File name(s)	Name of the file that we read data from or write into.	Type HR_Employee.csv.
Delimiters | Column	You can either choose from existing options: **Tab**, **Semicolon**, **Comma**, **Space**, or just type in your own custom delimiter as one character or a sequence of characters.	Choose **Comma**.
Delimiters | Text	You can specify whether you want character values to be wrapped in quotes / double quotes or not.	Choose ".
Skip row header	When you read from the file, use this option to skip the row header so it is not confused as a first data record.	We do not have to change this option as it would not make any effect because we are going to write to a flat file, not read from it.
Write row header	Same options as the previous one, but for cases when you write into a file. If set to **Yes**, the row header will be created as a first line in the file. If **No**, the first line in the file will be a data record.	Choose **Yes** to create a row header when writing to a file.

6. Click on the **Save & Close** button to close **File Format Editor** and save the new File Format.

7. Now you can open the **Local Object Library | Formats** tab and see your newly created file format F_EMPLOYEE.

8. Open the dataflow workspace and drag-and-drop this file format from the **Local Object Library** tab to a dataflow and choose the **Make Target...** option.

9. Link your **Query** transform to a target file object and validate your dataflow to make sure that there are no errors.

10. Run the job. You will see that the file HR_Employee.csv appears in C:\AW\Files and gets populated with 292 records (1 header record + 291 data records).

How it works...

File format configuration provides you with a flexible solution for reading data from and loading data into flat files. You can even set up automatic date recognition and configure an error handling mechanism to reject rows that do not fit into a defined file format structure.

Note that editing the file format from **Local Object Library** and editing it directly from the dataflow where it was placed to be used to read or write from flat files is not the same. If you edit it inside the dataflow, you will notice that some fields in the **File Format Editor** are grayed out. Opening the same file format for editing from **Local Object Library** makes those fields available for editing. This happens because when imported in a dataflow, the **File Format** object becomes an instance of the parent **File Format** object stored in a **Local Object Library**. and because all changes applied to an instance inside a dataflow are not propagated to other instances of this **File Format** object imported into other dataflows. Alternatively, when you modify the **File Format** definition in **Local Object Library**, changes made are propagated to all instances of this File Format object imported to different dataflows across ETL code.

> Some file format configuration parameters can be changed only on the parent file format object in **Local Object Library**.

You should also keep in mind that export to a flat file in Data Services is quite a forgiving process. For example, if your file format has the `varchar(2)` character field and you are trying to export a line of 50 characters to a file in this field, Data Services will allow you to do that. In fact Data Services does not care much about the columns specified in the file format at all if you use your file format to export data to a flat file. Data definition will be sourced from the output schema of the preceding transformation object linked to the target file object.

Importing from a flat file on the other hand is a very strict process. Data Services will reject the record immediately if it does not fit the file format definition.

There's more...

There are more ways to create a File Format object than shown in this recipe. Some are listed here:

- ▸ **Creating in Local Object Library**: Open the **Formats** tab in the **Local Object Library** window, right-click on **Flat Files**, choose **New** from the context menu. You can use the **Location**, **Root directory**, and **File Name(s)** options to automatically import the format from an external file. Otherwise, you will have to define all columns and their data types manually, one by one.

- ▸ **Replicating a file format from an existing File Format object in Local Object Library**: On the **Formats** tab, choose the object you want to replicate, right-click on it, and choose the **Replicate...** option in the context menu.

Loading data from a flat file

You can use the same File Format object created in the previous recipe to load data from a flat file. In the following section, we will take a closer look at file format options relevant to loading data from the files.

How to do it...

1. Create a new job and a new dataflow object in it.

2. Create a new text file, `Friends_30052015.txt`, with the following lines inside it:

   ```
   NAME|DOB|HEIGHT|HOBBY
   JANE|12.05.1985|176|HIKING
   JOHN|07-08-1982|182|FOOTBALL
   STEVE|01.09.1976|152|SLEEPING|10
   DAVE|27.12.1983|AB5
   ```

3. Go to **Local Object Library** and create a new file format by right-clicking on **Flat Files** and choosing **New.**

4. Populate the File Format options as shown in the following screenshot:

Type	Delimited
Name	FRIENDS
Adaptable Schema	No
Custom transfer program	No
Skip error handling	No
Parallel process threads	<default>
Data File(s)	
Location	Job Server
Root directory	c:\AW\Files
File name(s)	Friends_30052015.txt
Delimiters	
Column	|
Row	{new line}
Row within text string	Character
Text	{none}
Default Format	
Escape char	{none}
NULL indicator	NULL
Ignore row marker(s)	{none}
Date	dd.mm.yyyy
Time	hh24:mi:ss
Date-Time	yyyy.mm.dd hh24:mi:ss
Input/Output	
Style	Headers
Skipped rows	0
Skip row header	Yes
Write row header	No
Write BOM	No
Locale	
Language	<default>
Code page	<default>
Error handling	
Log data conversion warnings	Yes
Log row format warnings	Yes
Maximum warnings to log	5
Capture data conversion errors	Yes
Capture row format errors	Yes
Capture string truncation errors	Yes
Maximum errors to stop job	5
Write error rows to file	Yes
Error file root directory	C:\AW\Files
Error file name	Friends_rejected.txt

Field Name	Data Type	Field Size	Precision	Scale	Content Type	Format
NAME	varchar	10			Name	
DOB	date					{none}
HEIGHT	int					{none}
HOBBY	varchar	10				

	NAME	DOB	HEIGHT	HOBBY
1	JANE	12.05.1985	176	HIKING
2	JOHN	07-08-1982	182	FOOTBALL
3	STEVE	01.09.1976	152	SLEEPING
4	DAVE	27.12.1983	AB5	

- ❑ **Delimiters | Column** is set to | in this case as our file has the pipe as a delimiter.

- ❑ **NULL Indicator** was set to NULL, which means that only NULL values in the incoming file are interpreted as NULL when read by Data Services. The other "empty" values will be interpreted as empty strings.

- ❑ **Date format** is set to dd.mm.yyyy as we specified in the file format that we are loading the DOB (Date of Birth) column of the date data type. Imagine that you have configured the Query transform mapping for that column using the to_date(<date>, 'dd.mm.yyyy') function.

- ❑ **Skip row header** is set to **Yes** in order to specify that the file has a header row which has to be skipped.

- ❑ Then we set all options related to error capturing to **Yes** to catch all possible errors.

- ❑ **Write errors to a file** allows you to record the rejected records in a separate file for further analysis. We will be writing them to the Friends_rejected.txt file.

5. Import this file format object as a data source in your newly created dataflow.

6. Map all source columns to a **Query** transform and create the target template table FRIENDS in the DS_STAGE datastore.

7. Save and run the job.

As a result, you can see that two records were rejected, one because of an extra column in the row and the other because the row had one column less than the defined file format.

The contents of your target table should look like this:

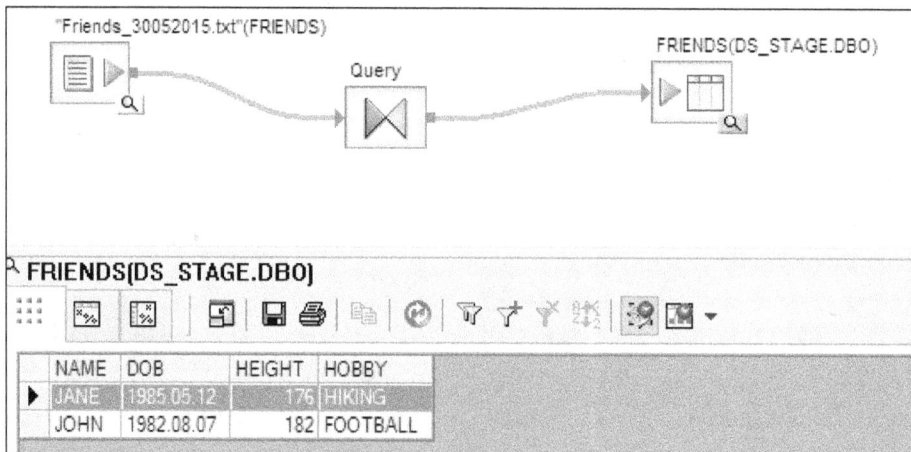

You can see that some lines are missing here due to the errors in the input file.

What's interesting is that Data Services was smart enough to correctly recognize and convert the date of birth for JOHN. Remember it was 07-08-1982 in the file and the date format we specified was dd.mm.yyyy.

How it works...

As you can see, most of the file format options we have used are useful for validating the contents of the source data file in order to reject records with data of incorrect data type or format.

The main question you have to ask yourself is whether you want all these records to be rejected. The alternative might be to build a dataflow that loads all records of the varchar data type and tries to cleanse and convert incorrect values to an acceptable format, or puts the default value instead of a wrong one to mark the field. Sometimes you do not want to lose the whole record if just one value is incorrect.

Now, let's fix the "number of columns" problem in the source file to see how Data Services deals with conversion problems. Do you remember we put the character symbol in one of the integer data type fields?

Change the records for Steve and Dave to the following lines and rerun the job:

```
STEVE|1976.01.01|152|SLEEPING
DAVE|27.12.1983|AB5|DREAMING
```

Both records are rejected with the following error messages appearing in the error log file when you execute the job:

Pid	Tid	Number	Time Stamp	Message
7972	6552	RUN-053001	22/10/2015 10:00:44 a.m.	|Data flow test|Transform FRIENDS1__AL_ReadFileMT_Process
7972	6552	RUN-053001	22/10/2015 10:00:44 a.m.	Invalid value <Month: 76> for date <1976.01.01>. Context: Column <Column DOB>.
7972	6552	RUN-050802	22/10/2015 10:00:44 a.m.	|Data flow test|Transform FRIENDS1__AL_ReadFileMT_Process
7972	6552	RUN-050802	22/10/2015 10:00:44 a.m.	Cannot convert data <AB5> into type <INTEGER>. Context: Column <Column HEIGHT>.

You can see those messages in the job error log and in the `Friends_rejected.txt` file along with the rejected records themselves. The name and location of the reject file is defined by two file format options: **Error file root directory** and **Error file name**. They become available when you open the file format object instance for editing from within a dataflow:

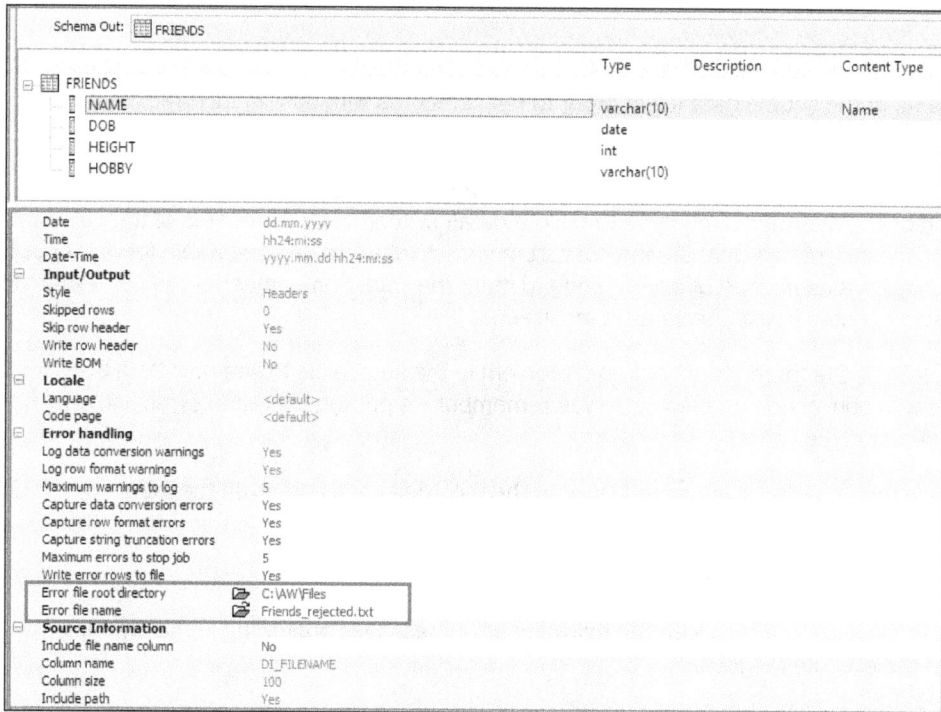

		Type	Description	Content Type
Schema Out: ⊞ FRIENDS				
⊟ ⊞ FRIENDS				
▯ NAME		varchar(10)		Name
▯ DOB		date		
▯ HEIGHT		int		
▯ HOBBY		varchar(10)		

Date	dd.mm.yyyy
Time	hh24:mi:ss
Date-Time	yyyy.mm.dd hh24:mi:ss
⊟ **Input/Output**	
Style	Headers
Skipped rows	0
Skip row header	Yes
Write row header	No
Write BOM	No
⊟ **Locale**	
Language	<default>
Code page	<default>
⊟ **Error handling**	
Log data conversion warnings	Yes
Log row format warnings	Yes
Maximum warnings to log	5
Capture data conversion errors	Yes
Capture row format errors	Yes
Capture string truncation errors	Yes
Maximum errors to stop job	5
Write error rows to file	Yes
Error file root directory	🗁 C:\AW\Files
Error file name	🗁 Friends_rejected.txt
⊟ **Source Information**	
Include file name column	No
Column name	DI_FILENAME
Column size	100
Include path	Yes

As we just stated, in order to load those records, you should put in some extra development effort and create a logic in your dataflow to deal with all possible scenarios in order to cleanse and correctly convert the data, and of course you should amend the file format, changing all data types to `varchar` in order to pass those records through for further cleansing.

> You can use masks in the **File name(s)** option when configuring the file object in your dataflow. For example, specifying `invoice_*.csv` as a file name will allow you to load both `invoice_number_1.csv` and `invoice_number_2.csv` files in a single execution of the dataflow. They will be loaded one after another.

There's more...

Try to experiment further with the contents of the `Friends_30052015.txt` file by adding extra rows with different data types to see whether they will be rejected or loaded, and which error messages you will get from Data Services.

Loading data from table to table – lookups and joins

When you specify a relational source table in the dataflow, Data Services executes simple SQL `SELECT` statements in the background to fetch the data. If you want to, you can see the list of statements executed for each source table. In this recipe, we explore what happens under the hood when you add multiple source tables and how Data Services optimizes the extraction of the data from these source tables and even joins them together, executing complex SQL queries instead of multiple `SELECT * FROM <table>`.

How to do it...

In this recipe, we will extract a person's name, address, and phone number from the source OLTP database and populate a new stage table **PERSON_DETAILS** with this data set.

1. Create a new job and a new dataflow. Specify your own names for the created objects.

2. To extract the required data, you will need to import the tables `PERSON`, `ADDRESS`, and `BUSINESSENTITYADDRESS` (which is a table linking the first two) into your source OLTP datastore. All these tables are located in the `Person` schema of the `AdventureWorks_OLTP` database.

3. Place the imported tables as source objects in your dataflow, as shown in the following figure, and link them with the **Query** transform. Insert the target template table `PERSON_DETAILS` to be created in the `DS_STAGE` datastore:

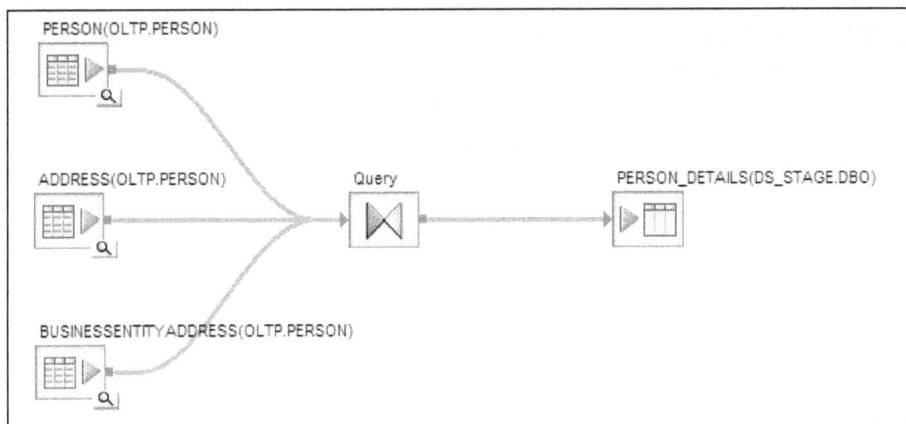

4. To set the required join conditions, you should use the **Join pairs** section located on the **FROM** tab of the **Query** transform. In this example, these join conditions should be generated automatically as soon as you open the **Query** transform. If they weren't, you can click on the icon with two intersecting green circles with the hint **Click to propose join** to generate them, or click on the **Join Condition** field and type required join conditions manually for each table pair to create join conditions manually. Please use the following screenshot as a reference to create two `Inner` join pairs (PERSON - BUSINESSENTITYADDRESS and BUSINESSENTITYADDRESS - ADDRESS):

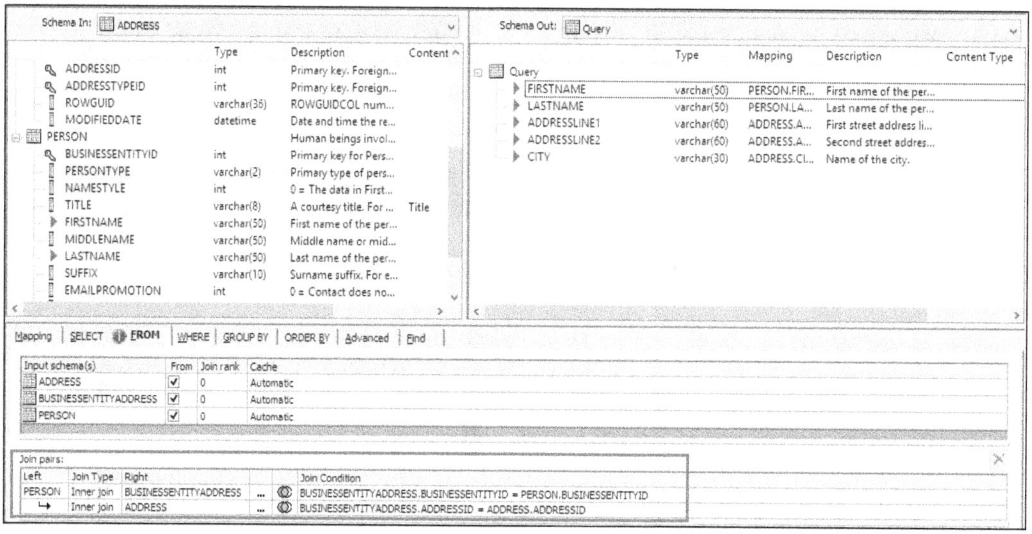

5. At this point, you are able to see which SQL statement DS uses to extract the required information by choosing **Validation | Display Optimized SQL** from the main menu. It opens the following window showing you the number of datastores queried in the window on the left and the full `SELECT` statement executed in each of them on the right:

Datastore:	Optimized SQL for:	OLTP
OLTP	SELECT "PERSON"."FIRSTNAME" , "PERSON"."LASTNAME" , "ADDRESS"."ADDRESSLINE1" , "ADDRESS"."ADDRESSLINE2" , "ADDRESS"."CITY" FROM {"PERSON"."PERSON" "PERSON" INNER JOIN "PERSON"."BUSINESSENTITYADDRESS" "BUSINESSENTITYADDRESS" ON ("BUSINESSENTITYADDRESS"."BUSINESSENTITYID" = "PERSON"."BUSINESSENTITYID")) INNER JOIN "PERSON"."ADDRESS" "ADDRESS" ON ("BUSINESSENTITYADDRESS"."ADDRESSID" = "ADDRESS"."ADDRESSID")	

6. We forgot to add country information for each person. It looks like the `Address` table has only street information and city but no country or state data. Import another two tables in the OLTP datastore: `STATEPROVINCE` and `COUNTRYREGION`.

7. Add them as source tables in the dataflow, but do not join them to already existing ones in the same **Query** transform. Create another **Query** transform and call it Get_Country. Use it to join the **Query** data set with two new source tables, as shown in the following figure:

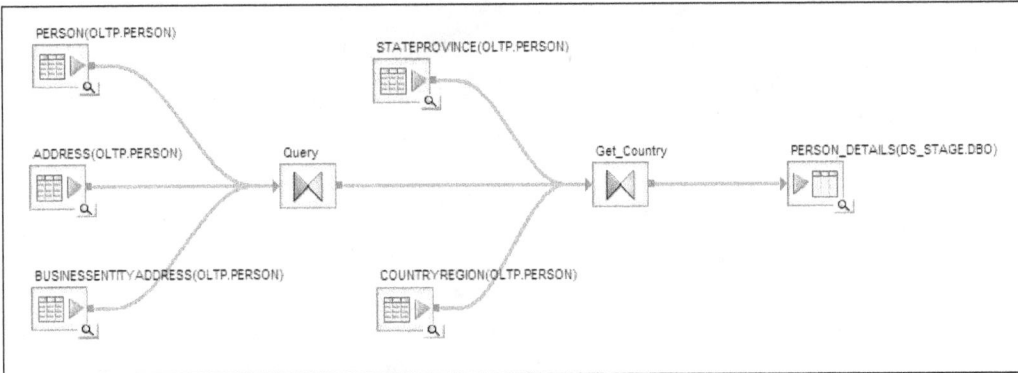

8. Add two new column mappings in the Get_Country Query transform: BUSINESSENTITYID, mapped from the field with the same name from the **Query** input schema, and the COUNTRY column, mapped from the NAME column of the COUNTRYREGION table input schema.

9. If you check **Validation | Display Optimized SQL** again, you will see that the SQL statement has changed, now including two new tables:

Datastore:	Optimized SQL for:	OLTP
OLTP	SELECT "BUSINESSENTITYADDRESS"."BUSINESSENTITYID" , "PERSON"."FIRSTNAME" , "PERSON"."LASTNAME" , "ADDRESS"."ADDRESSLINE1" , "ADDRESS"."ADDRESSLINE2" , "ADDRESS"."CITY" , "COUNTRYREGION"."NAME" FROM ((("PERSON"."PERSON" "PERSON" INNER JOIN "PERSON"."BUSINESSENTITYADDRESS" "BUSINESSENTITYADDRESS" ON ("BUSINESSENTITYADDRESS"."BUSINESSENTITYID" = "PERSON"."BUSINESSENTITYID")) INNER JOIN "PERSON"."ADDRESS" "ADDRESS" ON ("BUSINESSENTITYADDRESS"."ADDRESSID" = "ADDRESS"."ADDRESSID")) INNER JOIN "PERSON"."STATEPROVINCE" "STATEPROVINCE" ON ("STATEPROVINCE"."STATEPROVINCEID" = "ADDRESS"."STATEPROVINCEID")) INNER JOIN "PERSON"."COUNTRYREGION" "COUNTRYREGION" ON ("STATEPROVINCE"."COUNTRYREGIONCODE" = "COUNTRYREGION"."COUNTRYREGIONCODE")	

10. We still have missing phone information for our PERSON_DETAILS tables. Add a third **Query** transform on the right and call it Lookup_Phone. To look for the phone information, we will use the lookup_ext() function executed from a function call within a **Query** transform. The function lookup_ext() is most commonly used in column mappings to perform the lookup operation for the values from other tables.

11. Open the Lookup_Phone Query transform and map all source columns to the target ones except for the BUSINESSENTITYID and ADDRESSLINE2 columns (we are not going to propagate those).

12. Right-click on the last mapped column in the target schema (should be COUNTRY) and select the option **New Function Call...** from the context menu:

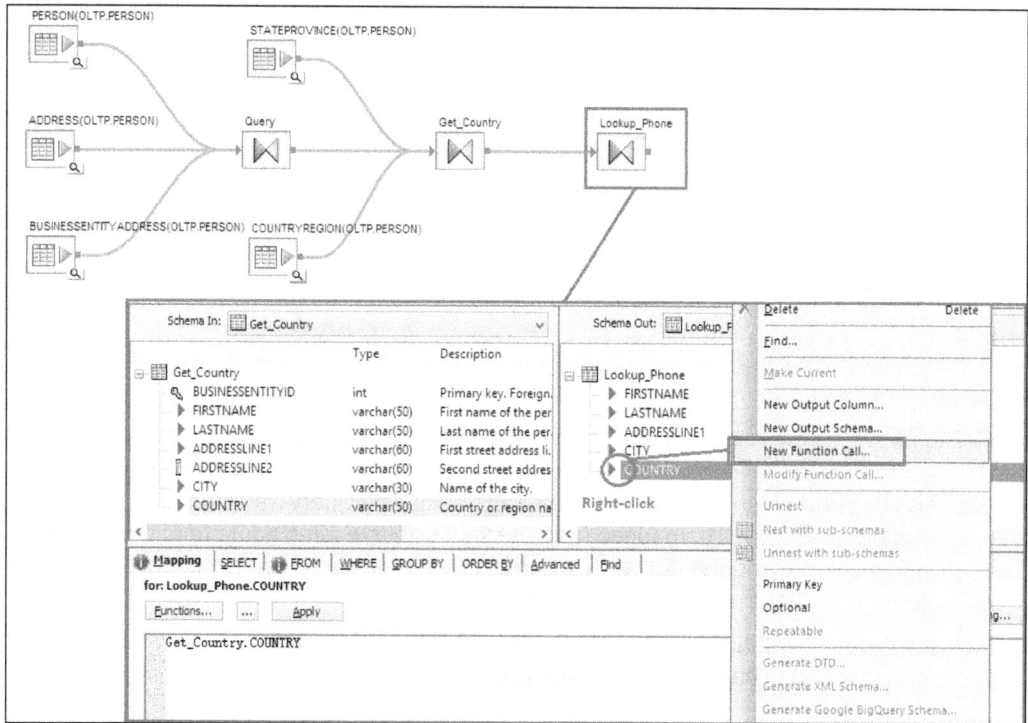

13. Choose **Insert Below...**, and in the opened **Select Function** window, choose **Lookup Functions | lookup_ext**

14. The opened **Lookup_ext | Select Parameters** window allows you to set lookup parameters for the table you want to extract information from. Remember that this is basically a form of a join, so you would have to specify the join conditions of the input data set to the lookup table. In our case, the lookup table is PERSONPHONE. If you did not import it earlier in your OLTP datastore, please do that now. Use the lookup parameter details shown in the following screenshot:

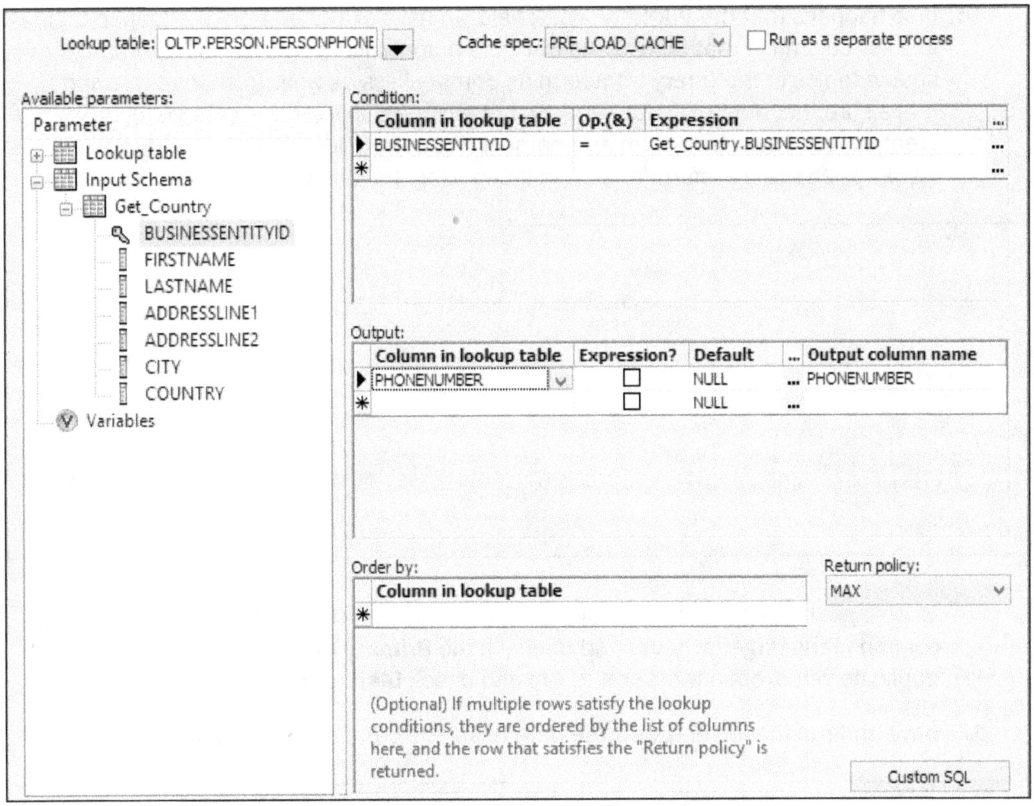

Lookup table:	OLTP.PERSON.PERSONPHONE ▼		Cache spec:	PRE_LOAD_CACHE ✓	☐ Run as a separate process

Available parameters:

Parameter

- ⊞ Lookup table
- ⊟ Input Schema
  - ⊟ Get_Country
    - 🔑 BUSINESSENTITYID
    - FIRSTNAME
    - LASTNAME
    - ADDRESSLINE1
    - ADDRESSLINE2
    - CITY
    - COUNTRY
- Ⓥ Variables

Condition:

Column in lookup table	Op.(&)	Expression	
▶ BUSINESSENTITYID	=	Get_Country.BUSINESSENTITYID	...
✳			...

Output:

Column in lookup table	Expression?	Default	...	Output column name
▶ PHONENUMBER ✓	☐	NULL	...	PHONENUMBER
✳	☐	NULL	...	

Order by:

Column in lookup table
✳

Return policy:

MAX ✓

(Optional) If multiple rows satisfy the lookup conditions, they are ordered by the list of columns here, and the row that satisfies the "Return policy" is returned.

[Custom SQL]

15. After you click on **Finish**, your target schema in the `Lookup_Phone` transform should look like this:

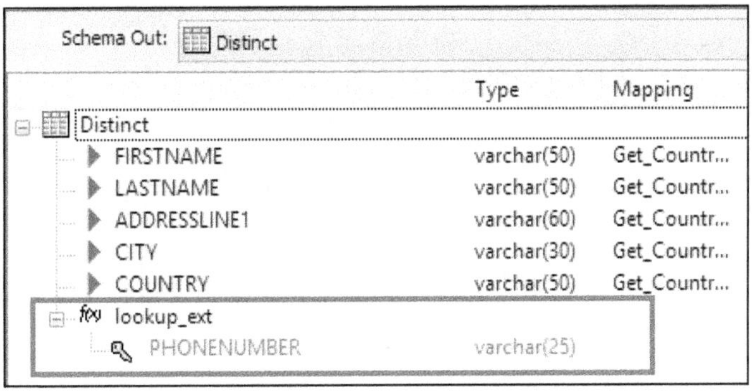

Schema Out: ⊞ Distinct	Type	Mapping
⊟ ⊞ Distinct		
▶ FIRSTNAME	varchar(50)	Get_Countr...
▶ LASTNAME	varchar(50)	Get_Countr...
▶ ADDRESSLINE1	varchar(60)	Get_Countr...
▶ CITY	varchar(30)	Get_Countr...
▶ COUNTRY	varchar(50)	Get_Countr...
⊟ *fx* lookup_ext		
🔑 PHONENUMBER	varchar(25)	

16. It so happens that the `PHONENUMBER` field we have extracted from the lookup table is a key column in that table. Data Services automatically defines key columns from source tables in the **Query** transform as primary keys as well. To change this and make sure that our final data set does not include duplicates, we are going to create a last **Query** transform and name it `Distinct`. Link it on the right to the `Lookup_Phone` transform and open it choosing the following options:

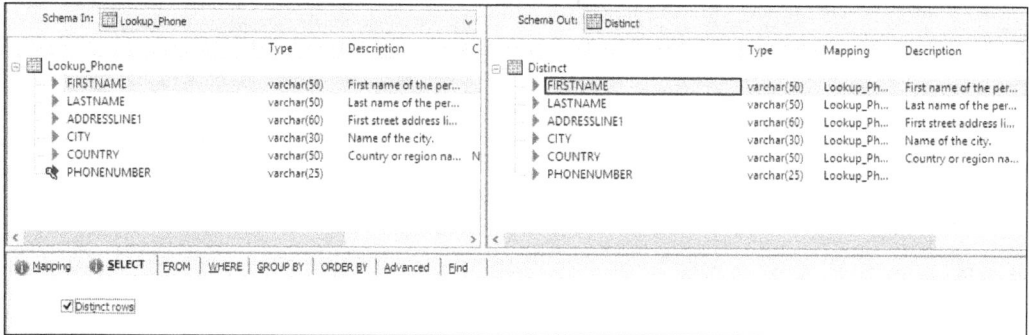

To change the `PHONENUMBER` column from being a primary key, double-click on the column in the target schema and uncheck the **Primary key** option. To get rid of the duplicate fields, open the `SELECT` tab and check **Distinct rows**.

17. Save and run the job and view the data using the dataflow target table option:

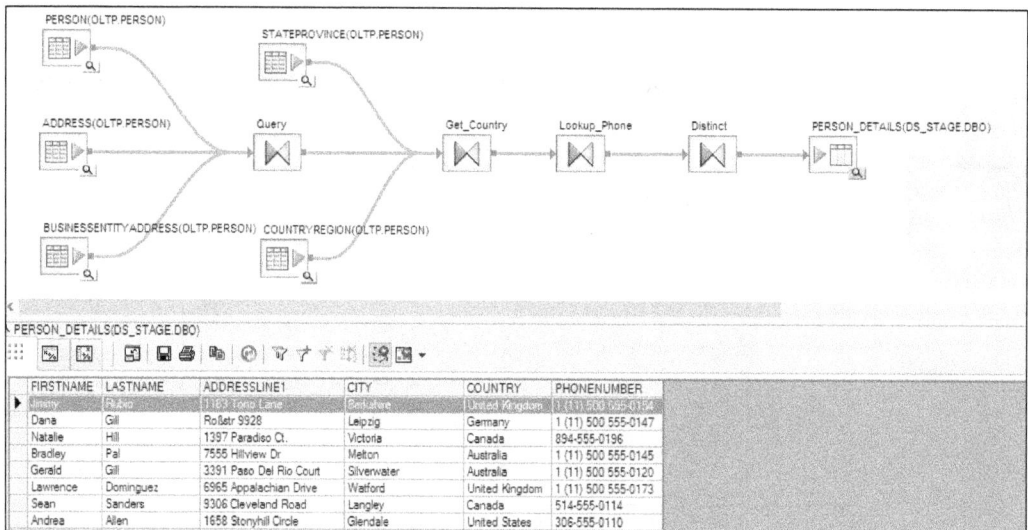

FIRSTNAME	LASTNAME	ADDRESSLINE1	CITY	COUNTRY	PHONENUMBER
Jimmy	Rubio	1183 Torro Lane	Berkshire	United Kingdom	1 (11) 500 555-0154
Dana	Gill	Roßstr 9928	Leipzig	Germany	1 (11) 500 555-0147
Natalie	Hill	1397 Paradiso Ct.	Victoria	Canada	894-555-0196
Bradley	Pal	7555 Hillview Dr	Melton	Australia	1 (11) 500 555-0145
Gerald	Gill	3391 Paso Del Rio Court	Silverwater	Australia	1 (11) 500 555-0120
Lawrence	Dominguez	6965 Appalachian Drive	Watford	United Kingdom	1 (11) 500 555-0173
Sean	Sanders	9306 Cleveland Road	Langley	Canada	514-555-0114
Andrea	Allen	1658 Stonyhill Circle	Glendale	United States	306-555-0110

As the final step, import the template table `PERSON_DETAILS` so it is converted into the normal table object inside the `DS_STAGE` datastore. To do that, right-click on the table either in **Local Object Library** or inside the dataflow workspace, as shown in the following screenshot, and choose the **Import Table** option from the object's context menu:

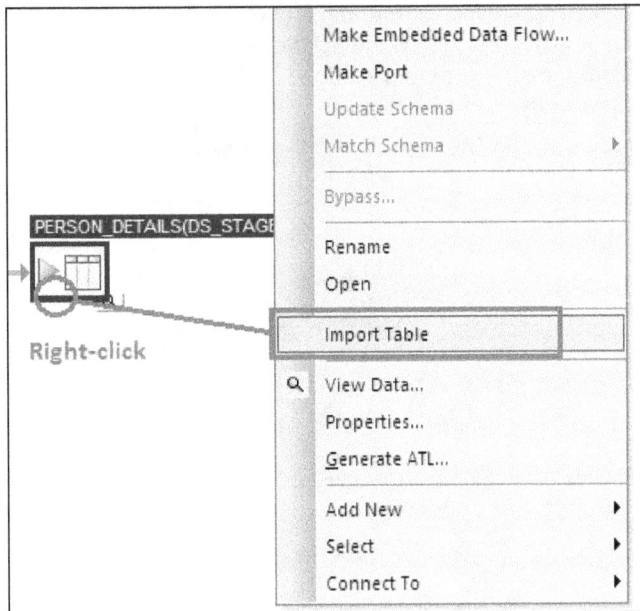

How it works...

You have seen an example of how multiple tables can be joined in Data Services. The **Query** transform represents the traditional SQL `SELECT` statement with the ability to group the incoming dataset, use various join conditions (`INNER`, `LEFT`, or `OUTER`), use the `DISTINCT` operator, sort data (on the **ORDER BY** tab), and apply filtering conditions in the **WHERE** tab.

The Data Services optimizer tries to build as few SQL statements as possible in order to extract the source data by joining tables in a complex `SELECT` statement. In a future chapters, we will see which factors prevent the propagation of dataflow logic to a database level.

We have also tried to use a function call in the mappings in order to join a table to extract additional data. It would be perfectly valid to import the `PERSONPHONE` table as a source table and join it with the rest of the tables with the help of the **Query** transform, but using the `lookup_ext()` functions gives you a great advantage. It always returns only one record from the lookup table for each record we look up values for. Whereas joining with a **Query** transform does not prevent you from getting duplicated or multiple records in the same way as if you have joined two tables in standard SQL query. Of course, if you want your Query transform to behave exactly like a `SELECT` statement joining tables in the database, producing multiple output records for each lookup record, the `lookup_ext()` function should not be used.

If you are writing a complex SQL `SELECT` statement, you are probably aware that joining multiple tables can lead to duplicate records in the result data set. This does not necessarily mean that joins are incorrectly specified. Sometimes it is the required behavior, or it can be a database design problem or simply the presence of "dirty" data in one of the source tables.

The function `lookup_ext()` makes sure that if it finds multiple records in the lookup table for your source record, it picks only one value according to the method specified in the **Return policy** field of the **Lookup_ext** parameters window:

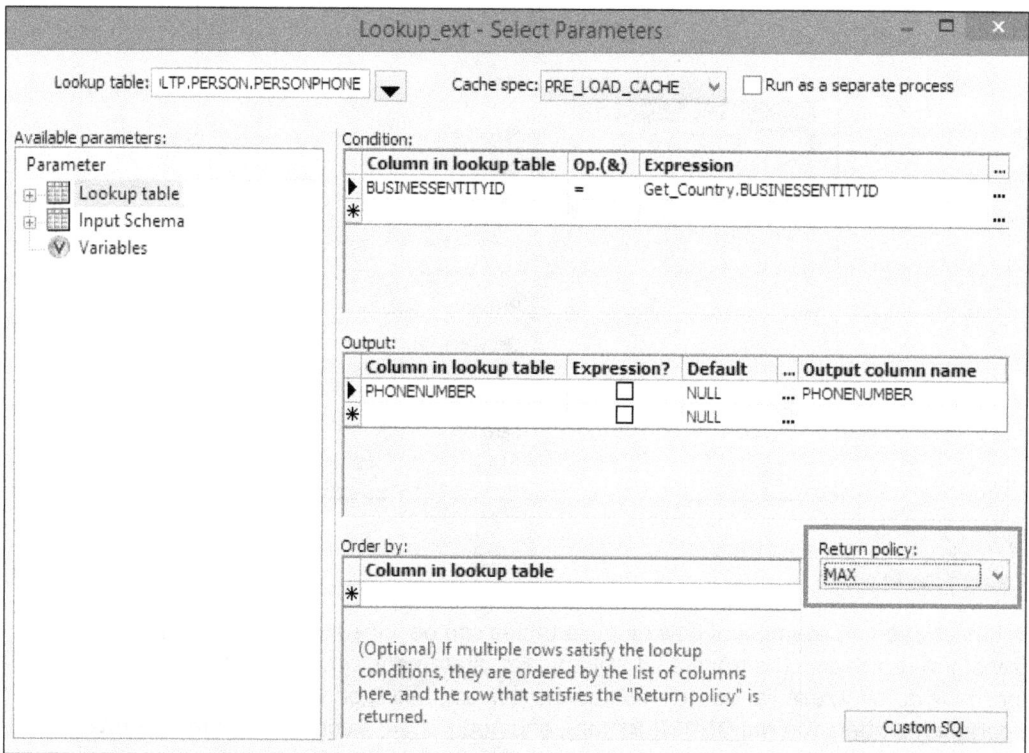

The main disadvantages of using the `lookup_ext()` function are low transparency of the ETL code—as it is hidden inside the Query transform—and the fact that `lookup_ext()` functions prevent the propagation of execution logic to a database level. Data Services always extracts the full table specified as the lookup table in the `lookup_ext()` function parameters.

Depending on which version of the product is used and on database environment configuration, Data Services can automatically generate all join conditions when you join tables in the Query transform and specify join pairs. This is because, when you import the source tables to a datastore, Data Services imports not just table definitions but also information about primary keys, indexes, and other table metadata. So, if Data Services sees that you are joining two tables with identically named fields which are marked as primary or foreign keys on the database level, it automatically assumes that those tables can be joined using those key fields.

Keep that in mind that if business rules or ETL logic dictates join conditions to be different from what Data Services automatically produces and you have to modify those values in **Query** transform logic or even write your own join conditions by manually entering them.

Using the Map_Operation transform

Here we explore a very interesting transformation available to you in Data Services. In fact, it does not perform any transformation of data per se. What it does is that it changes the type of the SQL **Data Modification Language** (**DML**) operation that should be applied to the row when it reaches the target object. As you probably know already, the DML operations in SQL language are the operations which modify the data, in other words, the INSERT, UPDATE, and DELETE statements.

First we will see the effect **Map_Operation** has when used in a dataflow, and then we will explain in detail how it works. In a few words, the **Map_Operation** transform allows you to choose what Data Services will do with the migrated row when passing it from **Map_Operation** to the next transform. **Map_Operation** assigns one of the four statuses to each record passing through: normal, insert, update, or delete. By default, the majority of transforms in Data Services produce records with a normal status. This means that the record will be inserted when it reaches the target table object in a dataflow. With **Map_Operation**, you can control this behavior.

How to do it...

In this exercise, we are going to slightly change the contents of our PERSON_DETAILS table. We will change country values for records belonging to *Samantha Smith* from *United States* to *USA* and remove the records for the same person with *United Kingdom* as the country. That means we will specify the same table both as a source and as a target:

1. Create a new job and new dataflow object and place the PERSON_DETAILS table from the DS_STAGE datastore as a source table.

2. Join the source table to a new **Query** transform named `Get_Samantha_Smith`. Map all columns from source to target and specify filtering conditions, as shown in the following screenshot. Also, double-click on each of the three columns, `FIRSTNAME`, `LASTNAME`, and `ADDRESSLINE1`, to define them as primary key columns:

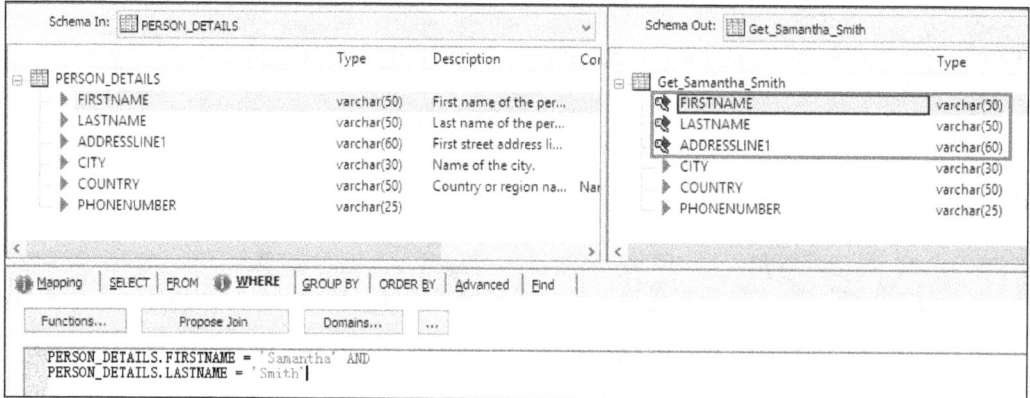

3. Split the dataflow in two by creating two new **Query** transforms: US and UK. Link them to two **Map_Operation** transforms imported from **Local Object Library | Transforms | Platform | Map_Operation** named `update` and `delete` respectively. Then merge the dataflows together with the **Merge** transform, which can be found in the same **Platform** category, and finally link it to the same table PERSON_DETAILS specified as a target table object. The **Merge** transform does not perform any transformations or does not have any configuration options as it simply merges two data sets together (like the UNION operation in SQL). Of course, input schema formats should be identical for the **Merge** transform to work. See what the dataflow should look like in the following figure:

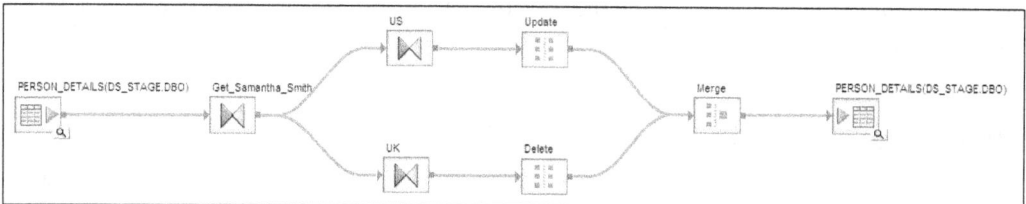

4. In the US transform, map all key columns and the COUNTRY column to target and change mapping for COUNTRY to a hardcoded value, USA. Most importantly, specify `Get_Samantha_Smith.COUNTRY = 'United States'` in the **WHERE** tab to select only *United States* records:

5. In the UK transform, map only key columns and the COUNTRY column to target it as well and put `Get_Samantha_Smith.COUNTRY = 'United Kingdom'` in the **WHERE** tab:

6. Now we have to tell Data Services that we want to update one set of records and delete the other. Double-click on your `update` **Map_Operation** transform and set up the following options:

Mapping	Map Operation
Input row type	**Output row type**
normal	update
update	discard
insert	discard
delete	discard

By doing this, we change row types for normal rows (the **Query** transform produces rows of `normal` type) to `update`. This means that Data Services will execute an UPDATE statement for those rows on the target table.

7. Repeat the same for the `Delete` **Map_Operation** transform but now change normal to delete and discard the rest of the row types:

Schema In: UK				Schema Out: Delete	
	Type	Description	Co		Type
⊟ UK				⊟ Delete	
🔍 FIRSTNAME	varchar(50)	First name of the per...		🔍 FIRSTNAME	varchar(50)
🔍 LASTNAME	varchar(50)	Last name of the per...		🔍 LASTNAME	varchar(50)
🔍 ADDRESSLINE1	varchar(60)	First street address li...		🔍 ADDRESSLINE1	varchar(60)
CITY	varchar(30)	Name of the city.		CITY	varchar(30)
COUNTRY	varchar(50)	Country or region na...	Na	COUNTRY	varchar(50)
PHONENUMBER	varchar(25)			PHONENUMBER	varchar(25)

Mapping   **Map Operation**

Input row type	Output row type
normal	delete
update	discard
insert	discard
delete	discard

8. For Data Services to correctly perform an update and delete operations, we have to define the correct target table key columns. Double-click on a target table object `PERSON_DETAILS` in the dataflow and change **Use input keys** to **Yes** in the **Options** tab. That tells Data Services to consider primary key information from the source dataset rather than using the target table primary keys:

Schema In: Merge				Schema Out: PERSON_DETAILS(DS_STAGE.DBO)	
	Type	Description	Co		Type
⊟ Merge				⊟ PERSON DETAILS(DS STAGE.DBO)	
🔍 FIRSTNAME	varchar(50)	First name of the per...		FIRSTNAME	varchar(50)
🔍 LASTNAME	varchar(50)	Last name of the per...		LASTNAME	varchar(50)
🔍 ADDRESSLINE1	varchar(60)	First street address li...		ADDRESSLINE1	varchar(60)
CITY	varchar(30)	Name of the city.		CITY	varchar(30)
COUNTRY	varchar(50)	Country or region na...	Na	COUNTRY	varchar(50)
PHONENUMBER	varchar(25)			PHONENUMBER	varchar(25)

Target   **Options**   Bulk Loader Options   Load Triggers   Pre-Load Commands   Post-Load Commands

Rows per commit: 1000

Delete data from table before loading: ☐

Advanced:

General	
Column comparison	Compare by name
Number of loaders	1
Error handling	
Use overflow file	No
File name	Not Applicable
File format	Not Applicable
Update control	
Use input keys	Yes
Update key columns	No
Auto correct load	No
Allow merge or upsert	Not Applicable

9. Before executing the job, let's check what our data looks like in the PERSON_
DETAILS table for Samantha Smith. Click on the **View data** button in the target table
and apply filters by clicking on the **Filters** button. Specify filters in the FIRSTNAME
and LASTNAME columns and check the records:

PERSON_DETAILS[DS_STAGE.DBO]

FIRSTNAME	LASTNAME	ADDRESSLINE1	CITY	COUNTRY	PHONENUMBER
Jimmy	Rubio	1183 Tono Lane	Berkshire	United Kingdom	1 (11) 500 555-0154
Dana	Gill	Roßstr 9928	Leipzig	Germany	1 (11) 500 555-0147
Natalie	Hill	1397 Paradiso Ct.	Victoria	Canada	894-555-0196
Bradley	Pal	7555 Hillview Dr	Melton	Australia	1 (11) 500 555-0145
Gerald	Gill	3391 Paso Del Rio Court	Silverwater	Australia	1 (11) 500 555-0120
Lawrence	Dominguez	6965 Appalachian Drive	Watford	United Kingdom	1 (11) 500 555-0173
Sean	Sanders	9306 Cleveland Road	Langley	Canada	514-555-0114
Andrea	Allen	1658 Stonyhill Circle	Glendale	United States	306-555-0110

10. Set the filters:

Filters

To create a filter, select a column name and operator; then enter a value.

Concatenate all filters using: AND ▾

Column	Operator	Value
FIRSTNAME	=	'Samantha'
LASTNAME	=	'Smith'

11. This is what the data in the table looks like before job execution:

PERSON_DETAILS(DS_STAGE.DBO)

FIRSTNAME	LASTNAME	ADDRESSLINE1	CITY	COUNTRY	PHONENUMBER
Samantha	Smith	205 Choctaw Court	Woodland Hills	United States	737-555-0151
Samantha	Smith	1648 Eastgate Lane	Bellevue	United States	587-555-0114
Samantha	Smith	9021 Onley Dr	Cheltenham	United Kingdom	978-555-0100

12. Run the job and view the data using the same filters to see the result:

PERSON_DETAILS(DS_STAGE.DBO)

FIRSTNAME	LASTNAME	ADDRESSLINE1	CITY	COUNTRY	PHONENUMBER
Samantha	Smith	205 Choctaw Court	Woodland Hills	USA	737-555-0151
Samantha	Smith	1648 Eastgate Lane	Bellevue	USA	587-555-0114

How it works...

This is the kind of task that would be much easier to accomplish with the following two SQL statements:

```
update dbo.person_details set country = 'USA'
where firstname = 'Samantha' and lastname = 'Smith' and country =
  'United States';

delete from dbo.person_details
where firstname = 'Samantha' and lastname = 'Smith' and country =
  'United Kingdom';
```

But for us, this example perfectly illustrates what can be done with the use of the **Map_ Operation** transform in Data Services.

Each row passed from the source to a target table in a dataflow through various transformation objects can be assigned one of the four types: `normal`, `insert`, `update`, and `delete`.

Some transformations can change the type of the row, while others just behave differently, depending on which type the incoming row has. For the target table object, the type of the row defines which DML instruction it has to execute on the target table using source row data. This is listed as follows:

- ▶ `insert`: If the row comes with normal or insert type, Data Services executes the `INSERT` statement in order to insert the source row into a target table. It will check the key columns defined on a target table in order to check for duplicates and prevent them from being inserted.

- ▶ `update`: If a row is marked as an update, Data Services determines the key columns it will use to find the corresponding record in the target table and updates all non-key column values of the target table record with the values from the source record.

- ▶ `delete`: Data Services determines the key columns to link source rows marked with the `delete` type with corresponding target row(s) and then deletes the row found in the target table.

- ▶ `normal`: This is treated as an insert when the row comes to a final target table object. It is the default type of row produced by the **Query** transform and the majority of other transforms in Data Services.

What the **Map_Operation** transform allows you to do is to change the type of the incoming row. This allows you to implement sophisticated logic in your dataflows, making your data transformation extremely flexible.

> Defining primary keys in Data Services objects, such as Query transforms, table and view objects, imported in datastores does not create the same primary key constraints for the correspondent tables on the database level. If you have them defined on the database level, they will be imported along with the table definition and will appear in Data Services automatically. Otherwise, you define primary key columns manually to help Data Services to efficiently and correctly process the data. Many Data Services transforms and target objects rely on this information to correctly process the passing records.

Setting **Output row type** to **Discard** in **Map_Operation** for a specific input row type will completely block the rows of the chosen type, not letting them pass through the **Map_ Operation** transform. This is a great way to make sure that your dataflow does not perform any unexpected inserts when it should, for example, always only update the target table.

Note how our target table in this recipe does not have the primary key constraints specified at the database level. It so happens that we analyzed the data in the PERSON_DETAILS table and know that the FIRSTNAME, LASTNAME, and ADDRESSLINE columns define the uniqueness of the record. That is why, we manually specify them as primary keys in Data Services transforms and use the **Update control** option **Use input keys** on the target table object so it knows where to get information regarding key columns to perform the correct execution of the INSERT, UPDATE, and DELETE statements. In case of UPDATE, all non-key columns will be updates with the values from the source row. That is why we propagated only the COUNTRY column as we wanted to update only this field. In case of DELETE, the set of non-key columns does not matter much as only source key columns will be considered in order to find the target row to delete.

The other option would be to modify the table object PERSON_DETAILS in datastore and specify primary keys there (see the following screenshot). In that case, we would not have to define keys in the transforms and use the target table loading option as Data Services would pick up this information from the target table object. To do that, expand the datastore object and double-click on the table to open the table editor, then double-click on the column and check **Primary key** in the newly opened window:

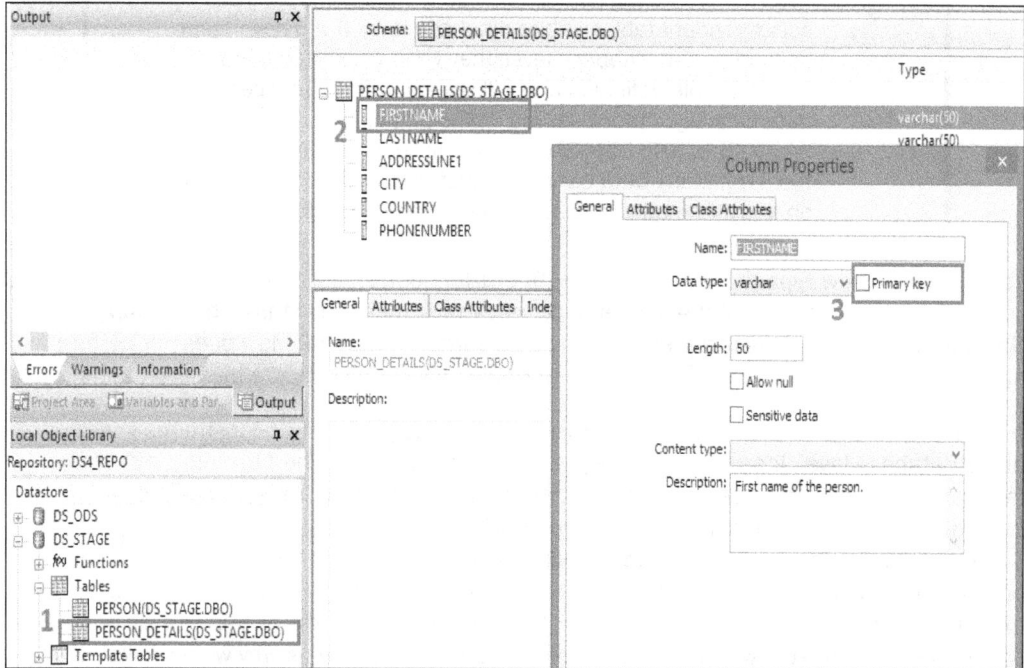

Using the Table_Comparison transform

The **Table_Comparison** transform compares a dataset generated inside a dataflow to a target table dataset and changes the statuses of data set rows to different types according to the conditions specified in the **Table_Comparison** transform.

Data Services uses primary key values for the row comparison and marks the passing row accordingly as: an *insert* row, which does not exist in the target table yet; an *update* row, the row for which primary key values exist in the target table but whose non-primary key fields (or comparison fields) have different values; and finally, a *delete* row (when the target dataset has rows with primary key values that do not exist in the source data set generated inside a dataflow). In some way, **Table_Comparison** does exactly the same thing as **Map_Operation**: it changes the row type of passing rows from normal to insert, update, or delete. The difference is that it does it in a smart way—after comparing the dataset to the target table.

Getting ready

In order to prepare the source data in the OLTP system for this recipe, please execute the following UPDATE in the AdventureWorks_OLTP database. It only updates one row in the table.

```
update Production.ProductDescription set Description = 'Enhanced
  Chromoly steel.'
where Description = 'Chromoly steel.';
```

We performed this modification of the source data so we can use this change to demonstrate the capabilities of the **Table_Comparison** transform.

How to do it...

Our goal in this recipe is simple. You remember that our DWH database sources data from the OLTP database. One of the tables in the target DWH database we are interested in right now is the DimProduct table, which is a dimension table that holds the information about all company products. In this recipe, we are going to build a job, which if executed, will check the product descriptions within source OLTP tables, and if necessary, will apply any changes to the product description in our data warehouse table DimProduct.

This is a small example of propagating data changes happening in the source systems to the data warehouse tables.

As an example, imagine that we need to change the name of one of the materials used to produce one of our products. Instead of the English description "Chromoly steel", we have to use "Enhanced Chromoly steel" now. People working with the OLTP database via applications systems have already made the required change, and now it is our responsibility to develop an ETL code that propagates this change from the source to the target data warehouse tables.

1. Create a new job with one dataflow, sourcing data from the following OLTP tables (Production schema):

    ❑ **Product**: This is a table containing products with some information (price, color, and so on)

    ❑ **ProductDescription**: This is a table containing product descriptions

    ❑ **ProductModelProductDescriptionCulture**: This is a linking table, which holds the key references of both **Product** and **ProductDescription** tables

2. If you do not have these tables imported already into your datastore, please do that in order to be able to reference them within your dataflow object.

3. Add a `DimProduct` table from DWH as a source table. Yes, do not be surprised, we are going to use the same table as a source and as a target within the same dataflow. The **Table_Comparison** transform will compare two datasets: the source dataset, which is based on the `DimProduct` table modified with the help of the source OLTP tables and the target dataset of the `DimProduct` table itself.

4. Create a new `Join` **Query** transform and modify its properties to join all four tables, as shown in the following screenshot:

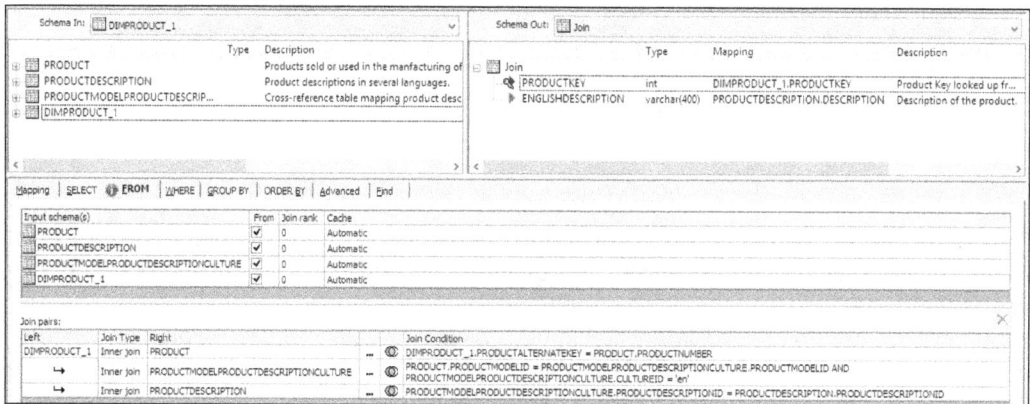

You can see that we use the `Product` and `ProductModelProductDescriptionCulture` tables just to link the `ProductDescription` table to our target `DimProduct` table in order to get a dataset of `DimProduct` primary key values and the corresponding English description values for specific products.

5. Next to your `Join` **Query** transform, place the **Table_Comparison** transform, which can be found in **Local Object Library | Transforms | Data Integrator | Table_Comparison**.

6. Open the **Table_Comparison** editor in the workspace and specify the following parameters:

7. Then, place the **Map_Operation** transform called `MO_Update` and discard all rows of `normal`, `insert`, and `delete` types, letting through only rows with the `update` status:

8. Finally, link `MO_Update` to the target `DimProduct` table and check whether your dataflow looks like the following figure:

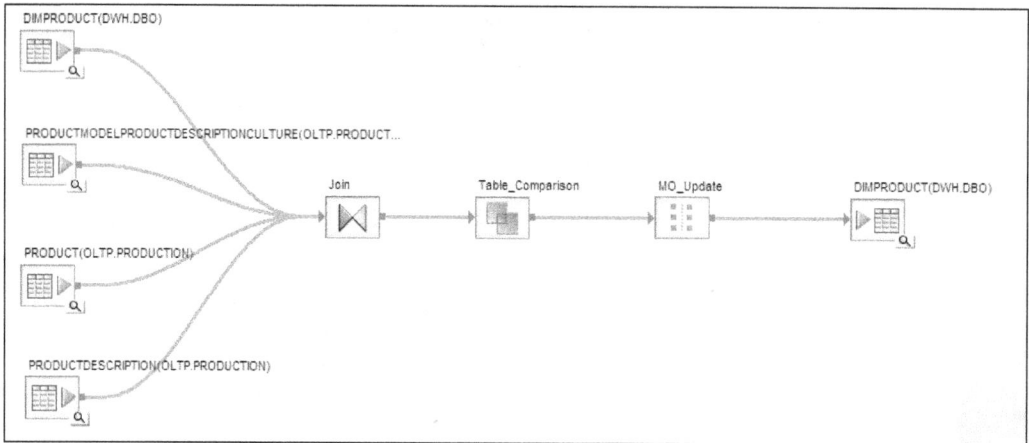

Now, save the job and execute it. Then, run the following command in SQL Server Management Studio to check the result data in the DimProduct table:

```
select EnglishDescription from dbo.DimProduct where
    EnglishDescription like '%Chromoly steel%';
```

You should get the following resulting value:

```
Enhanced Chromoly steel
```

How it works...

To see what exactly is happening with the data set before and after the **Table_Comparison** transform, replicate your dataflow and change the copy in the following manner:

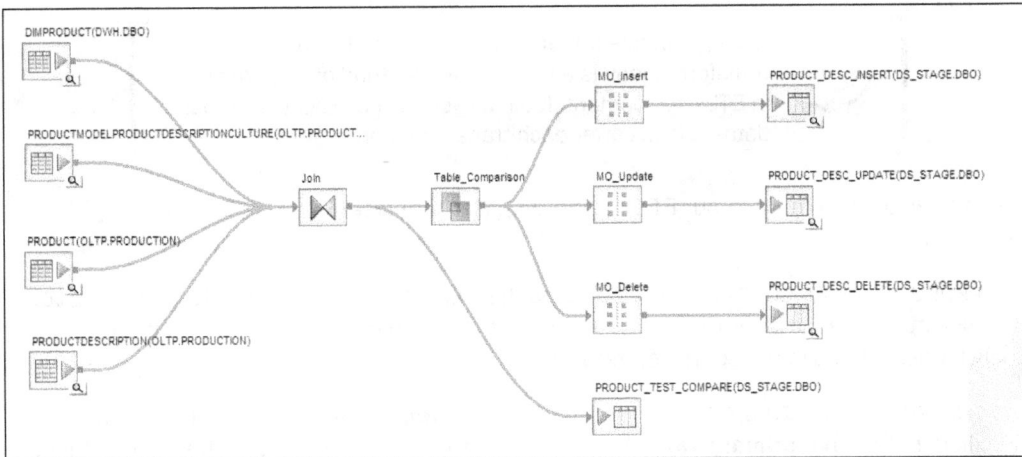

Here we dump the result of the `Join` **Query** transform in the temporary table to see which dataset we compare to the `DimProduct` table inside the **Table_Comparison** transform.

Extra **Map_Operation** transforms allow us to capture rows of different types coming out of **Table_Comparison**. Using **Map_Operation**, we convert all of them to `normal` type in order to insert them into temporary tables to see which rows were assigned which row types by the **Table_Comparison** transform:

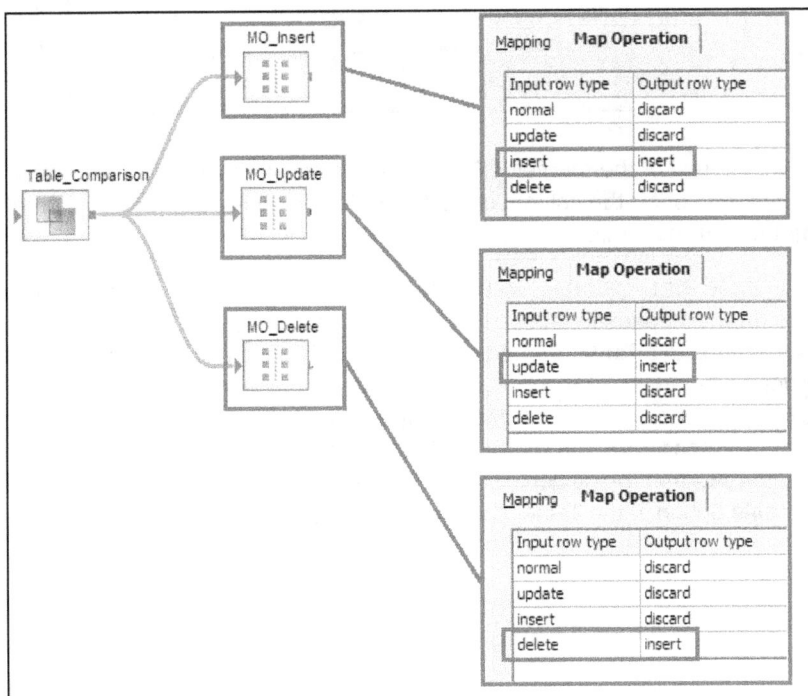

> Adding multiple target template tables after your transformations is a very popular method of debugging in ETL development. It allows you to see exactly how your dataset looks after each transformation.

Let's see what is going on in our ETL by analyzing the data inserted into the temporary target tables.

The `PRODUCT_TEST_COMPARE` table contains the rows starting from `ProductKey = 210`. This is simply because `ProductKeys < 210` in the `DimProduct` table does not have English descriptions in the source system.

The `PRODUCT_DESC_INSERT` table is empty. **Table_Comparison** uses the primary key specified in the **Input primary key columns** section to identify new rows in the input dataset that do not exist in the specified comparison table, `DWH.DBO.DIMPRODUCT`. As we used the `DimProduct` table as a source of the `PRODUCTKEY` values, there couldn't be any new values of course. So no rows were assigned the insert type.

`PRODUCT_DESC_UPDATE` contains exactly one row with a new `ENGLISHDESCRIPTION` value:

As you can see, the rest of the row fields Data Services has sourced from the comparison table. All of them except for the column specified in the **Compare columns** section of the **Table_Comparison** transform.

The `PRODUCT_DESC_DELETE` table, on the other hand, has a lot of records. Those are the target records (from comparison table `DimProduct`) for which primary key values do not exist in the dataset coming to a **Table_Comparison** transform from a `Join` **Query** transform. As you may remember, those are records that do not have English description records in the source tables. This is an optional feature of **Table_Comparison**. Data Services will use primary key values of those records to execute the DELETE statement on the target table. You can easily prevent `delete` rows from being generated by checking the **Detect deleted row(s) from comparison table** option in the **Table_Comparison** transform.

> The **Filter** section of **Table_Comparison** allows you to apply additional filters on the comparison table in order to restrict the number of rows you are comparing. This is very useful if your comparison table is large. This allows optimizing the resources consumed by Data Services in order to extract and store the comparison dataset and also speeds up the comparison process itself.

Exploring the Auto correct load option

The **Auto correct load** option is a convenient means Data Services provides for preventing the insertion of duplicates into your target table. This is the method of inserting data into a target table object inside the dataflow. It can easily be configured by setting the target table option to **Yes,** with no more configuration required. This recipe describes details regarding the usage of this load method.

Getting ready

For this recipe, we will create a new table in the STAGE database and populate it with a list of currencies from the DimCurrency dimension table in the AdventureWorks_DWH data warehouse.

Execute the following statements in SQL Server Management Studio:

```
SELECT CurrencyAlternateKey, CurrencyName
INTO STAGE.dbo.NewCurrency
FROM AdventureWorks_DWH.dbo.DimCurrency;

ALTER TABLE STAGE.dbo.NewCurrency
ADD PRIMARY KEY (CurrencyAlternateKey);
```

We will use the **Auto correct load** option to make sure that our dataflow does not insert rows already existing in the target table.

How to do it...

First, we are going to design the dataflow that will populate the target table NewCurrency.

In the dataflow, we will use the **Row_Generation** transform to generate three new rows, each for different currencies, and try to insert it into the previously created currency stage table NewCurrency. The NewCurrency table already has some data prepopulated from the DimCurrency table. That is required if we want to test the **Auto correct load** option.

The first generated row will be for EUR currency (the CURRENCYALTERNATEKEY column), which already exists in a target table but with a different currency name: CURRENCYNAME = 'NEW EURO'.

The second generated row will be a new currency which does not exist in the table yet: 'CRO' with CURRENCYNAME = 'CROWN'.

The third generated row will be 'NZD' with CURRENCYNAME = 'New Zealand Dollar', matching both values in fields CURRENCYALTERNATEKEY and CURRENCYNAME of the existing record in NewCurrency table.

1. Create a new job and a new dataflow, picking your own names for the created objects.

2. Open the dataflow in the workspace window to edit it and add three new **Row_Generation** transforms, which we will use as a source of data with default parameters. By default, this transform object generates one row with a single ID column populated with integer values starting with 0. Name the three newly added **Row_Generation** transforms Generate_EURO, Generate_NZD, and Generate_CROWN:

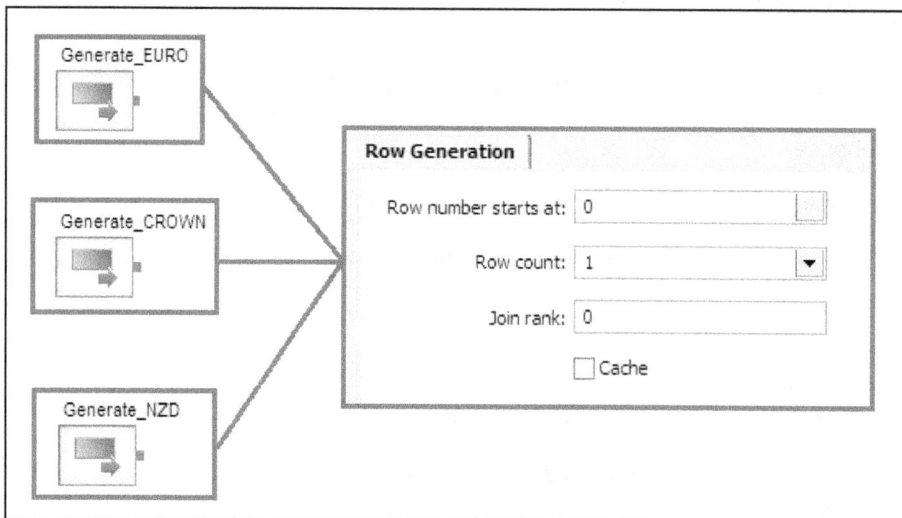

3. Link each **Row_Generation** transform to a respective **Query** transform to create an output schema matching the target table schema with two columns: CURRENCYALTERNATEKEY and CURRENCYNAME. See the example for EURO shown in the following screenshot:

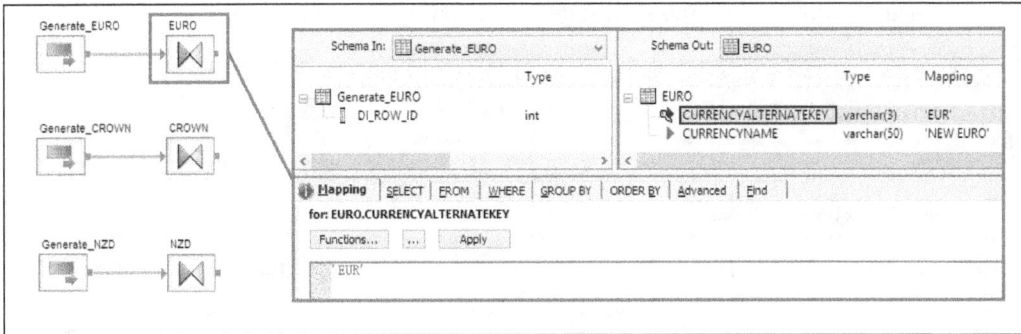

The other two are CRO (CROWN) and NZD (New Zealand Dollar)

4. Finally, merge these three rows into one dataset with the help of the **Merge** transform (**Local Object Library | Transforms | Platform | Merge**).

5. Map the **Merge** transform output to **Query** transform columns with the same names and link **Query** to the target table NewCurrency previously imported into the DS_ STAGE datastore.

6. Check the target data in the NewCurrency table before running this code. Apply filters in a **View Data** window of the target table, as shown in the following screenshot, to see the existing rows we are interested in:

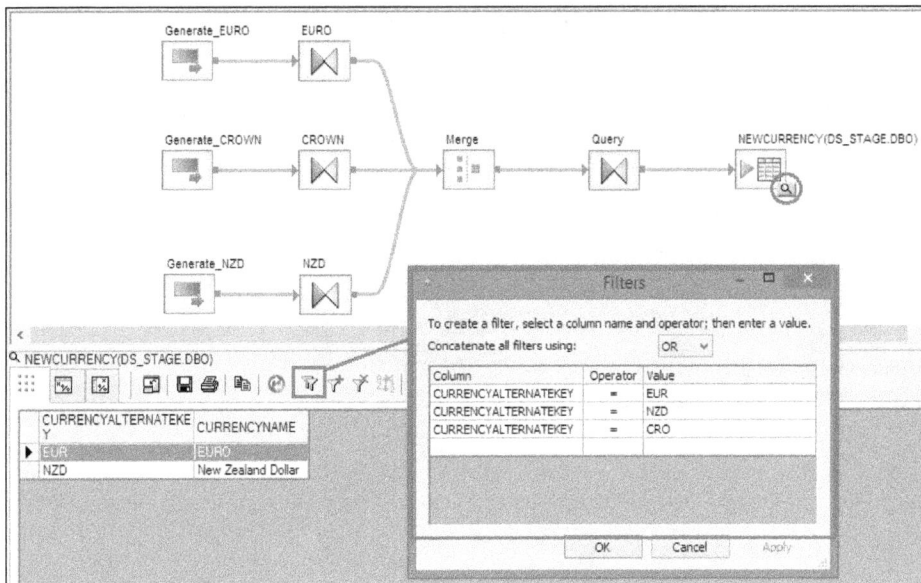

You can see that we have two records in the target table for EUR and NZD.

7. Save and run the job. You should get the following error message:

Pid	Tid	Number	Time Stamp	Message
9824	6608	DBS-070401	10/06/2015 11:03:09 p.m.	IData flow DF_Auto_Correct_Load|Loader Query_NEWCURRENCY
9824	6608	DBS-070401	10/06/2015 11:03:09 p.m.	ODBC data source <(local)\SQLEXPRESS> error message for operation <SQLExecute>: <[Microsoft][SQL Server Native Client 11.0][S
9824	6608	DBS-070401	10/06/2015 11:03:09 p.m.	Server]Violation of PRIMARY KEY constraint 'PK__NewCurre__DB88294D811F4D48'. Cannot insert duplicate key in object
9824	6608	DBS-070401	10/06/2015 11:03:09 p.m.	'dbo.NewCurrency'. The duplicate key value is (EUR).
9824	6608	DBS-070401	10/06/2015 11:03:09 p.m.	[Microsoft][SQL Server Native Client 11.0][SQL Server]The statement has been terminated.
9824	6608	DBS-070401	10/06/2015 11:03:09 p.m.	[Microsoft][SQL Server Native Client 11.0][SQL Server]Violation of PRIMARY KEY constraint 'PK__NewCurre__DB88294D811F4D48'.
9824	6608	DBS-070401	10/06/2015 11:03:09 p.m.	Cannot insert duplicate key in object 'dbo.NewCurrency'. The duplicate key value is (NZD).
9824	6608	DBS-070401	10/06/2015 11:03:09 p.m.	[Microsoft][SQL Server Native Client 11.0][SQL Server]The statement has been terminated. >.
9824	6608	RUN-051005	10/06/2015 11:03:09 p.m.	IData flow DF_Auto_Correct_Load|Loader Query_NEWCURRENCY
9824	6608	RUN-051005	10/06/2015 11:03:09 p.m.	Execution of <Regular Load Operations> for target <NEWCURRENCY> failed. Possible causes: (1) Error in the SQL syntax; (2)
9824	6608	RUN-051005	10/06/2015 11:03:09 p.m.	Database connection is broken; (3) Database related errors such as transaction log is full, etc.; (4) The user defined in the
9824	6608	RUN-051005	10/06/2015 11:03:09 p.m.	datastore has insufficient privileges to execute the SQL. If the error is for preload or postload operation, or if it is for
9824	6608	RUN-051005	10/06/2015 11:03:09 p.m.	regular load operation and load triggers are defined, check the SQL. Otherwise, for (3) and (4), contact your local DBA.

Recall how we applied the primary key constraint on the NewCurrency table. The Data Services job fails in an attempt to insert rows with the primary key values that already exist in the target table.

8. Now to enable the **Auto correct load** option, open the target table editor in the workspace. On the **Options** tab, change **Auto correct load** to **Yes**:

Target	Options	Bulk Loader Options	Load Triggers	Pre-Load Commands	Post-Load Commands

Rows per commit: 1000

Delete data from table before loading: ☐

Advanced:

General	
Column comparison	Compare by name
Number of loaders	1
Error handling	
Use overflow file	No
File name	Not Applicable
File format	Not Applicable
Update control	
Use input keys	No
Update key columns	No
Auto correct load	Yes
Allow merge or upsert	Yes
Ignore columns with value	
Ignore columns with null	No

9. Now save the job and run it again. It runs without errors, and if you browse the data in the target table using the same filters as before, you will see that the new CRO currency appears in the list and the EUR currency has a new currency name:

How it works...

Preventing duplicate data from being inserted is often one of the responsibilities of the ETL solution. In this example, we created a constraint object on our target table, delegating control to the database level. But this is not a common practice in modern data warehouses.

If not for that constraint, we would successfully have inserted duplicate rows on the first attempt and our job would not fail. The beauty of the **Auto correct load** option is its simplicity. All it takes is to set up a single option on a target object. When this option is enabled, Data Services checks each row before inserting it to a target table.

- ▶ If target table has a row identical to the incoming dataflow row, then the row is simply discarded.

- ▶ If the target table has the row with the same primary key values but different values in one or more columns, the Data Services executes the UPDATE statement, updating all non-primary key columns.

- ▶ And finally, if the target table does not have the row with the same primary key values, the Data Services executes the INSERT statement, inserting the row into the target table.

You can build a dataflow with the same logic, preventing duplicates from being inserted by using the **Table_Comparison** transform. **Auto correct load** performs the comparison between the dataflow dataset and the target table dataset just as well as **Table_Comparison** does. Both methods produce INSERT/UPDATE row types. The only difference is that **Auto correct load** cannot perform the deletion of target table records. Thus, the main purpose of the **Auto correct load** option is to provide you with a simple and efficient method of protecting your target data from incoming duplicate records.

We also used the **Merge** transform in this recipe. The **Merge** transform does the same thing as the SQL UNION operator and has the same requirements: the datasets should have the same format in order to be successfully merged:

Merge is often used in combination with **Table_Comparison**. First, you split your rows, assigning them different row types with **Table_Comparison**. Then, you deal with different types of rows, applying different transformations depending on whether the row is going to be inserted or updated in the target table. Finally, you join both split datasets back into one with the help of **Merge** transforms as you cannot link multiple transforms to a single target object.

Splitting the flow of data with the Case transform

The **Case** transform allows you to put branch logic in a single location inside a dataflow in order to split the dataset and send parts of it to different locations. They might be target dataflow objects, such as tables and files, or just other transforms. The use of the **Case** transform simplifies ETL development and increases the readability of your code.

Getting ready

In this recipe, we will build the dataflow that reads the contents of the dimension table DimEmployee and updates it according to the following business requirements:

- All male employees in the production department gets extra vacation hours
- All female employees in the production department get 10 extra sick hours
- All employees in the quality assurance department get their base rate increased by 1.5

So, before you begin developing your ETL, make sure you import the DimEmployee table in the DWH datastore. We are going to use it as both source and target object in our dataflow.

How to do it...

1. First of all, lets calculate average values per department and gender we are interested in. Execute the following queries in SQL Server Management Studio:

```
-- Average vacation hours for all males in Production department
select avg(VacationHours) as AvgVacHrs from dbo.DimEmployee where
    DepartmentName = 'Production' and Gender = 'M' and Status =
    'Current';

-- Average sick hours for all females in Production department
select avg(SickLeaveHours) as AvgSickHrs from dbo.DimEmployee
    where DepartmentName = 'Production' and Gender = 'F' and Status
    = 'Current';

-- Average base rate for all employees in Quality Assurance
    department
select avg(BaseRate) as AvgBaseRate from dbo.DimEmployee where
    DepartmentName = 'Quality Assurance' and Status = 'Current';
```

2. Please note the resultant values to compare them with the results when we run our dataflow after having updated those fields:

3. Create a new job and a new dataflow object, and open the dataflow in the workspace window for editing.

4. Put the `DimEmployee` table object as a source inside your new dataflow and link it to the **Case** transform, which can be found at **Local Object Library | Transforms | Platform | Case**.

5. Open Case Editor in the workspace by double-clicking on the Case transform. Here you can choose one of the tree options and specify conditions as **label-expression** pairs (by modifying the **Label** and **Expression** settings), according to which the row will be send to one output or another:

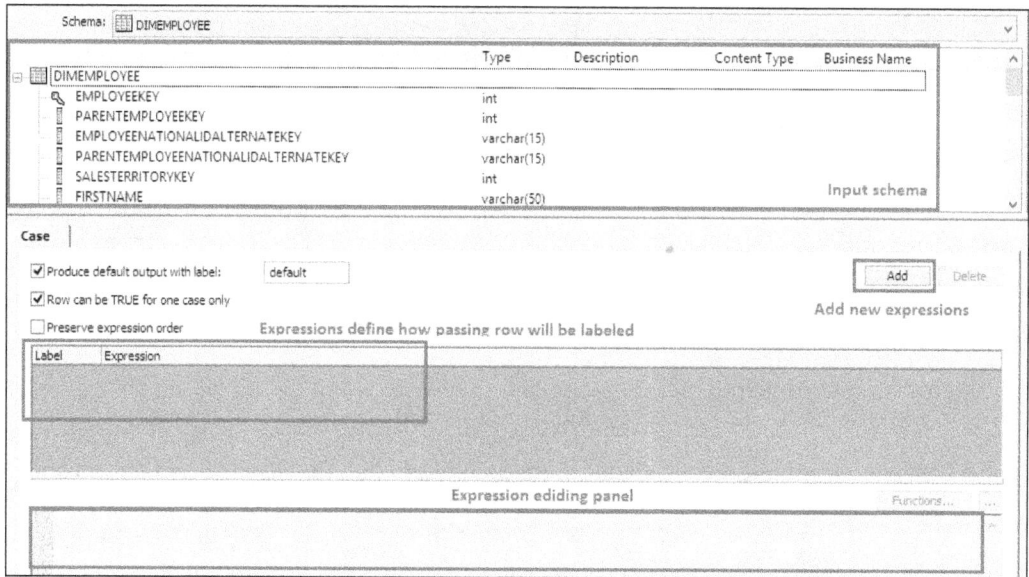

6. Label values are used to label different output. You will use these labels to output information to different transform objects when you are linking Case output to the next objects in a dataflow.

7. Check only the **Row can be TRUE for one case only** option and add the following condition expressions by clicking on the **Add** button:

Label	Expression
Female_in_Production	DIMEMPLOYEE.DEPARTMENTNAME = 'Production' AND DIMEMPLOYEE.STATUS = 'Current' AND DIMEMPLOYEE.GENDER = 'F'
Male_in_Production	DIMEMPLOYEE.DEPARTMENTNAME = 'Production' AND DIMEMPLOYEE.STATUS = 'Current' AND DIMEMPLOYEE.GENDER = 'M'
All_in_Quality_Assurance	DIMEMPLOYEE.DEPARTMENTNAME = 'Quality Assurance' AND DIMEMPLOYEE.STATUS = 'Current'

8. Your Case Editor should look like the following screenshot:

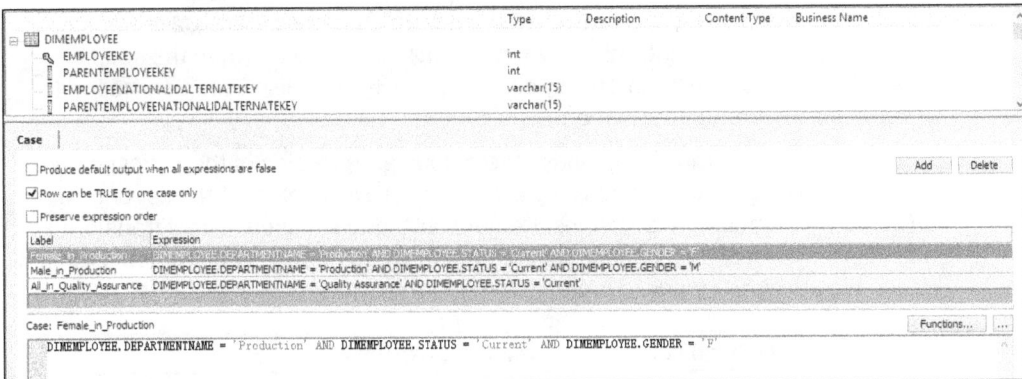

9. Now we have to link our **Case** transform output to three different **Query** transform objects. Each time you link the objects, you will be asked to choose the **Case** output from what we created before.

10. For Query transform names, lets choose meaningful values that represent the type of transformations we are going to perform inside them.

   ❑ The `Increase_Sick_Hours` **Query** transform is linked to the `Female_in_Production` **Case** output

   ❑ The `Increase_Vacation_Hours` **Query** transform is linked to the `Male_in_Production` **Case** output

   ❑ The `Increase_BaseRate` **Query** transform is linked to the `All_in_Quality_Assurance` **Case** output

11. Lastly, merge all **Query** outputs with the **Merge** transform object, link it to the **Map_Operation** transform object, and finally to the `DimEmployee` table object brought from the DWH datastore as a target table.

12. Please use the following screenshot as a reference for how your dataflow should look:

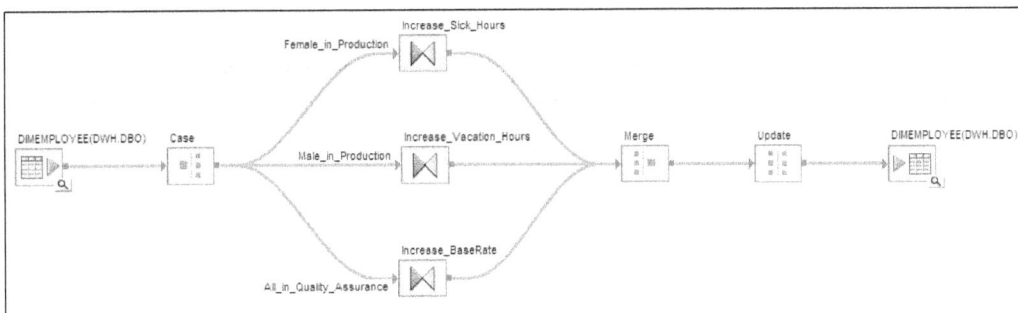

13. Now we have to configure output mappings in our Query transforms. As we are interested in updating only three target columns—`VacationHours`, `SickLeaveHours`, and `BaseRate`—we map them from the source **Case** transform. The Case transform inherits all column mappings automatically from the source object. We also map the primary key column `EmployeeKey` so Data Services will know which rows to update in the target.

14. Then in each Query transform, modify the mapping expression of the correspondent column according to the business logic. Use the following table for the list of columns and their new mapping expressions. Remember that each of our Query transforms modifies only one correspondent column; the other column mappings should remain intact. We are simply going to propagate them from the source object:

Query transform	Modified column	Mapping expression
Increase_Sick_Hours	SICKLEAVEHOURS	Case_Female_in_Production.SICK-LEAVEHOURS + 10
Increase_Va-cation_Hours	VACATIONHOURS	Case_Male_in_Production.VACATION-HOURS + 5
Increase_BaseRate	BASERATE	Case_All_in_Quality_Assurance.BASERATE * 1.5

15. See the example of the `Increase_Vacation_Hours` mapping configuration:

16. The last object we need to configure is the **Map_Operation** transform object named `Update`. You should already know by now that the **Query** transform generates the `normal` type of rows, which are inserted into a target object when they reach the end of the dataflow.

17. In our example, as we want to perform an update of non-key columns defined in our source dataset using matching primary key values in the target table, we need to modify the row type from `normal` to `update`:

18. To be absolutely clear about the purpose of this **Map_Operation** object, we change the other row types to discard, though we would never get the `insert`, `update`, or `delete` rows in this dataflow without modifying it.

19. Save and run the job and run the queries to see new average results for the columns updated in the table:

The difference between "before" and "after" values proves that Data Services correctly updates the required rows in the `DimEmployee` table.

How it works...

The developed dataflow is a good example of a dataflow performing an update of the target table.

We have split the rows according to the conditions specified, performed the required transformation of the data according to the logic provided in the conditions, and then merged all split datasets back together and modified all row types to update. We did this so that Data Services would execute **UPDATE** statements for the whole dataset, updating the corresponding rows that have the same primary key values.

As we used the target table as a source object as well, we can be sure that we will not have any extra rows in our update dataset that do not exist in the target.

Note that the dataset generated in your dataflow does not have to match exactly the target table structure. When you perform the update of the target table, make sure you have the primary key defined correctly and keep in mind that the target table will have updated all columns defined as non-primary columns in the source schema structure.

> Data Services uses primary key columns defined in the target table to find the matching rows. If you want to use a different set of columns to find the corresponding record to update in the target, set them up as primary key columns in the output schema of the Query transform inside a dataflow, and set **Use input keys** to Yes in the **Update control** section of the target table object.

There is another, less elegant way of doing the same thing that **Case** transform does. It involves using the **WHERE** tab of the Query transforms to filter the data required for transformation:

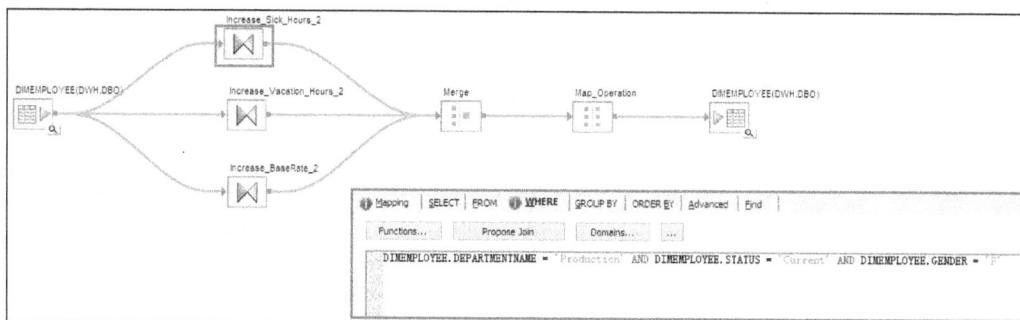

That does look like a simpler solution, but there are two main disadvantages:

▸ **You lose readability of your code**: With **Case** transform, you can see labels of the output, which can explain the conditions used to split the data.

▸ **You lose in performance**: Instead of splitting the dataset, you actually send it three times to different **Query** transforms, each of which performs the filtering. Technically, you are tripling the dataset, making your dataflow consume much more memory.

Monitoring and analyzing dataflow execution

When you execute the job, Data Services populates relevant execution information into three log files: the *trace*, *monitor*, and *error* logs. In later chapters, we will take a closer look at the configuration parameters available at the job level in order to gather more detailed information regarding job execution. Meanwhile, in this recipe, we will spend some time analyzing the monitor log file, which logs processing information from inside the dataflow components.

Getting ready

For simplicity, we will use the second dataflow from the recipe *Using the Table_Comparison transform* created for detailed explanation of the flow of the data before and after it passes the **Table_Comparison** transform object:

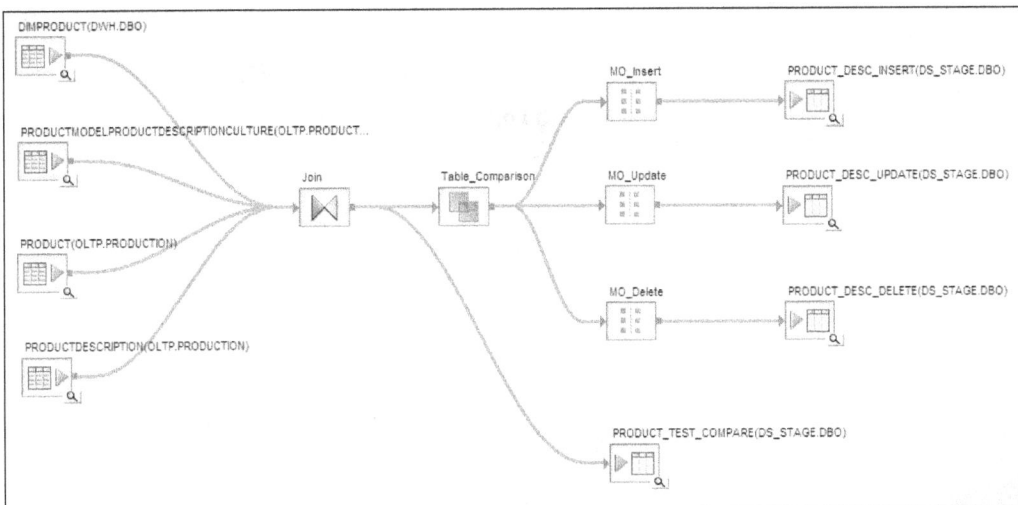

Open the **Table_Comparison** transform editor in the workspace and change the comparison method to **Cached comparison table**:

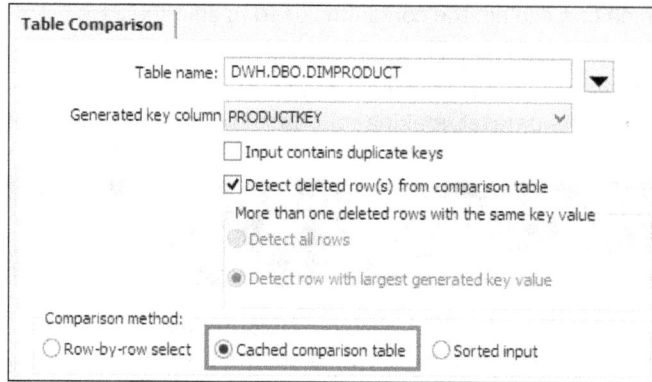

We change this option to slightly change the behavior of the Data Services optimizer. Now, instead of comparing data row by row, executing the SELECT statement against the comparison table in the database for each input row, Data Services will read the whole comparison table and cache it on the Data Services server side. Only after this will it perform the comparison of input dataset records with table records cached on the Data Services server side. That slightly speeds up the comparison process and changes how the information about dataflow execution is logged in the monitor log.

How to do it...

1. Save the dataflow and execute the job with the default parameters as usual.

2. In the main workspace, open the **Job Log** tab to show the *trace* log section, which contains information about job execution. To see the *monitor* log, click on the second button at the top of the workspace area. For convenience, you may select the records from the log you are interested in and copy and paste them into the Excel spreadsheet using the right-click context menu:

3. This monitor log section displays information about the number of records processed by each dataflow component and how long it takes to process them. The reader components shown in the following screenshot are responsible for extracting information from the source database tables. You can see that the `DimProduct` table is extracted by a separate process (probably because it is located in a different database), whereas the other three tables are joined and extracted with a single `SELECT` statement by a single component with quite a sophisticated name, as you can see:

/DF_Product_Desc_Compare/DIMPRODUCT_L1	STOP	606	0.000	3.686
/DF_Product_Desc_Compare/Join_PRODUCT_TEST_COMPARE	STOP	396	0.136	3.701
/DF_Product_Desc_Compare/Round_Robin_Split	STOP	606	0.002	3.687
/DF_Product_Desc_Compare/PRODUCT+BODIVView1+PRODUCTDESCRIPTION2	STOP	214	0.810	3.690

4. The component `Join_PRODUCT_TEST_COMPARE` passes the dataset from the `Join` **Query** transform to the first target table, `PRODUCT_TEST_COMPARE`. You can see that it has processed 396 rows in 0.136 seconds:

/DF_Product_Desc_Compare/Join_PRODUCT_TEST_COMPARE	STOP	396	0.136	3.701

5. Finally, information about dataflow components responsible for processing data in **Map_Operation** transforms shows that there were 210 rows processed by the **MO_Delete** transform and passed to a target **PRODUCT_DESC_DELETE** template table. Only one row was processed by **MO_Update** and passed to a corresponding target table and no rows were processed by `MO_Insert` as there weren't any rows with insert row type generated by this dataflow:

/DF_Product_Desc_Compare/MO_Insert_PRODUCT_DESC_INSERT	STOP	0	0.000	3.714
/DF_Product_Desc_Compare/Map_Operation[1]	STOP	211	0.009	3.715
/DF_Product_Desc_Compare/Join: 0	STOP	306	0.028	3.690
/DF_Product_Desc_Compare/Join: 1	STOP	214	0.003	3.691
/DF_Product_Desc_Compare/Join-Join8: 0	STOP	300	0.029	3.693
/DF_Product_Desc_Compare/MO_Update_PRODUCT_DESC_UPDATE	STOP	1	0.115	3.725
/DF_Product_Desc_Compare/Join-Join8: 1	STOP	182	0.003	3.693
/DF_Product_Desc_Compare/Join-JoinCache4	STOP	294	0.001	3.689
/DF_Product_Desc_Compare/MO_Delete_PRODUCT_DESC_DELETE	STOP	210	0.227	3.720

6. The last column shows the total time passed in the executed dataflow object when the component was processing records.

How it works...

Data Services puts processing information from all dataflow objects in a single place. If you have a job with 100 dataflows and some of them run in parallel, you can imagine that records in the monitor log could be mixed. That is why copying the log data to a spreadsheet for further search and filtering with functionality of Excel is quite useful.

Dataflow execution is a very complex process, and the components you see in the monitor log are not always in a one-to-one relationship with the objects placed inside a dataflow. There are various internal service components performing joins, splits, and the merging of data that will be displayed in the monitor log. Sometimes Data Services creates a few processing components for a single transform object.

If you know what you are looking for, reading the monitor log is much easier. Here is a summary of what the columns mean:

> ▸ The first column in the monitor log is the name of the component containing the name of the dataflow and the names of the components inside the dataflow.

> ▸ The second column is the status of the processing component. READY means that the component has not started processing data; in other words, no records have reached it yet. PROCEED means that the component is processing rows at the moment, and STOP means that all rows have passed the component and it has finished processing them by passing them further down the dataflow execution sequence.

> ▸ The third column shows you the number of rows processed by a component. This value is in flux while the component has the PROCEED status and attains a final value when the component's status changes to STOP.

> ▸ The fourth column shows you the execution time of the component.

> ▸ The fifth column shows you the total execution time of the dataflow while the component was processing the rows. As soon as the component's status changes to STOP, both execution time values freeze and stop changing.

To illustrate this even further, let's count the rows in the source tables to compare with what we have seen in the monitor log.

First, see the results of counting the number of records in the tables DIMPRODUCT and PRODUCTMODELPRODUCTDESCRIPTIONCULTURE with the help of the **View Data** function available on the **Profile Tab** for table objects inside a dataflow. Click on the **Records** button to calculate the number of records in the table:

DIMPRODUCT[DWH.DBO]							PRODUCTMODELPRODUCTDESCRIPTIONCULTURE[OLTP PRODUCTION]					
Update		Records : 606					Update		Records : 762			
Column	Distincts	Nulls	Min	Max	Timestamp		Column	Distincts	Nulls	Min	Max	Timestamp
PRODUCTKEY	0	0	<Blank>	<Blank>	<Blank>		PRODUCTMODELID	0	0	<Blank>	<Blank>	<Blank>
PRODUCTALTERNAT...	0	0	<Blank>	<Blank>	<Blank>		PRODUCTDESCRIPTI...	0	0	<Blank>	<Blank>	<Blank>
PRODUCTSUBCATEG...	0	0	<Blank>	<Blank>	<Blank>		CULTUREID	0	0	<Blank>	<Blank>	<Blank>
WEIGHTUNITMEASUR...	0	0	<Blank>	<Blank>	<Blank>		MODIFIEDDATE	0	0	<Blank>	<Blank>	<Blank>
SIZEUNITMEASUREC...	0	0	<Blank>	<Blank>	<Blank>							

Now see the result of counting the number of records in the tables `PRODUCT` and `PRODUCTDESCRIPTION` with the same **View Data | Profile** feature:

PRODUCT[OLTP.PRODUCTION]						
Update		Records : 504				
Column	Distincts	Nulls	Min	Max		Timestamp
PRODUCTIO	0	0	<Blank>	<Blank>		<Blank>
NAME	0	0	<Blank>	<Blank>		<Blank>
PRODUCTNUMBER	0	0	<Blank>	<Blank>		<Blank>
MAKEFLAG	0	0	<Blank>	<Blank>		<Blank>
FINISHEDGOODSFLAG	0	0	<Blank>	<Blank>		<Blank>
COLOR	0	0	<Blank>	<Blank>		<Blank>

PRODUCTDESCRIPTION[OLTP.PRODUCTION]						
Update		Records : 762				
Column	Distincts	Nulls	Min	Max		Timestamp
PRODUCTDESCRIPTI...	0	0	<Blank>	<Blank>		<Blank>
DESCRIPTION	0	0	<Blank>	<Blank>		<Blank>
ROWGUID	0	0	<Blank>	<Blank>		<Blank>
MODIFIEDDATE	0	0	<Blank>	<Blank>		<Blank>

By using the transform name `Join`, you can see the components related to the execution of the first Query transform.

You see the `DIMPRODUCT_11` component (**606** rows) as being not part of the Join transform components because it was executed separately. Data Services could not include it in a single `SELECT` statement (remember that this table is in the DWH database) with three other tables that had join conditions specified inside the Join transform. Data Services could recognize them as belonging to the same database and pushed down the single `SELECT` statement to the database level, extracting 294 rows.

Some components, that is **Map_Operation** related ones, are easily recognizable by name, which includes the name of the current transformation and the next target table object name: `Join_PRODUCT_TEST_COMPARE, MO_Update_PRODUCT_DESC_UPDATE`, and so on.

The **Table_Comparison** execution is the most complex one, as you can see from the monitor log. All compared datasets are first cached by separate components and then compared to each other by the other ones. You can identify components belonging to a **Table_Comparison** transform by using the keywords *TCRdr* and *Table_Comparison*.

There's more...

Reading the monitor log, which is the main source of the dataflow execution information, can require a lot of experience. In the following chapters, we will spend a lot of time peeking into the monitor log for different kinds of information about the dataflow execution. Often, it is very useful for identifying potential performance bottlenecks inside the dataflow.

5
Workflow – Controlling Execution Order

This chapter will explain in detail another type of Data Services object: workflow. Workflow objects allow you to group other workflows, dataflows and script objects into execution units. In this chapter, we will cover the following topics:

- ▶ Creating a workflow object
- ▶ Nesting workflows to control the execution order
- ▶ Using conditional and while loop objects to control the execution order
- ▶ Using the bypassing feature
- ▶ Controlling failures – try-catch objects
- ▶ Use case example – populating dimension tables
- ▶ Using a continuous workflow
- ▶ Peeking inside the repository – parent-child relationships between Data Services objects

Introduction

In this chapter, we will move to the next object in the Data Services hierarchy of objects used in ETL design: the workflow object. Workflows do not perform any movement of data themselves; their main purpose is to group dataflows, scripts, and other workflows together.

In other words, workflows are container objects grouping pieces of ETL code. They help define the dependencies between various pieces of ETL code in order to provide robust and flexible ETL architecture.

I will also show you how you can query the Data Services repository using database tools in order to query the hierarchy of objects directly and will show you how this hierarchy is stored in repository database tables. This may be very useful if you want to understand a bit more about how the software is functioning "under the hood".

Additionally, we will build a real-life use case ETL code by populating dimension tables in data warehouse. This use case example will include the functionality already reviewed in the previous chapters and will show you how you can augment existing ETL processes and migrate data (dataflows) with the help of workflow objects.

Creating a workflow object

A workflow object is a reusable object in Data Services. Once created, the same object can be used in different places of your ETL code. For example, you can place the same workflow in different jobs or nest it in other workflow objects by placing them in the workflow workspace.

> Note that a workflow object cannot be nested inside a dataflow object. Workflows are used to group dataflow objects and other workflows so that you can control their execution order.

Every workflow object has its own local variable scope and can have a set of input/output parameters so that it can "communicate" with the parent object (in which it is nested) by accepting input parameter values or sending values back through output parameters. A script object placed inside the workflow becomes part of the workflow and shares its variable scope. That is why all workflow local variables can be used within the scripts placed directly into the workflow or passed to the child objects by going to **Variables and Parameters | Calls**.

Later in this chapter, we will explore how this object hierarchy is stored within the Data Services repository.

How to do it...

There are few ways to create a workflow object. Follow these steps:

1. To create a workflow object in the workspace of the other parent object, you can use the tool pallet on the right-hand side of the Designer interface. Follow these steps:

    1. Create a new job and open it in the workspace for editing.

    2. Left-click on the **Work Flow** icon in the workspace tool palette (see the following screenshot), drag it to the job workspace, and left-click on the empty space in the workspace to place the new workflow object:

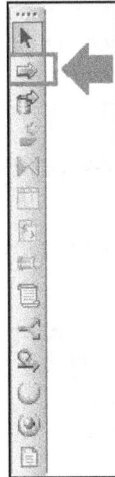

3. Name the object `WF_example` and press *Enter* to create it. Note that the object immediately appears in the **Local Object Library** workflow list. The parent object of the `WF_example` workflow is the job itself.

2. Create another workflow object inside `WF_example`. Now, we will use a different method to create workflows directly from **Local Object Library** rather than using the workspace tool palette. Then, perform these steps:

    1. Open `WF_example` in the main workspace window.

    2. Go to the **Local Object Library** window and select the **Work Flows** tab.

    3. Right-click on the **Local Object Library** empty area of this tab and choose **New** from the context menu.

    4. Fill in the workflow name, `WF_example_child,` and drag and drop the created object to the workspace area of `WF_example` from **Local Object Library**.

How it works...

A workflow object organizes and groups pieces of ETL processes (dataflow and sometimes scripts). It does not perform any data processing itself. When it is being executed, it simply starts executing sequentially (or in parallel) all its child objects in the order defined by the user.

You can think of a workflow as a container that holds the executable elements. Like a project object function is similar to a root folder, workflow serves the same "folder" functionality with a few extra features, which you will be able to get familiar with in the next few recipes.

Like the folder structure on your disk, you can create sophisticated nested tree structures with the help of workflow objects by putting them into each other.

One thing to remember is that each workflow has its own scope of variables or context. To pass variables from a parent workflow to a child object, select the **Calls** tab on the **Variables and Parameters** panel. It shows the list of input parameters from the child objects for the object currently open in the main workspace area.

To open the **Variables and Parameters** window, you can click on the **Variables** button in the tool menu at the top of your Designer screen.

Here, you see the context of the currently open object, that is, the list of defined local variables, input parameters, and available global variables inherited from the job context:

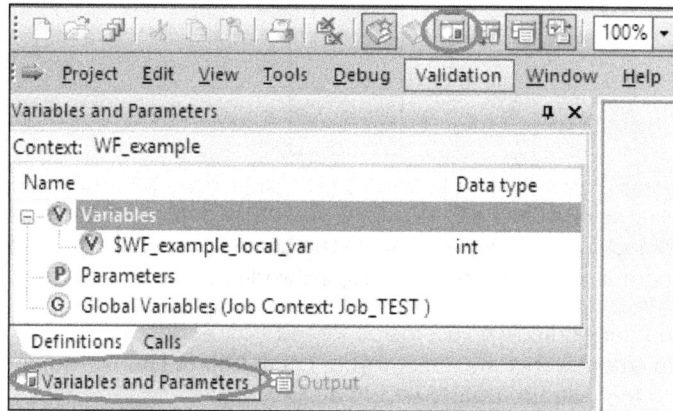

The **Calls** section allows you to pass your previously created local variable $WF_example_local_var of the WF_example workflow to the WF_example_child child workflow object's $WF_example_child_var1 input parameter, as shown here:

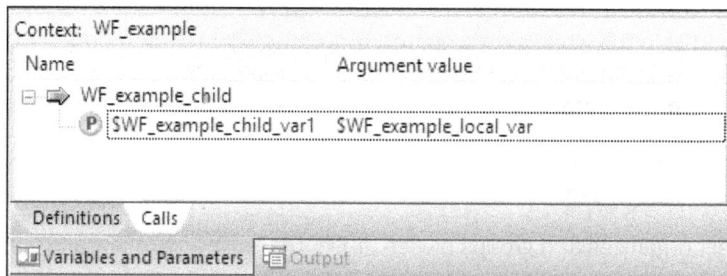

Of course, you have to open the child object context first and create an input parameter so that its call is visible in the context of the parent.

Scripts are not reusable objects and do not have local variable scope or parameters of their own. They belong to the workflow or job object they have been placed into. In other words, they can see and operate only on the local variables and parameters defined at the parent object level.

Of course, you can copy and paste the contents of a single script object to another script object in a different workflow. However, it will be a new instance of the script object that will be running in a new context of the different parent workflow. Hence, the variables and parameters used could be completely different.

Nesting workflows to control the execution order

In this recipe, we will see how workflow objects are executed in the nested structure.

Getting ready

We will not create dataflow objects in this recipe, so to prepare an environment, just create an empty job object.

How to do it

We will create a nested structure of a few workflow objects, each of which, when executed, will run the script. It will display the current workflow name and the full path to the root job context. Follow these steps:

1. In the job workspace, create a new workflow object, `WF_root`, and open it.
2. In the **Variables and Parameters** window, when in the `WF_root` context, create one local variable `$l_wf_name` and one input parameter `$p_wf_parent_name`, both of the `varchar(255)` data type.
3. Also, inside `WF_root`, add the new script object named `Script` with the following code:
    ```
    $l_wf_name = workflow_name();
    print('INFO: running {$l_wf_name} (parent={$p_wf_parent_name})');
    $l_wf_name = $p_wf_parent_name || ' > ' || $l_wf_name;
    ```
4. In the same `WF_root` workflow workspace, add two other workflow objects, `WF_level_1` and `WF_level_1_2`, and link all of them together.
5. Repeat steps 2 and 3 for both new workflows `WF_level_1` and `WF_level_1_2`.
6. Open `WF_level_1`, create a new workflow, `WF_parallel`, and link it to the script object.
7. Inside the `WF_level_1` workflow, create two other workflow objects, `WF_level_3_1` and `WF_level_3_2`. Then, create only one input parameter, `$p_wf_parent_name`, without creating a local variable.
8. Repeat steps 2 and 3 for both the `WF_level_3_1` and `WF_level_3_2` workflows.

9. Now, we have to specify mappings for the input parameters of the created workflows. To do this, double-click on parameter name `$p_wf_parent_name` by going to **Variables and Parameters | Calls** and input the name of the `$1_wf_name` local variable.

10. There are two exceptions to the input parameter mapping settings. In the context of the job for the input parameter of the `WF_root` workflow, you have to specify the `job_name()` function as a value. Perform these steps:

    1. Open the job in the main workspace (so that the `WF_root` workflow is visible on the screen).

    2. Choose **Variables and Parameters | Calls** and double-click on the `$p_wf_parent_name` input parameter name.

    3. In the **Value** field, enter the `job_name()` function and click on **OK**.

11. The second exception is the input parameter mappings for workflows `WF_level_3_1` and `WF_level_3_2`. Perform the following steps:

    1. Open the `WF_parallel` workflow to see both `WF_level_3_1` and `WF_level_3_2` displayed on the screen.

    2. Go to **Variables and Parameter | Calls** and specify the following value for both input parameter calls:

    ```
    (($p_wf_parent_name || ' > ') || workflow_name())
    ```

12. Your job should have the following workflow nested structure, as shown in the screenshot here:

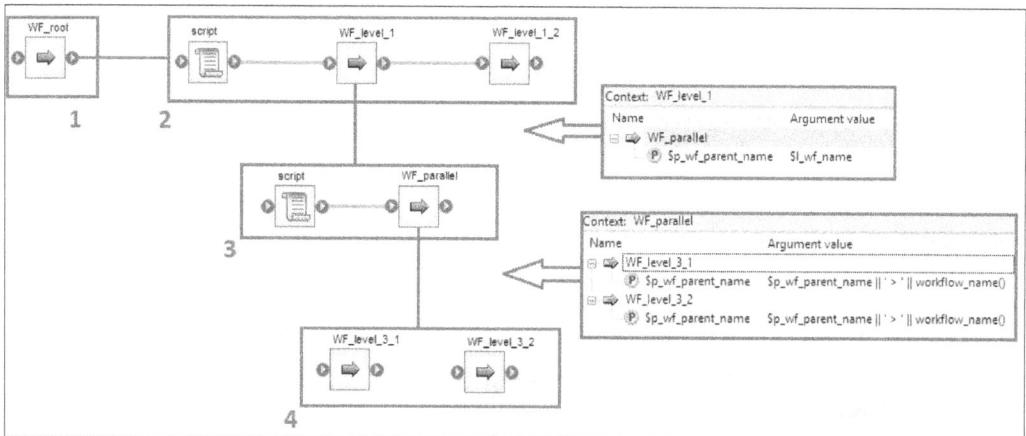

The only workflow object that does not have a script object inside it is `WF_parallel`. It will be explained later in the recipe.

13. Now, open the job in the workspace area and execute it.

14. The trace log shows the order of workflow executions, currently executed workflow names, and their location in the object hierarchy within the job. See the following screenshot:

Pid	Tid	Type	Time Stamp	Message
8264	10784	JOB	23/06/2015 2:20:19 p.m.	<14.2.4.0000>.
8264	10784	JOB	23/06/2015 2:20:19 p.m.	Current directory of job <bbf4f31e_b4c8_4797_ac09_a6e90d7d7c81> is <C:\EIM\Data Services\bin>.
8264	10784	JOB	23/06/2015 2:20:20 p.m.	Starting job on job server host <IVANSHOMNIKOV>, port <3500>.
8264	10784	JOB	23/06/2015 2:20:20 p.m.	Job <Job_TEST> of runid <20150623142020826410784> is initiated by user <ivan.shomnikov>.
8264	10784	JOB	23/06/2015 2:20:20 p.m.	Processing job <Job_TEST>.
8264	10784	JOB	23/06/2015 2:20:21 p.m.	Optimizing job <Job_TEST>.
8264	10784	JOB	23/06/2015 2:20:21 p.m.	Job <Job_TEST> is started.
8264	10784	WORKFLOW	23/06/2015 2:20:21 p.m.	Work flow <WF_root> is started.
8264	10784	PRINTFN	23/06/2015 2:20:21 p.m.	INFO: running 'WF_root' (parent='Job_TEST')
8264	10784	WORKFLOW	23/06/2015 2:20:21 p.m.	Work flow <WF_level_1> is started.
8264	10784	PRINTFN	23/06/2015 2:20:21 p.m.	INFO: running 'WF_level_1' (parent='Job_TEST > WF_root')
8264	10784	WORKFLOW	23/06/2015 2:20:21 p.m.	Work flow <WF_parallel> is started.
8264	11664	WORKFLOW	23/06/2015 2:20:21 p.m.	Work flow <WF_level_3_1> is started.
8264	6336	WORKFLOW	23/06/2015 2:20:21 p.m.	Work flow <WF_level_3_2> is started.
8264	11664	PRINTFN	23/06/2015 2:20:21 p.m.	INFO: running 'WF_level_3_1' (parent='Job_TEST > WF_root > WF_level_1 > WF_parallel')
8264	6336	PRINTFN	23/06/2015 2:20:21 p.m.	INFO: running 'WF_level_3_2' (parent='Job_TEST > WF_root > WF_level_1 > WF_parallel')
8264	10784	WORKFLOW	23/06/2015 2:20:21 p.m.	Work flow <WF_level_3_1> is completed successfully.
8264	10784	WORKFLOW	23/06/2015 2:20:21 p.m.	Work flow <WF_level_3_2> is completed successfully.
8264	10784	WORKFLOW	23/06/2015 2:20:21 p.m.	Work flow <WF_parallel> is completed successfully.
8264	10784	WORKFLOW	23/06/2015 2:20:21 p.m.	Work flow <WF_level_1> is completed successfully.
8264	10784	WORKFLOW	23/06/2015 2:20:21 p.m.	Work flow <WF_level_1_2> is started.
8264	10784	PRINTFN	23/06/2015 2:20:21 p.m.	INFO: running 'WF_level_1_2' (parent='Job_TEST > WF_root')
8264	10784	WORKFLOW	23/06/2015 2:20:21 p.m.	Work flow <WF_level_1_2> is completed successfully.
8264	10784	WORKFLOW	23/06/2015 2:20:21 p.m.	Work flow <WF_root> is completed successfully.
8264	10784	JOB	23/06/2015 2:20:21 p.m.	Job <Job_TEST> is completed successfully.

How it works...

As we have passed values to the input parameters of the objects in the previous chapter dedicated to the creation of dataflow objects, you probably already know how this mechanism works. The object calls for the input parameter value right before its execution in the parent object where it is located.

Every workflow in our structure (except `WF_parallel`) has a local variable that is used in the script object to save and display the current workflow name and concatenate it to the workflow path in the hierarchy received from the parent object in order to pass the concatenated value to the child object in their calls.

Let's follow the executions steps:

▶ When a job executes, it first runs the object that is located in the job context; in our case, it is `WF_root`. As we do not specify any local variable for the job, we cannot pass its value to the input parameter of the `WF_root` object. So, we simply pass it a `job_name()` function that returns the name of the job where it is being executed. The `job_name()` function generates the value that is passed to the input parameter right before the `WF_root` execution.

▶ The `WF_root` execution runs the script object from left to right. In the script, the local variable gets the value from the output of the `workflow_name()` function, which returns the name of the workflow where it is being executed. With the `print()` function, we display the local variable value and value of the input parameter received from the parent object (job). As the next step, the value of the local variable is being concatenated with the value of the input parameter to get the current location path in the hierarchy for the child objects `WF_level_1` and `WF_level_1_2`.

▶ As all objects inside `WF_root` are linked together, they are executed sequentially from left to right. Every next object only runs after successful completion of the previous object.

▶ Data Services runs `WF_level_1` and repeats the same sequence of displaying the current workflow name and current path with the consequent concatenation and passing of the value to the input parameter of the `WF_parallel` workflow.

▶ The `WF_parallel` workflow demonstrates how Data Services executes two workflow objects placed in the same level that are not linked to each other. Here, we cannot use the script to prepare to perform our usual sequence of script logic steps. If you try to add a script object not linked to the parallel workflows, Data Services gives you an error message from the job validation process:

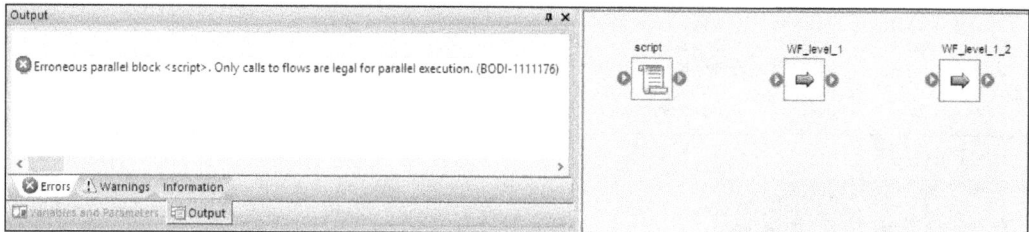

▶ If you try to link the script object to one of the workflows, you will get the following error message:

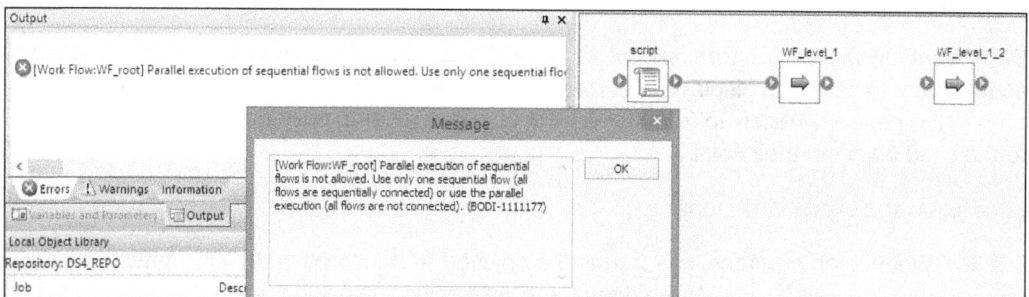

> Note how Data Services does not allow you to link the script object to both workflows.

If used within a job or a workflow, script objects disable parallel execution logic, allowing you only a sequential execution within the current context:

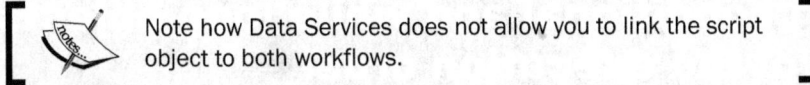

To make sure that your workflow executes simultaneously and runs in parallel, make sure that you do not use the script object in the same workspace.

- That is why, when we pass the values to the input parameters of two workflows executed in parallel, `WF_level_3_1` and `WF_level_3_2`, we specify the concatenation formula right in the input parameter value field:

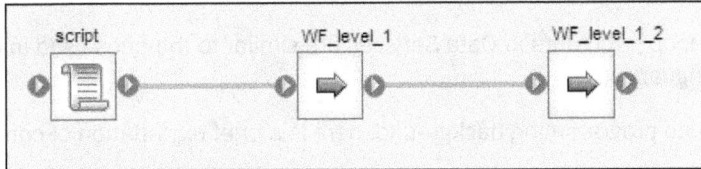

It's very important to understand that `$p_wf_parent_name` are two different parameters in the preceding screenshot. The one on the left-hand side is the `$p_wf_parent_name` input parameter belonging to the child object `WF_level_3_1`, which asks for a value. The one on the right-hand side belongs to the current workflow `WF_parallel`, in which context we are located at the moment, and it holds the value received from its parent object `WF_level_1`.

- After completion of `WF_level_3_1` and `WF_level_3_2`, Data Services completes the `WF_parallel` workflow, then the `WF_level_1` workflow, and finally runs the `WF_level_1_2` workflow. `WF_root` is the last workflow object that is finishing its execution within the job, so the job completes its execution successfully.

See the trace log again to follow the sequence of steps executed, and make sure that you understand why they were executed in this particular order.

Using conditional and while loop objects to control the execution order

Conditional and `while` loop objects are special control objects that branch the execution logic at the workflow level. In this recipe, we will modify the job from the previous recipe to make the execution of our workflow objects more flexible.

Conditional and loop structures in Data Services are similar to the ones used in other programming languages.

For readers with no programming background, here is a brief explanation of conditional and loop structures.

▸ The `IF-THEN-ELSE` structure allows you to check the result of the conditional expression presented in the `IF` block and executes either the `THEN` block or `ELSE` block depending on whether the result of the conditional expression is `TRUE` or `FALSE`.

▸ The `LOOP` structure in programming language allows you to execute the same code again and again in the loop until the specified condition is met. You should be very careful when creating loop structures in programming language and correctly specify the condition that exits or ends the loop. If incorrectly specified, the code in the loop could run indefinitely, making your program hang.

Getting ready

Open the job from the previous recipe.

How to do it...

We will get rid of our `WF_parallel` workflow and execute only one of the underlying `WF_level_3_1` or `WF_level_3_2` workflows randomly. This is not a common scenario you will see in real life, but it gives a perfect example of how Data Services allows you to control your execution logic. Perform these steps:

1. Open `WF_level_1` in the workspace and remove `WF_parallel` from it.
2. Using the tool palette on the right-hand side, create a conditional object, and link your script object to it. Name the conditional object `If_Then_Else`:

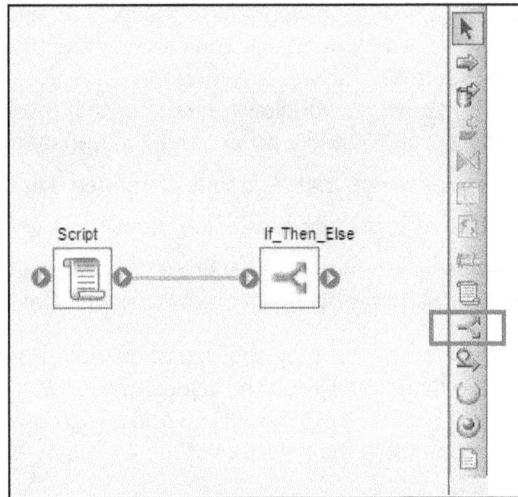

3. Double-click on the `If_Then_Else` conditional object or choose **Open** from the right-click context menu.

4. You can see three sections: **If**, **Then**, and **Else**. In the **Then** and **Else** sections, you can put any executional elements (workflows, scripts, or dataflows). The **If** field should contain the expression returning a Boolean value. If it returns TRUE, then all objects in the **Then** section are executed in sequential or parallel order, depending on their arrangement. If the expression returns FALSE, then all elements from the **Else** section are executed:

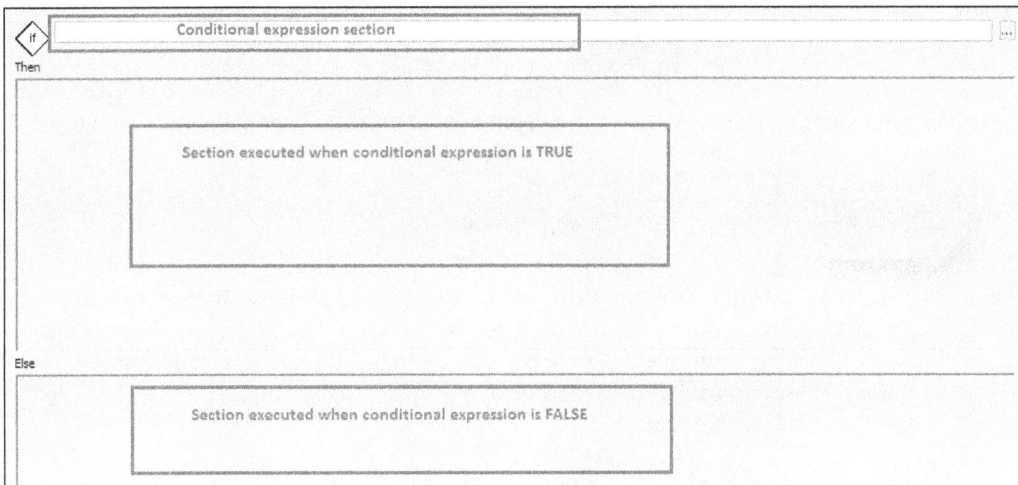

5. Put `WF_level_3_1` from **Local Object Library** into the **Then** section.

6. Put `WF_level_3_2` from **Local Object Library** into the **Else** section.

7. Map input parameter calls of each workflow to the local **$l_wf_name** variable of the parent `WF_level_1` workflow object. You can now see that without the `WF_parallel` workflow, both `WF_level_3_1` and `WF_level_3_2` are operating within the context of the `WF_level_1` workflow (remember that the conditional object does not have its own context and variable scope, and it is transparent in that aspect).

8. Type in the following expression that randomly generates 0 or 1 in the **If** section:

```
cast(round(rand_ext(),0),'integer') = 1
```

We will use this expression to randomly generate either 0 or 1 in order to execute the ETL placed in **THEN** or **ELSE** blocks every time we run the Data Services job.

9. Save and execute the job. The trace log shows that only one workflow, `WF_level_3_2`, was executed. To have more visibility on the values generated by the `If` expression, you can put in the script before `If_Then_Else` and assign its value to a local variable, which can be used after that in the **If** section of the `If_Then_Else` object to get the Boolean value:

4424	4056	JOB	25/06/2015 9:03:13 p.m.	Job <Job_TEST> is started.
4424	4056	WORKFLOW	25/06/2015 9:03:13 p.m.	Work flow <WF_root> is started.
4424	4056	PRINTFN	25/06/2015 9:03:13 p.m.	INFO: running 'WF_root' (parent='Job_TEST')
4424	4056	WORKFLOW	25/06/2015 9:03:13 p.m.	Work flow <WF_level_1> is started.
4424	4056	PRINTFN	25/06/2015 9:03:13 p.m.	INFO: running 'WF_level_1' (parent='Job_TEST > WF_root')
4424	4056	WORKFLOW	25/06/2015 9:03:13 p.m.	Work flow <WF_level_3_2> is started.
4424	4056	PRINTFN	25/06/2015 9:03:13 p.m.	INFO: running 'WF_level_3_2' (parent='Job_TEST > WF_root > WF_level_1')
4424	4056	WORKFLOW	25/06/2015 9:03:13 p.m.	Work flow <WF_level_3_2> is completed successfully.
4424	4056	WORKFLOW	25/06/2015 9:03:13 p.m.	Work flow <WF_level_1> is completed successfully.
4424	4056	WORKFLOW	25/06/2015 9:03:13 p.m.	Work flow <WF_level_1_2> is started.
4424	4056	PRINTFN	25/06/2015 9:03:13 p.m.	INFO: running 'WF_level_1_2' (parent='Job_TEST > WF_root')
4424	4056	WORKFLOW	25/06/2015 9:03:13 p.m.	Work flow <WF_level_1_2> is completed successfully.
4424	4056	WORKFLOW	25/06/2015 9:03:13 p.m.	Work flow <WF_root> is completed successfully.
4424	4056	JOB	25/06/2015 9:03:13 p.m.	Job <Job_TEST> is completed successfully.

Now, let's make our last workflow object in the job run 10 times in a loop, using these steps:

1. Open `WF_root` in the main workspace.

2. Delete `WF_level_1_2` from the workspace.

3. Add a `while` loop object from the tool palette, name it `While_Loop`, and link it to `WF_level_1`, as shown in the following screenshot. As we know that we are going to run a loop for 10 cycles, we need to create a counter that we will use in the loop condition. For this purpose, create a `$l_count` local integer variable for the `WF_root` workflow and assign it a value "1" in the initial script. Your code in the `Script` object should look like this:

```
$l_wf_name = workflow_name();
print('INFO: running {$l_wf_name} (parent={$p_wf_parent_name})');
$l_wf_name = $p_wf_parent_name || ' > ' || $l_wf_name;

$l_count = 1;
```

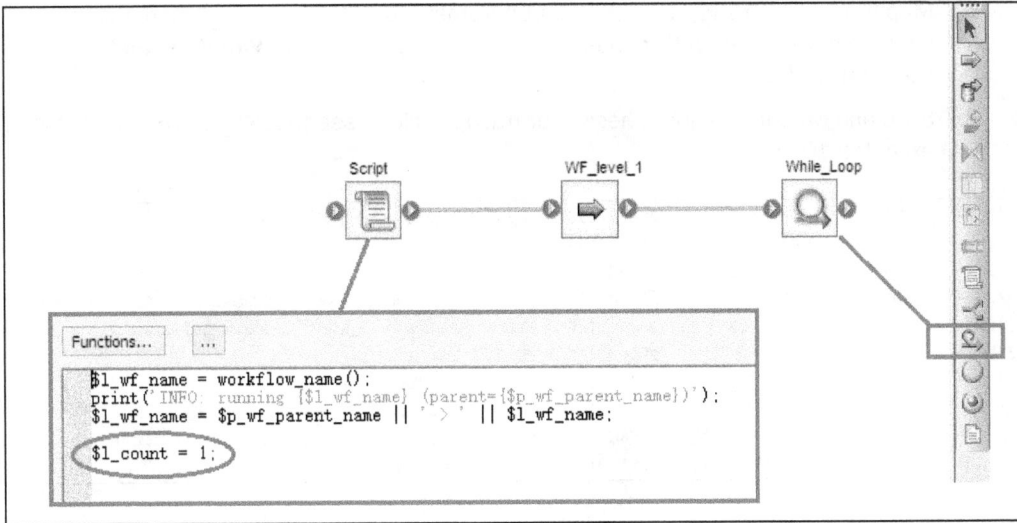

```
$l_wf_name = workflow_name();
print('INFO: running {$l_wf_name} (parent={$p_wf_parent_name})');
$l_wf_name = $p_wf_parent_name || ' > ' || $l_wf_name;

$l_count = 1;
```

4. Open the `While_Loop` in the workspace and place the `WF_level_1_2` workflow by copying or dragging it from **Local Object Library**.

5. Place two script objects, `script` and `increase_counter`, before and after the workflow and link all three objects together.

6. The initial script will contain the `print()` function displaying the current loop cycle, and the final script will increase the counter value by 1. You also have to put the conditional expression that checks the current counter value in the `while` field of the `While_Loop` object. The expression is `$l_count <= 10`:

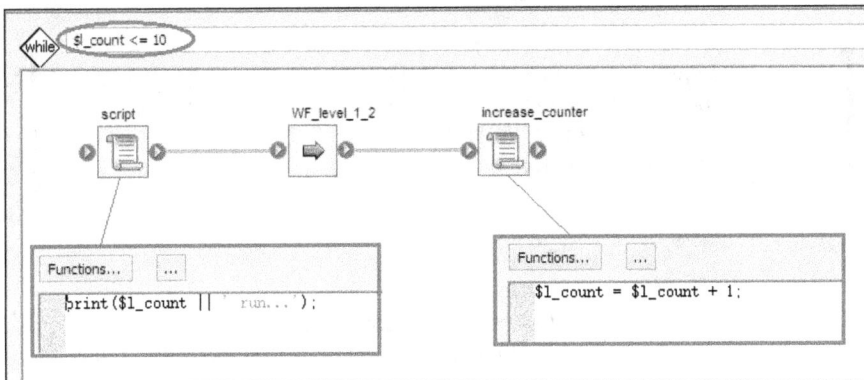

The conditional expression is checked after each loop cycle. The loop executes successfully as soon as the conditional expression returns FALSE.

7. Map the `$p_wf_parent_name` input parameter of `WF_level_1_2` to the local variable from the parent's context, `$l_wf_name`, by going to **Variables and Parameters | Calls**.

8. Save and execute the job. Check your trace log file to see that `WF_level_1_2` was executed 10 times:

11064	5004	WORKFLOW	25/06/2015 9:34:47 p.m.	Work flow <WF_level_1> is completed successfully.
11064	5004	PRINTFN	25/06/2015 9:34:47 p.m.	1 run...
11064	5004	WORKFLOW	25/06/2015 9:34:47 p.m.	Work flow <WF_level_1_2> is started.
11064	5004	PRINTFN	25/06/2015 9:34:47 p.m.	INFO: running 'WF_level_1_2' (parent='Job_TEST > WF_root')
11064	5004	WORKFLOW	25/06/2015 9:34:47 p.m.	Work flow <WF_level_1_2> is completed successfully.
11064	5004	PRINTFN	25/06/2015 9:34:47 p.m.	2 run...
11064	5004	WORKFLOW	25/06/2015 9:34:47 p.m.	Work flow <WF_level_1_2> is started.
11064	5004	PRINTFN	25/06/2015 9:34:47 p.m.	INFO: running 'WF_level_1_2' (parent='Job_TEST > WF_root')
11064	5004	WORKFLOW	25/06/2015 9:34:47 p.m.	Work flow <WF_level_1_2> is completed successfully.
11064	5004	PRINTFN	25/06/2015 9:34:47 p.m.	3 run...

How it works...

The `if-then-else` construction is available in the scripting language as well, but as you know already, the usage of script objects with workflows is quite limited—you can only join these objects sequentially. This is where conditional objects come in action.

The main characteristic of the `conditional` and `while` loop objects is that they are not workflows and do not have their own context. They operate within the variable scope of their parent objects and can only be placed within a workflow or job object. That is why, you need to create and define all local variables used in the `if-then-else` or `while` conditional expression inside the parent object context.

> Script objects have their own `if-then-else` and `while` loop constructions, and to branch logic within dataflows, you can use **Case**, **Validation**, or simply **Query** with filtering conditions transforms.

There is more...

Workflow objects themselves have a few options to control how they are executed within the job that adds some flexibility to the ETL design. They will be explained in the following recipes of this chapter. Now, we will just take a look at one of them.

This is the **Execute only once** option available in the workflow object properties window.

To open it, just right-click on the workflow either in the workspace or in **Local Object Library** and choose **Properties...** from the context menu:

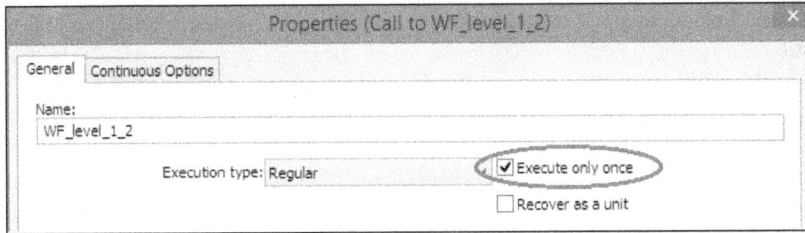

To see the effect this option has on workflow execution, take the job from this recipe and tick this option for the WF_level_1_2 workflow—the one that runs in loop.

Then, save the job and execute it. The trace log looks like this now:

13184	7896	PRINTFN	25/06/2015 9:38:22 p.m.	1 run...
13184	7896	WORKFLOW	25/06/2015 9:38:22 p.m.	Work flow <WF_level_1_2> is started.
13184	7896	PRINTFN	25/06/2015 9:38:22 p.m.	INFO: running 'WF_level_1_2' (parent='Job_TEST > WF_root')
13184	7896	WORKFLOW	25/06/2015 9:38:22 p.m.	Work flow <WF_level_1_2> is completed successfully.
13184	7896	PRINTFN	25/06/2015 9:38:22 p.m.	2 run...
13184	7896	WORKFLOW	25/06/2015 9:38:22 p.m.	Work flow <WF_level_1_2> is started.
13184	7896	WORKFLOW	25/06/2015 9:38:22 p.m.	Work flow <WF_level_1_2> is not run because of run once semantics.
13184	7896	WORKFLOW	25/06/2015 9:38:22 p.m.	Work flow <WF_level_1_2> is completed successfully.
13184	7896	PRINTFN	25/06/2015 9:38:22 p.m.	3 run...
13184	7896	WORKFLOW	25/06/2015 9:38:22 p.m.	Work flow <WF_level_1_2> is started.
13184	7896	WORKFLOW	25/06/2015 9:38:22 p.m.	Work flow <WF_level_1_2> is not run because of run once semantics.

What is happening here now is that after successfully executing the workflow for the first time in the first run, the while loop tries to do this another 9 times. However, as the workflow has already run within this job execution, it skips it with successful workflow completion status.

This option is rarely used within a loop as you, of course, do not put anything in loop that can be executed only once, but it shows how Data Services deals with workflows like this.

The most common scenario is when you put the specific workflow in multiple branches of the workflow hierarchy as a dependency for other workflows and you only need it to be executed once without caring which branch it will be executed in first as long as it completes successfully.

The scope of this option is restricted by a job level. If you place the workflow with this option enabled in multiple jobs and run them in parallel, the workflow will be executed once in each job.

Using the bypassing feature

The bypassing option allows you to configure a workflow or dataflow object to be skipped during the job execution.

Getting ready...

We will use the same job as in the previous recipe.

How to do it...

Let's configure the WF_level_1 workflow object that belongs to the parent WF_root workflow to be skipped permanently when the job runs.

The configuration of this feature requires two steps: creating a bypassing substitution parameter and enabling the bypassing feature for the workflow using a created substitution parameter.

1. To create a bypassing substitution parameter, follow these steps:

   1. Go to **Tools | Substitution Parameter Configurations...**.

   2. On the **Substitution Parameter Editor** window, you can see the list of default substitution parameters used by Data Services.

   3. Click on the empty field at the bottom of the list to create a new substitution parameter.

   4. You can choose any name you want, but remember that all substitution parameters start with the double dollar sign.

   5. Call your new substitution parameter $$BypassEnabled and choose the default value **YES** in the **Configuration** column to the right:

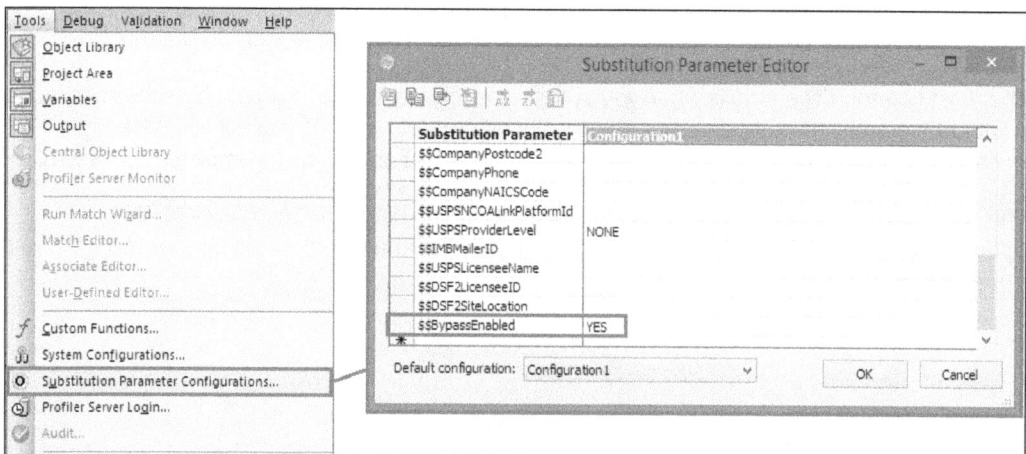

6. As a final step, click on **OK** to create the substitution parameter.

2. Now, you can "label" any workflow object with this substitution parameter if you want it to be bypassed during job execution. Follow these steps:

    1. Open the `WF_root` workflow within your job to see `WF_level_1` in the main workspace window.

    2. Right-click on the `WF_level_1` workflow and choose **Properties...** from the context menu to open the workflow properties window.

    3. Click on the **Bypass** field combobox and choose the newly created substitution parameter from the list, `[$$BypassEnabled]`. By default, the `{No Bypass}` value is chosen in this field:

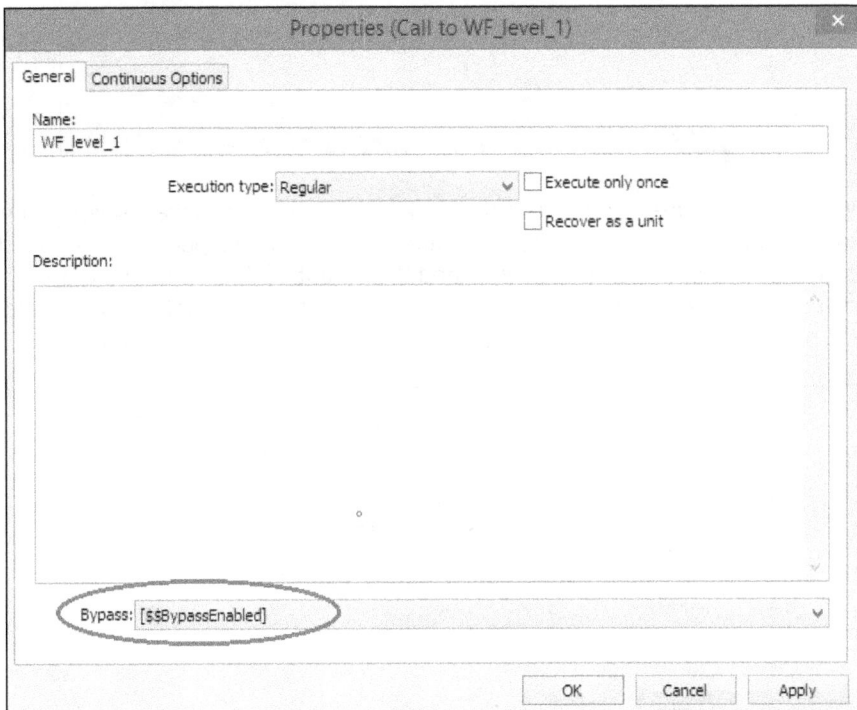

    4. Click on **OK**. The workflow becomes marked with a crossed red-circle icon. This means that during the job execution, this workflow will be skipped, and the next object in the sequence will be executed straight away:

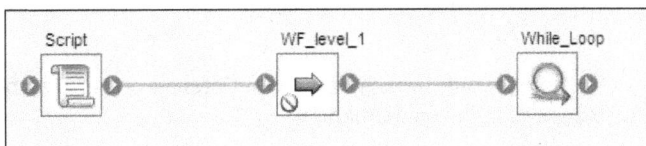

How it works...

Now, let's see what happens when you run the job:

▸ During job validation, you can see a warning message telling you that a particular workflow will be bypassed:

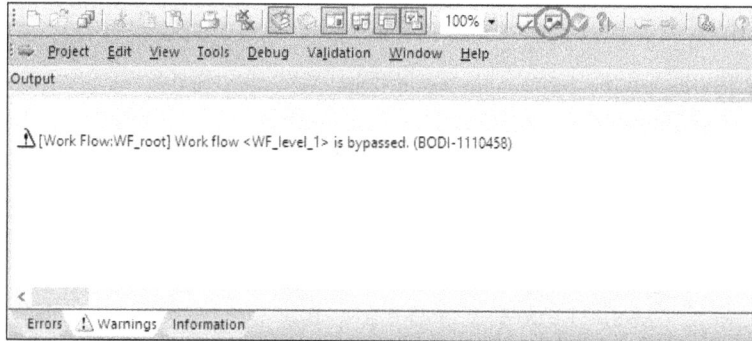

▸ When the job is executed, it runs the workflow sequence as usual, except when it gets to the bypassed workflow object. The workflow object is skipped and all dependent objects, the object next in sequence and the parent workflow where the bypassed object resides, consider its execution to be successful. If you take a look at the trace log of the job execution, you will see something similar to this screenshot:

10036	14700	JOB	26/06/2015 6:43:02 p.m.	Processing job <Job_TEST>.
10036	14700	WORKFLOW	26/06/2015 6:43:02 p.m.	Work flow <WF_level_1> is bypassed.
10036	14700	JOB	26/06/2015 6:43:03 p.m.	Optimizing job <Job_TEST>.
10036	14700	JOB	26/06/2015 6:43:03 p.m.	Job <Job_TEST> is started.
10036	14700	WORKFLOW	26/06/2015 6:43:03 p.m.	Work flow <WF_root> is started.
10036	14700	PRINTFN	26/06/2015 6:43:03 p.m.	INFO: running 'WF_root' (parent='Job_TEST')
10036	14700	PRINTFN	26/06/2015 6:43:03 p.m.	1 run...
10036	14700	WORKFLOW	26/06/2015 6:43:03 p.m.	Work flow <WF_level_1_2> is started.
10036	14700	PRINTFN	26/06/2015 6:43:03 p.m.	INFO: running 'WF_level_1_2' (parent='Job_TEST > WF_root')
10036	14700	WORKFLOW	26/06/2015 6:43:03 p.m.	Work flow <WF_level_1_2> is completed successfully.

There is more...

In Data Services, there is more than one way to set up the workflow object as bypassed. If you right-click on the workflow object, you will see that the **Bypass** option is available in the context menu directly. It opens the **Set Bypass** window with the same combobox list of substitution parameter values available for this option.

> You can not only bypass workflows. Dataflow objects can be bypassed in the same manner.

Controlling failures – try-catch objects

In the *Creating custom functions* recipe in *Chapter 3, Data Services Basics - Data Types, Scripting Language, and Functions*, we created a custom function showing an example of the try-catch block exception handling in the scripting language. Like in the case of if-then-else and while loop, Data Services has a variation of the try-catch construction for the workflow/dataflow object level as well. You can put the sequence of the executable objects (workflows/dataflows) between Try and Catch objects and then catch potential errors in the Catch object where you can put scripts, dataflows, or workflows that you want to run to handle the caught errors.

How to do it...

The steps to deploy and enable the exception handling block in your workflow structure are extremely easy and quick to implement.

All you have to do is place an object or sequence of objects from which you want to catch possible exceptions between two special objects, Try and Catch. Then, follow these steps:

1. Open the job from the previous recipe.

2. Open WF_root in the workspace.

3. Choose the Try object from the right-side tool palette and place it at the beginning of the object sequence. Name it Try:

4. Choose the Catch object from the right-side tool palette and place it at the end of the object sequence. Name it Catch:

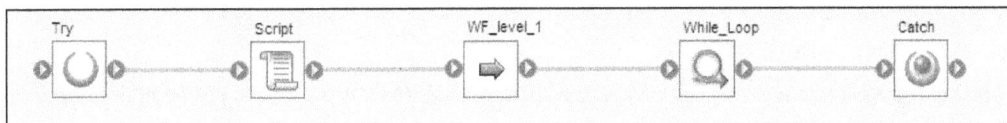

5. The Try object is not modifiable and does not have any properties except description. Its only purpose is to mark the beginning of the sequence for which you want to handle an exception.

6. Double-click on the `Catch` object to open it in the main workspace. Note that all exception types are selected by default. This way, we make sure that we catch any possible failures that can happen during our code execution. Of course, there can be scenarios when you want the ETL to fail and do not want to run the code in the `Catch` block for some types of errors. In this case, you can deselect the exception to be handled in the `Catch` block. In our example, we just want our code to continue to run putting the error message in the trace log.

7. Create the script object with the following line in it:

```
print('ERROR: exception has been caught and handled
    successfully');
```

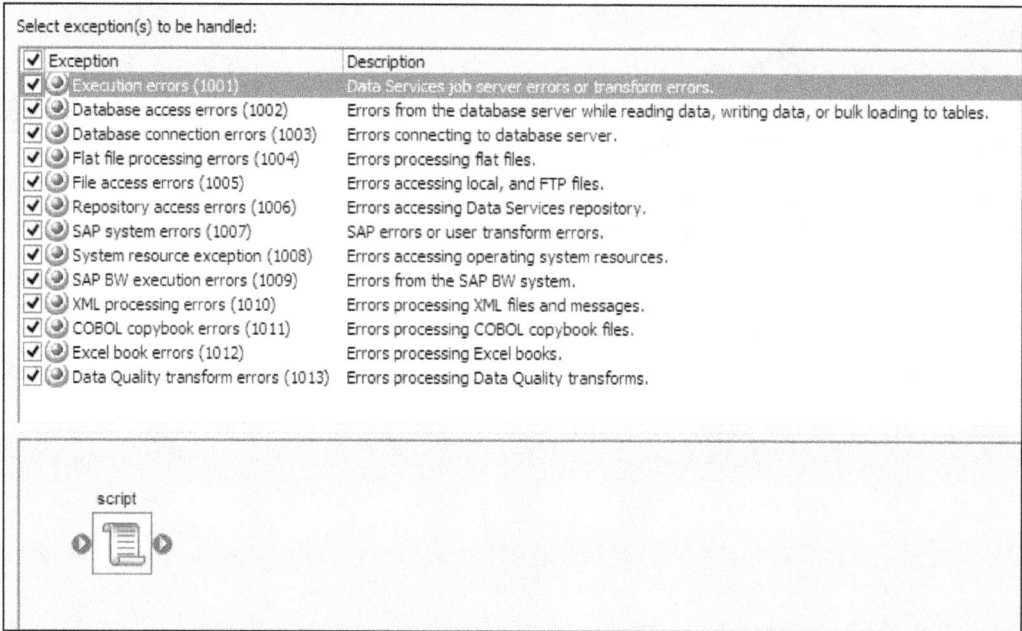

Select exception(s) to be handled:

Exception	Description
✔ Execution errors (1001)	Data Services job server errors or transform errors.
✔ Database access errors (1002)	Errors from the database server while reading data, writing data, or bulk loading to tables.
✔ Database connection errors (1003)	Errors connecting to database server.
✔ Flat file processing errors (1004)	Errors processing flat files.
✔ File access errors (1005)	Errors accessing local, and FTP files.
✔ Repository access errors (1006)	Errors accessing Data Services repository.
✔ SAP system errors (1007)	SAP errors or user transform errors.
✔ System resource exception (1008)	Errors accessing operating system resources.
✔ SAP BW execution errors (1009)	Errors from the SAP BW system.
✔ XML processing errors (1010)	Errors processing XML files and messages.
✔ COBOL copybook errors (1011)	Errors processing COBOL copybook files.
✔ Excel book errors (1012)	Errors processing Excel books.
✔ Data Quality transform errors (1013)	Errors processing Data Quality transforms.

script

8. Save and execute the job. The exception you generated in the script is successfully handled by the `try-catch` construction, and the job completes successfully.

How it works...

If you take a look at the trace log of your job run, you can see that the `WF_level_3_1` and `WF_level_1` workflows failed:

Pid	Tid	Type	Time Stamp	Message
3060	10984	JOB	29/06/2015 7:59:06 a.m.	Reading job <bbf4f31e_b4c8_4797_ac09_a6e90d7d7c81> from the repository; Server version is <14.2.4.668>; Repository version is
3060	10984	JOB	29/06/2015 7:59:06 a.m.	<14.2.4.0000>.
3060	10984	JOB	29/06/2015 7:59:06 a.m.	Current directory of job <bbf4f31e_b4c8_4797_ac09_a6e90d7d7c81> is <C:\EIM\Data Services\bin>.
3060	10984	JOB	29/06/2015 7:59:07 a.m.	Starting job on job server host <IVANSHOMNIKOV>, port <3500>.
3060	10984	JOB	29/06/2015 7:59:08 a.m.	Job <Job_TEST> of runid <201506290759073060109984> is initiated by user <ivan.shomnikov>.
3060	10984	JOB	29/06/2015 7:59:08 a.m.	Processing job <Job_TEST>.
3060	10984	JOB	29/06/2015 7:59:08 a.m.	Optimizing job <Job_TEST>.
3060	10984	JOB	29/06/2015 7:59:08 a.m.	Job <Job_TEST> is started.
3060	10984	WORKFLOW	29/06/2015 7:59:08 a.m.	Work flow <WF_root> is started.
3060	10984	PRINTFN	29/06/2015 7:59:08 a.m.	INFO: running 'WF_root' (parent='Job_TEST')
3060	10984	WORKFLOW	29/06/2015 7:59:08 a.m.	Work flow <WF_level_1> is started.
3060	10984	PRINTFN	29/06/2015 7:59:08 a.m.	INFO: running 'WF_level_1' (parent='Job_TEST > WF_root')
3060	10984	WORKFLOW	29/06/2015 7:59:08 a.m.	Work flow <WF_level_3_1> is started.
3060	10984	PRINTFN	29/06/2015 7:59:08 a.m.	INFO: running 'WF_level_3_1' (parent='Job_TEST > WF_root > WF_level_1')
3060	10984	WORKFLOW	29/06/2015 7:59:08 a.m.	Work flow <WF_level_3_1> is terminated due to an error <50316>.
3060	10984	WORKFLOW	29/06/2015 7:59:08 a.m.	Work flow <WF_level_1> is terminated due to an error <50316>.
3060	10984	PRINTFN	29/06/2015 7:59:08 a.m.	ERROR: exception has been caught and handled successfully.
3060	10984	WORKFLOW	29/06/2015 7:59:08 a.m.	Work flow <WF_root> is completed successfully.
3060	10984	JOB	29/06/2015 7:59:08 a.m.	Job <Job_TEST> is completed successfully.

`WF_level_3_1` failed as the exception was raised in the script inside it, and `WF_level_1` failed because its execution depends on the child object `WF_level_3_1`. You should remember that if any child objects within a workflow fail (another workflow, dataflow, or script), the parent object fails immediately. Then, the parent's parent object fails as well, and so on, until the root level of the job hierarchy is reached and the job itself fails and stops it's execution.

By placing the `try-catch` sequence inside `WF_root`, we made it possible to catch all exceptions inside it, making sure that our `WF_root` workflow never fails.

> Try-catch objects do not prevent a job from failing in the case of the crash of the job server itself. This is, of course, because the successful execution of the try-catch logic depends on the work of the Data Services job server.

Note that the error log is still generated in spite of the successful job execution. In there, you can see the logging message that was generated by the logic from the catch object and the context in which the initial exception happened:

Pid	Tid	Number	Time Stamp	Message
3060	10984	RUN-050316	29/06/2015 7:59:08 a.m.	|Session Job_TEST|Work flow WF_root|Work flow WF_level_1|Work flow WF_level_3_1
3060	10984	RUN-050316	29/06/2015 7:59:08 a.m.	INFO: raising exception in the workflow 'WF_level_3_1'
3060	10984	RUN-050304	29/06/2015 7:59:08 a.m.	|Session Job_TEST|Work flow WF_root|Work flow WF_level_1|Work flow WF_level_3_1
3060	10984	RUN-050304	29/06/2015 7:59:08 a.m.	Function call <raise_exception (INFO: raising exception in the workflow 'WF_level_3_1') > failed, due to error <50316>:
3060	10984	RUN-050304	29/06/2015 7:59:08 a.m.	<INFO: raising exception in the workflow 'WF_level_3_1'>.
3060	10984	RUN-053008	29/06/2015 7:59:08 a.m.	|Session Job_TEST|Work flow WF_root|Work flow WF_level_1|Work flow WF_level_3_1
3060	10984	RUN-053008	29/06/2015 7:59:08 a.m.	INFO: The above error occurs in the context <|Session Job_TEST|Work flow WF_root|Work flow WF_level_1|Work flow
3060	10984	RUN-053008	29/06/2015 7:59:08 a.m.	WF_level_3_1|raise_exception(...) Function Body|>.

`Try-catch` objects can be a vital part of your recovery strategy. If your workflow contains a few steps that you can think of as a transactional unit, you would want to clean up when some of these steps fail before running the sequence again. As explained in the recipe dedicated to the recovery topic, the Data Services automatic recovery strategy just simply skips the steps that have already been executed, and sometimes, this is simply not enough.

It all depends on how thorough you have to be during your recovery.

Another very important aspect is to understand that `try-catch` blocks prevent the failure of the workflow in which context they are put. This means that the error is hidden inside the `try-catch` and parent workflow, and all subsequent objects down the execution path will be executed by Data Services.

There are situations when you definitely want to fail the whole job to prevent any further execution if some of the data processing inside it fails. You can still use `try-catch` blocks to catch the error in order to log it properly or do some extra steps, but after all this is done, the `raise_exception()` function at the end of the `catch` block is put to fail the workflow.

Use case example – populating dimension tables

In this recipe, we will build the ETL job to populate two dimension tables in the `AdventureWorks_DWH` database, `DimGeography` and `DimSalesTerritory`, with the data from the operational database `AdventureWorks_OLTP`.

Getting ready

For this recipe, you will have to create new job. Also, create two new schemas in the `STAGE` database: `Extract` and `Transform`. To do this, open the SQL Server Management Studio, expand **Databases | STAGE | Security | Schemas**, right-click on the **Schemas** folder, and choose the **New Schema...** option from the context menu. Specify your administrator user account as a schema owner.

How to do it...

1. In the first step, we will create extraction processes using these steps:
    1. Open the job context and create the `WF_extract` workflow.

2. Open the `WF_extract` workflow in the workspace and create four workflows: each for every source table we extract from the OLTP database: `WF_Extract_SalesTerritory`, `WF_Extract_Address`, `WF_Extract_StateProvince`, `WF_Extract_CountryRegion`. Do not link these workflow objects to make them run in parallel.

3. Open `WF_Extract_SalesTerritory` in the main workspace area and create the `DF_Extract_SalesTerritory` dataflow.

4. Open `DF_Extract_SalesTerritory` in the workspace area.

5. Add a source table from the OLTP datastore: `SalesTerritory`.

6. Place the **Query** transform after the source table, link them, open the Query transform object in the workspace, and map all source columns to the target schema by selecting them together and dragging them to the target schema empty section.

7. Exit **Query Editor** and add the target template table, `SalesTerritory`. Choose `DS_STAGE` as a datastore object and `Extract` as the owner to create a target stage table in the `Extract` schema of the `STAGE` database.

8. Your dataflow and Query transform mapping should look as shown in the screenshots here:

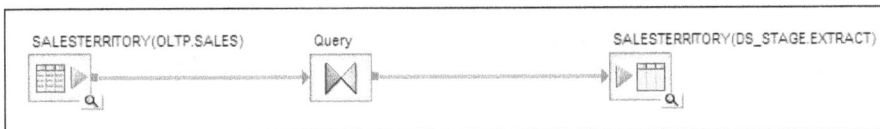

Schema In: SALESTERRITORY				
	Type	Description	Cc	
SALESTERRITORY		Sales territory looku...		
TERRITORYID	int	Primary key for Sales...		
NAME	varchar(50)	Sales territory descri...	Na	
COUNTRYREGIONCODE	varchar(3)	ISO standard countr...		
GROUP	varchar(50)	Geographic area to ...		
SALESYTD	decimal(19,4)	Sales in the territory ...		
SALESLASTYEAR	decimal(19,4)	Sales in the territory ...		
COSTYTD	decimal(19,4)	Business costs in the...		
COSTLASTYEAR	decimal(19,4)	Business costs in the...		
ROWGUID	varchar(36)	ROWGUIDCOL num...		
MODIFIEDDATE	datetime	Date and time the re...		

Schema Out: Query				
	Type	Mapping	Description	
Query				
TERRITORYID	int	SALESTERRI...	Primary key for Sales...	
NAME	varchar(50)	SALESTERRI...	Sales territory descri...	
COUNTRYREGIONCODE	varchar(3)	SALESTERRI...	ISO standard countr...	
GROUP	varchar(50)	SALESTERRI...	Geographic area to ...	
SALESYTD	decimal(19,4)	SALESTERRI...	Sales in the territory ...	
SALESLASTYEAR	decimal(19,4)	SALESTERRI...	Sales in the territory ...	
COSTYTD	decimal(19,4)	SALESTERRI...	Business costs in the...	
COSTLASTYEAR	decimal(19,4)	SALESTERRI...	Business costs in the...	
ROWGUID	varchar(36)	SALESTERRI...	ROWGUIDCOL num...	
MODIFIEDDATE	datetime	SALESTERRI...	Date and time the re...	

9. In the same manner, using steps 3 to 8, create extract dataflow objects for the other OLTP tables: Address (dataflow DF_Extract_Address), StateProvince (dataflow DF_Extract_StateProvince), and CountryRegion (dataflow DF_Extract_CountryRegion). Place each of the created dataflows inside the parent object with the same name, substituting the prefix DF_ with WF_ and put all extract workflows to run in parallel inside the WF_extract workflow object. To name the target template tables inside each of the dataflows, choose the same name as of the source table object and select DS_STAGE as a database for the table to be created in and Extract as the owner/schema:

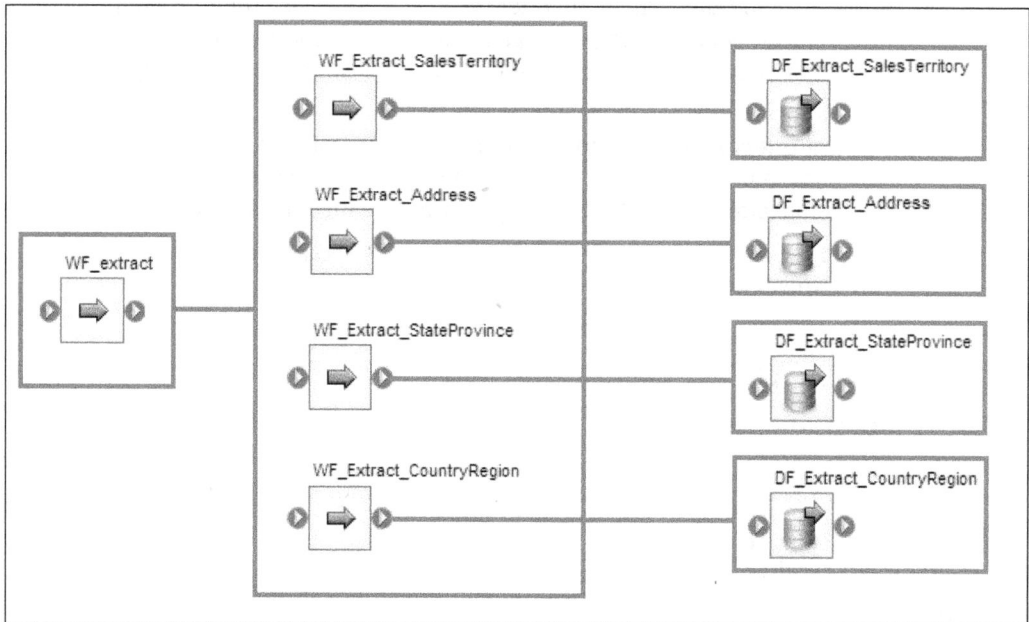

2. Now, let's create transformation processes using these steps:

   1. Go to the job context level in your Designer and open the WF_transform object.

   2. As we will populate two dimension tables, we will create two transformation workflows running in parallel for each one of them: WF_Transform_DimSalesTerritory and WF_Transform_DimGeography.

   3. Open WF_transform_DimSalesTerritory and create a new dataflow in its workspace: DF_Transform_DimSalesTerritory.

4. Open the dataflow object and design it as shown in the following screenshot:

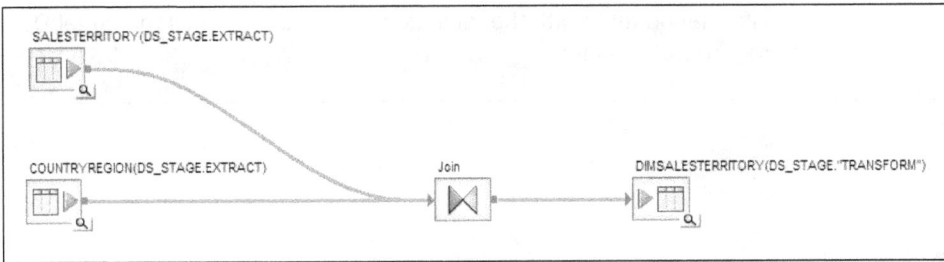

5. It is now important for the transformation dataflows to create target template tables in the `Transform` schema created earlier. The name of the target table template object should be the same as the target dimension table in DWH.

6. The `Join` Query transform performs the join of two source tables and maps the columns from each one of them to the **Query** output schema. As we do not migrate image columns, specify `NULL` as a mapping for the `SalesTerritoryImage` output column. Also, specify `NULL` as a mapping for `SalesTerritoryKey`, as its value will be generated in one of the load processes:

7. To create the transformation process for `DimGeography`, go back to the `WF_transform` workflow context level and create a new workflow `WF_Transform_DimGeography` with a dataflow `DF_Transform_DimGeography` inside.

8. In the dataflow, we will source the data from three OLTP tables, `Address`, `StateProvince`, and `CountryRegion`, to populate the stage transformation table with the table definition that matches the target DWH `DimGeography` table:

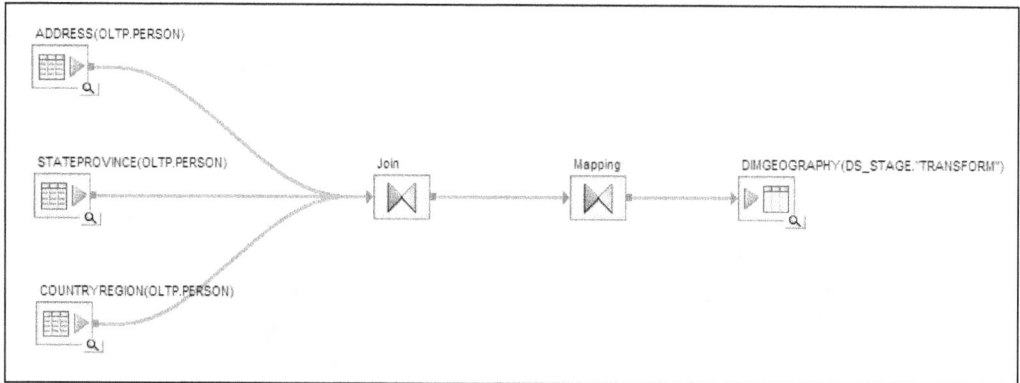

9. Specify join conditions for all three source tables in the `Join` Query transform and map the source column to the target output schema:

10. Place another Query transform and name it `Mapping`. Link the `Join` Query transform to the `Mapping` Query transform and map the source columns to the target schema columns which match the table definition of the DWH `DimGeography` table. Map one extra column `TERRITORYID` from source to target:

Schema In: Join				Schema Out: Mapping			
	Type	Description	Cd		Type	Mapping	
Join				Mapping			
CITY	varchar(30)	Name of the city.		TERRITORYID	int	Join.TERRITORYID	
POSTALCODE	varchar(15)	Postal code for the s...		GEOGRAPHYKEY	int	NULL	
COUNTRYREGIONCODE	varchar(3)	ISO standard code fo...		CITY	varchar(30)	Join.CITY	
COUNTRYREGION_NAME	varchar(50)	Country or region na... Na		STATEPROVINCECODE	varchar(3)	Join.STATEPROVINCECODE	
STATEPROVINCECODE	varchar(3)	ISO standard state or...		STATEPROVINCENAME	varchar(50)	Join.STATEPROVINCE_NAME	
STATEPROVINCE_NAME	varchar(50)	State or province des... Na		COUNTRYREGIONCODE	varchar(3)	Join.COUNTRYREGIONCODE	
TERRITORYID	int	ID of the territory in ...		ENGLISHCOUNTRYREGIONNAME	varchar(50)	Join.COUNTRYREGION_NAME	
				SPANISHCOUNTRYREGIONNAME	varchar(50)	NULL	
				FRENCHCOUNTRYREGIONNAME	varchar(50)	NULL	
				POSTALCODE	varchar(15)	Join.POSTALCODE	
				IPADDRESSLOCATOR	varchar(15)	NULL	

11. In the `Mapping` Query transform, place `NULL` in the mapping sections for the columns that we are not going to populate values for.

3. Now, we need to create final load processes that will move the data from the stage transformation tables into the target DWH dimension tables. Perform these steps:

    1. Open the `WF_load` workflow, add two workflow objects `WF_Load_DimSalesTerritory` and `WF_Load_DimGeography`, and link them together to run sequentially.

    2. Open `WF_Load_DimSalesTerritory` and create a dataflow object, `DF_Load_DimSalesTerritory`, inside it.

    3. This dataflow will perform a comparison of source data to a target `DimSalesTerritory` dimension table data and will produce the set of updates for the existing records whose values have changed in the source system, or will insert records with key column values that do not exist in the dimension table yet:

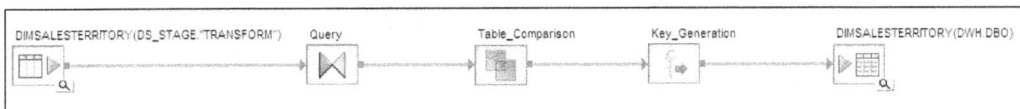

4. In the Query transform, simply map all source columns from the `DimSalesTerritory` transformation table to the output schema.

5. Inside the `Table_Comparison` object, define target DWH `DimSalesTerritory` as a comparison table and specify `SalesTerritoryAlternateKey` as a key column and three compare columns `SalesTerritoryRegion`, `SalesTerritoryCountry`, and `SalesTerrtoryGroup`, as shown here:

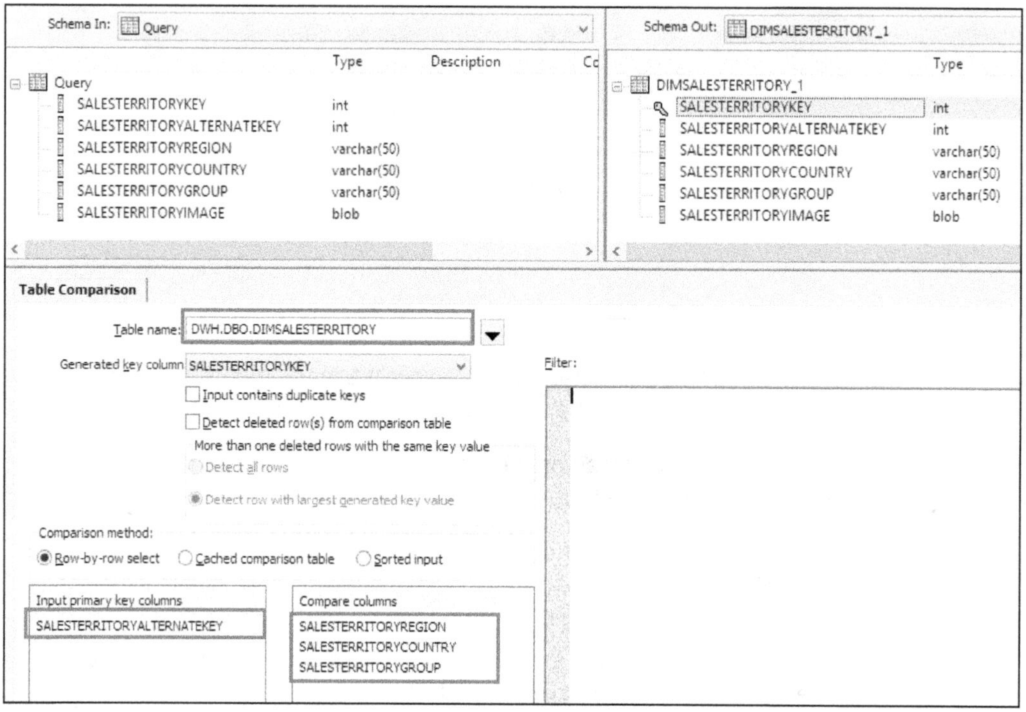

6. As the final step in the dataflow, before inserting data into target table object, the `Key_Generation` transform helps you to populate the `SalesTerritoryKey` column of the target dimension table with sequential surrogate keys. Surrogate keys are the keys usually generated during the population of DWH tables. Surrogate key columns can identify the uniqueness of the record. This way, you have a single column with a unique ID that you can use instead of referencing multiple columns in the table, which defines the uniqueness of the record:

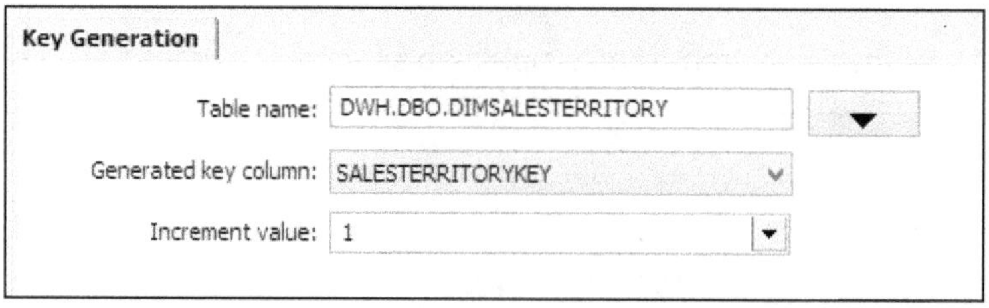

7. By default, all dimension tables in the DWH database we are using have identity columns. In SQL Server, the identity columns feature allows you to delegate the process of surrogate keys creation to the SQL Server database. You simply insert the record without specifying values for the identity column, and the SQL Server populates the field for you with the sequential unique number. In our case, we want to have control over the key creation ourselves to be able to generate the keys in the ETL before inserting the data. To do this, we have to enable `IDENTITY INSERT` before inserting the records and disable it after the insert. Otherwise, you will receive the error message from the SQL Server informing you that you cannot populate identity columns with values as it is done automatically by the database engine.

To switch the ability to insert surrogate keys in identity columns from Data Services, open **Target Table Editor** of the `DimSalesTerritory` table and populate the **Pre-Load Commands** and **Post-Load Commands** tabs with the following two commands correspondingly:

```
set identity_insert dimsalesterritory on
set identity_insert dimsalesterritory off
```

8. Now, let's create the second load process of populating the `DimGeography` dimension table. Open the `DF_Load_DimGeography` dataflow in the workspace area.

9. The dataflow will have the same structure as the previous one, except that we will look up to the already populated `DimSalesTerritory` dimension table for `SalesTerritoryKey`:

10. In the Query transform, map all columns from the stage `Transform.DimGeography` table and one `SalesTerritoryKey` from the DWH `DimSalesTerritory` table to the output schema. For the join condition, specify the following one:

```
DIMGEOGRAPHY.TERRITORYID =
   DIMSALESTERRITORY.SALESTERRITORYALTERNATEKEY
```

11. Mapping transform output schema definition matches the target table definition, and here, we will finally drop the `TERRITORYID` column from the mappings, as we do not need it anymore.

12. Specify the following settings in the **Table_Comparison** transform:

Table Comparison	
Table name:	DWH.DBO.DIMGEOGRAPHY
Generated key column	GEOGRAPHYKEY
	☐ Input contains duplicate keys
	☐ Detect deleted row(s) from comparison table
	More than one deleted rows with the same key value
	○ Detect all rows
	● Detect row with largest generated key value

Comparison method:
● Row-by-row select   ○ Cached comparison table   ○ Sorted input

Input primary key columns	Compare columns
CITY	POSTALCODE
STATEPROVINCECODE	SALESTERRITORYKEY
COUNTRYREGIONCODE	ENGLISHCOUNTRYREGIONNAME

13. In the **Key_Generation** transform, specify `DWH.DBO.DIMGEOGRAPHY` as the table name and `GEOGRAPHYKEY` as the generated key column.

14. Also, do not forget to define the commands in `Pre-Load` and `Post-Load` target table settings to switch on `IDENTITY_INSERT` and switch it off after the insert is complete. Use the following commands:

```
set identity_insert dimgeography on
set identity_insert dimgeography off
```

How it works...

Let's review the different aspects of the example we just implemented in the previous steps.

Mapping

Before you start the ETL development in Data Services, you have to define the mapping between source columns of operational database tables, target columns of Data Warehouse tables, and transformation rules for the migrated data, if required. At this step, you also have to identify dependencies between source data structures to correctly identify types of join required to extract the correct dataset.

Target column	Source table	Source column	Transformation rule
SalesTerritoryKey	NULL		Generated surrogate key in DWH
SalesTerritoryAlternateKey	SalesTerritory	TerritoryID	Direct mapping
SalesTerritoryRegion	SalesTerritory	Name	Direct mapping
SalesTerritoryCountry	CountryRegion	Name	Direct mapping
SalesTerritoryGroup	SalesTerritory	Group	Direct mapping
SalesTerritoryImage			Not migrating

Table 1: Mappings for the DimSalesTerritory dimension

Here, you can find the mapping table for the DimGeography dimension:

Target column	Source table	Source column	Transformation rule
GeographyKey	NULL		Generated surrogate key in DWH
City	Address	City	Direct mapping
StateProvinceCode	StateProvince	StateProvinceCode	Direct mapping
StateProvinceName	StateProvince	Name	Direct mapping
CountryRegionCode	CountryRegion	CountryRegionCode	Direct mapping
EnglishCountryRegionName	CountryRegion	Name	Direct mapping
SpanishCountryRegionName	NULL		Not migrated
FrenchCountryRegionName	NULL		Not migrated
PostalCode	Address	PostalCode	Direct mapping
SalesTerritoryKey	DimSales Territory	SalesTerritoryKey	Lookup
IpAddressLocator	NULL		Not migrated

Table 2: Mappings for DimGeography dimension

The majority are direct mappings, which means that we do not change the migrated data and move it as is from source to target. The information in these mapping tables is used primarily in the **Query** transforms inside the dataflows to join the source table together and map source columns from source to target schema:

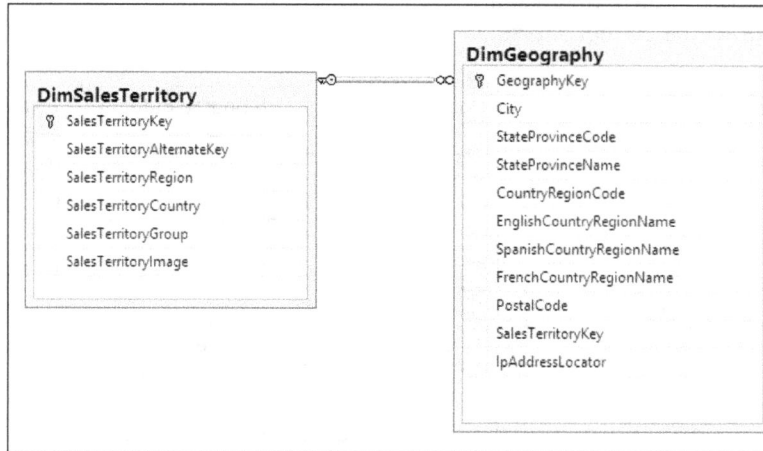

Dependencies

The next step is to define the dependencies between populated target tables to understand in which order ETL processes loading data into them should be executed. The preceding diagram shows that SalesTerritoryKey from the DimSalesTerritory dimension table is used as a reference key in the DimGeography dimension table. This means that ETL processes populating each of these tables cannot be executed in parallel and should run sequentially, as when we populate the DimGeography table, we will require the information in DimSalesTerritory to be already updated.

Development

After defining the mappings and transformation rules and making the decision about the execution order of ETL elements, you can finally open the Designer application and start developing the ETL job.

> The naming conventions for the workflow, dataflow, scripts, and different transformation objects as well as for staging table objects is very important. It allows you to easily read the ETL code and understand what resides in one table or another and what type of operation is performed by a specific dataflow or transformation object within a dataflow.

Our ETL job contains three main stages that are defined by three workflow objects created in the job's workspace. Each of these workflows plays a role of the container for the underlying workflow objects containing dataflows:

- ▶ The first workflow container `WF_extract` contains the processing units that extract the data from the OLTP system into the DWH staging area. There are different advantages of this approach rather than extracting and transforming data within the same dataflow. The main reason is that by copying the data as is in the staging area, you access the production OLTP system only once, creating a consistent snapshot of the OLTP data at specific time. You can query extracted tables in staging as many times as you want, without affecting the live production system's performance. We do not apply any transformations or mapping logic in these extraction processes and are simply copying the contents of the source tables as is.

- ▶ The second workflow container `WF_transform` selects the data from the stage tables, assembles it, and transforms to match the target table definition. At this stage, we will leave all surrogate key columns empty and NULL-out the columns for which we are not going to migrate values.

> In the `DF_Transform_DimGeography` dataflow, the target template table does not exactly match the DWH table's `DimGeography` definition. We will keep one extra column from the source `TERRITORYID` to reference another dimension table `DimSalesTerritory` at the load stage. Without this column, we would not be able to link these two dimension tables together.

- ▶ The third workflow container, `WF_load`, loads the transformed datasets into the target DWH dimension tables. Another important operation this step performs is generating surrogate keys for the new records to be inserted into the target dimension table.

Another important decision you have to make when you populate dimension tables using the **Table_Comparison** transform is which set of keys define a new record in the target dimension table and which columns you are checking for updated values.

In this example, we made a decision to select only two comparison columns, `PostalCode` and `SalesTerritoryKey`. Whenever there is a new location (*City + State + Country*), the record is inserted, and if the location exists, Data Services checks whether the source record coming from the OLTP system contains new values in the `PostalCode` or `SalesTerritoryKey` column. If yes, then the existing record in the target dimension table would be updated.

> Note that in the transformation processes we developed, we did not generate DWH surrogate keys for our new records. The main goal of the transformation process is to assemble the dataset for it to match the target table definition and apply all required transformation if the source data do not comply with the data warehouse requirements.

Execution order

All three steps or three workflows, WF_extract, WF_transform, and WF_load, run sequentially one after another. The next workflow starts execution only after successful completion of the previous one.

Child objects of both WF_extract and WF_transform run in parallel as at those stages, we are not trying to link the migrated datasets to each other with reference keys.

At the final load stage, WF_Load, contains two workflow objects that run sequentially. First, we will fully populate and update the DimSalesTerritory dimension, and then after it's done, we can safely reference it when populating the DimGeography table.

Testing ETL

The best way to test ETL is to make changes to the source system, run the ETL job, and check the contents of the target data warehouse tables.

Preparing test data to populate DimSalesTerritory

Let's make some changes to the source data. We will add a new sales territory in the Sales. SalesTerritory table and a new state in the Person.StateProvince table. Run the following code in the SQL Server Management Studio:

```
-- Insert new records into source OLTP tables to test ETL
-- populating DimSalesTerritory

USE [AdventureWorks_OLTP]
GO

-- Insert new sales territory
INSERT INTO [Sales].[SalesTerritory]
  ([Name], [CountryRegionCode], [Group], [SalesYTD],
    [SalesLastYear]
      ,[CostYTD], [CostLastYear], [rowguid], [ModifiedDate])
  VALUES
  ('Russia', 'RU', 'Russia', 9000000.00, 0.00
    ,0.00, 0.00, NEWID(), GETDATE());
```

```
-- Insert new state
INSERT INTO [Person].[StateProvince]
   ([StateProvinceCode], [CountryRegionCode],
    [IsOnlyStateProvinceFlag]
      , [Name], [TerritoryID], [rowguid], [ModifiedDate])
  VALUES
  ('CR','RU', 1, 'Crimea', 12, NEWID(), GETDATE());


GO
```

Preparing test data to populate DimGeography

To update the source tables, run the following script in the SQL Server Management Studio. This should create a new address with a new city which does not yet exist in the DimGeography dimension. You could skip this step as, by default, the OLTP database has multiple address records that do not have correspondent rows in the target DWH dimension, but to make the test more transparent, it is recommended that you create your own new record in the source system:

```
-- Insert new records into source OLTP tables to test ETL
-- populating DimGeography dimension

USE [AdventureWorks_OLTP]
GO


-- Insert new address
INSERT INTO [Person].[Address]
   ([AddressLine1], [AddressLine2], [City],
    [StateProvinceID]
      , [PostalCode], [SpatialLocation], [rowguid],
       [ModifiedDate])
  VALUES
  ('10 Suvorova St.',NULL, 'Sevastopol', 182, '299011', NULL,
    NEWID(), GETDATE());


GO
```

Now, execute the job and query both dimension tables. There is one new row inserted in DimSalesTerritory with SalesTerritoryKey = 12 and multiple records were inserted into and updated in the DimGeography table.

Among the new records in DimGeography, you should be able to see the record for the new city of *Sevastopol* that we inserted manually with the help of the preceding script.

> If you run the job again without making changes to the source system's data, it should not create or update any records in the target dimension tables, as all changes have already been propagated from OLTP to DWH by the first job run. The main object in our ETL driving the changes tracking is the **Table_Comparison** transform.

Using a continuous workflow

In this recipe, we will take a close look at one of the workflow object features that controls how the workflow runs within a job.

How to do it...

1. Create a job with a single workflow inside named `WF_continuous`. Create a single global variable `$g_count` of the `integer` type at the job level context.

2. Open the workflow properties by right-clicking on the workflow object and selecting the **Properties...** option from the context menu and change the workflow execution type to **Continuous** on the **General** workflow properties tab:

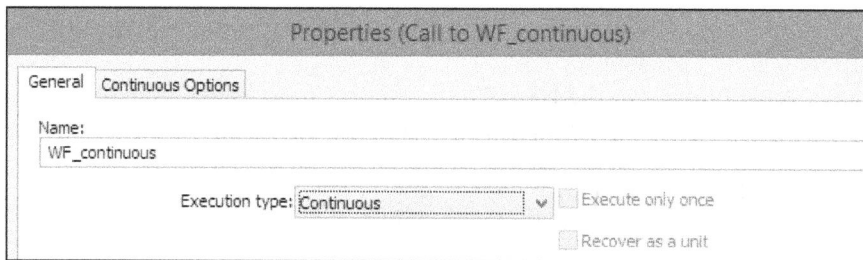

Properties (Call to WF_continuous)

General	Continuous Options

Name:
WF_continuous

Execution type: Continuous ☐ Execute only once
                              ☐ Recover as a unit

3. Exit the workflow properties by clicking on **OK**. See how the icon of the workflow object changes when its execution type is changed from **Regular** to **Continuous**:

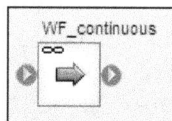

WF_continuous

4. Go to **Local Object Library | Custom Functions**.

5. Right-click on the **Custom Functions** list and select **New** from the context menu.

6. Name the custom function `fn_check_flag` and click on **Next** to open the custom function editor.

7. Create the following parameters and variables:

Variable/parameter	Description
$p_Directory	Input parameter of the varchar(255) type to store the directory path value
$p_File	Input parameter of the varchar(255) type to store the filename value
$l_exist	Local variable of the integer type to store the result of the file_exists() function

8. Add the following code to the custom function body:

```
$l_exist = file_exists($p_Directory||$p_File);

if ($l_exist = 1)
  begin
  print('Check: file exists');
  Return 0;
  end
else
  begin
  print('Check: file does not exist');
  Return 1;
  End
```

Your custom function should look like this:

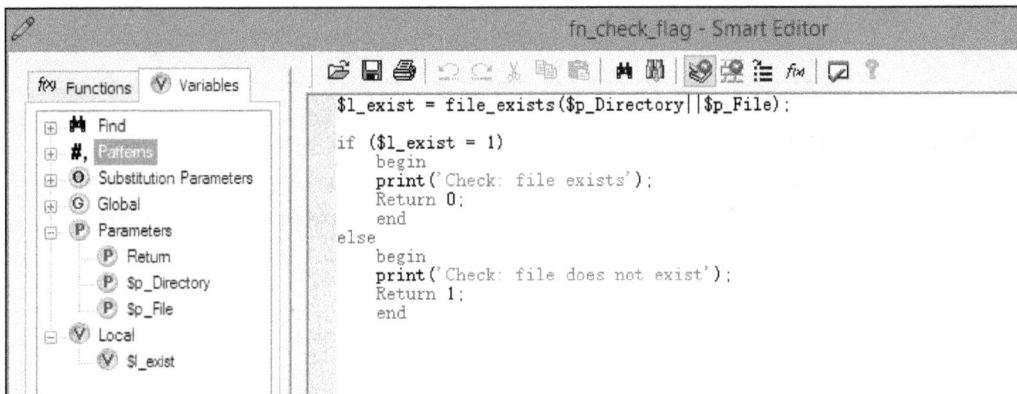

9. Open the workflow properties again to edit the continuous options using the **Continuous Options** tab.

10. On the **Continuous Options** tab, tick the checkbox when the result of the function is zero in the **Stop** section at the bottom and input the following line in the empty box: `fn_check_flag($1_Directory, $1_File)`.

11. Click on **OK** to exit the workflow properties and save the changes.

12. Open the workflow in the main workspace and create two local variables in the **Variables and Parameters** window: `$1_Directory` of the `varchar(255)` type and `$1_File` of the `varchar(255)` type.

13. Create a single script object within a workflow and add the following code in it:

```
$1_Directory = 'C:\\AW\\Files\\';
$1_File = 'flag.txt';

$g_count = $g_count + 1;

print('Execution #'||$g_count);
print('Starting   '||workflow_name()||' ...');
sleep(10000);
print('Finishing '||workflow_name()||' ...');
```

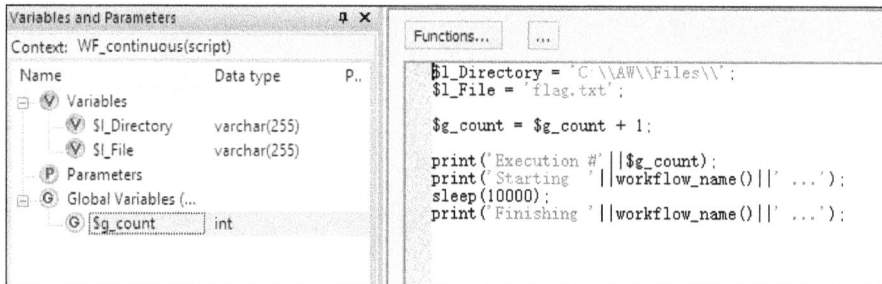

14. Save and validate the job to make sure that there are no errors.

15. Run the job and after few workflow execution cycles add the `flag.txt` file in the `C:\AW\Files\` directory to stop the continuous workflow execution sequence and the job itself.

How it works...

Continuous execution type allows you to run the workflow object an indefinite number of times in a loop. There are many restrictions of using the continuous workflow execution mode. Some of them are as follows:

- ▸ You cannot nest continuous workflow in another workflow object
- ▸ Some dataflow transforms are not available for use when placed under a continuous workflow hierarchy structure
- ▸ A continuous workflow object can be used only in the batch job

The main purpose of the continuous workflow is not to substitute the `while` loop as you might have thought at a first glance, but to save memory and processing resources for the tasks that have to be executed again and again, indefinitely in the non-stop mode or for a very long period of time. Data Services is saving resources by initializing and optimizing for execution all the underlying structures such as dataflows, datastores, and memory structures required for dataflow processing only once the continuous workflow object is executed for the first time.

The release resources section inside the **Continuous** option controls how often resources used by the underlying objects are released and reinitialized.

It is not possible to specify the exact number of cycles for the continuous workflow directly. The only option to add the stop logic is to write a custom function that is executed after every cycle, and if it returns zero, the value stops the continuous workflow execution sequence.

In the preceding recipe, we created a custom function that checks the presence of the file in the specified folder. If the file appears in there, it returns 0. The job will be running indefinitely until the file appears in the folder, or the job itself is killed manually, or the job server crashes.

To check the existence of the file, the `file_exists()` function is used. It returns 1 if the file exists and 0 if it does not. The function accepts a single parameter: a full filename that includes the path. As in our case, we are interested in stopping continuous workflow execution. When the function returns 0, we had to invert the returned value of the function and created a custom function for that.

We added the `sleep()` function to imitate the execution of the workflow so that it would be easy to place the file while the execution cycle is still running. The `Sleep()` function accepts integer parameters in milliseconds, so 10000 is equal to 10 seconds.

The global variable `$g_count` was added to control the number of cycles that were executed in the continuous workflow sequence.

Another interesting fact about how continuous workflow behaves is that it always executes another cycle after the stop function returns the zero value. Look at the following screenshot:

15056	14432	WORKFLOW	5/07/2015 12:17:16 p.m.	Work flow <WF_continuous> is started.
15056	14432	PRINTFN	5/07/2015 12:17:16 p.m.	Execution #1
15056	14432	PRINTFN	5/07/2015 12:17:16 p.m.	Starting WF_continuous ...
15056	14432	PRINTFN	5/07/2015 12:17:26 p.m.	Finishing WF_continuous ...
15056	14432	WORKFLOW	5/07/2015 12:17:26 p.m.	Work flow <WF_continuous> is completed successfully.
15056	14432	PRINTFN	5/07/2015 12:17:26 p.m.	Check: file does not exist
15056	14432	WORKFLOW	5/07/2015 12:17:26 p.m.	Work flow <WF_continuous> is started.
15056	14432	PRINTFN	5/07/2015 12:17:26 p.m.	Execution #2
15056	14432	PRINTFN	5/07/2015 12:17:26 p.m.	Starting WF_continuous ...
15056	14432	PRINTFN	5/07/2015 12:17:36 p.m.	Finishing WF_continuous ...
15056	14432	WORKFLOW	5/07/2015 12:17:36 p.m.	Work flow <WF_continuous> is completed successfully.
15056	14432	PRINTFN	5/07/2015 12:17:36 p.m.	Check: file does not exist
15056	14432	WORKFLOW	5/07/2015 12:17:36 p.m.	Work flow <WF_continuous> is started.
15056	14432	PRINTFN	5/07/2015 12:17:36 p.m.	Execution #3
15056	14432	PRINTFN	5/07/2015 12:17:36 p.m.	Starting WF_continuous ... ◀▬▬ Filed placed during 3rd run
15056	14432	PRINTFN	5/07/2015 12:17:46 p.m.	Finishing WF_continuous ...
15056	14432	WORKFLOW	5/07/2015 12:17:46 p.m.	Work flow <WF_continuous> is completed successfully.
15056	14432	PRINTFN	5/07/2015 12:17:46 p.m.	Check: file exists
15056	14432	WORKFLOW	5/07/2015 12:17:46 p.m.	Work flow <WF_continuous> is started.
15056	14432	PRINTFN	5/07/2015 12:17:46 p.m.	Execution #4
15056	14432	PRINTFN	5/07/2015 12:17:46 p.m.	Starting WF_continuous ...
15056	14432	PRINTFN	5/07/2015 12:17:56 p.m.	Finishing WF_continuous ...
15056	14432	WORKFLOW	5/07/2015 12:17:56 p.m.	Work flow <WF_continuous> is completed successfully.
15056	14432	WORKFLOW	5/07/2015 12:17:56 p.m.	Continuous execution type work flow <WF_continuous> is completed successfully.

See that in spite of the fact that we placed the `flag.txt` file during the third execution cycle and the stop function found it and returned a zero value (see the `Check: file exists` print message in the trace log), the fourth cycle still was executed.

Let's try another test to confirm this. Place the `flag.txt` file before the job is executed and then run it. This is what you see in the trace log file:

11992	13688	WORKFLOW	5/07/2015 12:15:11 p.m.	Continuous execution type work flow <WF_continuous> is started.
11992	13688	WORKFLOW	5/07/2015 12:15:11 p.m.	Work flow <WF_continuous> is started.
11992	13688	PRINTFN	5/07/2015 12:15:11 p.m.	Execution #1
11992	13688	PRINTFN	5/07/2015 12:15:11 p.m.	Starting WF_continuous ...
11992	13688	PRINTFN	5/07/2015 12:15:21 p.m.	Finishing WF_continuous ...
11992	13688	WORKFLOW	5/07/2015 12:15:21 p.m.	Work flow <WF_continuous> is completed successfully.
11992	13688	PRINTFN	5/07/2015 12:15:21 p.m.	Check: file exists
11992	13688	WORKFLOW	5/07/2015 12:15:21 p.m.	Work flow <WF_continuous> is started.
11992	13688	PRINTFN	5/07/2015 12:15:21 p.m.	Execution #2
11992	13688	PRINTFN	5/07/2015 12:15:21 p.m.	Starting WF_continuous ...
11992	13688	PRINTFN	5/07/2015 12:15:31 p.m.	Finishing WF_continuous ...
11992	13688	WORKFLOW	5/07/2015 12:15:31 p.m.	Work flow <WF_continuous> is completed successfully.
11992	13688	WORKFLOW	5/07/2015 12:15:31 p.m.	Continuous execution type work flow <WF_continuous> is completed successfully.

You can see that after the custom function returned 0 after the first cycle, the continuous workflow was executed the second time.

There is more...

You have to understand that continuous workflow usage is very limited in real life because of functional restrictions and also because of the nature of the loop in which the workflow is executed. In the majority of cases, the `while` loop object is a preferable option to run the workflow or underlying processing sequence of objects.

Peeking inside the repository – parent-child relationships between Data Services objects

With the introduction of workflow objects, which allow the nesting and grouping of objects, you can see that ETL code executed within the Data Services job is a hierarchical structure of objects that can be quite complex. Just imagine if real-life jobs have hundreds of workflows in their structure and twice as many dataflows.

In this recipe, we will look under the hood of Data Services to see how it stores the object information (our ETL code) in the local Data Services repository. Techniques learned in this recipe can help you browse the hierarchy of objects within your local repository with the help of the database SQL language toolset. This often proves to be a very convenient method to use.

Getting ready

You will not create any jobs or other objects in the Data Services Designer as we are just going to browse the ETL code and run a few queries in the SQL Server Management Studio.

How to do it...

Follow these simple steps to access the contents of the Data Services local repository in this recipe:

1. Start the SQL Server Management Studio and connect to the DS_LOCAL_REPO database created in *Chapter 2, Configuring the Data Services Environment*.

2. Query the dbo.AL_PARENT_CHILD table for references between Data Services objects and additional info.

3. Query the dbo.AL_LANGTEXT table for extra object properties and script object contents.

How it works...

Querying object-related information from the Data Services repository could be useful if you want to build the report on ETL metadata that does not exist out of the box in Data Services. It also could be useful when troubleshooting potential problems with your ETL code. We will take a look at the different scenarios and briefly explain each case.

Get a list of object types and their codes in the Data Services repository

Use the following query:

```
select
    descen_obj_type, descen_obj_r_type, count(*)
from
    dbo.al_parent_child
group by
    descen_obj_type, descen_obj_r_type;
```

The main table of the reference is the AL_PARENT_CHILD table. It contains the full hierarchy of the objects starting from the job object level and finishing with the table object level. The preceding query shows all the possible object types that Data Services registers in the repository.

Display information about the DF_Transform_DimGeography dataflow

Use the query to get this information:

```
select *
from
    dbo.al_parent_child
where
    descen_obj = 'DF_Transform_DimGeography';
```

All columns and their values are explained in this table:

Column name	Value	Description
PARENT_OBJ	WF_Transform_DimGeography	This is the name of the parent object DF_Transform_DimGeography belongs to. See the following figure.
PARENT_OBJ_TYPE	WorkFlow	This is the type of the parent object.
PARENT_OBJ_R_TYPE	0	This is the type code of the parent object.

Column name	Value	Description
PARENT_OBJ_DESC	No description available	This is the description of the parent object. This is what you input in the Description field inside the workflow properties window in the Designer. If empty, Data Services uses "No description available" in the repo table.
PARENT_OBJ_KEY	175	This is the internal parent object key (ID).
DESCEN_OBJ	DF_Transform_DimGeography	This is the object name we are looking up information for.
DESCEN_OBJ_TYPE	DataFlow	This is the type of the object.
DESCEN_OBJ_R_TYPE	1	This is the type code of the object.
DESCEN_OBJ_DESC	No description available	This is the contents of the **Description** field of dataflow properties in the Designer. It is empty for this specific dataflow.
DESCEN_OBJ_USAGE	NULL	This indicates whether the object is a source or a target within a dataflow. As the object itself is a dataflow, this field is not populated.
DESCEN_OBJ_KEY	174	This is the internal object key (ID).
DESCEN_OBJ_DS	NULL	This indicates what the datastore object belongs to. As the object we are looking up is a dataflow. this field is not populated.
DESCEN_OBJ_OWNER	NULL	This is the database owner of the object. It is not applicable to dataflow objects either.

Display information about the SalesTerritory table object

Use the following query:

```
select
  parent_obj, descen_obj_desc, descen_obj_usage, descen_obj_key,
descen_obj_ds, descen_obj_owner
from
  dbo.al_parent_child
where descen_obj = 'SALESTERRITORY';
```

The result is in the following screenshot:

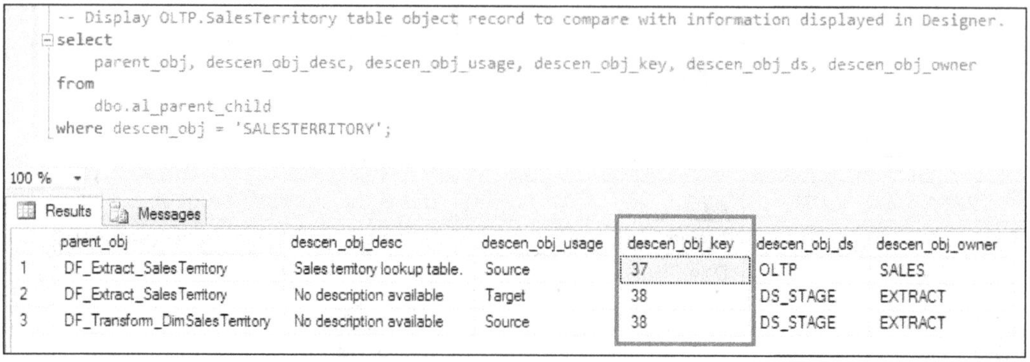

```
    -- Display OLTP.SalesTerritory table object record to compare with information displayed in Designer.
⊟ select
      parent_obj, descen_obj_desc, descen_obj_usage, descen_obj_key, descen_obj_ds, descen_obj_owner
  from
      dbo.al_parent_child
  where descen_obj = 'SALESTERRITORY';
```

100 % ▼

▦ Results | 🛢 Messages

	parent_obj	descen_obj_desc	descen_obj_usage	descen_obj_key	descen_obj_ds	descen_obj_owner
1	DF_Extract_SalesTerritory	Sales territory lookup table.	Source	37	OLTP	SALES
2	DF_Extract_SalesTerritory	No description available	Target	38	DS_STAGE	EXTRACT
3	DF_Transform_DimSalesTerritory	No description available	Source	38	DS_STAGE	EXTRACT

From the preceding screenshot, you can see that two different objects with the same name SALESTERRITORY exist in the Data Services repository with unique keys 37 and 38.

The one with OBJ_KEY as 37 is imported in the OLTP datastore and belongs to the Sales schema. It is used only DF_Extract_SalesTerritory as it has only one record with the parent object of that name.

The SALESTERRITORY object with OBJ_KEY as 38 is a stage area table and is imported into the DS_STAGE datastore and belongs to the Extract database schema. It has two different parent objects, as in Designer, it was placed into two different dataflows: as a target table object in DF_Extract_SalesTerritory (you can see it from the DESCEN_OBJ_USAGE column) and as a source table object in DF_Transform_DimSalesTerritory.

See the contents of the script object

The one thing you have probably noticed already from the result of the very first query in this recipe is that Data Services does not have a script object type.

As you probably remember, script objects do not have their own context in Data Services and operate in the context of the workflow object they belong to. That is why, you have to query the information about workflow properties using another table AL_LANGTEXT to find the information about script contents in the Data Services repository.

Use the following query:

```
select *
from dbo.al_langtext txt
  JOIN dbo.al_parent_child pc
  on txt.parent_objid = pc.descen_obj_key
where
  pc.descen_obj = 'WF_continuous';
```

We are extracting information about the script object created in the `WF_continuous` workflow.

All workflow properties with the contents of all scripts that belong to it are stored in a plain text format.

In this table, we are only interested in two columns `SEQNUM`, which represents the number of properties text row, and `TEXTVALUE`, which stores the properties text row itself.

See the concatenated version of information stored in the `TEXTVALUE` column of the `AL_LANGTEXT` repository table here:

```
AlGUIComment ("ActaName_1" = 'RSavedAfterCheckOut', "ActaName_2" =
    'RDate_created', "ActaName_3" = 'RDate_modified', "ActaValue_1"
    = 'YES', "ActaValue_2" = 'Sat Jul 04 16:52:33 2015',
    "ActaValue_3" = 'Sun Jul 05 11:18:02 2015', "x" = '-1', "y" = '-
    1')
CREATE PLAN WF_continuous::'7bb26cd4-3e0c-412a-81f3-b5fdd687f507'(
    )
DECLARE
    $l_Directory VARCHAR(255) ;
    $l_File VARCHAR(255) ;
BEGIN
 AlGUIComment ("UI_DATA_XML" = '<UIDATA><MAINICON><LOCATION><X>
    0</X><Y>0</Y></LOCATION><SIZE><CX>216</CX><CY>-
    179</CY></SIZE></MAINICON><DESCRIPTION><LOCATION><X>0</X><Y>-
    190</Y></LOCATION><SIZE><CX>200</CX><CY>200
    </CY></SIZE><VISIBLE>0</VISIBLE></DESCRIPTION></U
IDATA>', "ui_display_name" = 'script', "ui_script_text" =
    '$l_Directory = \'C:\\\\AW\\\\Files\\\\\';
$l_File = \'flag.txt\';

$g_count = $g_count + 1;

print(\'Execution #\'||$g_count);
print(\'Starting \'||workflow_name()||\' ...\');
sleep(10000);
print(\'Finishing \'||workflow_name()||\' ...\');', "x" = '116',
    "y" = '-175')
BEGIN_SCRIPT
$l_Directory = 'C:\\AW\\Files\\';$l_File = 'flag.txt';$g_count =
    ($g_count + 1);print(('Execution #' ||
    $g_count));print((('Starting ' || workflow_name()) || '
    ...'));sleep(10000);print((('Finishing ' || workflow_name()) ||
    ' ...'));END
END
```

```
SET ("loop_exit" = 'fn_check_flag($1_Directory, $1_File)',
  "loop_exit
_option" = 'yes', "restart_condition" = 'no', "restart_count" =
  '10', "restart_count_option" = 'yes', "workflow_type" =
  'Continuous')
```

The first highlighted section of the preceding code is the declaration section of local workflow variables created for `WF_continuous`. The second highlighted section is marking the text that belongs to the underlying script object. You can see that the script object is not considered by Data Services as a separate object entity and is just a property of the parent workflow object. To compare, take a look at how the script contents look like in Designer:

```
$1_Directory = 'C:\\AW\\Files\\';
$1_File = 'flag.txt';

$g_count = $g_count + 1;

print('Execution #'||$g_count);
print('Starting  '||workflow_name()||' ...');
sleep(10000);
print('Finishing '||workflow_name()||' ...');
```

You can see that formatting of the same information stored in the TEXTVALUE field is a bit different. So, be careful when extracting and parsing this data from the local repository.

Finally, the third highlighted section marks the workflow properties configured with the **Properties...** context menu option in Designer.

> There is another version of the AL_LANGTEXT table that contains the same properties information but in the XML format. It is the AL_LANGXMLTEXT table.

6
Job – Building the ETL Architecture

In this chapter, we will cover the following topics:

- Projects and jobs – organizing ETL
- Using object replication
- Migrating ETL code through the central repository
- Migrating ETL code with export/import
- Debugging job execution
- Monitoring job execution
- Building an external ETL audit and audit reporting
- Using built-in Data Services ETL audit and reporting functionality
- Auto Documentation in Data Services

Introduction

In this chapter, we will go up to the job level and review the steps in the development process that make a successful and robust ETL solution. All recipes presented in this chapter can fall into one of the three categories: ETL development, ETL troubleshooting, and ETL reporting. These categories include design techniques and processes usually implemented and executed sequentially in order within the ETL life cycle.

Here, you can see which topics fall under which category.

- **Developing ETL**:
  - ❑ Projects and jobs – organizing ETL
  - ❑ Using object replication
  - ❑ Migrating ETL code through the central repository
  - ❑ Migrating ETL code with export/import

  The **developing** category discusses issues faced by ETL developers on a daily basis when they work on designing and implementing an ETL solution in Data Services.

- **Troubleshooting ETL**:
  - ❑ Debugging job execution
  - ❑ Monitoring job execution

  The **troubleshooting** category explains in detail the troubleshooting techniques that can be used in Data Services Designer to troubleshoot the ETL code.

- **Reporting on ETL**:
  - ❑ Building external ETL audit and audit reporting
  - ❑ Using built-in Data Services ETL audit and reporting functionality
  - ❑ Auto Documentation in Data Services

  The **reporting** category reviews the methods used to report on ETL metadata and also explains the Auto Documentation feature available in Data Services to quickly generate and export documentation for the developed ETL code.

Projects and jobs – organizing ETL

Projects are a simple and great mechanism to group your ETL jobs together. They are also mandatory components of ETL code organization for various Data Services features, such as Auto Documentation and batch job configuration available in the Data Services Management Console.

Getting ready

There are no preparation steps. You have everything you need in your local repository that has already been created. In this recipe, we will use `Job_DWH_DimGeography` developed in *Chapter 5, Workflow – Controlling Execution Order*, to populate the DWH dimension tables `DimSalesTerritory` and `DimGeography`.

How to do it...

To create a project object in Data Services, follow these steps:

1. Open the **Local Object Library** window and choose the **Projects** tab.

2. Right-click in the empty space of the **Projects** tab and select **New** from the context menu. The **Project – New** window appears on the screen.

3. Input the project name as DWH_Dimensions in the **Project Name** field.

4. Open the **Project Area** window using the **Project Area** button on the tool bar at the top:

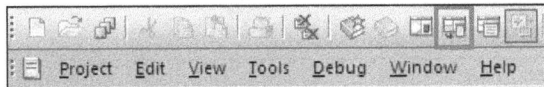

5. Go to **Project Area | Designer**. You will only see the contents of one selected project. To select the project or make it visible in the **Project Area | Designer** window, go to **Local Object Library | Projects** and either double-click on the project you are interested in (in our case, it has only one project created) or choose **Open** from the context menu of the selected project.

6. To add the job in the project, drag and drop the selected job from **Local Object Library | Jobs** into **the Project Area | Designer** tab window or right-click on the job object in **Local Object Library** and choose the **Add To Project** option from the context menu. Add Job_DWH_DimGeography created in the previous recipe to the DWH_Dimensions project:

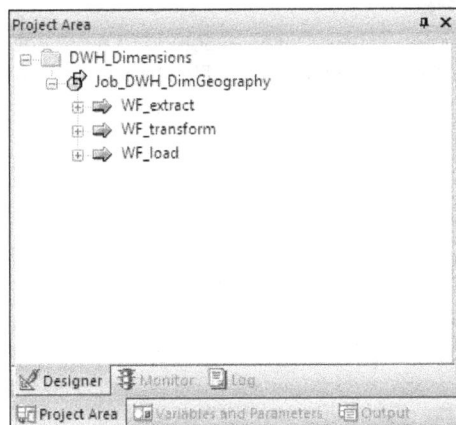

How it works...

This is all you need to do to create a project and place jobs in it. It is a very simple process that, in fact, brings you a few extra advantages that you can use in ETL development. The process also reveals new functionality not accessible otherwise in Data Services. Let's take a look at some of them.

Hierarchical object view

Available in the **Project Area | Designer**, this view allows you to quickly access any child object within a job. In the following screenshot, the expanding tree shows workflow, dataflow, and transformation objects; by clicking on any of them, you open them in the main workspace window:

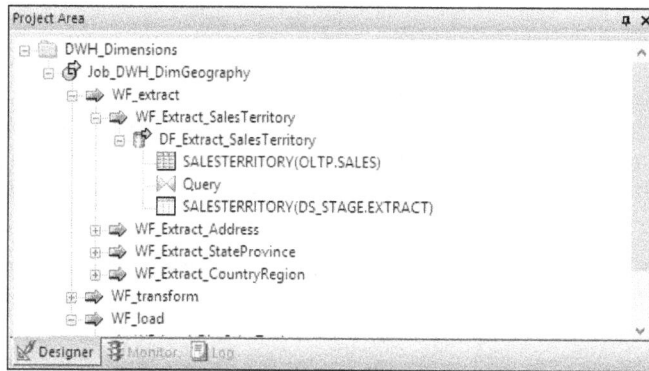

History execution log files

These log files are available only if the job was assigned to a project. The **Project Area | Log** tab allows you to see and access all available log files (trace, performance, and error logs) kept by Data Services for specific jobs:

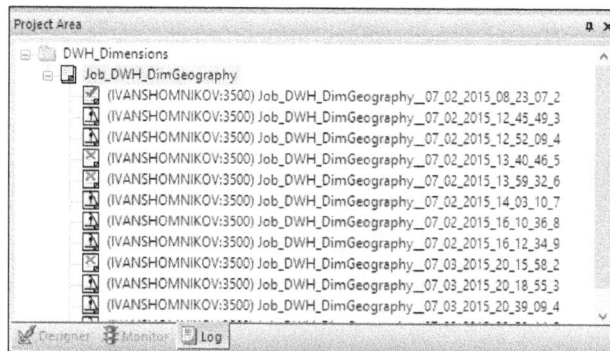

Executing/scheduling jobs from the Management Console

Yes, this option is available only for jobs that belong to a project.

Use `http://localhost:8080/DataServices` to start your Data Services Management Console.

Log in to the Management Console using the `etl` user account created in the *Configuring user access* recipe of *Chapter 2, Configuring the Data Services Environment*. It is the same user you use to connect to Data Services Designer.

Go to **Administrator | Batch | DS4_REPO**.

If you open the **Batch Job Configuration** tab, you will see that only `Job_DWH_DimGeography` is available for being executed/scheduled/exported for execution, as it was the only job in our local repository that we added to a created project:

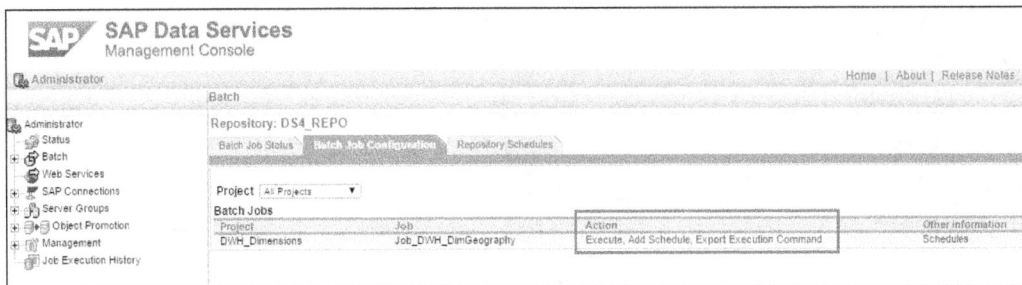

As you can see, projects are the containers for your jobs, allowing you to organize and display your ETL code and perform additional tasks from the Management Console application. Keep in mind that you cannot add anything else except the job object directly into the project level.

Using object replication

Data Services allows you to instantly create an exact replica of almost any object type you are using in ETL development. This feature is useful to create new versions of an existing workflow or dataflow to test or just to create backups at the object level.

How to do it...

We will replicate a job object using these steps:

1. Go to **Local Object Library | Jobs**.

2. Right-click on the `Job_DWH_DimGeography` job and select **Replicate** from the context menu:

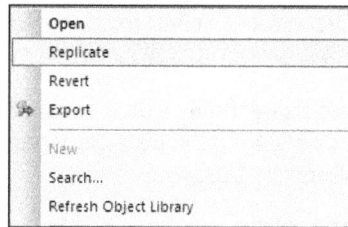

	Open
	Replicate
	Revert
✈	Export
	New
	Search...
	Refresh Object Library

3. Copy of the job with the new name is created in the **Local Object Library**:

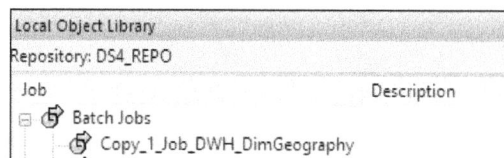

Local Object Library	
Repository: DS4_REPO	
Job	Description
⊟ ⑤ Batch Jobs	
⑤ Copy_1_Job_DWH_DimGeography	

How it works...

All objects in Data Services can be identified as either reusable or not reusable.

A reusable object can be used in multiple locations, that is, a table object imported in a datastore can be used as a source or target object in different dataflows. Nevertheless, all these dataflows will reference the same object, and if changed in one place, it would change everywhere it is used.

Not reusable objects represent the instances of a specific object type. For example, if you copy and paste the script object from one workflow to another, these two copies will be two different objects, and by changing one of them, you are not making changes to another.

Let's take another example of a dataflow object. Dataflows are reusable objects. If you copy and paste the selected dataflow object into another workflow, you would create a reference to the same dataflow object.

To be able to make a copy of a reusable object so that the copy does not reference the original object, it has been copied from the **replication** feature used in Data Services. Note that the replicated object cannot have the same name as the original object it has been replicated from. That is because for reusable objects such as workflows and dataflows, their names uniquely identify the object.

> The rule of thumb for checking whether an object type is reusable or not, is to check if it exists in the **Local Object Library** panel. All objects that can be found on **Local Object Library** panel tabs are reusable objects, except **Projects**, as it is not part of executable ETL code. Instead, it is a location folder that is used to organize job objects. Nevertheless, you cannot create two projects with the same tool like you can with the script objects.

The following table shows which object type can be replicated in Data Services and how the replication process behaves for each one of them. All these are reusable object types.

Job	New object automatically created in **Local Object Library** named as `Copy_<ID>_<original job name>`
Workflow	New object automatically created in **Local Object Library** named as `Copy_<ID>_<original workflow name>`
Dataflow	New object automatically created in **Local Object Library** named as `Copy_<ID>_<original dataflow name>`
File format	New **File Format Editor** window is opened. The new name is already defined as `Copy_<ID>_<Original File Format name>`, but you can change it by adding a new value into the name field
Custom functions	New **Customer Function** window is opened. You have to select a new name for the replicated function

The replication process is a convenient and easy way to perform object-level backups. All you have to do to create a copy of the object before editing it is to click on the **Replicate** option from the context menu of the object you are replicating.

It is also an easy way to test the code changes before you decide to update the production version of the ETL.

For example, if you want to see how your dataflow object behaves after you change the properties of the **Table_Comparison** transform inside it, you can perform the following sequence of steps:

1. Replicate the dataflow and set it up to run separately within a test job.
2. Run the test job and test the output dataset to make sure that it generates the expected result.
3. Rename the original dataflow by adding the `_archive` or `_old` prefix to it.
4. Rename the new replicated version to the original dataflow name.
5. Replace the archive dataflow object everywhere it is used with a new version.

To see all parent objects the specific object belongs to you. In other words, to see all the locations where the specific object was placed, you can use one of the following steps:

1. Choose the DIMGEOGRAPHY object from the DWH datastore in **Local Object Library**. Right-click on it and choose the **View Where Used** option from the context menu.

   The parent objects that the table object belongs to are displayed in the **Information** tab of the **Output** window:

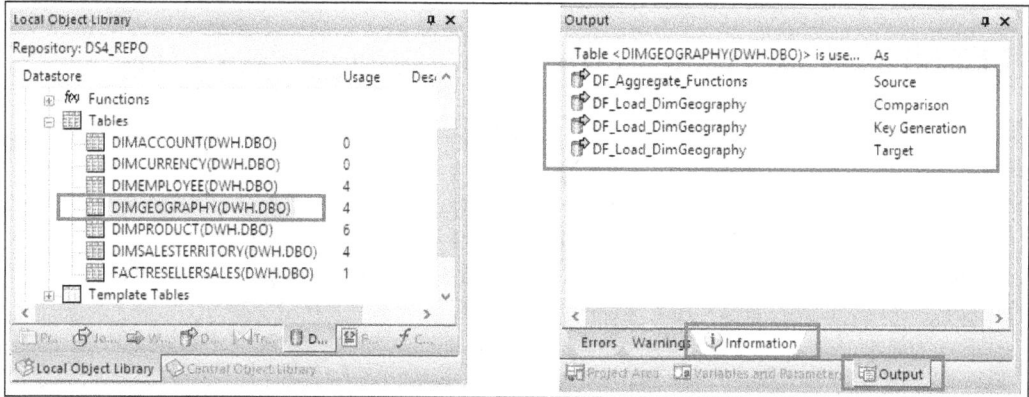

You can also see the number of parent objects (locations) for the object right away in **Local Object Library** in the **Usage** column available next to the object name. This is useful information that can help you identify unused or "orphaned" objects.

2. Pick the object of interest in the workspace area (for example, a dataflow placed within a workflow workspace or table object placed in the dataflow), right-click on it, and choose **View Where Used** from the context menu. The list of parent objects will appear in the **Output | Information** window:

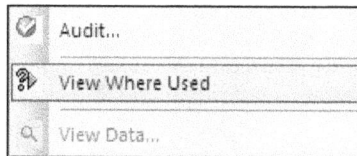

3. Finally, it is possible to check where the currently opened object is used. When you have the object opened in the workspace area and do not have the ability to right-click on it, instead of going to the **Local Object Library** lists in order to find the object, try to just click on the **View Where Used** button from the top tool menu panel:

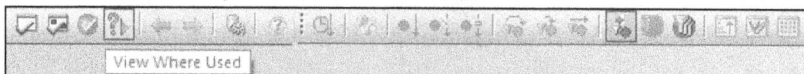

> Remember that it displays the used locations list for the object currently displayed on the active tab of the main workspace area.

Migrating ETL code through the central repository

In this recipe, we will take a brief look at the aspects of working in the multiple-user development environment and how Data Services accommodates the need to migrate the ETL code between local repositories belonging to different ETL developers.

Getting ready

To use all functionality available in Data Services to work in a multiuser development environment, we miss a very important component: the configured central repository. So, to get ready, and before we explore this functionality, we have to create and deploy the central repository into our Data Services environment.

Perform all the following steps to create, configure, and deploy the central repository:

1. Open the SQL Server Management Studio and connect to the SQLEXPRESS server engine.

2. Right-click on **Databases** and choose the **New Database...** option from the context menu.

3. Name the new database as DS_CENTRAL_REPO and keep all its parameters with default values.

4. Start the SAP Data Services Repository Manager application.

5. Choose **Repository type** as **Central** and specify connectivity settings to the new database DS_CENTRAL_REPO. When you finish, click on the **Create** button to create central Data Services repository objects in the selected database:

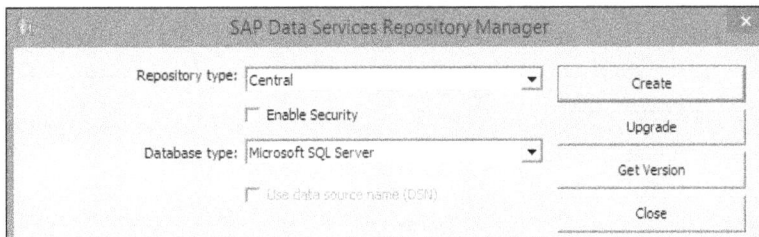

6. The process of creating a repository can take a few minutes. If it is successful, you should see the following output on the screen:

```
BODI-300130: Adding Associate transform...
BODI-300131: Adding USA Regulatory Address Cleanse transform...
BODI-300132: Adding User Defined transform...
BODI-300189: Adding Global Geocoder transform...
BODI-300212: Adding Extraction transform...
BODI-300226: Adding DSF2WS transform...
BODI-300230: Installing the JIT viewdata job...
BODI-300246: Adding CTID transform...
BODI-300257: Adding DataMask transform...
The central repository was successfully created. (BODI-300021)
```

7. Now, we need to register our newly created central repository within Data Services and the **Information Platform Services** (**IPS**) configuration. Start the Central Management Console web application by going to `http://localhost:8080/BOE/CMC` and log in to the **administrator** account. It is the same account that was created during the installation of Data Services (see *Chapter 2, Configuring the Data Services Environment*, for details).

8. Choose the **Data Services** link on the home screen to open the Data Services repository configuration area.

9. Right-click on the **Repositories** folder or in the empty area of the main window and choose the **Configure repository** option from the context menu:

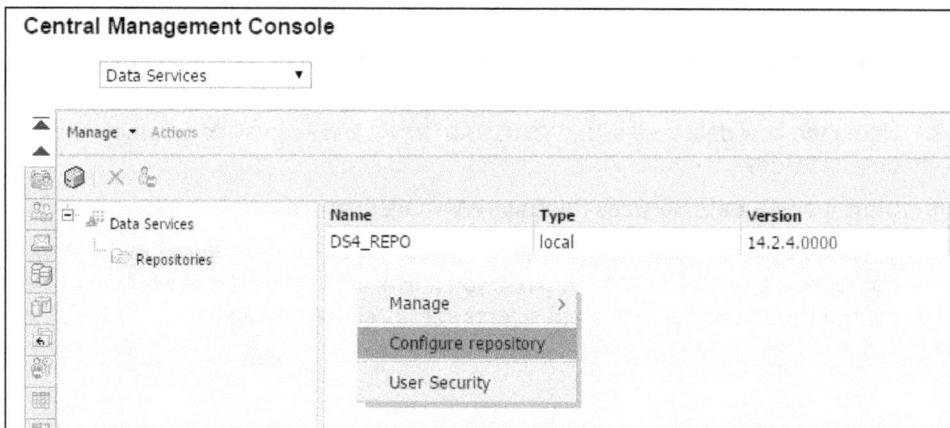

10. Name the newly configured repository as DS4_CENTRAL and input connectivity settings. After that, click on **Test Connection** to see the successful connection message:

11. Close the repository properties window. You should see the new non-secured central repository, DS4_CENTRAL, displayed on the screen along with local repository DS4_REPO:

12. Right-click on DS4_CENTRAL and choose the **User Security** option from the context menu.

13. Choose **Data Services Administrator Users** and click on the **Assign Security** button.

14. On the **Assign Security** window, go to the **Advanced** tab and click on the **Add/Remove Rights** link.

15. On the **Add/Remove Rights** window, choose **Application | Data Services Repository** and select/grant the following options in the right-hand side under the **Specific Rights for Data Services Repository** section:

16. Click on **OK** to save the changes and close the **User Security** window.

17. The final step of configuration is to specify the central repository in your **Designer** configuration settings. This can be configured on the **Designer Option** window, or you can open the **Central Repository Connections** section by going to **Tools | Central Repositories...** from the top menu.

18. In the **Central Repository Connections** section, click on the **Add** button to open the list of repositories available and select **DS4_CENTRAL**.

19. The **Activate** button activates the central repository from the list (if you add multiple ones, only one of them can be active at a time). You can also specify the **Reactivate automatically** flag for the central repository to reactivate automatically when the Designer application restarts:

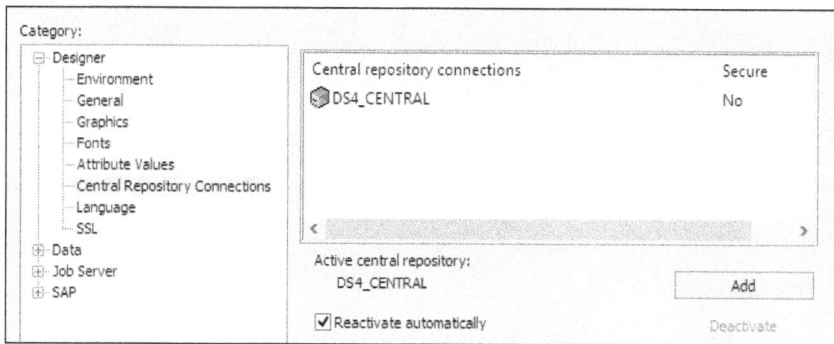

20. After performing all these steps, you should be able to activate the **Central Object Library** window (see the top tool panel), which looks almost exactly like **Local Object Library**:

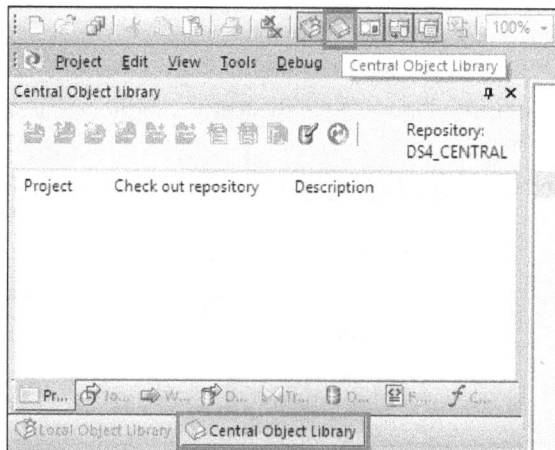

The preceding steps showed you how to create, configure, and deploy the central repository in Data Services. Next, we will see how you can actually use the central repository to migrate the ETL between different local repositories.

How to do it...

The central repository or **Central Object Library** is a location shared by different ETL developers to exchange and synchronize the ETL code. In this recipe, we will copy the existing job into **Central Object Library** and see which operations are available in Data Services on the objects stored there. Follow these steps:

1. Go to **Local Object Library | Jobs**.

2. Right-click on the `Job_DWH_DimGeography` job object and go to **Add to Central Repository | Object and Dependents** from the context menu.

3. Open **Central Object Library** and see that the job object and all dependent objects, workflows, and dataflows appeared on the **Central Object Library** tab sections. The ETL code for `Job_DWH_DimGeography` has been successfully migrated to the central repository.

4. Now, go to the **Local Object Library | Dataflows**, find the `DF_Load_DimGeography` dataflow object, and double-click on it to open it in the workspace area for editing.

5. Rename the first **Query** transform from **Query** to **Join** and save the dataflow.

6. Now that you have changed the ETL code migrated from local to central repository, you can compare the two versions of your job and see the differences displayed in **Differences Viewer**. Right-click on the job in **Local Object Library** and go to **Compare | Object and dependents to Central** from the context menu:

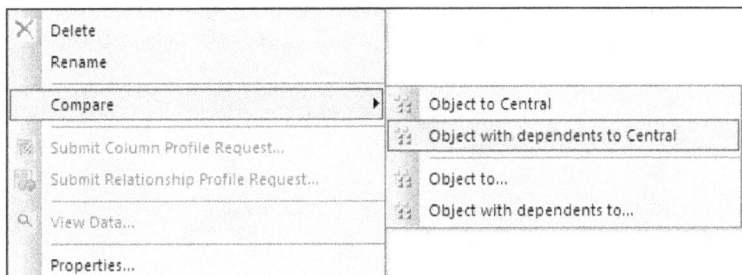

7. When in **Central Object Library**, you can do the same thing by clicking on a specific object and choosing the preferable option from the **Compare** context menu.

8. To get the version of the object from the central repository to a local one, select the `DF_Load_DimGeography` dataflow object in the **Central Object Library**, right-click on it, and go to **Get Latest Version | Object** from the context menu.

9. If you compare the local object version to the one stored in the central repository now, you will see that there is no difference, as the central object version has overwritten the local object version.

How it works...

The purpose of the central repository is to provide a centralized location to store ETL code.

The **Central Object Library** represents the contents of the central repository in the same way that the **Local Object Library** represents the contents of the local repository.

The ETL code stored in the central repository cannot be changed directly as in the local repository. So, it provides a level of security to make sure that the central repository changes can be tracked, and the history of all operations performed on its objects can be displayed.

Adding objects to and from the Central Object Library

If the object does not exist in the central repository, you can add it using the **Add to Central Repository** option from the objects context menu.

If the object already exists in the central repository, there are a few extra steps required to update it with a newer version from the local one. We will take a close look at this functionality in the upcoming chapters.

Getting the object from the central to the local repository is much more simple. All you need to do is use the **Get Latest Version** option from the objects context menu in **Central Object Library**. It does not matter if the object exists or not in the local repository—it will be created or overwritten. This means that it will be deleted and copied from the central repository.

Another important aspect of copying an object into, and from, the central repository is the availability of three modes: **Object**, **Object and dependents**, and **With filtering**:

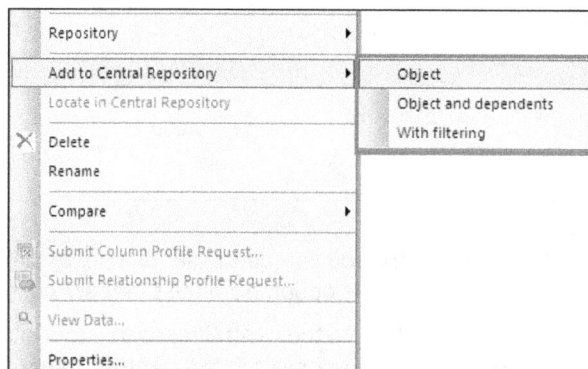

Repository	▶	
Add to Central Repository	▶	Object
Locate in Central Repository		Object and dependents
✕ Delete		With filtering
Rename		
Compare	▶	
Submit Column Profile Request...		
Submit Relationship Profile Request...		
🔍 View Data...		
Properties...		

▶ **Object**: In this mode, it does not matter which operation you perform, whether it is getting the latest object version from central to local, comparing object versions between central and local, or just placing objects from local to central. The operation is performed on this object only.

▶ **Object and dependents**: This operation affects all the child objects belonging to the selected object, their child objects, their child objects, and so on until the lowest level down the hierarchy (which is usually a table/file format level).

▶ **With filtering**: This mode is basically the same as **Object and dependents**, but with the ability to exclude the specific object from the affected objects. When chosen, the new window opens, allowing you to exclude specific objects from the hierarchy tree. Here is the result of choosing **Add to Central Repository | With filtering** for the Job_ DWH_DimGeography object:

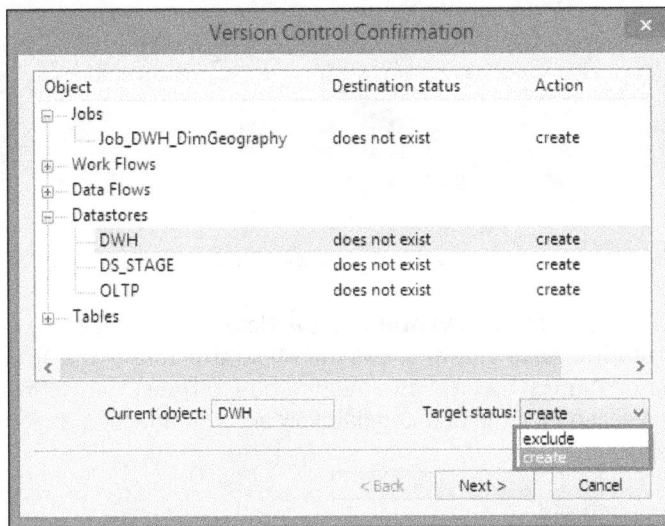

Comparing objects between the Local and Central repositories

Designer has a very useful Compare function available for all objects stored in the local or central repositories. When selected from the context menu of the object stored in a central repository location, there are two Compare methods available: **Object to Local** and **Object with dependents to Local**.

When selected from the context menu of the object stored in a local repository location, there are two Compare methods available: **Object to Central** and **Object with dependents to Central**.

The result is presented in the **Difference Viewer** window, which opens in the main workspace area in a separate tab and looks similar to the following screenshot:

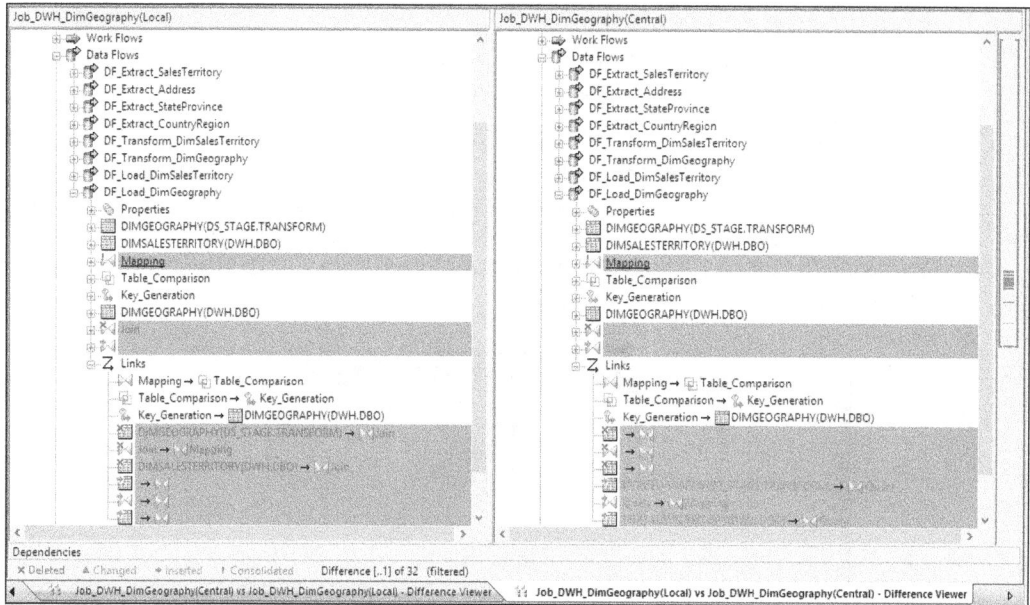

This is an example of the **Difference Viewer** window. Note how we have only renamed the **Query** transform, yet **Difference Viewer** shows the whole structure of the Join **Query** object as deleted, and on the **Central** tab, it shows the new Query **Query** transform structure. The **Mapping** and **Links** sections of the updated dataflow are also affected, as you can see in the preceding screenshot.

There is more...

I have not described one of the most important concepts of the central repository: the ability to check out and check in objects and view the history of changes in the multiuser development environment. I have left it for more advanced chapters, and it will be explained further in the book.

Migrating ETL code with export/import

Data Services Designer has various options to import/export ETL code.

In this recipe, we will review all possible import/export scenarios and take a closer look at the file formats used for import/export in Data Services: ATL files (the main export file format for the Data Services code) and XML structures.

Getting ready

To complete this recipe, you will need another local repository created in your environment. Refer to the first two chapters of the book to create another repository named DS4_LOCAL_EXT in the new database, DS_LOCAL_REPO. Do not forget to assign the proper security settings for Data Services Administrator users in CMC after registering the new repository.

How to do it...

Data Services has two main import/export options:

- ▸ Using ATL/XML external files
- ▸ Direct import into another local repository

Import/Export using ATL files

In the following steps, I will show you an example of how to export ETL code from the Data Services Designer into an ATL file.

1. Export Job_DWH_DimGeography into an ATL file. Right-click on the job object in **Local Object Library | Jobs** and select **Export** from the context menu. The **Export** window opens in the main workspace area. Look at the following screenshot:

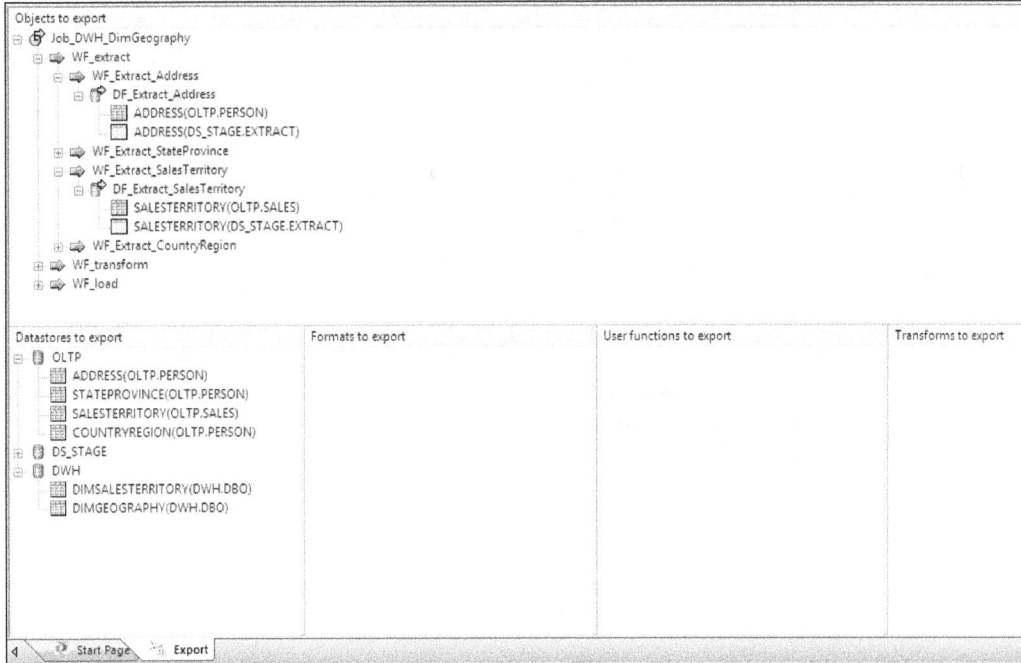

2. Using the context menu by right-clicking on the specific object or objects in the **Export** window, you can exclude selected objects with the **Exclude** option or selected objects with all their dependencies using the **Exclude Tree** option. Exclude the DF_ Extract_SalesTerritory dataflow and all its dependencies from the export, as shown in the following screenshot using the **Exclude Tree** option:

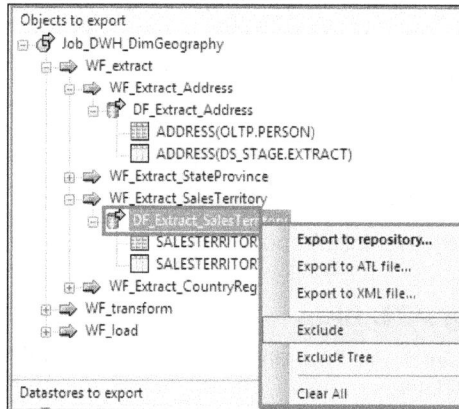

3. Objects excluded from the export are marked with red crosses. See both the **Objects to export** and **Datastores to export** areas on the **Export** tab for the objects excluded by the **Exclude Tree** command executed in the previous step:

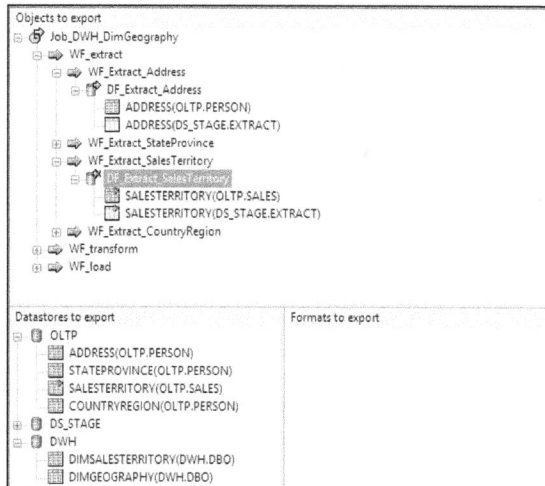

4. To execute the export operation, right-click in any area of the **Export** workspace tab and choose the **Export to ATL file...** option from the context menu. On the opened **Save As** screen, choose the name of the ATL file, export.atl, and its location. Then, click on **OK** and specify the security passphrase for the ATL file.

5. Export could take anything from a few seconds up to a few minutes, depending on the number of objects you are exporting. When it is finished, you will see the following output in the **Output | Information** window. If you check the chosen location, you should see that the export.atl file was created:

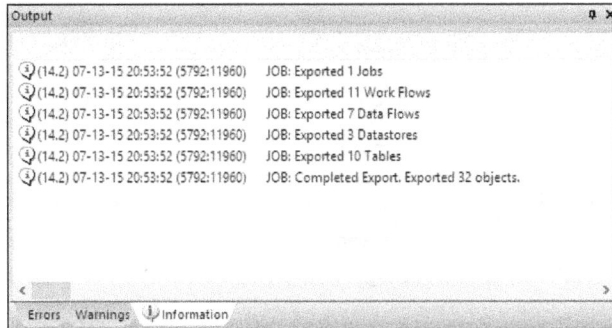

6. Now, log in to the second local repository with Designer. For this, exit the Designer to restart the application. On the logon screen, choose to connect to another local repository:

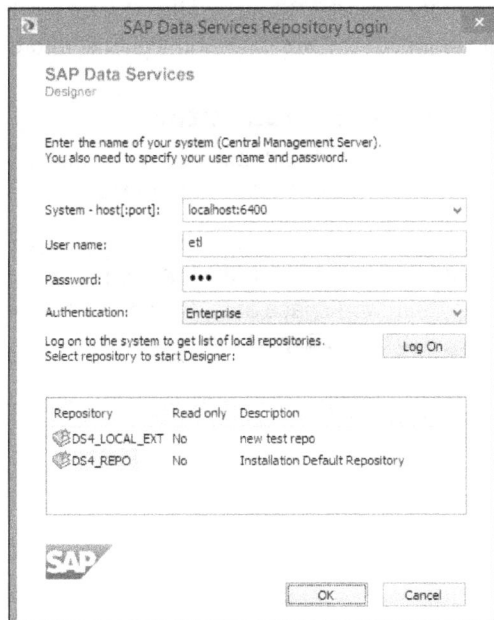

7. The new local repository is completely empty. We will use the `export.atl` file created in the previous step to import the job and its dependent objects into this new repository. Select the **Import From File...** option from the top **Tools** menu list. Then, select the `export.atl` file and click on OK, thus agreeing to import all objects from the file into the currently open local repository.

8. As we exported the job object and its dependents, it does not belong to any project in a new repository. Create a new project called `TEST` and place the job in it to expand its structure:

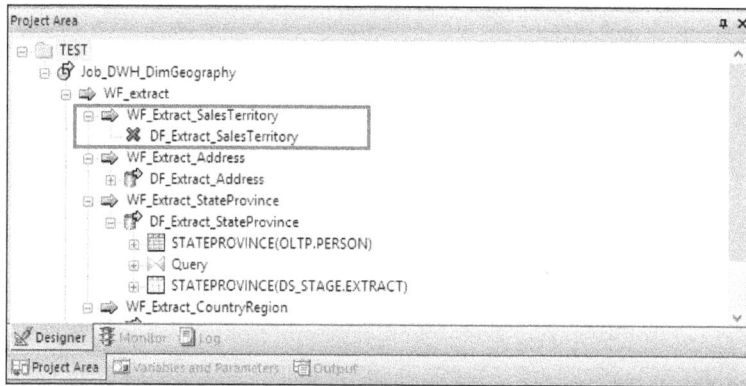

```
Project Area                                                            ↕ ✕
⊟ 📁 TEST                                                                 ∧
   ⊟ 🔗 Job_DWH_DimGeography
      ⊟ ➡ WF_extract
         ⊟ ➡ WF_Extract_SalesTerritory
              ✘ DF_Extract_SalesTerritory
         ⊟ ➡ WF_Extract_Address
            ⊞ 🗗 DF_Extract_Address
         ⊟ ➡ WF_Extract_StateProvince
            ⊟ 🗗 DF_Extract_StateProvince
               ⊞ 🗐 STATEPROVINCE(OLTP.PERSON)
               ⊞ 🔀 Query
               ⊞ 🗐 STATEPROVINCE(DS_STAGE.EXTRACT)
         ⊟ ➡ WF_Extract_CountryRegion                                    ∨
📝 Designer  🛠 Monitor  📄 Log
🗂 Project Area  📇 Variables and Parameters  🗒 Output
```

See that `DF_Extract_SalesTerritory` and the tables belonging to it are missing from the job structure, although Data Services keeps reference for `WF_Extract_SalesTerritory`. If the dataflow is imported in the future, it would automatically be assigned as a child object to the workflow and would fit into the job structure.

Direct export to another local repository

Let's perform a direct export of the missing `DF_Extract_SalesTerritory` object and its dependents from the `DS4_REPO to DS4_LOCAL_EXT` repository:

1. Log in to `DS4_REPO`, right-click on the `DF_Extract_SalesTerritory` dataflow object in the **Local Object Library**, and select **Export** from the context menu to open the **Export** tab in the main workspace area. By default, the selected objects and all its dependents are added to the **Export** tab.

2. Right-click on the **Export** tab and choose the **Export to repository...** menu item displayed with bold text. Select DS4_LOCAL_EXT as the target repository:

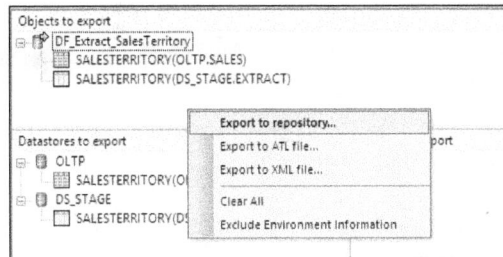

3. On the **Export Confirmation** window, which opens next, exclude all objects that already exist in the target repository. These are the datastore objects OLTP and DS_STAGE:

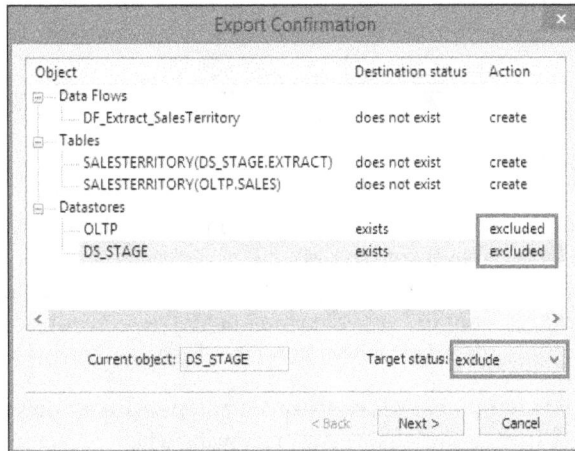

4. The output of the direct export command is displayed in the **Output | Information** window:

```
(14.2) 07-13-15 21:06:51 (1000:6636) JOB: Exported 1 Data Flows

(14.2) 07-13-15 21:06:51 (1000:6636) JOB: Exported 2 Tables

(14.2) 07-13-15 21:06:51 (1000:6636) JOB: Completed Export.
Exported 3 objects.
```

5. Now, exit the Designer and reopen it by connecting to the DS4_LOCAL_EXT repository. Expand the full project TEST structure to see that all missing dependent objects were imported into the structure of the Job_DWH_DimGeography job:

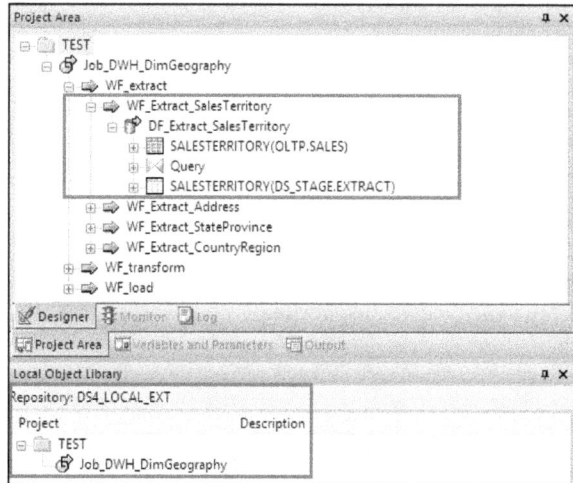

How it works...

Manipulating objects on the **Export** tab is a preparation step that allows you to exclude the objects that you do not want to export to the ATL file or directly to another local repository. After preparing the ETL structure for export by excluding specific objects that you do not want to export, in case you do not want to overwrite versions of the same objects in the target repository or are just not interested in migrating them, you have three options:

▶ Direct export into another local repository (a comparison window opens, allowing you exclude objects from being exported and showing which object exists in the target repository)

▶ Export to an ATL file

▶ Export to an XML file (this is exactly the same as the previous option, except that a different flat file format is used to store the ETL code)

An ATL file is a structured file that contains properties, links, and references for the objects exported.

An ATL file can be opened in any text editor. It can be useful to browse its contents if you want to check which specific object included in the export file. For function objects, it is easy to see the text of the exported function if you want to check its version and so on.

For example, if you open the `export.atl` file generated in this recipe with Notepad and search for `DF_Load_DimGeography`, you will see that it can be found in two places within a file:

```
CREATE    DATAFLOW  DF_Load_DimGeography::'cdeade8b-189e-451d-b0b4-8e98bd82357b'
BEGIN
```

```
CALL DATAFLOW DF_Load_DimGeography::'cdeade8b-189e-451d-b0b4-8e98bd82357b'();
```

The first section defines the properties of the object, and the second defines its place within an execution structure.

Debugging job execution

Here, I will explain the use of Data Services Interactive Debugger. In this recipe, I will debug the `DF_Transform_DimGeography` dataflow.

The debugging process is the process of defining the points in the ETL code (dataflow in particular) that you want to monitor closely during job execution. By monitoring it closely, I mean to actually see the rows passing through or even to have control to pause the execution at those points to investigate the current passing record more closely.

Those points in code are called breakpoints, and they are usually placed before and after particular transform objects in order to see the effect made by particular a transformation on the passing row.

Getting ready...

The easiest way to debug a specific dataflow is to copy it in a separate test job. Create a new job called `Job_Debug` and copy `DF_Transform_DimGeography` in it from the workflow workspace that it's currently located in, or just drag and drop the dataflow object in the `Job_Debug` workspace from **Local Object Library | Dataflows**.

How to do it...

Here are the steps to create a breakpoint and execute the job in the debug mode:

1. First, define the breakpoint inside a dataflow. To do this, double-click on the link connecting the two transform objects, `Join` and `Mapping`:

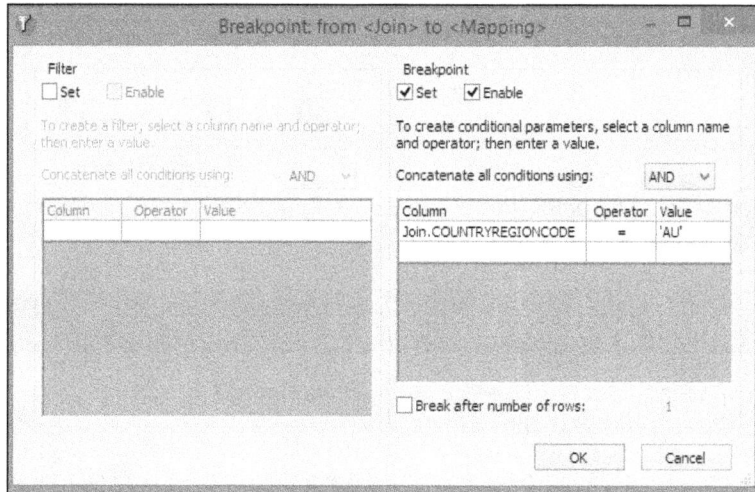

2. Created breakpoints are displayed as red dots on the links between transform objects. You can toggle them on/off using the **Show Filters/Breakpoints** button from the top instrument panel:

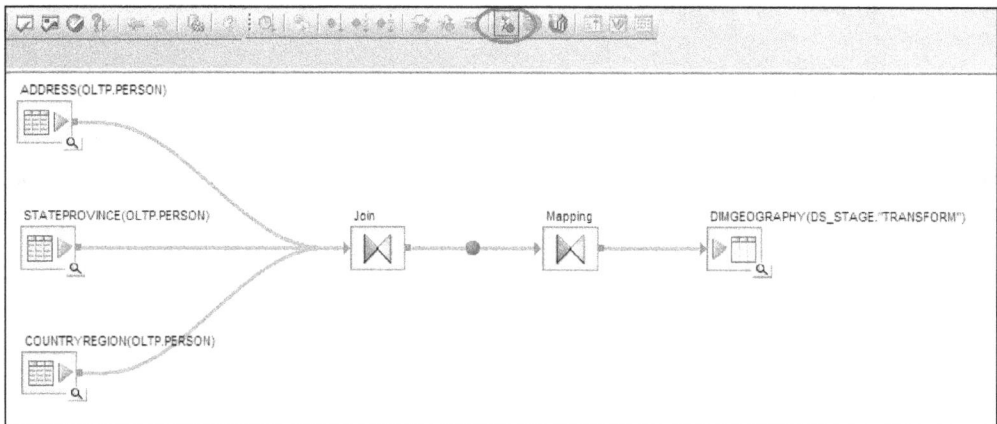

3. Go to the `Job_Debug` context and choose **Debug | Start Debug...** from the top menu, or just click on the **Start Debug...** (*Ctrl* + *F8*) button on the top instrument panel:

4. The **Debug Properties** window opens, allowing you to specify or change the debug properties. Do not change them—the default values are suitable for most debugging cases:

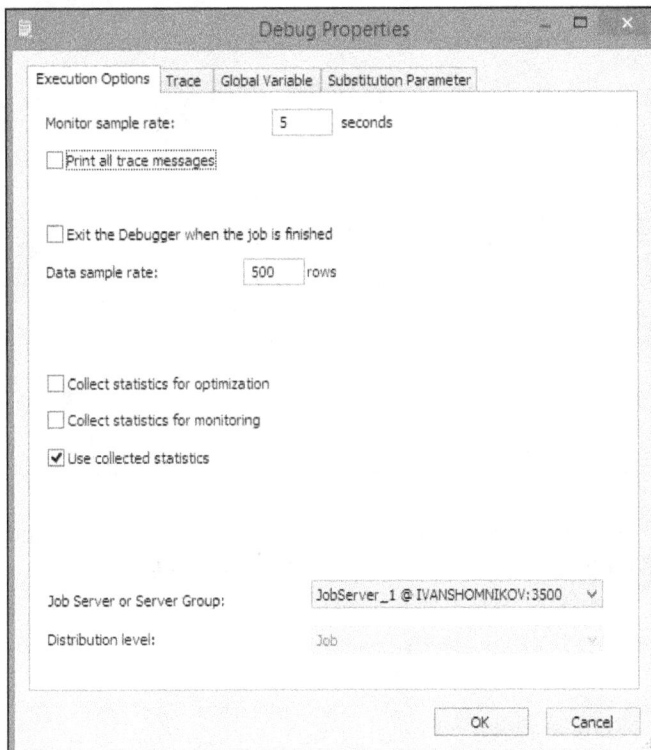

5. In the debugging mode, the job executes in the same manner as in the normal execution mode, except that it is possible to pause it at any moment to browse the data between transforms. In our case, the job paused automatically as soon as the first passing row meets the specified breakpoint condition. To view the dataset passed between the transforms, click on the magnifying glass icon on the link between the transform objects:

6. When paused or running, the top-level instrument panel changes the activating debugging buttons, allowing you to stop/continue debugging:

Alternatively, step through the passing rows one by one when viewing the dataset between transforms:

7. Along with the breakpoints, you can define the filter in the same window:

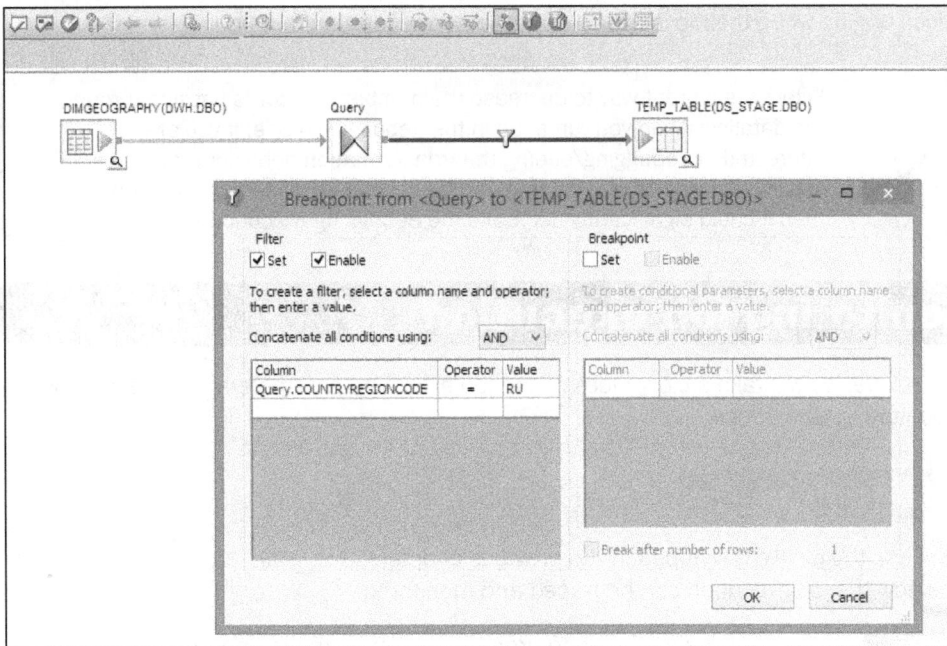

The filter is displayed with a different icon in the dataflow and allows you to filter datasets passing through the dataflow in the debugging mode.

How it works...

Two-step process:

1. Define the breakpoints where you want the job execution to pause.
2. Run the job in the debugging mode.

Breakpoints allow you to pause job execution on a specific condition so that you are able to investigate the data flowing through you dataflow process. In the debugging mode, it is possible to see all records passed between transform objects inside a dataflow. You can see how a specific record extracted from the source object is transformed and changed while it is making its way into the target object. It is also easy to detect when the record is filtered by the WHERE clause condition, as it will not appear after the Query transform that filters it out.

Managing filters/breakpoints with the **Filters/Breakpoints...** (*Alt* + *F9*) button from the instrument panel.

Filters applied to links between transform objects are considered only when the job is executed in the debugging mode. Filters as well as breakpoints are not visible for the Data Services engine when the job is executed in the normal execution mode.

> Filters are a great way to decrease the number of records passing through the dataflow when you run a job in the debugging mode. If you are interested in debugging/seeing the transformation behavior for a small, specific amount of records that can be defined with filtering conditions, then it could significantly decrease the debugging execution time.

Monitoring job execution

In this recipe, we will take a closer look at the job execution parameters, tracing options, and job monitoring techniques.

Getting ready

We will use the job we developed in the previous chapters, `Job_DWH_DimGeography`, to see how the job execution can be traced and monitored.

Let's perform minor changes to the job to prepare the job for the recipe examples using these steps:

1. On the job-level context, create a global variable, `$g_RunDate`, of the **date** data type and assign the `sysdate()` function to it as a value.

2. At the same job level, before the sequence of workflows, place a new script object with the following code and link it to the first workflow. This script will be the first object executed within a job:

    ```
    print('************************************************');
    print('INFO: Job '||job_name()||' started on '||$g_RunDate);
    print('************************************************');
    ```

How to do it...

Click on the **Execute...** button to execute the job. Before the job runs, the **Execution Properties** window opens, allowing you to set up execution options, configure the tracing of the job, or change the predefined values of the global variables for that particular job run to a different one.

Let's take a closer look at the tabs available on this window:

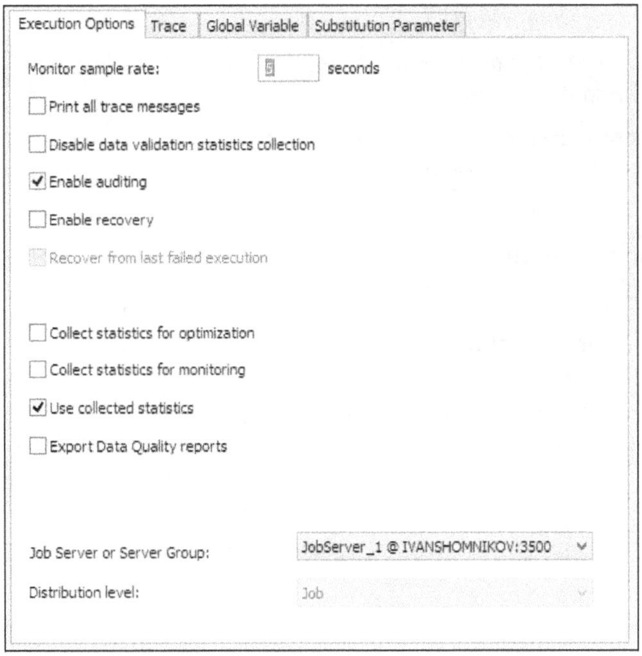

Execution Options	Trace	Global Variable	Substitution Parameter

Monitor sample rate: 5   seconds

☐ Print all trace messages

☐ Disable data validation statistics collection

☑ Enable auditing

☐ Enable recovery

☐ Recover from last failed execution

☐ Collect statistics for optimization

☐ Collect statistics for monitoring

☑ Use collected statistics

☐ Export Data Quality reports

Job Server or Server Group: JobServer_1 @ IVANSHOMNIKOV:3500 ⌄

Distribution level: Job ⌄

Click on the Execution Options tab.

Here are the options available on this tab:

▶ **Print all trace messages**: This option displays all the possible trace messages from all components participating in the job execution: object parameters and options, internal system queries and internally executed commands, loader parameters, the data itself, and many other different kinds of information. The log generated is so enormous that we do not recommend that you use this option if you have a few workflow/dataflow objects inside your job or if the data passing your dataflows is big enough to not want to see every row of it passing through the transformations.

This option literally shows what is happening in every Data Services internal component participating in the data processing, and all this information is displayed for every row passing those components.

▶ **Monitor sample rate**: This option defines how often your logs get updated when the job runs. The default is 5 seconds.

- ▸ **Collect statistics for optimization**: This option collects optimization statistics, allowing Data Services to choose optimal cache types for various components when executing dataflows. We will talk about it in more detail in the upcoming chapters.

- ▸ **Collect statistics for monitoring**: If set, Data Services will display cache sizes in the trace log when the job runs.

- ▸ **Use collected statistics**: This makes Data Services use the statistics collected when the job was executed previously with the **Collect statistics for optimization** option set up.

Click on the second Trace tab.

This tab has a list of various trace options. Setting up each of these options adds extra information to the contents of the trace log file when the job runs:

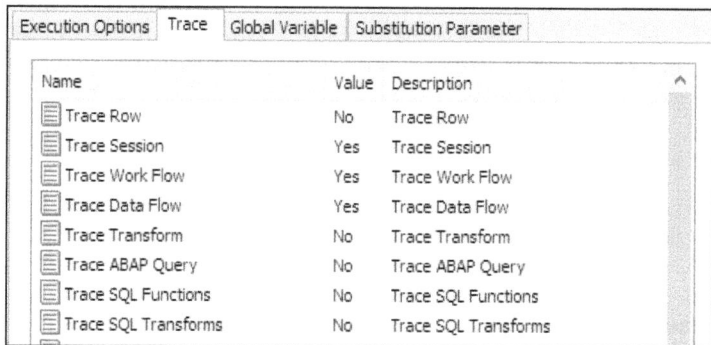

Execution Options	Trace	Global Variable	Substitution Parameter		
Name			Value	Description	
Trace Row			No	Trace Row	
Trace Session			Yes	Trace Session	
Trace Work Flow			Yes	Trace Work Flow	
Trace Data Flow			Yes	Trace Data Flow	
Trace Transform			No	Trace Transform	
Trace ABAP Query			No	Trace ABAP Query	
Trace SQL Functions			No	Trace SQL Functions	
Trace SQL Transforms			No	Trace SQL Transforms	

By default, only **Trace Session**, **Trace Work Flow**, and **Trace Data Flow** are enabled. Switch their values to **No** and enable only **Trace Row** by changing its value to **Yes**. After you execute the job, you will see the following trace log:

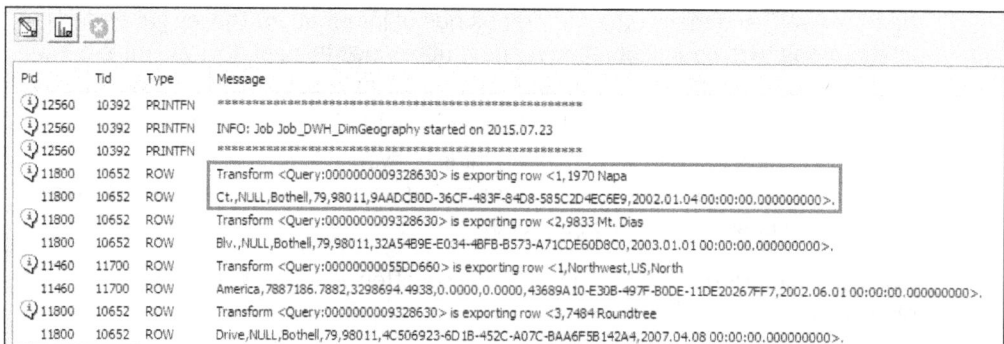

Pid	Tid	Type	Message
12560	10392	PRINTFN	===
12560	10392	PRINTFN	INFO: Job Job_DWH_DimGeography started on 2015.07.23
12560	10392	PRINTFN	===
11800	10652	ROW	Transform <Query:0000000009328630> is exporting row <1,1970 Napa
11800	10652	ROW	Ct.,NULL,Bothell,79,98011,9AADCB0D-36CF-483F-84D8-585C2D4EC6E9,2002.01.04 00:00:00.000000000>.
11800	10652	ROW	Transform <Query:0000000009328630> is exporting row <2,9833 Mt. Dias
11800	10652	ROW	Blv.,NULL,Bothell,79,98011,32A54B9E-E034-48FB-B573-A71CDE60D8C0,2003.01.01 00:00:00.000000000>.
11460	11700	ROW	Transform <Query:00000000055DD660> is exporting row <1,Northwest,US,North
11460	11700	ROW	America,7887186.7882,3298694.4938,0.0000,0.0000,43689A10-E30B-497F-80DE-11DE20267FF7,2002.06.01 00:00:00.000000000>.
11800	10652	ROW	Transform <Query:0000000009328630> is exporting row <3,7484 Roundtree
11800	10652	ROW	Drive,NULL,Bothell,79,98011,4C506923-6D1B-452C-A07C-BAA6F5B142A4,2007.04.08 00:00:00.000000000>.

You can see that you do not see information about the statuses of the workflow and dataflow execution that you normally see. The trace log file now displays only the output of the `print()` functions from user script objects and rows passing through the dataflows. Be extra careful—this is a lot of data. Avoid using this option unless you are specifically in a design test environment with just a few rows red from the source table.

Click on the third Global Variable tab.

This tab displays the list of all global variables created within the job, allowing you to modify their values for this specific job execution without changing these values in the job context level:

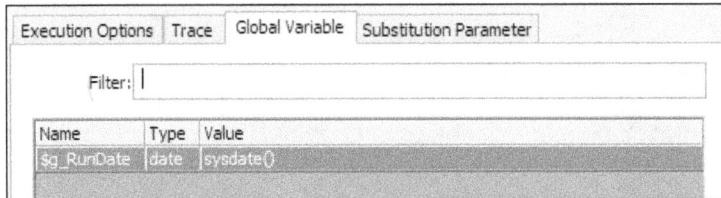

Execution Options	Trace	Global Variable	Substitution Parameter

Filter: |

Name	Type	Value
$g_RunDate	date	sysdate()

To change the value, just double-click on the **Value** field of the specific global variable row and input the new value. Remember that this change applies only to this current job execution. When you run the job next time and open this tab, the global variables will have their default values defined again.

Log in to the Data Services Management Console to monitor job execution and go to Administrator | Batch | DS4_REPO.

The Management Console not just allows the Web access to the same three log files, trace, log, and monitor, but also to another one, **Performance Monitor**:

Repository: DS4_REPO

Batch Job Status	Batch Job Configuration	Repository Schedules

Page: 1

Job name:
Job_DWH_DimGeography ▼

Display:
○ Last execution of job
● Last [5 ▼] Days
○ All executions   From:
To:

Wildcard search string (optional)

[Search]

Batch jobs history (Jobs: Executed job All batch jobs in last 5 days.)

Select	Status	Job name	System configuration	Job Server	Job information	Start time	End time	Duration
☐	✪	Job_DWH_DimGeography		IVANSHOMNIKOV:3500	Trace,Monitor,Error,Performance Monitor	23/07/2015 8:51:48 PM	23/07/2015 8:57:32 PM	0s
☐	♨	Job_DWH_DimGeography		IVANSHOMNIKOV:3500	Trace,Monitor,Error,Performance Monitor	23/07/2015 8:50:30 PM	23/07/2015 8:50:46 PM	16s
☐	♨	Job_DWH_DimGeography		IVANSHOMNIKOV:3500	Trace,Monitor,Error,Performance Monitor	23/07/2015 8:44:20 PM	23/07/2015 8:44:35 PM	15s
☐	♨	Job_DWH_DimGeography		IVANSHOMNIKOV:3500	Trace,Monitor,Error,Performance Monitor	23/07/2015 8:42:32 PM	23/07/2015 8:42:47 PM	15s
☐	♨	Job_DWH_DimGeography		IVANSHOMNIKOV:3500	Trace,Monitor,Error,Performance Monitor	23/07/2015 8:42:03 PM	23/07/2015 8:42:19 PM	18s
☐	♨	Job_DWH_DimGeography		IVANSHOMNIKOV:3500	Trace,Monitor,Error,Performance Monitor	23/07/2015 3:49:55 PM	23/07/2015 3:58:21 PM	8m 26s
☐	♨	Job_DWH_DimGeography		IVANSHOMNIKOV:3500	Trace,Monitor,Error,Performance Monitor	23/07/2015 3:31:37 PM	23/07/2015 3:31:53 PM	16s
☐	♨	Job_DWH_DimGeography		IVANSHOMNIKOV:3500	Trace,Monitor,Error,Performance Monitor	23/07/2015 3:27:15 PM	23/07/2015 3:27:40 PM	25s

The top-level section allows easy access to the previous versions of the log files for a specific job. It does not matter whether the job has been placed in the `Project` folder or not.

In the preceding screenshot, we displayed all log files for the last 5 days for the `Job_DWH_DimGeography` job.

Click on the **Performance Monitor** link of the last job execution to open the **Performance Monitor** page:

The first page of **Performance Monitor** displays the list of dataflows from the job structure. When clicking on the specific dataflow, it is possible to drill in on the dataflow components level to see how many records passed through the specific dataflow components and the execution time of each them.

In fact, the information displayed in **Performance Monitor** is based on the same data as the information displayed in the **Monitor** log. It is just presented differently, in making it sometimes more convenient for analysis.

How it works...

It is simply a matter of personal choice when deciding what to use to monitor job execution: the web application of **Data Services Management Console** or the **Designer** client. Sometimes, due to restricted access to the environment, the Web option is more preferable. It is also easier to use if you need to find any old log files of a specific job for analysis, performance comparison, or simply need to copy and paste few rows from the trace log file.

Building an external ETL audit and audit reporting

In this recipe, we will implement the external user-built ETL audit mechanism. Our ETL audit will include information about the start and stop times of the workflows running within the job, their statuses, names, and information about which job they belong to.

Getting ready...

We need to create an ETL audit table in our database where we will store the audit results.

Connect to the STAGE database using the SQL Server Management Studio and execute the following statement to create the ETL audit table:

```
create table dbo.etl_audit (
  job_run_id integer,
  workflow_status varchar(50),
  job_name varchar(255),
  start_dt datetime,
  end_dt datetime,
  process_name varchar(255)
);
```

How to do it...

First, we need to choose objects for auditing. The following steps should be implemented for every workflow or dataflow that you want to collect auditing information about. In this particular example, we will enable ETL auditing for the job object itself.

1. Create extra variables for the job object:

   ```
   $v_process_name varchar(255)
   $v_job_run_id integer
   ```

2. Add the following code in the script that starts the job execution:

   ```
   $v_process_name = job_name();
   $v_job_run_id = job_run_id();

   # Insert audit record
   sql('DS_STAGE',
   ```

```
' insert into dbo.etl_audit (job_run_id, workflow_status,
  job_name, start_dt, end_dt, process_name) '||
' values('|| $v_job_run_id ||', '|| '\'STARTED\'' ||',
  \''|| job_name() ||'\', SYSDATETIME(), NULL, \''|| $v_process_
name ||'\')'
);
```

3. Create a new script, `ETL_audit_update`, at the end of the execution sequence inside the job context and put the following code in it:

```
# Update ETL audit record
sql('DS_STAGE',
  ' update dbo.etl_audit '||
  '    set workflow_status = '||'\'COMPLETED\''||', end_dt =
  SYSDATETIME() '||
  ' where job_run_id = '|| $v_job_run_id ||' and
    process_name = \''|| $v_process_name ||'\''
);
```

4. The job content has now been wrapped in the auditing insert/update commands placed in the initial and final scripts:

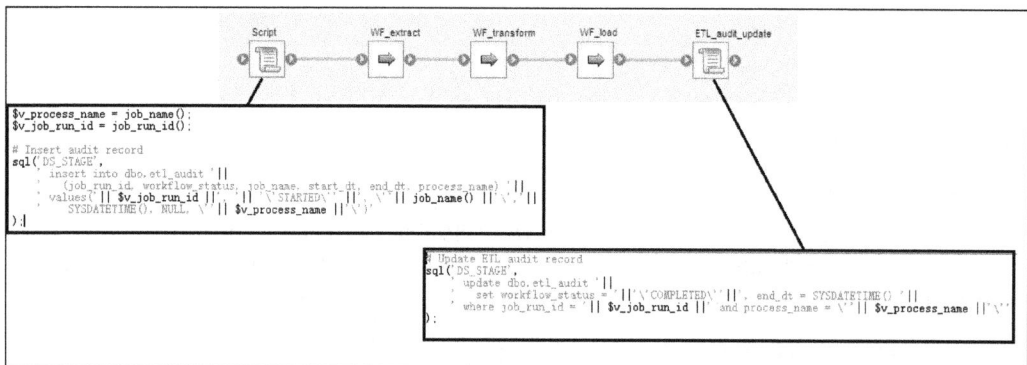

5. Implement the preceding steps for `WF_Extract_SalesTerritory`, which can be found in the `WF_extract` workflow container to enable the ETL audit for that object as well. The only change is that in the initial script, the `$v_process_name` variable value should be changed to the `workflow_name()` function instead of the `job_name()` function, how it was done for the job:

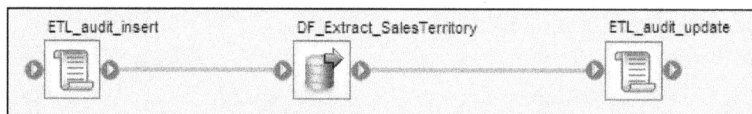

How it works...

Now, if you execute the job and query the contents of the ETL audit table in a few seconds, you should see some thing like this:

	job_run_id	workflow_status	job_name	start_dt	end_dt	process_name
1	224	STARTED	Job_DWH_DimGeography	2015-07-24 16:33:10.967	NULL	Job_DWH_DimGeography
2	224	COMPLETED	Job_DWH_DimGeography	2015-07-24 16:33:10.977	2015-07-24 16:33:13.520	WF_Extract_SalesTerritory

A few seconds later, after the job successfully completes, your ETL audit table will look like this:

	job_run_id	workflow_status	job_name	start_dt	end_dt	process_name
1	224	COMPLETED	Job_DWH_DimGeography	2015-07-24 16:33:10.967	2015-07-24 16:33:25.113	Job_DWH_DimGeography
2	224	COMPLETED	Job_DWH_DimGeography	2015-07-24 16:33:10.977	2015-07-24 16:33:13.520	WF_Extract_SalesTerritory

A simple analysis of this table can answer the following questions:

▶ *Which objects are running within the currently running job?* This is very useful information, especially if your job contains hundreds of workflows, with 20 of them running in parallel. In this case, it is hard to obtain this information from the trace log.

▶ *What was the status of the object when it was executed last time?* To be precise, you also have to implement another piece of logic, the third update that changes the status of the workflow to "ERROR" if something unexpected happens and the workflow cannot be considered as successfully completed. This third update usually goes into the catch section of the try-catch block.

▶ *What was the execution time for the specific object?* The answer speaks for itself.

▶ *What was the execution order of the objects?* You can compare the execution times. If you know when the objects started and ended, you can easily derive the execution order. When comparable workflows are not directly linked and run within different branches of logic, it is sometimes useful to know which one started or finished earlier.

The advantage of the external user-built ETL audit is that you can build a flexible solution that gathers any information that you want it to gather.

> Note that with insert/update ETL audit statements, you can define the logical borders of a successful object completion. Theoretically, a workflow object and the job itself can still fail right after it successfully executes the `sql()` command and updates its status in the ETL audit table as successful. However, this is often a good thing as it is exactly what you are interested in when you make the decision of if you should rerun a specific workflow or not – has the workflow completed the work it was supposed to?

Information in ETL audit tables can be utilized not only in the reports showing the execution statistics of your jobs but also to implement execution logic inside the job.

For example, if you want to run the specific workflow only once a week but it is being executed within a daily job, you could add the script objects in your workflow. You could check from ETL audit tables when the workflow was run the last time and skip it if it was executed and successfully completed less than a week ago.

Finally, it is even possible to not only audit a Data Services object (dataflow, workflow, job, or script object) but to audit any piece of code—part of the script or a single branch of the logic. You can wrap anything in the insert/update statements sent to an external table to store audit information.

That is the true power of custom ETL auditing. You can collect all the information you want and easily query this information from ETL itself to make various decisions.

Using built-in Data Services ETL audit and reporting functionality

Data Services provides ETL reporting functionality through the Management Console web application. It is available in the form of the **Operational Dashboard** application on the main Management Console Hope page.

Getting ready

You do not have to configure or prepare the operational dashboards feature. It is available by default, and all you have to do to access it is start the Data Services Management Console.

How to do it...

Let's review which ETL reporting capabilities are available in Data Services. Perform these steps:

1. Start the **Data Services Management Console**.

2. Choose the **Operational Dashboard** application from the home page:

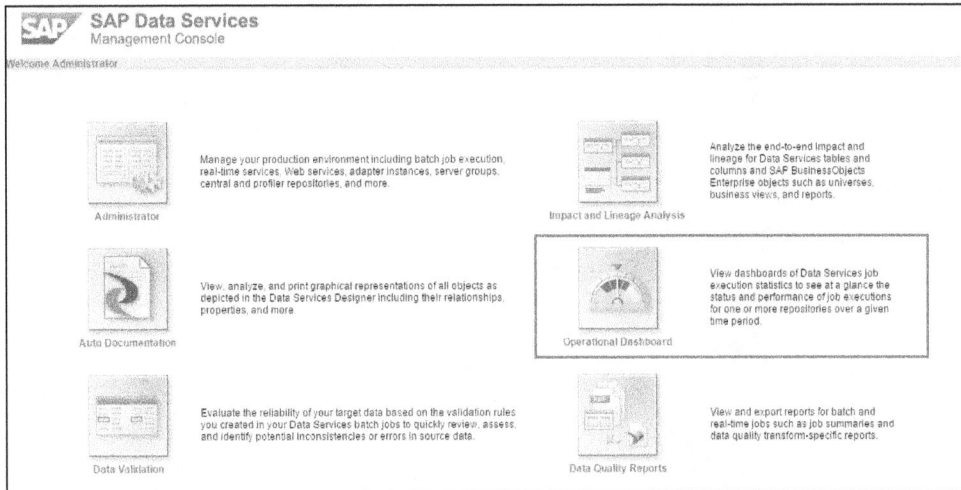

3. The main interface of **Operational Dashboard** includes three sections. It includes the pie chart of the general job status statistics per interval for a selected repository. Green shows the number of successfully completed jobs for a specific period of time, yellow shows jobs successfully completed with warning messages, and red shows failed jobs:

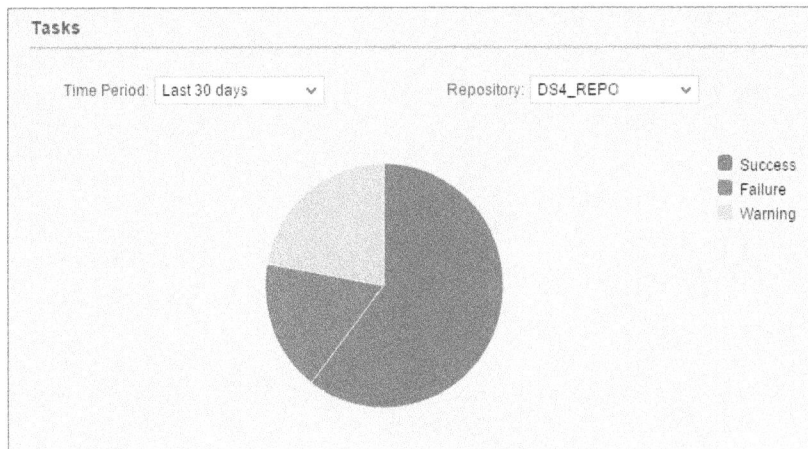

4. The section below shows more detailed job execution statistics in the form of a vertical bar chart for specific days or interval of days. Try to hover your mouse cursor over the bars to see the actual numbers behind the graph. The vertical line shows the number of jobs executed on specific days with different statuses: successfully with no errors (green), successfully with warning messages (yellow), and failed (red):

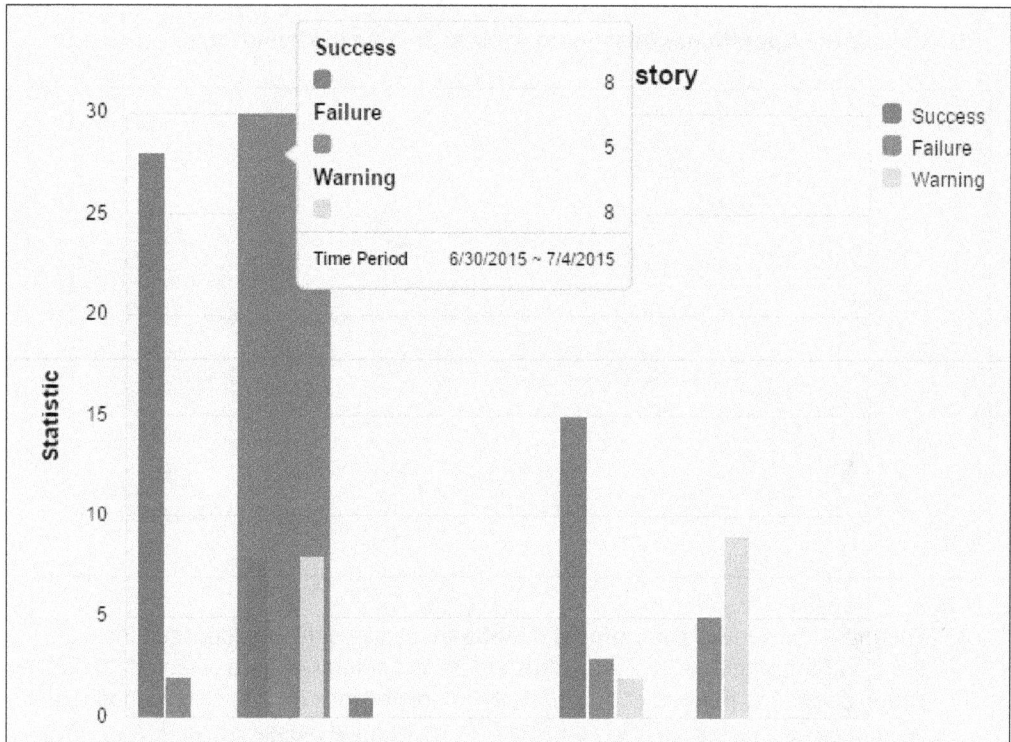

5. At the right-hand side, you can see the list of jobs whose execution statistics are represented by graphs on the left-hand side. By clicking on a specific row, you can drill down to see the list of executions for this specific job. The most useful information here is the execution time displayed in seconds, the run ID of the job, and status of the job, as you can see in the following screenshot:

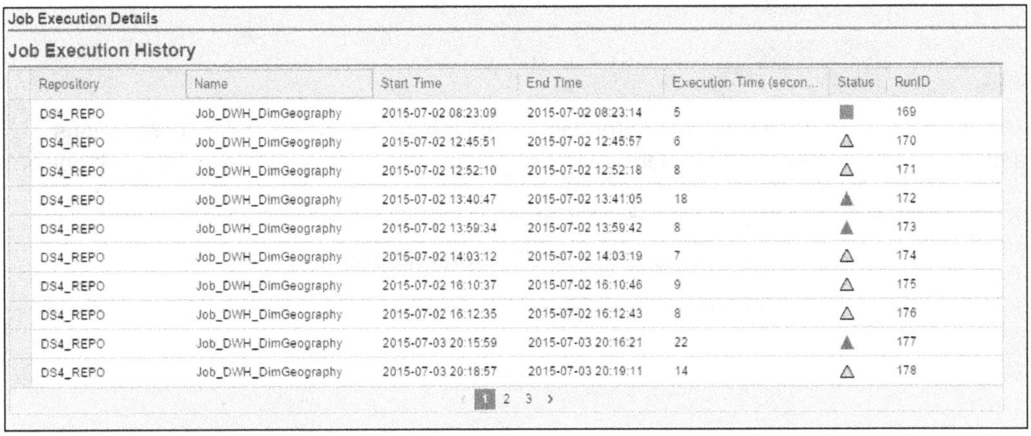

Job Execution Details

Job Execution History

Repository	Name	Start Time	End Time	Execution Time (secon...	Status	RunID
DS4_REPO	Job_DWH_DimGeography	2015-07-02 08:23:09	2015-07-02 08:23:14	5	■	169
DS4_REPO	Job_DWH_DimGeography	2015-07-02 12:45:51	2015-07-02 12:45:57	6	△	170
DS4_REPO	Job_DWH_DimGeography	2015-07-02 12:52:10	2015-07-02 12:52:18	8	△	171
DS4_REPO	Job_DWH_DimGeography	2015-07-02 13:40:47	2015-07-02 13:41:05	18	▲	172
DS4_REPO	Job_DWH_DimGeography	2015-07-02 13:59:34	2015-07-02 13:59:42	8	▲	173
DS4_REPO	Job_DWH_DimGeography	2015-07-02 14:03:12	2015-07-02 14:03:19	7	△	174
DS4_REPO	Job_DWH_DimGeography	2015-07-02 16:10:37	2015-07-02 16:10:46	9	△	175
DS4_REPO	Job_DWH_DimGeography	2015-07-02 16:12:35	2015-07-02 16:12:43	8	△	176
DS4_REPO	Job_DWH_DimGeography	2015-07-03 20:15:59	2015-07-03 20:16:21	22	▲	177
DS4_REPO	Job_DWH_DimGeography	2015-07-03 20:18:57	2015-07-03 20:19:11	14	△	178

1 2 3 >

How it works...

Operational Dashboard reporting can be used to provide job execution history data, analyze the percentage of failed jobs for a specific time interval, and compare those numbers between different days or time intervals.

That is pretty much it. To do more, you would have to build your own ETL metadata collection and build your own reporting functionality on top of this data.

Auto Documentation in Data Services

This recipe will guide you through the Auto Documentation feature available in Data Services. Like **Operational Dashboard**, this feature is also part of functionality available in the Data Services Management Console.

How to do it...

These steps will create a PDF document containing graphical representation, descriptions, and relationships between all underlying objects of the `Job_DWH_DimGeography` job object:

1. Log in to the Data Services Management Console web application.

2. On the home page, click on the **Auto Documentation** icon:

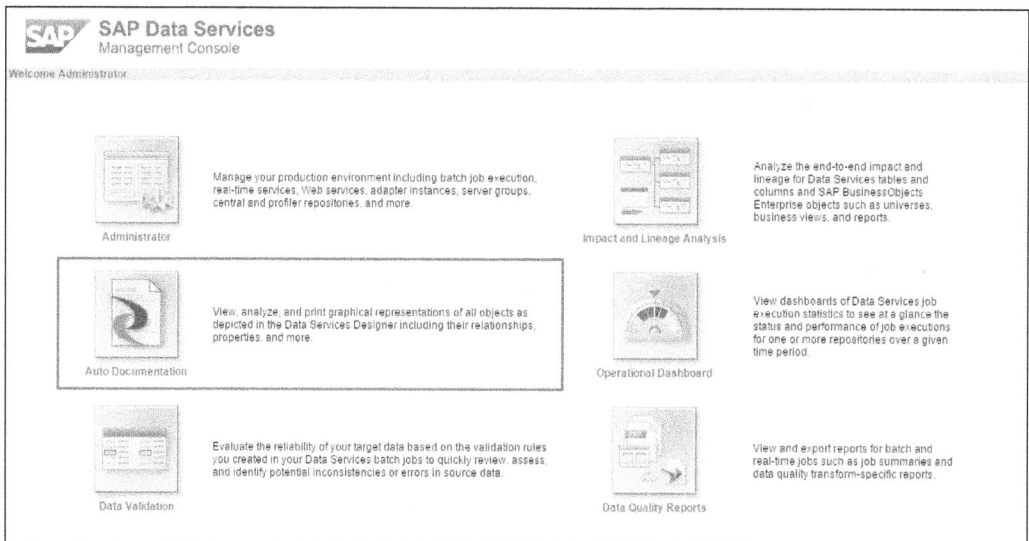

3. In the following screen, expand the project tree and left-click on the job object. You can see which object is displayed as current by checking the object name in the top tab name on the right-hand side of the window:

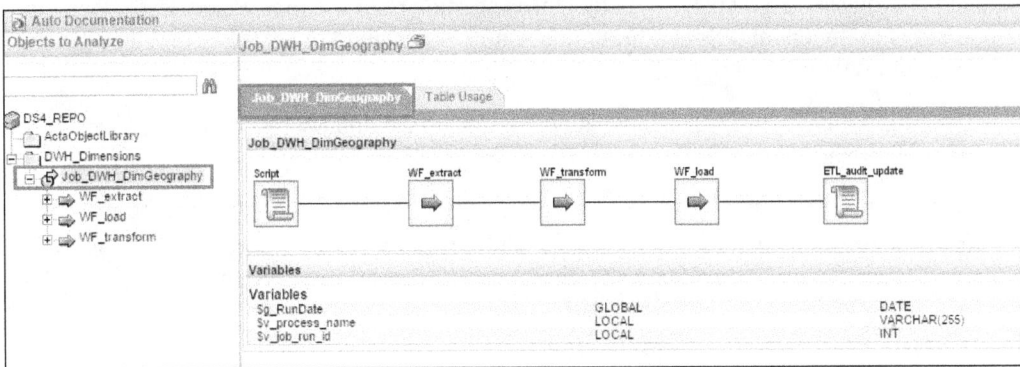

4. Then, click on the small printer icon located at the top of the window:

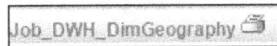

5. In the pop-up window, just click on the **Print** button, leaving all options with default values.

6. Data Services, by default, generates a PDF document in the browser's default Downloads folder:

1. ETL Documentation

1.1. Job_DWH_DimGeography

Variables

$g_RunDate	DATE	sysdate()
$v_process_name	VARCHAR	
$v_job_run_id	INT	

How it works...

As you have probably noticed, the Auto Documentation feature is only available for the jobs included in projects as it displays the object tree starting from the root Project level. Jobs that were created in the **Local Object Library** and were not assigned to a specific project will not be visible for auto-documenting.

Auto Documentation export is available in two formats: PDF and Microsoft Word (see the following screenshot):

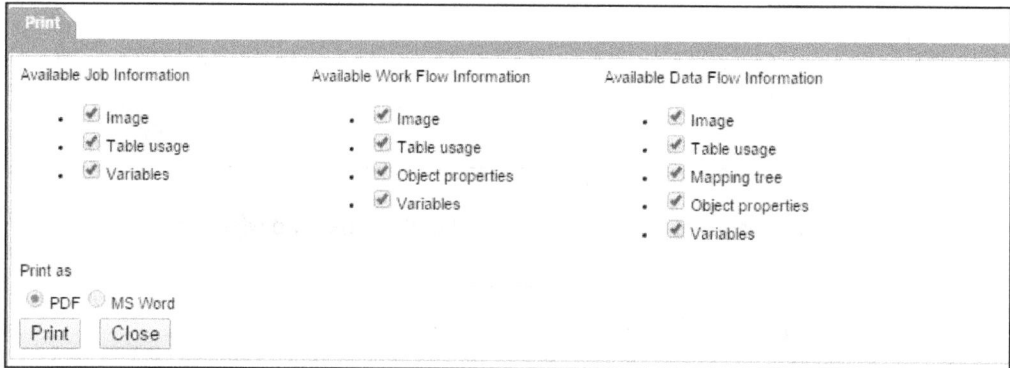

On the same screen, you can display types of information to be included in the documentation file.

> Note that dataflow documentation includes mapping of each and every column from source to target through all dataflow transformations. This is a very detailed level, and even our dataflow inside Job_DWH_DimGeography is not at all complex. The datasets we are migrating are relatively small, but we still get a 34-pages document. So, you can see that the documentation level is extremely detailed.

Another extremely useful feature of Data Services Auto Documentation is the **Table Usage** tab:

It allows us to see which source and target table objects are used within the `Job_DWH_ DimGeography` object tree.

Information like this about relationships between objects within ETL is extremely useful as during development, some objects often change, and you need to evaluate how it impacts the ETL code. If the table column is changed (renamed and data type changed) on the database level and you have to apply the same changes to your ETL code. Otherwise, it will fail the next time it runs, as Data Services is not aware of the table changes and still operates with old version of the table.

Table object dependencies can also be visualized with another Data Services feature: **Impact and Linage Analysis**. This functionality will be discussed in *Chapter 12, Introduction to Information Steward*.

7

Validating and Cleansing Data

Here are the recipes presented in this chapter:

- ▶ Creating validation functions
- ▶ Using validation functions with the Validation transform
- ▶ Reporting data validation results
- ▶ Using regular expression support to validate data
- ▶ Enabling dataflow audit
- ▶ Data Quality transforms – cleansing your data

Introduction

This chapter introduces the concepts of validating methods that can be applied to the data passing through ETL processes in order to cleanse and conform it according to the defined Data Quality standards. It includes validation methods that consist of defining validation expressions with the help of validation functions and then splitting data into two data sets: valid and invalid data. Invalid data that does not pass the validation function conditions usually gets inserted into a separate target table for further investigation.

Another topic discussed in this chapter is dataflow audit. This feature of Data Services allows the collection of executional statistical information about the data processed by the dataflow and even controls the executional behavior depending on the numbers collected.

Finally, we will discuss the Data Quality transforms—the powerful set of instruments available in Data Services in order to parse, categorize, and make cleansing suggestions in order to increase the reliability and quality of the transformed data.

Creating validation functions

One of the ways to implement the data validation process in Data Services is to use validation functions along with the Validation transform in your dataflow to split the flow of data into two: records that pass the defined validation rule and those that do not. Those validation rules can be combined into validation function objects for your convenience and traceability.

In this recipe, we will create a standard but quite simple validation function. We will deploy it in our dataflow, which extracts the address data from the source system into a staging area. The `Validation` function will check to see whether the city in the migrated record has `Paris` as a value, and if it does, it will send the records to a separate reject table.

Getting ready

First, we need to create another schema in our `STAGE` database to contain reject tables. Creating the `Reject` schema to store these tables allows the keeping of the original table names; that makes writing queries and reporting against those tables as well as locating them much easier.

1. Open **SQL Server Management Studio**.

2. Go to **STAGE | Security | Schemas** in the **Object Explorer** window.

3. Right-click on the list and choose **New Schema...** in the context menu.

4. Choose **Reject** for schema name and **dbo** as schema owner.

5. Click on **OK** to create the schema.

How to do it...

Follow these steps to create a validation function:

1. Log in to **Data Services Designer** and connect to the local repository.

2. Go to **Local Object Library | Custom Functions**.

3. Right-click on **Validation Functions** and select **New** from the context menu.

4. Input the function name `fn_Check_Paris`, check **Validation function**, as shown in the following screenshot, and populate the description field.

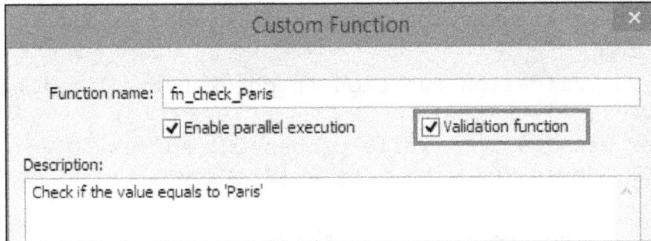

5. Click on **Next** and input the following code in the main section of **Smart Editor**:

```
# Validation function to check if the passed value equals
# to 'Paris'

# Wrap the function in the try-catch block. We do not want
# to fail the dataflow process
# if the function itself fails.

try
  begin

    # Assign input parameter value to a local variable
    $l_City = $p_City;
    $l_AddressID = $p_AddressID;

    # Default "Success" result status
    $l_Result = 1;

    if ($l_City = 'Paris')
    begin
      # Change to "Failure" result status

      $l_Result = 0;
    end

    # Returning result status
    Return $l_Result;
```

```
      end
catch ( all )
  begin
    # writing information about the failure in the
# trace log
    print('Validation function fn_check_Paris() failed with
      error: '||
    error_message()||' while processing AddressID =
      {$l_AddressID} with City = {$l_City}');

    # Returning the result status
    Return $l_Result;
  end
```

6. In the same **Smart Editor** window, create local variables $l_AddressID int, $l_
    City varchar(100), and $l_Result int and the function's input parameters,
    $p_City varchar(100) and $p_AddressID int.

7. Click on the **Validate** button to validate the function and click **OK** to close **Smart
    Editor** and save all changes.

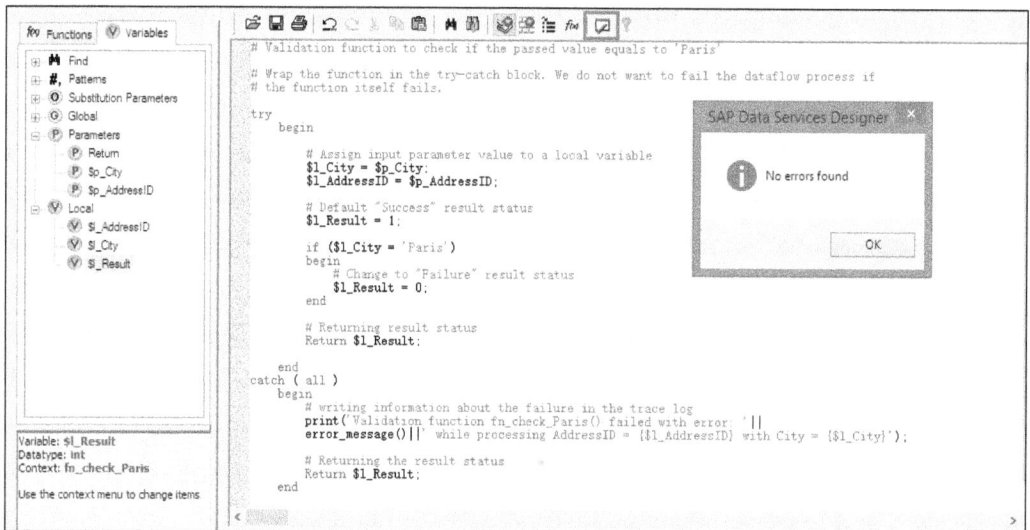

How it works...

The function's body is wrapped in `try-catch` block to prevent our main dataflow processes from failing if something goes wrong with the validation function. The validation function is executed for each row passing through, so it would be ineffective at allowing the execution of the function to determine the execution behavior of the main process.

Try to imagine a situation when you your dataflow process 2 million records from the source table and 50 of them make the function fail for some reason or other. To process all 2 million records in one go, you would need to wrap the logic of the entire function in `try-catch` and output extra information into the trace log or into an external table in the catch section to perform further analysis of the data after processing is done.

In our example, we only pass the `AddressID` field for traceability purposes, so it would be easy to find the exact row on which the function failed.

The validation function should return either 1 or 0. The value 1 means that the processed row against which the validation function was executed successfully passed the validation; 0 means failure.

See in the following screenshot that, in **Local Object Library**, validation functions are displayed separately from custom functions:

Using validation functions with the Validation transform

This recipe will demonstrate how validation functions are deployed and configured within a dataflow. As the validation function that we created in the previous recipe validates city values, we will deploy it in the `DF_Extract_Address` dataflow object to perform the validation of data extracted from the `Address` table located in the source OLTP database.

Getting ready

Open the job-containing dataflow, DF_Extract_Address, already created in the *Use case example – populating dimension tables* recipe in *Chapter 5, Workflow – Controlling Execution Order*, and copy it into a new job to be able to execute it as a standalone process.

How to do it...

1. Open DF_Extract_Address in the main workspace for editing.

2. Go to **Local Object Library | Transform**, find the **Validation** transform under **Platform**, and drag it into the DF_Extract_Address dataflow right after the Query transform.

3. Link the output of the **Query** transform to the **Validation** transform and double-click on the **Validation** transform to open it for editing.

4. Open the **Validation** transform in the workspace and see how **Validation** splits the flow into three output schemas: **Validation_Pass**, **Validation_Fail**, and **Validation_RuleViolation**:

The **Validation_Pass** and **Validation_Fail** output schemas are identical, except that **Validation_Fail** contains three extra columns: DI_ERRORACTION, DI_ERRORCOLUMNS, and DI_ROWID.

5. Inside the **Validation** transform, click on the **Add** button located on the **Validation Rules** tab to create the first validation rule. Choose the **Validation Function** option for the created rule and map columns sent from the previous transform output to the input parameters, also choosing **Send To Fail** as the value for **Action on Fail**. Do not forget to specify the validation rule name and description.

6. Click on **OK** to create the validation rule. It is now displayed in the Validation transform.

7. Now close the **Validation** transform editor window and add three Query transforms, one for each validation schema output. Name them `Validation_Pass`, `Validation_Fail`, and `Validation_Rules`. Link the Validation transform output to all Query transforms choosing the correct logic branch each time Data Services asks you to.

8. Map all input schema columns to the output schemas in all created Query transforms without making any changes to the mappings.

9. Create two additional template target tables to output data from the **Rules** and **Fail** transforms. Specify the `REJECT` owner schema for both of them as follows:

   ❑ The `ADDRESS` template table for the **Fail** output

   ❑ The `ADDRESS_RULES` template table for the **Rules** output

10. Your final dataflow version should look like the one in the following screenshot:

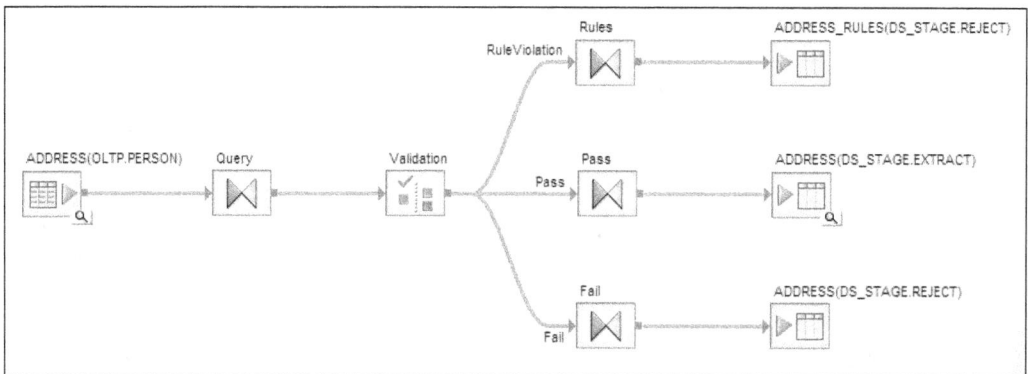

11. Save and execute the job.

12. After the execution is finished, open the dataflow again and view the data in the `REJECT.ADDRESS` and `REJECT.ADDRESS_RULES` tables:

ADDRESSID	ADDRESSLINE1	CITY	DI...	DI_ERRORCOLUMNS	DI_ROWID
676	21,105, Rue de Vaugirard	Paris	F	Validation failed rule(s): ADDRESSID: CITY	1.000000
683	36, avenue de la Gare	Paris	F	Validation failed rule(s): ADDRESSID: CITY	2.000000
689	39, route de Marseille	Paris	F	Validation failed rule(s): ADDRESSID: CITY	3.000000

DI_ROWID	DI_RULENAME	DI_COLUMNNAME
100001.000000	City_not_Paris	ADDRESSID
100001.000000	City_not_Paris	CITY
100002.000000	City_not_Paris	ADDRESSID
100002.000000	City_not_Paris	CITY
100003.000000	City_not_Paris	ADDRESSID
100003.000000	City_not_Paris	CITY

> Note that the rows where the value of CITY equals Paris are not passed to the Transform.ADDRESS stage table anymore.

How it works...

Usually, the **Validation** transform is deployed right before the target object to perform the validation of data changed by previous transformations.

The **Pass** output schema of the **Validation** transform is used to output records that have successfully passed the validation rule defined by either validation function(s) or column condition(s).

Note that you can define as many validation functions or column condition rules as you like, and Data Services is very flexible in allowing you to define different **Action on Fail** options for different functions. This makes it possible to send some "failed" records to both **Pass** and **Fail** outputs or others only to the **Fail** output, depending on the severity of the validation rule.

Let's review another feature of the **Validation** transform—the ability to modify the values of the passing rows depending on the result of validation rule. Follow these steps:

1. Open the Validation transform for editing in the main workspace.

2. As we are validating the city name, let's change the behavior of the Validation transform to send the rows which did not pass validation to both **Pass** and **Fail**. However, in the rows sent to the **Pass** output, change the city name value from `Paris` to `New Paris`. To do that in the section located at the bottom of the **Validation** transform editor, choose the `Query.CITY` column and specify `'New Paris'` in the expression field, as shown here:

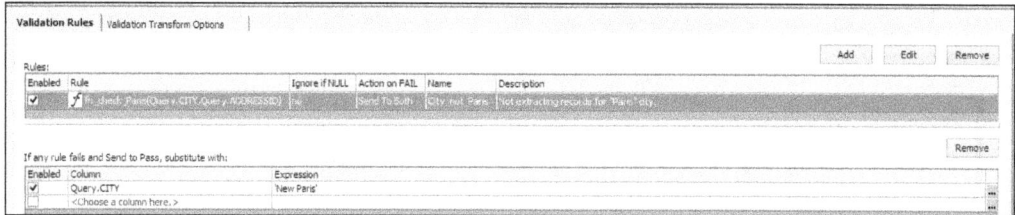

3. Save and execute the job.

4. Open the dataflow again and view the data from both the `Transform.ADDRESS` and `Reject.ADDRESS` tables. You will see that records with the same `ADDRESSID` field were inserted in both the tables, but in the main staging table, the values for city name were substituted with `New Paris`.

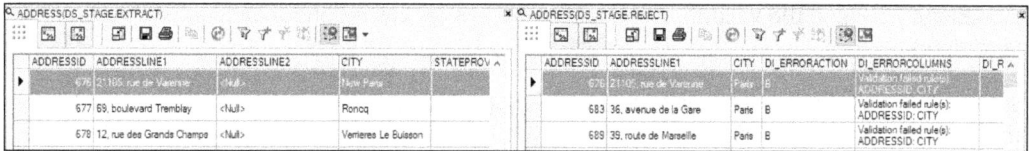

See the following table for a description of the extra columns from the **Fail** and **RuleViolation** Validation transform output schemas:

DI_ERRORACTION	This shows where the output for the specific rule was sent: B means "both", F means "fail", and P means "pass".
DI_ERRORCOLUMNS	This shows the specific columns that were validated (as part of input values for the validation function or simply as a source for column validation).
DI_ROWID	This is the unique identifier of the failed row.
DI_RULENAME	This is the name of the rule which generated the failed row.

DI_COLUMNNAME	This is the validated column (part of the validation function input values or source for column validation in the validation rule). Note that in ADDRESS_RULE output, one row is generated for each validated column separately. So, if your validation function was using five columns from the source object, all five of them are considered to be validated columns, and in case of failure, five rows will be created in the ADDRESS_RULE table for each column with the same ROWID (see the figure showing the contents of the ADDRESS_RULE table in the first example of job execution in this recipe).

Reporting data validation results

One of the advantages of using the **Validation** transform is that Data Services provides the reporting functionality which is based on validation statistics and collected sample data during validation processes.

Validation reports can be viewed in the **Data Services Management Console**. In this recipe, we will learn how to collect data for validation reports and access them in the **Data Services Management Console**.

Getting ready

Use the same job and dataflow, DF_Extract_Address, updated with the Validation transform as in the previous recipes of the current chapter.

How to do it...

1. Open the dataflow DF_Extract_Address and double-click on the **Validation** transform object to open it for editing.

> To be able to use Data Services validation reports, the validation statistics collection has to be enabled first for a Validation transform object in the ETL code structure that you want to collect the reporting data for.

2. Open the **Validation Transform Options** tab in the **Validation** transform editor.

3. Tick both check-boxes, **Collect data validation statistics** and **Collect sample data**.

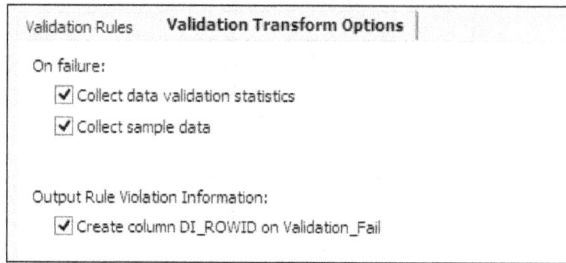

Validation Rules   **Validation Transform Options**

On failure:
- ☑ Collect data validation statistics
- ☑ Collect sample data

Output Rule Violation Information:
- ☑ Create column DI_ROWID on Validation_Fail

4. Save and run the job to collect the data validation statistics for the data set processed by DF_Extract_Address. Make sure that you do not have the option **Disable data validation statistics collection** selected on the job's **Execution Properties** window:

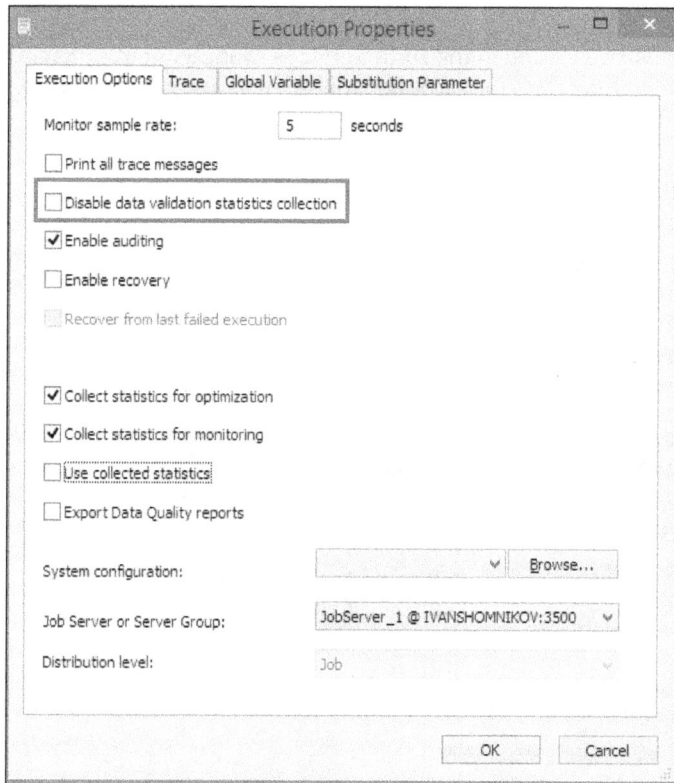

Execution Properties

Execution Options   Trace   Global Variable   Substitution Parameter

Monitor sample rate: 5   seconds

- ☐ Print all trace messages
- ☐ Disable data validation statistics collection
- ☑ Enable auditing
- ☐ Enable recovery
- ☐ Recover from last failed execution

- ☑ Collect statistics for optimization
- ☑ Collect statistics for monitoring
- ☐ Use collected statistics
- ☐ Export Data Quality reports

System configuration: [⌄]   Browse...

Job Server or Server Group: JobServer_1 @ IVANSHOMNIKOV:3500 ⌄

Distribution level: Job

OK   Cancel

5. Launch the **Data Services Management Console** and log into it.

6. On the **Home** page, click on the **Data Validation** link to start the **Data Validation** dashboard web application:

7. Experiment and hover your mouse over the pie chart to see the detailed information about passed and failed records for your validation rule.

8. Click on a specific area in the pie chart to drill down into another bar chart report showing validation rules. As we only have one validation rule defined in our **Validation** transform and in all repository, there is only one bar displayed for the City_not_Paris validation rule.

How it works...

The options **Collect Data Validation Statistics** and **Collect sample data** enable Data Services to collect execution statistics for specific Validation transform rules. In our case, we defined one, so there is not much diversity in the presented dashboard reports that you can see in the **Data Services Management Console**.

Here is the pie chart you see after implementing steps 7-8 of this recipe:

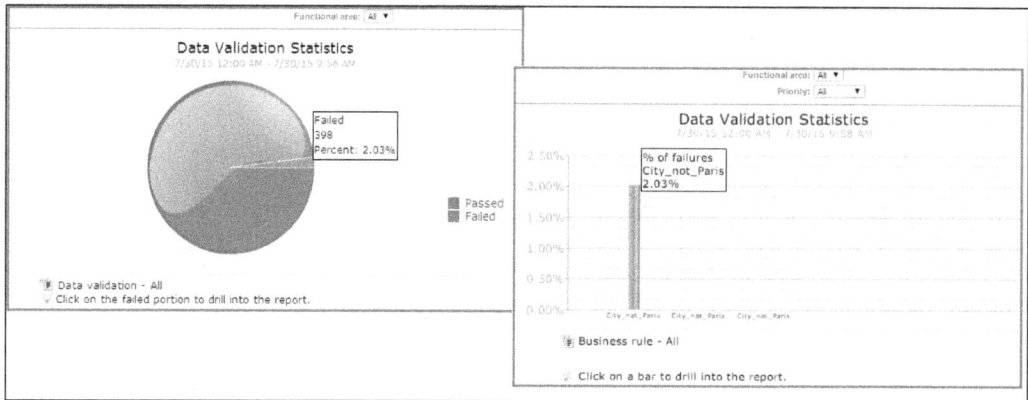

By clicking on the object in the bar chart, you can drill down to the actual data sample of the failed rows collected by the Validation transform during job execution.

The information presented in these dashboard reports is a very useful graphical representation of the quality of the data which passes through dataflow objects and gets validated. You can easily see what percentage of data does not pass the validation rules, the comparison of validation statistics between different periods of time, and even the actual rows that did not pass the specific validation rule without running SQL queries on your database tables, or using any other application except **Data Services Management Console**.

Using regular expression support to validate data

In this recipe, we will see how you can use regular expressions to validate your data. We will take a simple example of validating phone numbers extracted from the source OLTP table PERSONPHONE located in the PERSON schema. The validation rule would be to identify all records which have phone numbers different from this pattern: *ddd-ddd-dddd* (*d* being a numeral). Let's say that we do not want to reject any data. Our goal is to generate a dashboard report showing the percentage of records in the source table which do not comply with the specified requirement for the phone number pattern.

Getting ready

Make sure that you have the PERSON.PERSONPHONE table imported into the OLTP datastore. We will create a new job and new dataflow, DF_Extract_PersonPhone, which will be migrating PersonPhone records from OLTP to a STAGE database, at the same time as validating them.

How to do it...

1. Create a new job with a new dataflow, DF_Extract_PersonPhone, designed as a standard extract dataflow with a deployed Validation transform, as shown in the following figure:

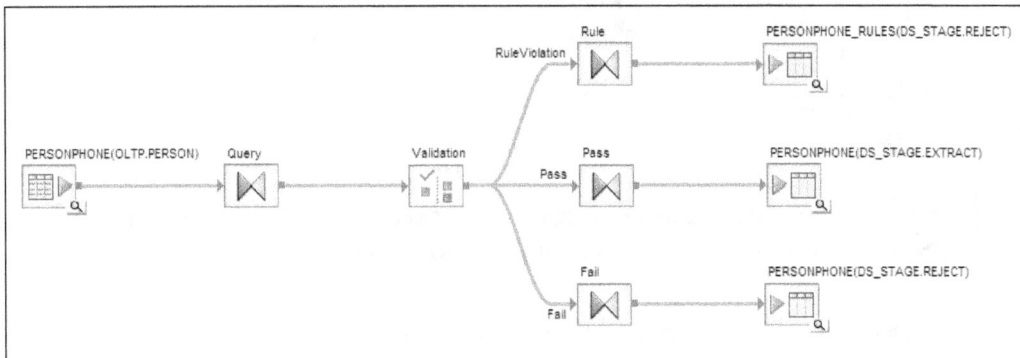

2. You should also create target tables for the RuleViolation and Fail output schemas in the Reject schema of the STAGE database.

3. To configure the validation rule, open the Validation transform for editing in the main workspace. Use **Column Validation** instead of **Validation Function** and put the following custom condition into Query.PHONENUMBER:

```
match_regex(Query.PHONENUMBER,'^\d{3}-\d{3}-\d{4}$',NULL) =
    1
```

The validation rule configuration should look like in the following screenshot:

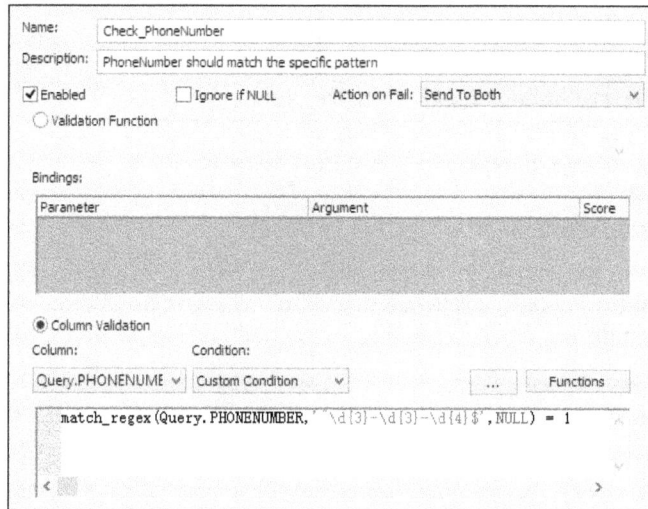

4. Click on **OK** to create and save the validation rule.

5. Now go to the second tab, **Validation Transform Options**, and check all three options: **Collect data validation statistics**, **Collect sample data**, and **Create column DI_ROWID on Validation_Fail**.

6. Your Validation transform should look like this now:

7. Save and execute the job to extract the records into the staging table and collect the validation data for the dashboard report.

How it works...

Regular expressions are a powerful way to validate the data passing through. The `match_regex()` function used in this recipe returns `1` if the value in the input column matches the pattern specified as the second input parameter.

Data Services supports standard POSIX regular expressions. See the *match_regex* section (section *6.3.96*) in *Chapter 6, Functions and Procedures*, of the *Data Services 4.2 Reference Guide* for full syntax and regular expression support details.

Note that in this recipe, we did not reject the records which failed the validation rule. As our goal was to simply evaluate the number of records which do not comply with the phone number standard, both failed and passed records were forwarded to the target main staging table.

Let's see how the dashboard validation report for our job execution looks:

1. Launch the **Data Services Management Console** and log in into it.

2. Open the **Data Validation** application on the main **Home** page.

3. By default, Data Services shows the data validation statistics for all functional areas for the current date (starting from midnight).

4. Hover your mouse pointer and click on the failed red section of the pie chart to see the following details: the percentage and number of rows which did not pass the validation rule.

5. If you did not run any jobs gathering validation statistics today, the pie chart for `DF_Extract_PersonPhone` created and executed in this recipe shows that 9,188 records (46%) in the `PERSONPHONE` table have a phone number in a pattern different from *ddd-ddd-dddd,* and 10,784 records (54%) have phone numbers matching this pattern.

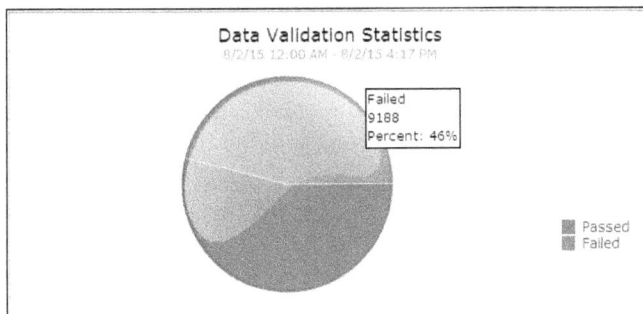

Enabling dataflow audit

Auditing in Data Services allows the collection of additional information about the data migrated from the source to the target by a specific dataflow on which the audit is enabled, and even allows making decisions according to the rules applied on the audit data. In this recipe, we will see how audit can be enabled and utilized during the extraction of data from the source system.

Getting ready

For this recipe, you can use the dataflow `DF_Extract_Address` from the previous recipes of this chapter.

How to do it...

Perform the following steps to enable the auditing for the specific dataflow.

1. Open `DF_Extract_Address` in the workspace window and select **Tools | Audit** from the top-level menu.

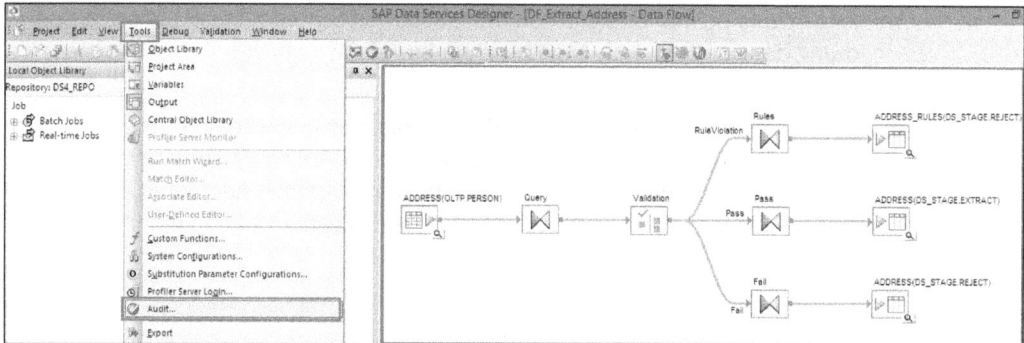

2. In the newly opened window, select the **Label** tab, right-click in the empty space, and choose **Show All Objects** from the context menu.

3. The **Label** tab displays the list of objects from within a dataflow. Enable auditing on the **Query** and **Pass** Query transform objects by right-clicking on them and selecting the **Count** option from the context menu.

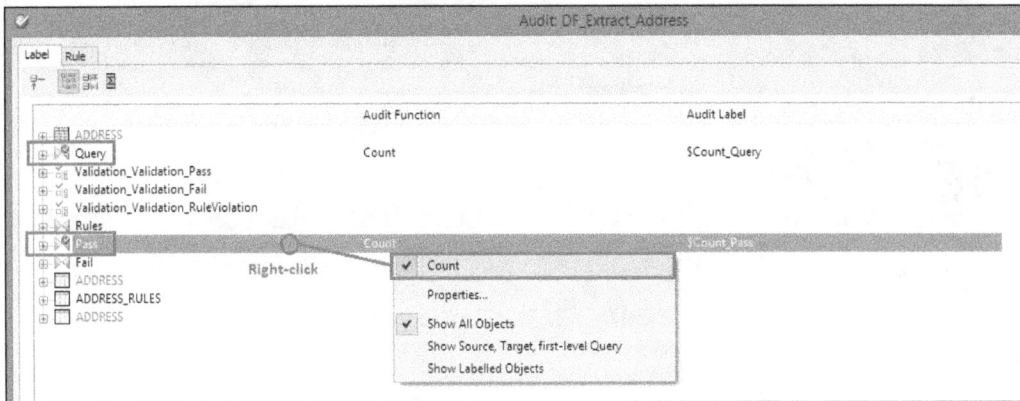

4. Another way to enable auditing on specific objects from within a dataflow is to right-click on it and select the **Properties** option from the context menu.

5. Then, go to the **Audit** tab in the newly open **Schema Properties** window and select the respective audit function from the combobox menu. In our case, both audit points were enabled for Query transforms, and the only audit option available in this case is **Count**.

6. Data Services creates two variables which are used to store the audit value. For the **Pass** Query transform, two variables were created by default: $Count_Pass, to store the number of successfully passed records, and $CountError_Pass to store the number of incorrect or rejected records.

7. Let's change the default audit variable names for the Query object by opening its properties and selecting the **Audit** tab on the **Schema Properties** window.

8. Specify the audit variable names to be $Count\_Extract$ and $CountError\_Extract$. Then, close the window by clicking on the **OK** button.

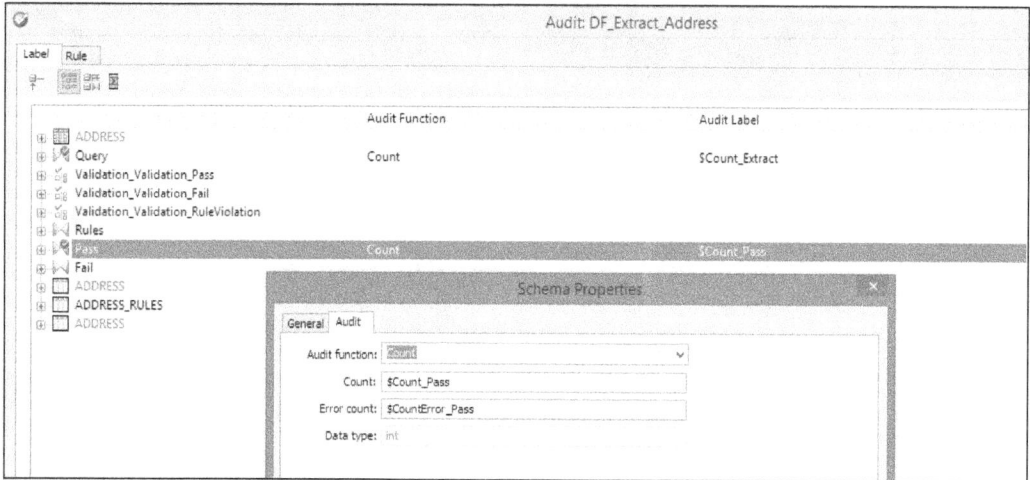

9. Now, close the **Audit: DF_Extract_Address** window by clicking on the **Close** button.

10. If you take a look at the dataflow objects in the workspace window, you can see that the created audit points were marked with small green icons. To access the dataflow audit configuration, you also can just click on the **Audit** button in the tools menu.

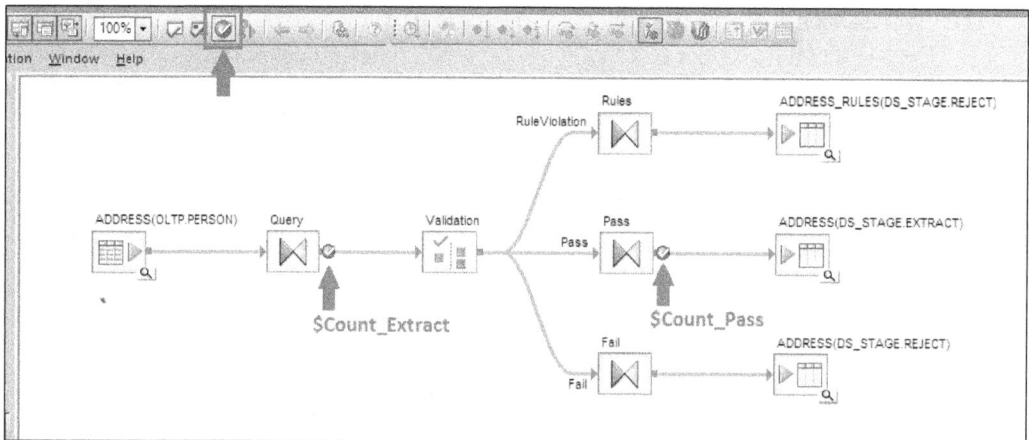

How it works...

At this point, you have configured the audit collection for rows passing two Query objects in the `DF_Extract_Address` dataflow. Auditing, if enabled at the object level, allows only single-audit function usage: count audit function. This audit function simply keeps track of the number of records passing the specific object inside the dataflow.

Auditing can also be enabled on the column level inside the object which resides inside the dataflow, usually on the columns in the Query transforms. In that case, three additional audit functions are available—`Sum`, `Average`, and `Checksum`—if the column is of numeric data type and only `Checksum` is available if the column is of the `varchar` data type. As you might have guessed, these functions allow you to store either the summary or the average of values in the specific columns for all passing records or calculate the checksum.

As you can see, the collected audit data can later be accessed from the **Operational Dashboard** tab in the **Data Services Management Console**. However, the most useful purpose of the *audit* feature is the ability to define the rules on the collected audit data and perform the actions depending on the result of the audit rule implemented.

Here are the steps showing you how to implement the rule on collected audit data:

1. Open `DF_Extract_Address` in the workspace and click on the **Audit** button to open the **Audit** configuration window for this dataflow.

2. Go to the **Rule** tab.

3. Click on the **Add** button to add a new audit rule.

4. Choose the **Custom** option to define a custom audit rule.

5. Input the custom function shown in the following screenshot:

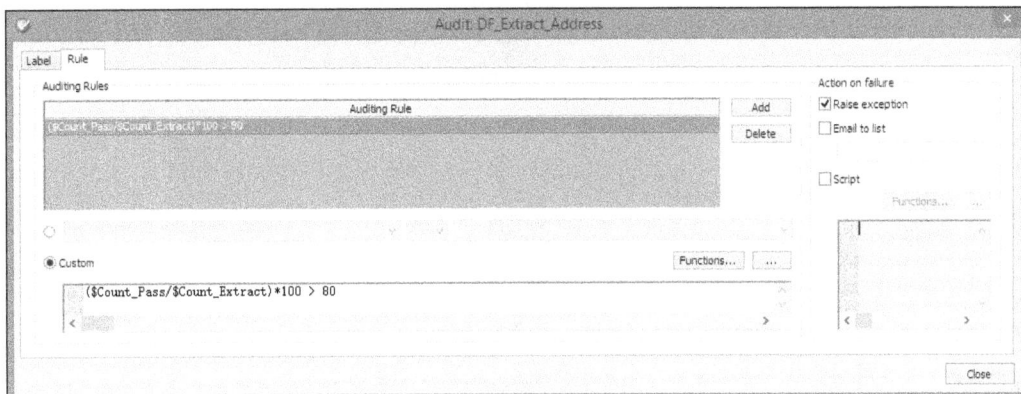

6. Check the option **Raise exception** in the **Action on failure** section. Other options are **Email to list** and **Script**.

   ❑ The **Email to list** option allows you to send notifications about rule violations to specific email recipients. Note that to use this functionality, you have to specify SMTP server details in your Data Services configuration.

   ❑ The **Script** option allows you to execute scripts written in a standard Data Services scripting language.

7. The rule that we specified is applied at the very end of the dataflow execution and checks that the percentage of rows which passed the validation rule taken from the total amount of rows extracted from the source table is higher than 80 percent. Remember that our validation rule checks and rejects all `Paris` records. We know that the number of records with a city value equal to `Paris` is significantly less than 20 percent of the rows, which should be rejected during validation to fail the defined audit rule. So, if you run your dataflow now, nothing will happen; the audit rule will not be violated and the job will be successfully completed. To make the audit rule fail, let's change our validation function to reject all records with a city value not equal to `Paris`, as shown in the following screenshot:

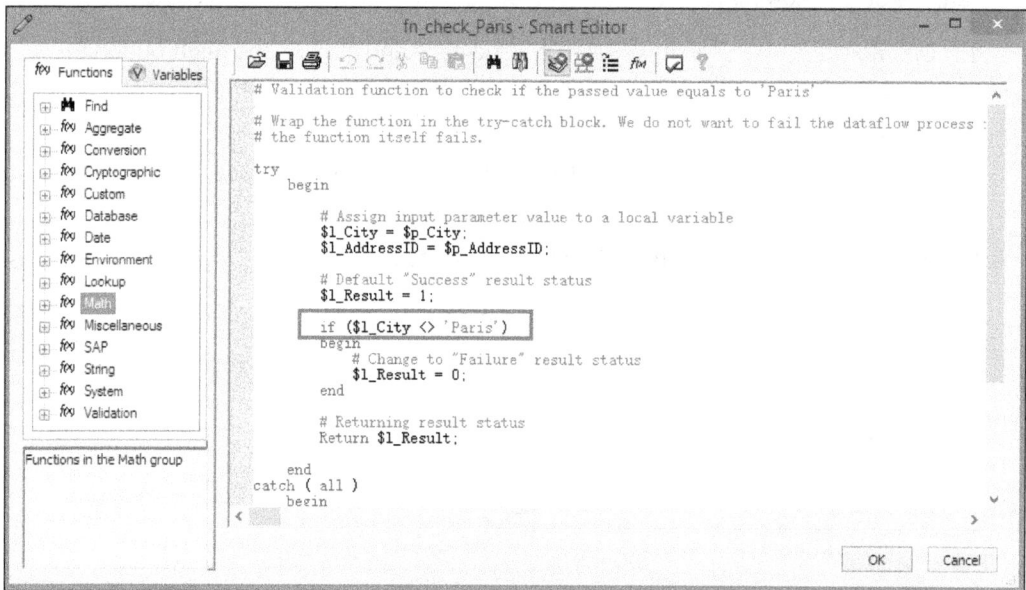

8. As the final step for utilizing audit functionality on the job's **Execution Properties** window, you should check the **Enable auditing** option. If this is not checked, audit data will not be collected and audit rules will not work.

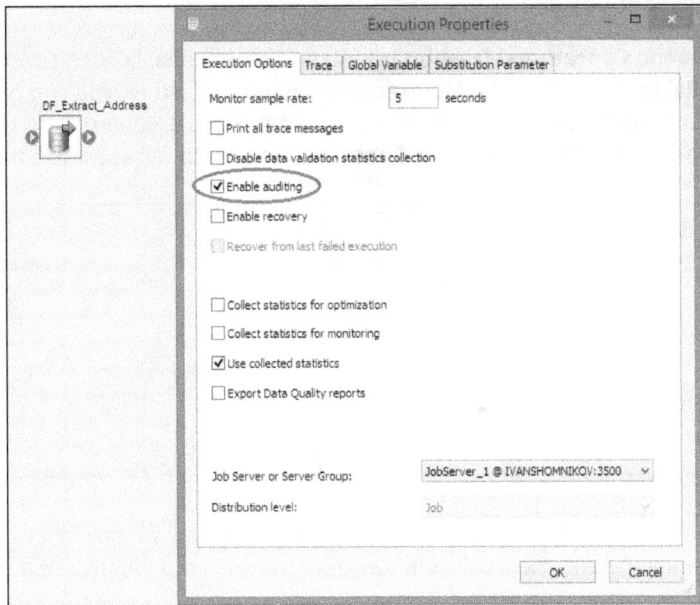

9. Save and execute the job. Dataflow execution fails and relevant information is displayed in the error log, as shown here:

Remember that although the dataflow `DF_Extract_Address` fails, the audit rule check happens after it completes all the previous steps and the data is successfully inserted into all targets.

There's more...

Collected audit numbers can be accessed via the **Operational Dashboard** tab from the **Data Services Management Console**.

To access it, open the **Operational Dashboard** tab and select specific jobs to open **Job Execution Details**. By clicking on the job execution instances further, you can open a **Job Details** view, which will contain information about all dataflows executed within a job. If the dataflow has audit enabled for it columns, **Contains Audit Data** will show you that.

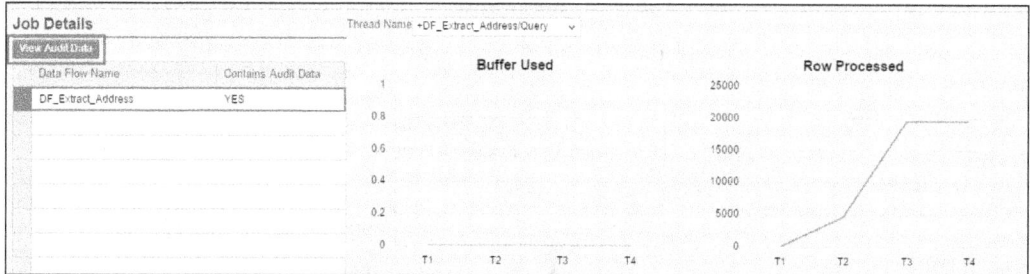

By clicking on the **View Audit Data** button, you can open the new window showing values collected during auditing and the audit rule result for the selected job instance execution.

Data Quality transforms – cleansing your data

Data Quality transforms are available in the **Data Quality** section of the **Local Object Library Transforms** tab. These transforms help you to build a cleansing solution for your migrated data.

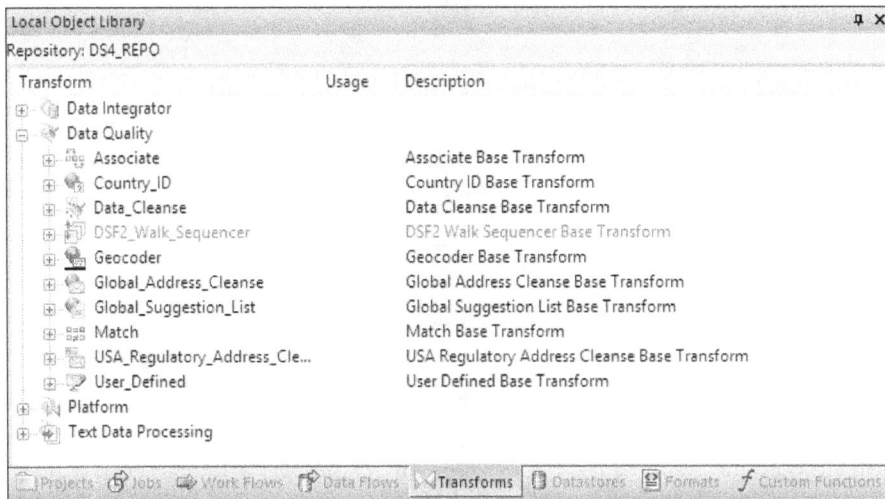

Local Object Library			📌 ✕
Repository: DS4_REPO			
Transform	**Usage**	**Description**	
⊞ 🗗 Data Integrator			
⊟ ☀ Data Quality			
⊞ 🔤 Associate		Associate Base Transform	
⊞ 🌐 Country_ID		Country ID Base Transform	
⊞ 🗗 Data_Cleanse		Data Cleanse Base Transform	
⊞ 📑 DSF2_Walk_Sequencer		DSF2 Walk Sequencer Base Transform	
⊞ 🌐 Geocoder		Geocoder Base Transform	
⊞ 🌐 Global_Address_Cleanse		Global Address Cleanse Base Transform	
⊞ 🌐 Global_Suggestion_List		Global Suggestion List Base Transform	
⊞ 🔢 Match		Match Base Transform	
⊞ 🗗 USA_Regulatory_Address_Cle...		USA Regulatory Address Cleanse Base Transform	
⊞ 🗗 User_Defined		User Defined Base Transform	
⊞ 🗗 Platform			
⊞ 🗗 Text Data Processing			

📄 Projects 🗗 Jobs 🗗 Work Flows 🗗 Data Flows ⬡ Transforms 🗗 Datastores 🔱 Formats 𝑓 Custom Functions

The subject of implementing Data Quality solutions in ETL processes is so vast that it probably requires a whole chapter, or even a whole book, dedicated to it. That is why we will just scratch the surface in this recipe by showing you how to use the most popular of Data Quality transforms, **Data_Cleanse**, to perform the simplest data cleansing task.

Getting ready

To build a data cleansing process, it would be ideal if we had source data which required cleansing. Unfortunately, our OLTP data source, and especially DWH data source, already contain pretty conformed and clean data. Therefore, we are going to create dirty data by concatenating multiple fields together to see how Data Services cleansing packages will automatically parse and cleanse the data out of the concatenated text field.

As a preparation step, make sure that you have imported these three tables in your OLTP datastore: PERSON, PERSONPHONE, and EMAILADDRESS (all of them are from the PERSON schema of the SQL Server's AdventureWorks_OLTP database).

How to do it...

1. As the first step, create a new job with a new dataflow object in it. Name the dataflow `DF_Cleanse_Person_Details`.

2. Import three tables—`PERSON`, `PERSONPHONE`, and `EMAILADDRESS`—from the OLTP datastore as a source table inside the dataflow.

3. Join these tables using the Query transform with the join conditions, as shown in the following screenshot:

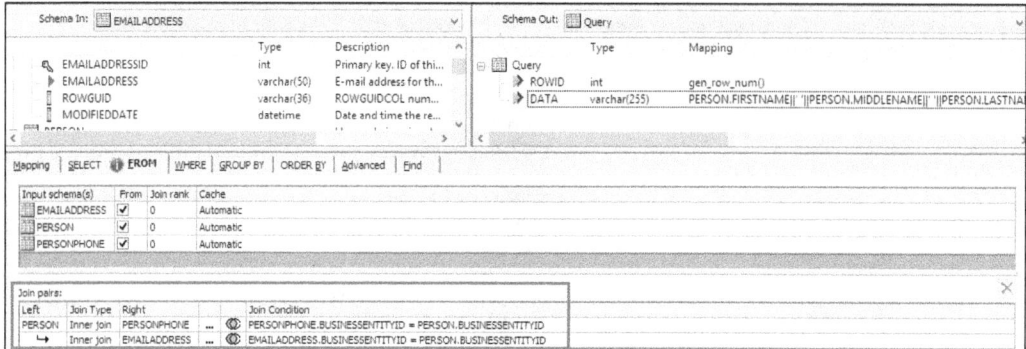

4. In the output schema of the Query transform, create two columns: `ROWID` of the data type integer, with the following function as a mapping: `gen_row_num()`, and `DATA` column of the data type `varchar(255)`, with the following mapping:

```
PERSON.FIRSTNAME||' '||PERSON.MIDDLENAME||'
    '||PERSON.LASTNAME||' '||PERSONPHONE.PHONENUMBER||'
    '||EMAILADDRESS.EMAILADDRESS
```

5. Now, when we have prepared the source field that we will be cleansing, let's import and configure the **Data_Cleanse** transforms themselves. Drag and drop the **Data_Cleanse** transform objects from **Local Object Library | Transforms | Data Quality** to your dataflow. Please refer to the following steps as each **Data_Cleanse** transform object will be imported and configured differently.

6. The first **Data_Cleanse** object will be parsing our **DATA** column to extract the email address of the person. When importing the transform object into the dataflow, choose the **Base_DataCleanse** configuration.

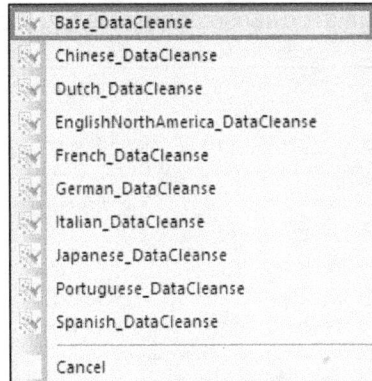

Base_DataCleanse
Chinese_DataCleanse
Dutch_DataCleanse
EnglishNorthAmerica_DataCleanse
French_DataCleanse
German_DataCleanse
Italian_DataCleanse
Japanese_DataCleanse
Portuguese_DataCleanse
Spanish_DataCleanse
Cancel

7. Rename the imported **Data_Cleanse** transform to `Email_DataCleanse` and join the Query transform output to it.

8. Open the **Email_DataCleanse** transform editor in the workspace to configure it.

9. On the **Input** tab, select **EMAIL1** in the **Transform Input Field Name** column and map it to the `DATA` source field.

10. On the **Options** tab, choose **PERSON_FIRM** as a cleansing package name and configure the rest of the options, as shown in the following screenshot:

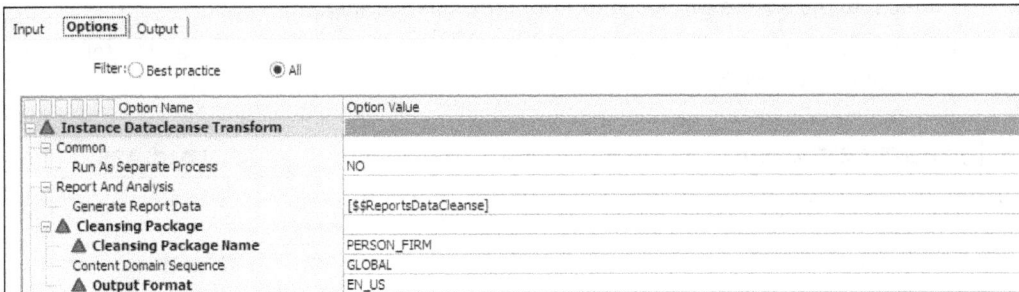

Input [Options] Output	
Filter: ○ Best practice ● All	
Option Name	Option Value
⊟ ▲ **Instance Datacleanse Transform**	
⊟ Common	
Run As Separate Process	NO
⊟ Report And Analysis	
Generate Report Data	[$$ReportsDataCleanse]
⊟ ▲ **Cleansing Package**	
▲ **Cleansing Package Name**	PERSON_FIRM
Content Domain Sequence	GLOBAL
▲ **Output Format**	EN_US

11. On the **Output** tab, select the EMAIL field (of the PARSED field class related to the EMAIL1 parent component) to be produced by the **Email_DataCleanse** transform. That will create the EMAIL1_EMAIL_PARSED column in the output schema of the **Email_DataCleanse** transform. Propagate the source RO0057ID column as well, which will be used to join the cleansed data sets together in the later steps.

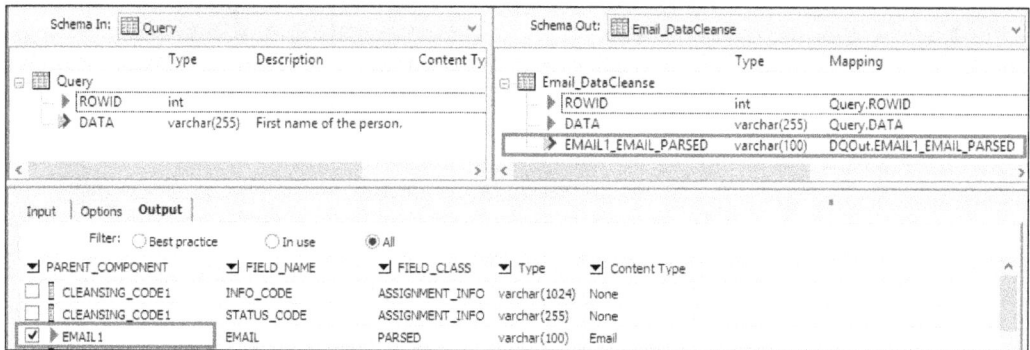

12. Close the **Email_DataCleanse** editor and import the second **Data_Cleanse** transform with the same **Base_DataCleanse** configuration. Rename the imported transform object to Phone_DataCleanse, join it to the Query transform output, and open it in the main workspace for editing.

13. Select the same transform options on the **Options** tab as for the **Email_DataCleanse** transform example we just saw.

14. Choose PHONE1 as the input parsing component (**Transform Input Field Name**) and map it to the source DATA column from the Query transform output.

15. On the **Output** tab of the **Phone_DataCleanse** transform editor, choose the following output fields from the list:

PARENT_COMPONENT	FIELD_NAME	FIELD_CLASS
NORTH_AMERICAN_ PHONE1	NORTH_AMERICAN_PHONE	PARSED
NORTH_AMERICAN_ PHONE1	NORTH_AMERICAN_PHONE_EX- TENSION	PARSED
NORTH_AMERICAN_ PHONE1	NORTH_AMERICAN_PHONE_LINE	PARSED
NORTH_AMERICAN_ PHONE1	NORTH_AMERICAN_PHONE_PRE- FIX	PARSED
PHONE1	PHONE	PARSED

16. Also propagate two source fields, ROWID and DATA, into the output schema of the **Phone_DataCleanse** transform. Close it to finish editing.

17. When importing the third **Data_Cleanse** transform, select the predefined EnglishNorthAmerica_DataCleanse configuration and rename the transform to Name_DataCleanse.

18. Open the transform in the workspace for editing. You do not have to configure anything on the **Options** tab this time. So, select the component **NAME_LINE1** on the **Input** tab and the following fields on the **Output** tab:

PARENT_COMPONENT	FIELD_NAME	FIELD_CLASS
PERSON1	FAMILY_NAME1	PARSED
PERSON1	GENDER	STANDARDIZED
PERSON1	GIVEN_NAME1	PARSED
PERSON1	GIVEN_NAME2	PARSED
PERSON1	PERSON	PARSED

19. Close the **Name_DataCleanse** transform editor and join all three **Data_Cleanse** outputs with a single Join Query transform. Use the ROWID column to join the datasets together and remap the default **Data_Cleanse** output names to more meaningful names, as shown in the following screenshot:

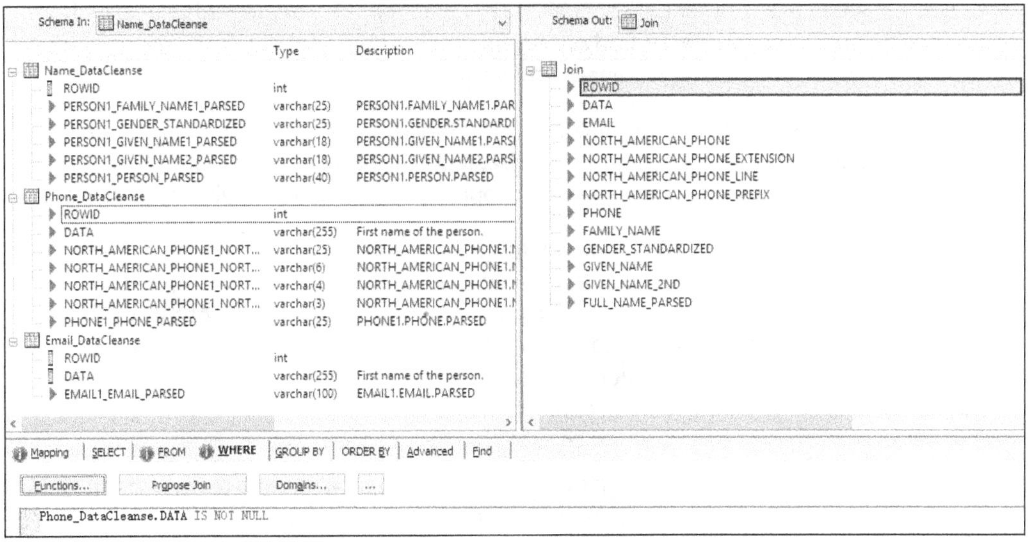

20. Specify `Phone_DataCleanse.DATA IS NOT NULL` as a join filter in the `Join` Query transform to exclude the empty records from the migration.

21. Import the target template table `CLEANSE_RESULT` stored in the `STAGE` datastore to save the cleansing results in.

22. Finally, your dataflow should look like this:

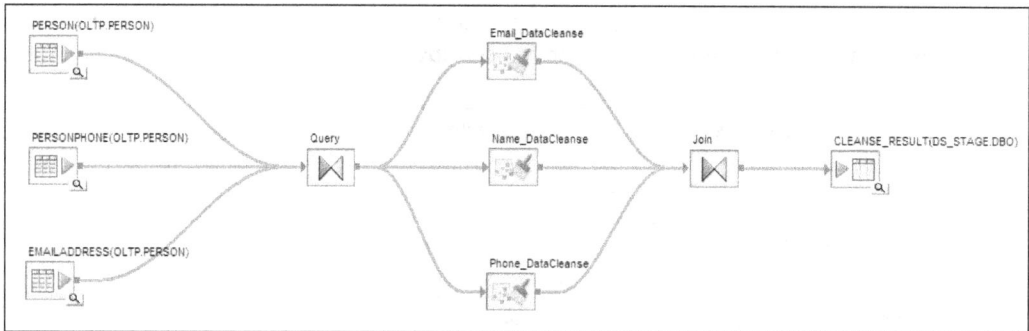

23. Save and execute the job to see the cleansing results in the `CLEANSE_RESULT` table.

How it works...

In the first few steps of the preceding sequence, by concatenation of the multiple fields from the source OLTP database, we prepared our "dirty" data column, `DATA`, which was used as a source column for all three **Data_Cleanse** transforms.

When importing the **Data_Cleanse** transform, Data Services offers you the option to choose from one of the predefined configurations. The **Base_DataCleanse** configuration requires you to configure the mandatory options manually or your imported transform object will not work.

The **Data_Cleanse** transform is a mere mapping tool to map your input columns to the required parsing rules and desired output. Parsing rules and reference data are defined in the cleansing package, which could be developed and configured by the **Information Steward Cleansing Package Builder** tool. This tool provides a graphical user interface for this task. In this recipe, we are using the default cleansing package `PERSON_FIRM` available in Data Services without the need to have Information Steward installed.

> The default `PERSON_FIRM` cleansing package allows you to parse and standardize dates, emails, firm data, person names, social security numbers, and phone numbers.

The **Input** tab allows you to choose the type of component you would like to parse from the input data set. Please note that you cannot specify the same field as a source of data for multiple components. That is why we have to create three distinct **Data_Cleanse** transform objects to parse the same DATA column for email, person name, and phone data. Each has its own configuration and mappings from input components to a desired set of output fields.

The set of fields available on the **Output** tab depend on which component you have chosen to be recognized and parsed on the **Input** tab, but it basically includes all possible information that can be extracted for a selected component. For example, if it is a Person name component, output data cleanse fields include given name, second given name, last name, gender, and similar others.

Propagation of an artificial ROWID column allows us to join the split datasets together after they are processed by **Data_Cleanse** transforms.

To view the result data use the **View data** option on the target table object in the dataflow or open **SQL Server Management Studio** and run the following query to see the parsed results:

```
select DATA,EMAIL,PHONE,GIVEN_NAME,GIVEN_NAME_2ND,FAMILY_NAME,
   GENDER_STANDARDIZED
from dbo.CLEANSE_RESULT
```

As you can see in the following screenshot, **Data_Cleanse** transforms did a pretty good job of parsing the input DATA field:

An interesting result is stored in the GENDER_STANDARDIZED column. Based on the parsing rules and reference data available, Data Services suggests how accurate the determination of gender could be based solely on the available given and last names.

There's more...

As mentioned before, Data Services has great Data Quality capabilities. This is a huge topic for discussion, and we've just scratched the surface by showing you one transform from this toolset. This powerful functionality works best when Data Services is integrated with Information Steward. You can build your own cleansing packages to parse the migrated data more efficiently and accurately. Please refer to *Chapter 12, Introduction to Information Steward*, for more details.

8
Optimizing ETL Performance

If you tried all the previous recipes from the book, you can consider yourself familiar with the basic design techniques available in Data Services and can perform pretty much any ETL development task. Starting from this chapter, we will begin using advance development techniques available in Data Services. This particular chapter will help you to understand how the existing ETL processes can be optimized further to make sure that they run quickly and efficiently, consuming as less computer resources as possible with the least amount of execution time.

- ▶ Optimizing dataflow execution – push-down techniques
- ▶ Optimizing dataflow execution – the SQL transform
- ▶ Optimizing dataflow execution – the Data_Transfer transform
- ▶ Optimizing dataflow readers – lookup methods
- ▶ Optimizing dataflow loaders – bulk-loading methods
- ▶ Optimizing dataflow execution – performance options

Introduction

Data Services is a powerful development tool. It supports a lot of different source and target environments, all of which work differently with regard to loading and extracting data from them. This is why it is required of you, as an ETL developer, to be able to apply different design methods, depending on the requirements of your data migration processes and the environment that you are working with.

In this chapter, we will review the methods and techniques that you can use to develop data migration processes in order to perform transformations and migrate data from the source to target more effectively. The techniques described in this chapter are often considered as best practices, but do keep in mind that their usage has to be justified. They allow you to move and transform your data faster, consuming fewer processing resources on the ETL engine's server side.

Optimizing dataflow execution – push-down techniques

The Extract, Transform, and Load sequence can be modified to Extract, Load, and Transform by delegating the power of processing and transforming data to the database itself where the data is being loaded to.

We know that to apply transformation logic to a specific dataset we have to first extract it from the database, then pass it through transform objects, and finally load it back to the database. Data Services can (and most of the time, should, if possible) delegate some transformation logic to the database itself from which it performs the extract. The simplest example is when you are using multiple source tables in your dataflow joined with a single Query transform. Instead of extracting each table's contents separately onto an ETL box by sending multiple `SELECT * FROM <table>` requests, Data Services can send the generated single `SELECT` statement with proper SQL join conditions defined in the Query transform's `FROM` and `WHERE` tabs. As you can probably understand, this can be very efficient: instead of pulling millions of records into the ETL box, you might end up with getting only a few, depending on the nature of your Query joins. Sometimes this process shortens to a complete zero processing on the Data Services side. Then, Data Services does not even have to extract the data to perform transformations. What happens in this scenario is that Data Services simply sends the SQL statement instructions in the form of `INSERT INTO … SELECT` or `UPDATE … FROM` statements to a database when all the transformations are hardcoded in those SQL statements directly.

The scenarios when Data Services delegates the parts of or all the processing logic to the underlying database are called push-down operations.

In this recipe, we will take a look at different kinds of push-down operations, what rules you have to follow to make push-down work from your designed ETL processes, and what prevents push-downs from happening.

Getting ready

As a starting example, let's use the dataflow developed in the *Loading data from table to table – lookups and joins* recipe in *Chapter 4, Dataflow – Extract, Transform, and Load*. Please refer to this recipe to rebuild the dataflow if, for some reason, you do not have it in your local repository any more.

Push-down operations can be of two different types:

- ▶ **Partial push-downs**: A **partial push-down** is when Optimizer sends the SELECT query joining multiple source tables used in a dataflow or sends one SELECT statement to extract data from a particular table with mapping instructions and filtering conditions from the Query transform hardcoded in this SELECT statement.

- ▶ **Full push-downs**: A **full push-down** is when all dataflow logic is reformed by Optimizer in a single SQL statement and sent to the database. The most common statements generated in these cases are complex INSERT/UPDATE and MERGE statements, which include all source tables from the dataflow joined together and transformations in the form of database functions applied to the table columns.

How to do it...

1. To be able to see what SQL queries have been pushed down to the database, open the dataflow in the workspace window and select **Validation | Display Optimized SQL....**

2. The **Optimized SQL** window shows all queries generated by Data Services Optimizer and pushed down to the database level. In the following screenshot, you can see the ELECT query and part of the dataflow logic which this statement represents:

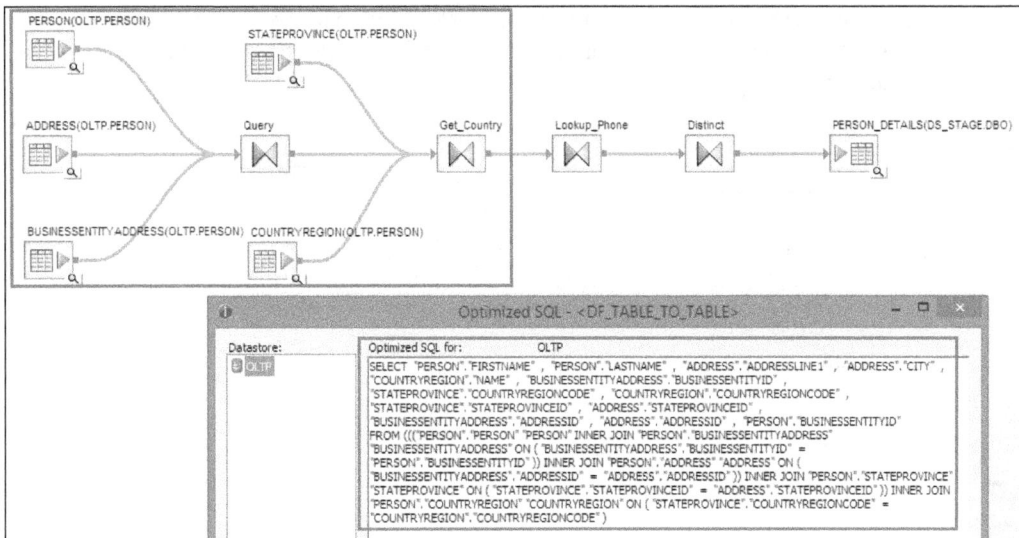

3. Let's try to push down logic from the rest of the Query transforms. Ideally, we would like to perform a full push-down to the database level.

4. The **Lookup_Phone** Query transform contains a function call which extracts the PHONENUMBER column from another table. This logic cannot be included as is because Optimizer cannot translate internal function calls into SQL construction, which could be included in the push-down statement.

5. Let's temporarily remove this function call by specifying a hardcoded NULL value for the PHONENUMBER column. Just delete a function call and create a new output column instead of the varchar(25) data type.

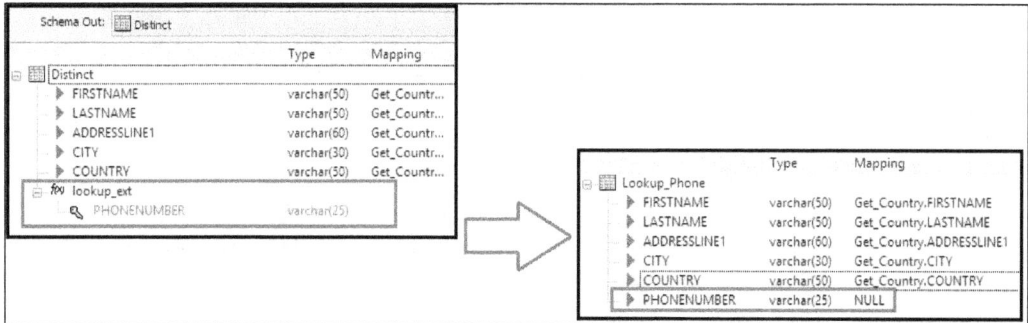

6. Validate and save the dataflow and open the **Optimized SQL** window again to see the result of the changes. Straight away, you can see how logic from both the Lookup_ Phone and Distinct Query transforms were included in the SELECT statement: the default NULL value for a new column and DISTINCT operator at the beginning of the statement:

7. What remains for the full push-down is the loading part when all transformations and selected datasets are inserted into the target table PERSON_DETAILS. The reason why this does not happen in this particular example is because the source tables and target tables reside in different datastores which connect to the different databases: OLTP (AdventureWorks_OLTP) and STAGE.

8. Substitute the PERSON_DETAILS target table from the DS_STAGE datastore with a new template table, PERSON_DETAILS, created in the DBO schema of OLTP.

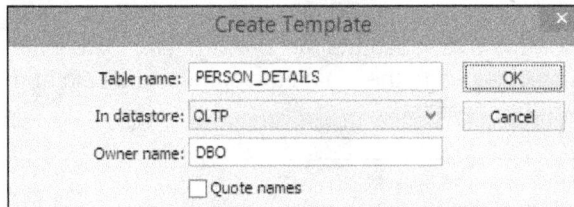

9. As a change, you can see that Optimizer *now* fully transforms dataflow logic into a pushed-down SQL statement.

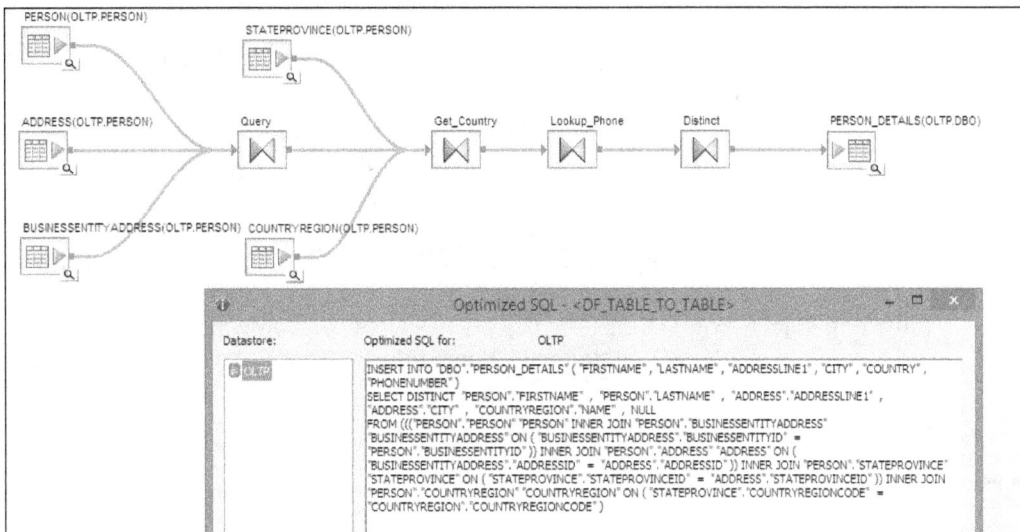

How it works...

Data Services Optimizer wants to perform push-down operations whenever possible. The most common reasons, as we demonstrated during the preceding steps, for push-down operations not working are as follows:

- ▶ **Functions**: When functions used in mappings cannot be converted by Optimizer to similar database functions in generated SQL statements. In our example, the `lookup_ext ()` function prevents push-down from happening. One of the workarounds for this is to substitute the `lookup_ext ()` function with an imported source table object joined to the main data set with the help of the Query transform (see the following screenshot):

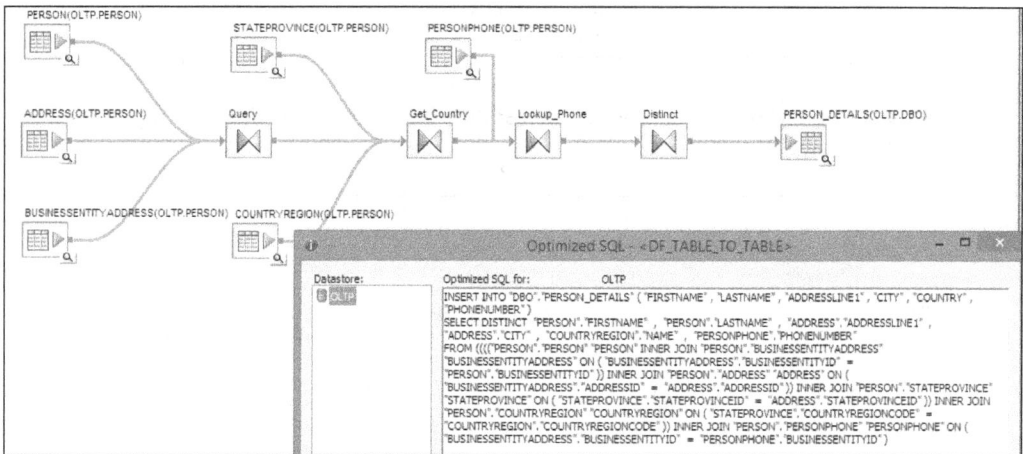

- ▶ **Transform objects**: When transform objects used in a dataflow cannot be converted by Optimizer to relative SQL statements. Some transforms are simply not supported for push-down.

- ▶ **Automatic data type conversions**: These can sometimes prevent push-down from happening.

▶ **Different data sources**: For push-down operations to work for the list of source or target objects, those objects must reside in the same database or must be imported into the same datastore. If they reside in different databases, **dblink** connectivity should be configured on the database level between those databases, and it should be enabled as a configuration option in the datastore object properties. All Data Services can do is send a SQL statement to one database source, so it is logical that if you want to join multiple tables from different databases in a single SQL statement, you have to make sure that connectivity is configured between databases, and then you can run SQL directly on the database level before even starting to develop the ETL code in Data Services.

What is also important to remember is that Data Services Optimizer capabilities depend on the type of underlying database that holds your source and target table objects. Of course, it has to be a database that supports the SQL standard language as Optimizer can send the push-down instructions only in the form of SQL statements.

Sometimes, you actually want to prevent push-downs from happening. This can be the case if:

▶ The database is busy to the extent that it would be quicker to do the processing on the ETL box side. This is a rare scenario, but still sometimes occurs in real life. If this is the case, you can use one of the methods we just discussed to artificially prevent the push-down from happening.

▶ You want to actually make rows go through the ETL box for auditing purposes or to apply special Data Services functions which do not exist at the database level. In these cases, the push-down will automatically be disabled and will not be used by Data Services anyway.

Optimizing dataflow execution – the SQL transform

Simply put, the SQL transform allows you to specify SQL statements directly inside the dataflow to extract source data instead of using imported source table objects. Technically, it has nothing to do with optimizing the performance of ETL as it is not a generally recommended practice to substitute the source table objects with the SQL transform containing hard-coded SELECT SQL statements.

How to do it...

1. Take the dataflow used in the previous recipe and select **Validation | Display Optimized SQL...** to see the query pushed down to the database level. We are going to use this query to configure our SQL transform object, which will substitute all source table objects on the left-hand side of the dataflow.

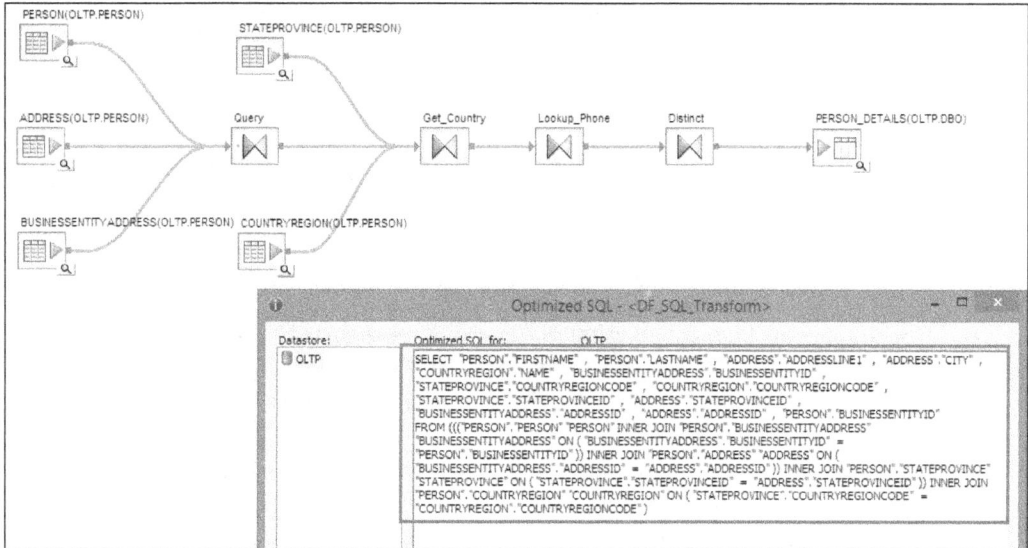

2. On the Optimized SQL window, click on **Save As...** to save this push-down query to the file.

3. Drag-and-drop the SQL transform from **Local Object Library | Transforms | Platform** into your dataflow.

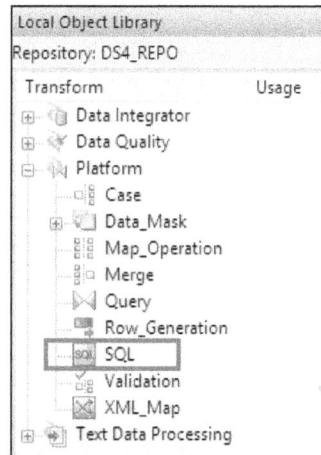

4. Now you can remove all objects on the left-hand side of the dataflow prior to the **Lookup_Phone** Query transform.

5. Open the SQL transform for editing in a workspace window. Choose **OLTP** as a datastore and copy and paste the query saved previously from your file into the **SQL text** field. To complete the SQL transform configuration, create output schema fields of appropriate data types which match the fields returned by the SELECT statement.

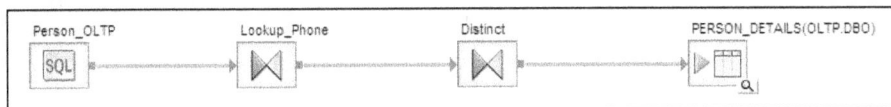

6. Exit the SQL transform editor and link it to the next **Lookup_Phone** Query transform. Open **Lookup_Phone** and map the source columns to target.

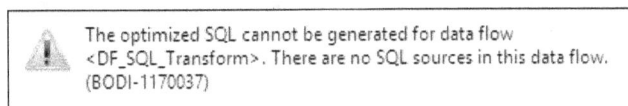

7. Please note that the dataflow does not perform any native push-down queries anymore, and will give you the following warning message if you try to display optimized SQL:

> The optimized SQL cannot be generated for data flow
> <DF_SQL_Transform>. There are no SQL sources in this data flow.
> (BODI-1170037)

8. Validate the job before executing it to make sure there are no errors.

How it works...

As you can see, the structure of the SQL transform is pretty simple. There are not many options available for configuration.

- **Datastore**: This option defines which database connection will be used to pass the SELECT query to

- **Database type**: This option pretty much duplicates the value defined for the specified datastore object

- **Cache**: This option defines whether the dataset returned by the query has to be cached on the ETL box

- **Array fetch size**: This option basically controls the amount of network traffic generated during dataset transfer from database to ETL box

- **Update schema**: This button allows you to quickly build the list of schema output columns from the SQL SELECT statement specified in the SQL text field

The two most common reasons why would you want to use SQL transform instead of defining source table objects are as follows:

- **Simplicity**: Sometimes, you do not care about anything else except getting things done as fast as possible. Sometimes you can get the extract requirements in the form of a SELECT statement, or if you want to use a tested SELECT query in your ETL code straight away.

- **To utilize database functionality which does not exist in Data Services**: This is usually a poor excuse as experienced ETL developers can do pretty much anything with standard Data Services objects. However, some databases can have internal non-standard SQL functions implemented which can perform complex transformations. For example, in Netezza you can have functions written in C++, which can be utilized in standard SQL statements and, most importantly, will be using the massive-parallel processing functionality of the Netezza engine. Of course, Data Services Optimizer is not aware of these functions and the only way to use them is to run direct SELECT SQL statements against the database. If you want to call a SQL statement like this from Data Services, the most convenient way to do it from within a dataflow is to use the SQL transform object inside the dataflow.

- **Performance reasons**: Once in a while, you can get a set of source tables joined to each in a dataflow for which Optimizer—for some reason or other—does not perform a push-down operation. You are very restricted in the ways you can create and utilize database objects in this particular database environment. In such cases, using a hard-coded SELECT SQL statement can help you to maintain an adequate level of ETL performance.

As a general practice, I would recommend that you avoid SQL transforms as much as possible. They can come in handy sometimes, but when using them. you not only lose the advantage of utilizing Data Services, the Information Steward reporting functionality, and ability to perform auditing operations, you also potentially create big problems for yourself in terms of ETL development process. Tables used in the SELECT statements cannot be traced with the **View were used** feature. They can be missing from your datastores, which means you do not have a comprehensive view of your environment and underlying database objects utilized by hiding source database tables inside the ETL code rather than having them on display in **Local Object Library**.

This obviously makes ETL code harder to maintain and support. Not to mention that migration to another database becomes a problem as you would most likely have to rewrite all the queries used in your SQL transforms.

> The **SQL** transform prevents the full push-down from happening, so be careful. Only the SELECT query inside the SQL transform is pushed down to database level. The rest of the dataflow logic will be executed on the ETL box even if the full push-down was working before, when you had source table objects instead of the SQL transform.
>
> In other words, the result data set for the SQL transform always transferred to the ETL box. That can affect the decisions around ETL design. From the performance perspective, it is preferable to spend more time building a dataflow based on the source object tables but for which Data Services performs the full push-down (producing the INSERT INTO ... SELECT statement), rather than quickly building the dataflow which will transfer datasets back and forth to the database, increasing the load time significantly.

Optimizing dataflow execution – the Data_Transfer transform

The transform object **Data_Transfer** is a pure optimization tool helping you to push down resource-consuming operations and transformations like JOIN and GROUP BY to the database level.

Getting ready

1. Take the dataflow from the *Loading data from a flat file* recipe in *Chapter 4, Dataflow – Extract, Transform, and Load*. This dataflow loads the *Friends_*.txt* file into a STAGE.FRIENDS table.

2. Modify the Friends_30052015.txt file and remove all lines except the ones about Jane and Dave.

3. In the dataflow, add another source table, OLTP.PERSON, and join it to a source file object in the Query transform by the first-name field. Propagate the PERSONTYPE and LASTNAME columns from the source OLTP.PERSON table into the output Query transform schema, as shown here:

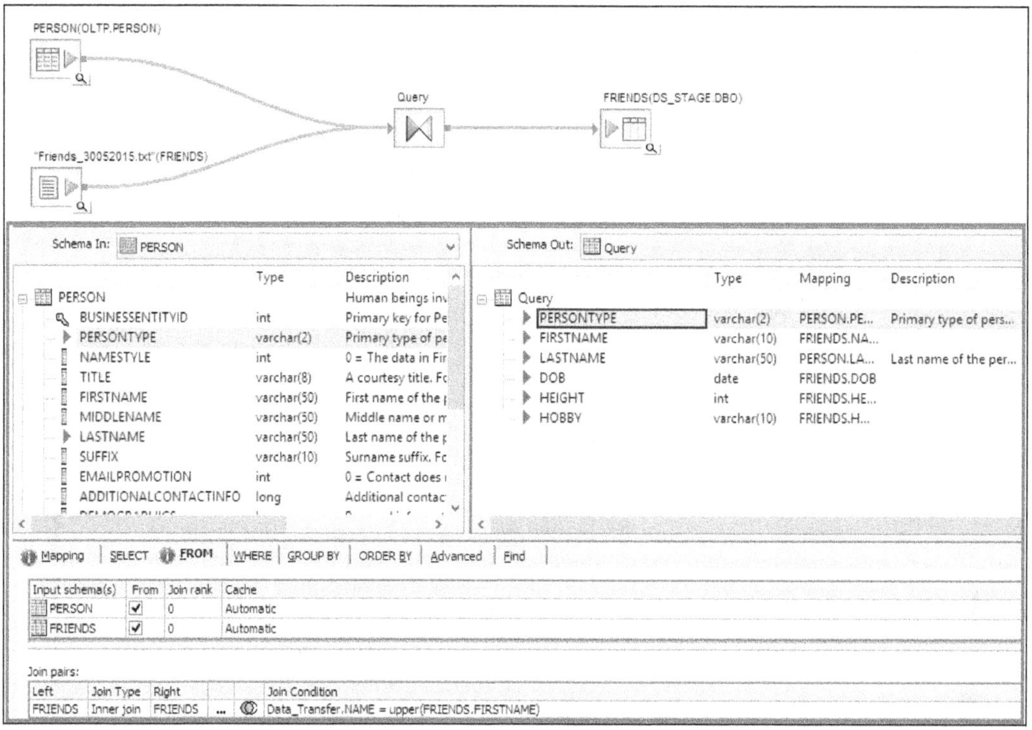

How to do it...

Our goal will be to configure this new dataflow to push down the insert of the joined dataset of data coming from the file and data coming from the OLTP.PERSON table to a database level.

By checking the **Optimized SQL** window, you will see that the only query sent to a database from this dataflow is the SELECT statement pulling all records from the database table OLTP. PERSON to the ETL box, where Data Services will perform an in-memory join of this data with data coming from the file. It's easy to see that this type of processing may be extremely inefficient if the PERSON table has millions of records and the FRIENDS table has only a couple of them. That is why we do not want to pull all records from the PERSON table for the join and want to push down this join to the database level.

Looking at the dataflow, we already know that for the logic to be pushed down, the database should be aware of all the source data sets and should be able to access them by running a single SQL statement. The **Data_Transfer** transform will help us to make sure that the **Friends** file is presented to a database as a table. Follow these steps to see how it can be done:

1. Add the **Data_Transfer** object from **Local Object Library | Transforms | Data Integrator** into your dataflow, putting it between the source file object and the Query transform.

2. Edit the `Data_Transfer` object by opening it in a workspace window. Set **Transfer type** to **Table** and specify the new transfer table in the **Table options** section with `STAGE.DBO.FRIENDS_FILE`.

General	Options	Bulk Loader Options	Pre-Load Commands	Post-Load Commands

✔ Enable transfer

Transfer type: Table

Join rank: 0

File options

Root directory:

File name:

Table options

Table name: DS_STAGE.DBO.FRIENDS_FILE

Database type: Microsoft SQL Server 2012   Array fetch size: 1000

3. Close the **Data Transfer transform** editor and select **Validation | Display Optimized SQL...** to see the queries pushed down to a database. You can see that there are now two SELECT statements generated to pull data from the OLTP.PERSON and STAGE.FRIENDS_FILE tables.

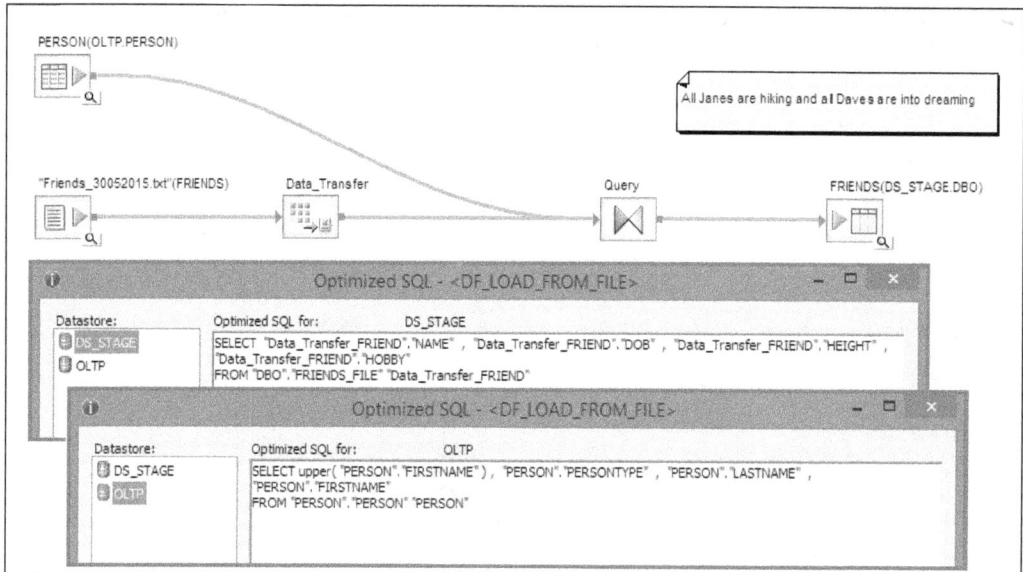

   ❑ The join between these two datasets happens on the ETL box. Then the merged data set is sent back to the database to be inserted into the DS_STAGE.FRIENDS table.

4. Add another **Data_Transfer** transformation between the source table PERSON and the Query transform. In the **Data_Transfer** configuration window, set **Transfer type** to **Table** and specify DS_STAGE.DBO.DT_PERSON as the data transfer table.

5. Validate and save the dataflow and display the **Optimized SQL** window.

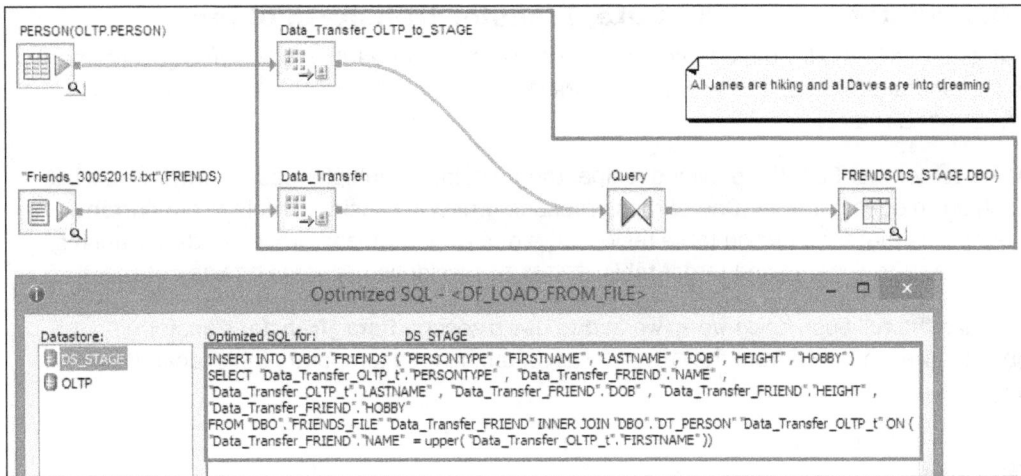

Now you can see that we successfully implemented a **full push-down** of dataflow logic, inserting merged data from two source objects (one of which is a flat file) into a staging table. In the preceding screenshot, logic in the section marked as red is represented by a SQL statement `INSERT` pushed down to the database level.

How it works...

Under the hood, **Data_Transfer** transform creates a subprocess that transfers the data to the specified location (file or table). Simply put, **Data_Transfer** is a target dataflow object in the middle of a dataflow. It has a lot of options similar to what other target table objects have; in other words, you can set up a bulk-loading mechanism, run **Pre-Load Commands** and **Post-Load Commands**, and so on.

The reason why I called **Data_Transfer** a pure optimization tool is because you can redesign any dataflow to do the same thing that **Data_Transfer** does without using it. All you have to do is to simply split your dataflow in two (or three, for the dataflow in our example). Instead of forwarding your data into a **Data_Transfer** transform, you forward it to a normal target object and then, in the next dataflow, you use this object as a source.

> What **Data_Transfer** still does, which cannot be done easily when you are splitting dataflows, is automatically clean up temporary data transfer tables.

It is critical to understand how push-down mechanisms work in Data Services to be able to effectively use the **Data_Transfer** transform. Putting it to use at the wrong place in a dataflow can decrease performance drastically.

Why we used a second Data_Transfer transform object

Our goal was to modify the dataflow in such a way as to get a full push-down SQL statement to be generated: `INSERT INTO STAGE.FRIENDS SELECT <joined PERSON and FRIENDS data sets>`.

As we remember from the previous recipe, there could be multiple reasons why full push-down does not work. One of these reasons, which is causing trouble in our current example, is that the `PERSON` table resides in a different database, while our data transfer table, `FRIENDS_FILE`, and target table, `FRIENDS`, reside in the same `STAGE` database.

To make the full push-down work, we had to use a second **Data_Transfer** transform object to transfer data from the `OLTP.PERSON` table into a temporary table located in a `STAGE` database.

When to use Data_Transfer transform

Whenever you encounter a situation where a dataflow has to perform a very "heavy" transformation (say the `GROUP BY` operation, for example) or join two very big data sets and this operation is happening on an ETL box. In these cases, it is much quicker to transfer the required data sets to the database level so that the resource-intensive operation can be completed there by the database.

There's more...

One of the good examples of a use case for the **Data_Transfer** transform is when you have to perform the `GROUP BY` operation in a Query transform right before inserting data into a target table object. By placing **Data_Transfer** right before the Query transform at the end of the dataflow, you can quickly insert the dataset processed by dataflow logic before the Query transform with the `GROUP BY` operation and then push down the `INSERT` and `GROUP BY` operations in a single SQL statement to a database level.

When you perform the transformations on datasets which include millions of records, using the **Data_Transfer** transform can save you minutes, and sometimes hours, depending on your environment and the number of processed records.

Optimizing dataflow readers – lookup methods

There are different ways in which to perform the lookup of a record from another table in Data Services. The three most popular ones are: a table join with a Query transform, using the `lookup_ext()` function, and using the `sql()` function.

In this recipe, we will take a look at all these methods and discuss how they affect the performance of ETL code execution and their impact on a database used to source data from.

Getting ready

We will be using the same dataflow as in the first recipe, the one which populates the PERSON_DETAILS stage table from multiple OLTP tables.

How to do it...

We will perform a lookup for the PHONENUMBER column of a person from the OLTP table PERSONPHONE in three different ways.

Lookup with the Query transform join

1. Import the lookup table into a datastore and add the table object as a source in the dataflow where you need to perform the lookup.

2. Use the **Query** transform to join your main dataset with the lookup table using the BUSINESSENTITYID reference key column, which resides in both tables.

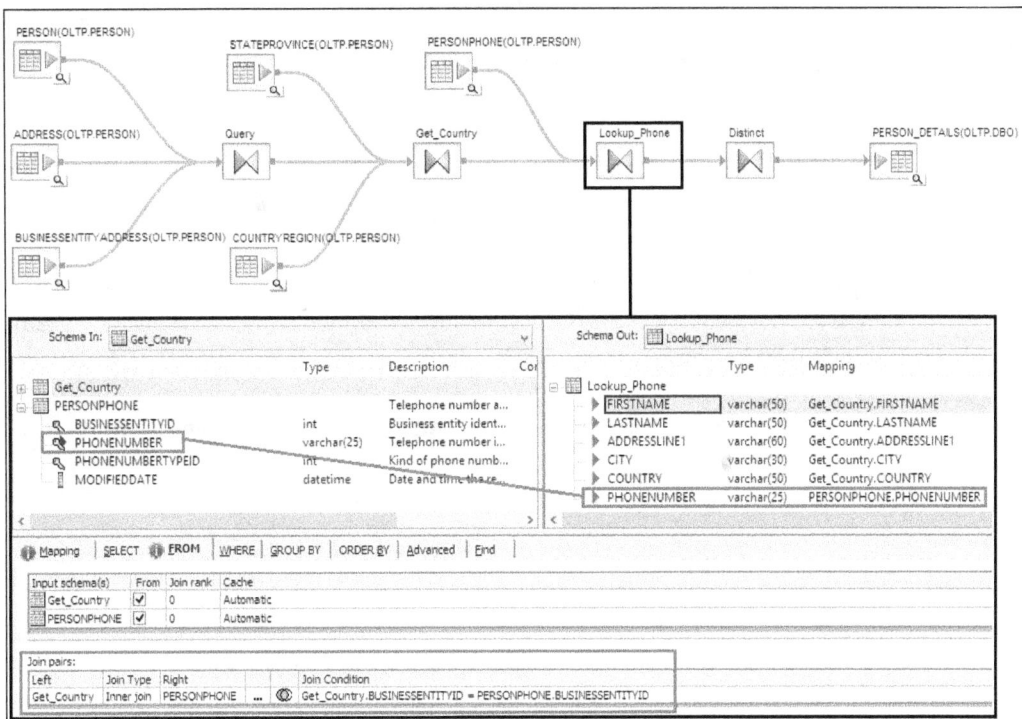

Lookup with the lookup_ext() function

1. Remove the PERSONPHONE source table from your dataflow and clear out the join conditions in the **Lookup_Phone** Query transform.

2. As you have seen in the recipes in previous chapters, the lookup_ext() function can be executed as a function call in the Query transform output columns list. The other option is to call the lookup_ext() function in the column mapping section. For example, say that we want to put an extra condition on when we want to perform a lookup for specific value.

   Instead of creating a new function call for looking up the PHONENUMBER column for all migrated records, let's put in the condition that we want to execute the lookup_ext() function only when the row has nonempty ADDRESSLINE1, CITY, and COUNTRY columns; otherwise, we want to use the default value UNKNOWN LOCATION.

3. Insert the following lines in the **Mapping** section of the PHONENUMBER column inside the **Lookup_Phone** Query transform:

```
ifthenelse(
   (Get_Country.ADDRESSLINE1 IS NULL) OR
   (Get_Country.CITY IS NULL) OR
   (Get_Country.COUNTRY IS NULL), 'UNKNOWN
     LOCATION',
lookup_ext()
)
```

4. Now double-click on the lookup_ext() text to highlight only the lookup_ext function and right-click on the highlighted area for the context menu.

5. From this context menu, select **Modify Function Call** to open the Lookup_ext parameter configuration window. Configure it to perform a lookup for a PHONENUMBER field value from the PERSONPHONE table.

After closing the function configuration window, you can see the full code generated by Data Services for the `lookup_ext()` function in the **Mapping** section.

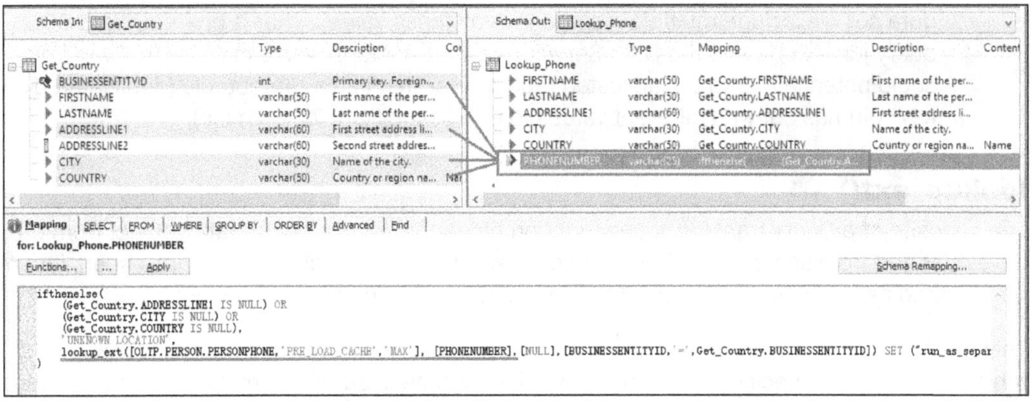

When selecting the output field, you can see all source fields used in its **Mapping** section highlighted in the **Schema In** section on the left-hand side.

Lookup with the sql() function

1. Open the **Lookup_Phone** Query transform for editing in the workspace and clear out all code from the **PHONENUMBER** mapping section.

2. Put the following code in the **Mapping** section:

```
sql('OLTP','select PHONENUMBER from
    Person.PERSONPHONE where BUSINESSENTITYID =
    [Get_Country.BUSINESSENTITYID]')
```

How it works...

Query transform joins

The advantages of this method are:

▶ **Code readability**: It is very clear which source tables are used in transformation when you open the dataflow in a workspace.

▶ **Push-down lookup to the database level**: This can be achieved by including a lookup table in the same SELECT statement. Yes, as soon as you have placed the source table object in the dataflow and joined it properly with other data sources using the Query transform, there is a chance that it will be pushed down as a single SQL SELECT statement, allowing the joining of source tables at the database level.

▶ **DS metadata report functionality and impact analysis**: The main disadvantage of this method comes naturally from its advantage. If a record from the main dataset references multiple records in the lookup table by the key column used, the output data set will include multiple records with all these values. That is how standard SQL query joins work, and the Data Services Query transform works in the same way. This could potentially lead to duplicated records inserted into a target table (duplicated by key columns but with different values in the lookup field, for example).

lookup_ext()

The opposite of a Query transform, this function hides the source lookup table object from the developer and from some of the Data Services reporting functionality. As you have seen, it can be executed as a function call or used in the mapping logic for a specific column.

This function's main advantage is that it will always return a single value from the lookup table. You can even specify the return policy, which will be used to determine the single value to return—MAX or MIN—with the ability to order the lookup table dataset by any column.

sql()

Similar to the `lookup_ext()` function in the presented example, it is rarely used that way as `lookup_ext()` fetches rows from the lookup table more efficiently, if all you want to do is to extract values from the lookup table referencing key columns.

At the same time, the `sql()` function makes possible the implementation of very complex and flexible solutions as it allows you to pass any SQL statement that can be executed on the database side. This can be the execution of stored procedures, the generation of the sequence numbers, running analytical queries, and so on.

As a general rule, though, the usage of the `sql()` function in the dataflow column mappings is not recommended. The main reason for this is performance, as you will see further on. Data Services has a rich set of instruments to perform the same task but with a proper set of objects and ETL code design.

Performance review

Let's quickly review dataflow execution times for each of the explained methods.

▶ **The first method**: The lookup with the **Query** transform took 6.4 seconds.

Path Name	State	Row Count	Elapsed Time (sec)	Absolute Time (sec)
/DF_TABLE_TO_TABLE/Distinct_PERSON_DETAILS	STOP	18798	0.000	6.430
/DF_TABLE_TO_TABLE/Distinct	STOP	18798	0.000	6.410

▶ **The second method**: The lookup with the `lookup_ext ()` function took 6.6 seconds.

Path Name	State	Row Count	Elapsed Time (sec)	Absolute Time (sec)
/DF_TABLE_TO_TABLE/Distinct_PERSON_DETAILS	STOP	18798	0.512	6.650
/DF_TABLE_TO_TABLE/Round_Robin_Split	STOP	18798	0.208	6.612
/DF_TABLE_TO_TABLE/Distinct-Mapping2	STOP	9400	0.209	6.614
/DF_TABLE_TO_TABLE/Distinct	STOP	18798	0.147	6.631
/DF_TABLE_TO_TABLE/Distinct-Mapping3	STOP	9398	0.209	6.624
/DF_TABLE_TO_TABLE/PERSON+BUSINESSENTITYADD...	STOP	18798	0.208	6.611
/DF_TABLE_TO_TABLE/Merge: 0	STOP	18798	0.147	6.627

▶ **The third method**: This used the `sql ()` function and took 73.3 seconds.

Path Name	State	Row Count	Elapsed Time (sec)	Absolute Time (sec)
/DF_TABLE_TO_TABLE/Distinct_PERSON_DETAILS	STOP	18798	1.166	73.349
/DF_TABLE_TO_TABLE/Get_Country	STOP	18798	63.742	73.320
/DF_TABLE_TO_TABLE/Distinct	STOP	18798	65.798	73.326
/DF_TABLE_TO_TABLE/Lookup_Phone	STOP	18798	66.193	73.322

The first two methods look like the methods with similar effectiveness, but that is only because the number of rows and the size of the dataset used is very small. The `lookup_ext ()` function allows the usage of the different cache methods for the lookup dataset, which makes it possible to tune and configure it depending on the nature of your main data and that of the lookup data. It can also be executed as a separate OS process, increasing the effectiveness of fetching the lookup data from the database.

The third figure for the `sql ()` function, on the contrary, shows the perfect example of extremely poor performance when the `sql ()` function is used in the column mappings.

Optimizing dataflow loaders – bulk-loading methods

By default, all records inside a dataflow coming to a target table object are sent as separate `INSERT` commands to a target table at the database level. If millions of records pass the dataflow and transformation happens on the ETL box without push-downs, the performance of sending millions of `INSERT` commands over the network back to a database for insertion could be extremely slow. That is why it is possible to configure the alternative load methods on the target table object inside a dataflow. These types of loads are called **bulk-load** loads. Bulk-load methods are different in nature, but all of them have the main principle and achieve the same goal—they avoid the execution of millions of `INSERT` statements for each migrated record, providing alternative ways of inserting data.

Bulk-load methods executed by Data Services for inserting data into a target table are completely dependent on the type of target database. For example, Oracle Database Data Services can implement bulk-loading through the files or through the Oracle API.

Bulk-loading mechanisms for inserting data into Netezza or Teradata are completely different. You will notice this straightaway if you create different datastores connecting to different types of databases and compare the target table **Bulk Loader Options** tab to the target table object from each of these datastores.

For detailed information about each bulk-load method available for each database, please refer to official SAP documentation.

How to do it...

To see the difference between loading data in normal mode—row by row—and bulk loading, we have to generate quite a significant number of rows. To do this, take the dataflow from a previous recipe, *Optimizing dataflow execution – the SQL transform*, and replicate it to create another copy for using in this recipe. Name it `DF_Bulk_Load`.

Open the dataflow in the workspace window for editing.

1. Add a new **Row_Generation** transform from **Local Object Library | Transforms | Platform** as a source object and configure it to generate 50 rows, starting with row number 1.

2. The **Row_Generation** transform is used to multiply the number of rows currently being transformed by the dataflow logic. Previously, the number of rows returned by the `Person_OLTP` SQL transform was approximately 19,000. By performing a Cartesian join of these records to 50 artificially generated records, we can get almost 1 million records inserted in a target `PERSON_DETAILS` table. To implement Cartesian join, use the Query transform but without specifying any join conditions and leaving the section empty.

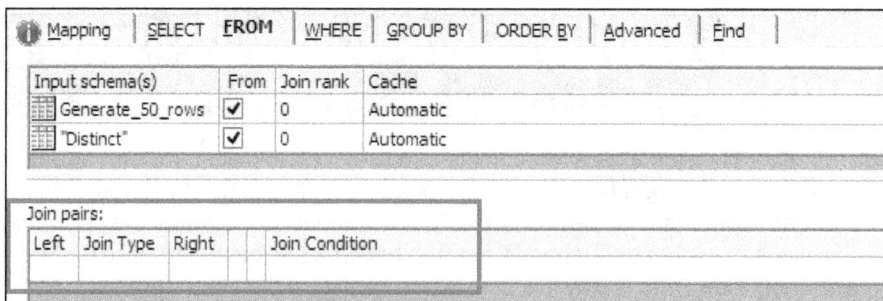

Mapping	SELECT	FROM	WHERE	GROUP BY	ORDER BY	Advanced	Find

Input schema(s)	From	Join rank	Cache
Generate_50_rows	✔	0	Automatic
"Distinct"	✔	0	Automatic

Join pairs:

Left	Join Type	Right		Join Condition

3. Your dataflow should look like this:

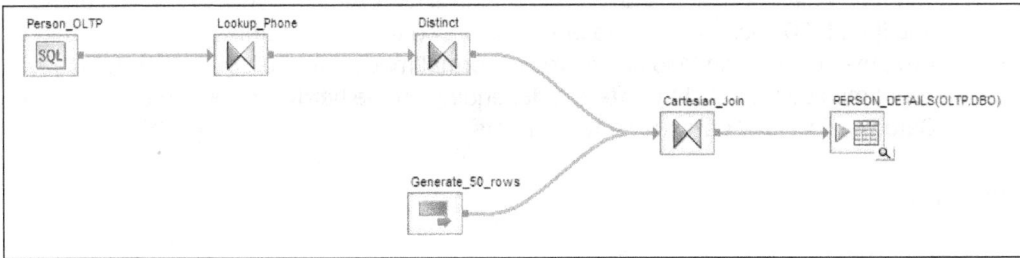

4. To test the current dataflow execution time, save and run the job, which includes this dataflow. Your target table's **Bulk Loader Option** tab should be disabled, and on the **Options** tab, the **Delete data from table before loading** flag should be selected.

5. The execution time of the dataflow is 49 seconds, and as you can see, it took 42 seconds for Data Services to insert 9,39,900 records into the target table.

Path Name	State	Row Count	Elapsed Time (sec)	Absolute Time (sec)
/DF_SQL_Transform/Round_Robin_Split	STOP	50	0.000	48.956
/DF_SQL_Transform/CacheSplit	STOP	18798	0.014	48.975
/DF_SQL_Transform/Round_Robin_Split[1]	STOP	18798	0.581	48.960
/DF_SQL_Transform/Distinct	STOP	18798	0.383	48.973
/DF_SQL_Transform/Lookup_Phone	STOP	9400	0.583	48.961
/DF_SQL_Transform/Cartesian_Join: 0	STOP	50	42.695	48.979
/DF_SQL_Transform/Cartesian_Join_PERSON_DETAILS	STOP	939900	42.069	49.013
/DF_SQL_Transform/Cartesian_Join: 1	STOP	939900	42.010	48.981
/DF_SQL_Transform/Lookup_Phone-Mapping1	STOP	9398	0.582	48.968
/DF_SQL_Transform/Merge: 0	STOP	18798	0.386	48.970
/DF_SQL_Transform/CacheSplitMemoryReader	STOP	939900	42.014	48.977
/DF_SQL_Transform/Cartesian_Join-Join2: 0	STOP	0	0.000	48.984
/DF_SQL_Transform/SQL	STOP	18798	0.580	48.958
/DF_SQL_Transform/Merge[1]: 0	STOP	939900	42.744	48.988
/DF_SQL_Transform/Cartesian_Join-Join2: 1	STOP	0	0.004	48.986
/DF_SQL_Transform/Row_Generation	STOP	50	0.000	48.954
/DF_SQL_Transform/CacheSplitMemoryReader[1]	STOP	0	6.145	48.982

6. To enable bulk loading, open the target table configuration in the workspace for editing, go to the **Bulk Loader Options** tab, and check **Bulk load**. After that, set **Mode** to **truncate** and leave other options at their default values.

7. Save and execute the job again.

8. The following screenshot shows that total dataflow execution time was 27 seconds, and it took 20 seconds for Data Services to load the same number of records. That is two times faster than loading records in normal mode into the SQL Server database. Your time could be slightly different depending on the hardware you are using for your Data Services and database environments.

Path Name	State	Row Count	Elapsed Time (sec)	Absolute Time (sec)
/DF_SQL_Transform/Round_Robin_Split	STOP	50	0.000	27.449
/DF_SQL_Transform/CacheSplit	STOP	18798	0.044	27.472
/DF_SQL_Transform/Round_Robin_Split[1]	STOP	18798	0.590	27.453
/DF_SQL_Transform/Distinct	STOP	18798	0.309	27.470
/DF_SQL_Transform/Lookup_Phone	STOP	9400	0.592	27.455
/DF_SQL_Transform/Cartesian_Join: 0	STOP	50	21.114	27.476
/DF_SQL_Transform/Cartesian_Join_PERSON_DETAILS	STOP	939900	20.328	27.529
/DF_SQL_Transform/Cartesian_Join: 1	STOP	939900	20.291	27.478
/DF_SQL_Transform/Lookup_Phone-Mapping1	STOP	9398	0.593	27.463
/DF_SQL_Transform/Merge: 0	STOP	18798	0.310	27.466
/DF_SQL_Transform/CacheSplitMemoryReader	STOP	939900	20.294	27.474
/DF_SQL_Transform/Cartesian_Join-Join2: 0	STOP	0	0.000	27.481
/DF_SQL_Transform/SQL	STOP	18798	0.589	27.451
/DF_SQL_Transform/Merge[1]: 0	STOP	939900	21.135	27.485
/DF_SQL_Transform/Cartesian_Join-Join2: 1	STOP	0	0.002	27.483
/DF_SQL_Transform/Row_Generation	STOP	50	0.000	27.447
/DF_SQL_Transform/CacheSplitMemoryReader[1]	STOP	0	6.249	27.480

How it works...

Availability of the bulk-load methods is totally dependent on which database you use as a target. Data Services does not perform any magic; it simply utilizes bulk-loading methods available in a database.

These methods are different for different databases, but the principle of bulk loading is usually as follows: Data Services sends the rows to the database host as quickly as possible, writing them into a local file. Then, Data Services uses the external table mechanism available in the database to present the file as a relational table. Finally, it executes a few UPDATE/ INSERT commands to query this external table and insert data into a target table specified as a target object in a Data Services dataflow.

To run one INSERT ... SELECT FROM command is much faster than to execute 1 million INSERT commands.

Some databases perform these small insert operations quite effectively, while for others this could be a really big problem. In almost all cases, if we talk about a significant number of records, the bulk-loading method will always be the quicker way to insert data.

When to enable bulk loading?

You have probably noticed that as soon as you enable bulk loading in target table configuration, the **Options** tab becomes grayed out. Unfortunately, by enabling bulk loading, you lose all extra functionality available for loading data, such as autocorrect load, for example. This happens because of the nature of the bulk-load operation. Data Services simply passes the data to the database for insertion and cannot perform extra comparison operations, which are available for row-by-row inserts.

The other reason for not using bulk loading is that enabled bulk loading prevents full push-downs from occurring. Of course, in most of the cases push-down is the best possible option in terms of execution performance, so you would never think about enabling bulk loading if you have full push-down working. For partial push-downs, when you push down only SELECT queries to get data onto the ETL box for transformation, bulk loading is perfectly valid. You still want to send records back to the database for insertion and want to do it as quickly as possible.

Most of the time, bulk loading does a perfect job when you are passing a big number of rows for insertion from the ETL box and do not utilize any extra loading options available in Data Services.

The best advice in terms of making decisions to enable or not enable bulk loading on your target table is to experiment and try different ways of inserting data. This is a decision which should take into account all parameters, such as environment configuration, workload on a Data Services ETL box, workload on a database, and of course, the number of rows to be inserted into a target table.

Optimizing dataflow execution – performance options

We will review a few extra options available for different transforms and objects in Data Services which affect performance and, sometimes, the way ETL processes and transforms data.

Getting ready

For this recipe, use the dataflow from the recipe *Optimizing dataflow readers – lookup methods* in this chapter. Please refer to this recipe if you need to create or rebuild this dataflow.

How to do it...

Data Services performance-related configuration options can be put under the following categories:

- ▸ Dataflow performance options
- ▸ Source table performance options
- ▸ Query transform performance options
- ▸ Lookup functions performance options
- ▸ Target table performance options

In the following sections, we will review and explain all of them in details.

Dataflow performance options

To access dataflow performance options, right-click on a dataflow object and select **Properties** from the context menu.

General
Name: DF_TABLE_TO_TABLE
☐ Execute only once   ☑ Use database links

Degree of parallelism: 2   Cache type: Pageable ⌄
                                          In-Memory
                                          Pageable

Description:

The **Degree of parallelism** option replicates transform processes inside the dataflow according to the number specified. Data Services creates separate subdataflow processes and executes them in parallel. At the points in the dataflow where the processing cannot be parallelized, data is merged back together from different subdataflow processes in the main dataflow process. If the source table used in the dataflow is partitioned and the value in the **Degree of parallelism** option is higher than 1, Data Services can use multiple reader processes to read the data from the same table. Each reader reads data from corresponding partitions. Then, data is merged or continued to be processed in parallel if the next transform object allows parallelization.

For detailed information on how the **Degree of Parallelism** option works, please refer to the official documentation, *SAP Data Services: Performance Optimization Guide*. You should be very careful with this parameter. The usage and value of **Degree of parallelism** should depend on the complexity of the dataflow and on the resources available on your Data Services ETL server, such as the number of CPUs and amount of memory used.

If the **Use database links** option is configured on both database and Data Services datastore levels, database links can help to produce push-down operations. Use this option to enable or disable database links usage inside a dataflow.

Cache type defines which type of cache will be used inside a dataflow for caching datasets. A **Pageable** cache is stored on the ETL server's physical disk and **In-Memory** keeps the cached dataset in memory. If the dataflow processes very large datasets, it is recommended that you use a pageable cache to not run out of memory.

Source table performance options

Open your dataflow in the workspace and double-click on any source table object to open the table configuration window.

Array fetch size allows you to optimize the number of requests Data Services sends to fetch the source data set onto the ETL box. The higher the number used, the fewer the requests that Data Services has to send to fetch the data. This setting should be dependent on the speed of your network. The faster your network is, the higher the number you can specify to move the data in bigger chunks. By decreasing the number of requests, you can potentially also decrease the CPU usage consumption on your ETL box.

Join rank specifies the "weight" of the table used in Query transforms when you join multiple tables. The higher the rank, the earlier the table will be joined to the other tables. If you have ever optimized SQL statements, you know that specifying big tables in the join conditions earlier can potentially decrease the execution time. This is because the number of records after the first join pair can be decreased dramatically through inner joins, for example. This makes the join pairs further on produce smaller datasets and run quicker. The same principle applies here in Data Services but to specify the order of join pairs, you can use the rank option.

Cache can be set up if you want the source table to be cached on the ETL server. The type of cache used is determined by the dataflow cache type option.

Query transform performance options

Open the Query transform in the workspace window:

Mapping	SELECT	FROM	WHERE	GROUP BY	ORDER BY	Advanced	Find

Input schema(s)	From	Join rank	Cache
BUSINESSENTITYADDRESS	✔	2	Yes
PERSON	✔	1	Automatic
ADDRESS	✔	3	Automatic

Join rank offers the same options as described earlier and allows you to specify the order in which the tables are joined.

Cache is, again, the same as described earlier and defines whether the table will be cached on the ETL server.

lookup_ext() performance options

Right-click on the selected `lookup_ext` function in the column mapping section or on the function call in the output schema of the Query transform and select **Modify Function Call** in the context menu:

Lookup table:	OLTP.PERSON.PERSONPHONE	▼		Cache spec:	PRE_LOAD_CACHE ∨	✔ Run as a separate process

DEMAND_LOAD_CACHE
NO_CACHE
PRE_LOAD_CACHE

Available parameters:		Condition:		
Parameter		**Column in lookup table**	Op.(&) Expression	...
Lookup table		▶ BUSINESSENTITYID	= Get_Country.BUSINESSENTITYID	...
Input Schema		＊		...
Variables				

Cache spec defines the type of cache method used for the lookup table. **NO_CACHE** means that, for every row in the main dataset, a separate SELECT lookup query is generated, extracting value from the database lookup table. When **PRE_LOAD_CACHE** is used, the lookup table first pulled to the ETL box and cached in memory or on the physical disk (depending on the dataflow cache type option). **DEMAND_LOAD_CACHE** is a more complex method best used when you are looking up repetitive values. Only then is it most efficient. Data Services caches only values already extracted from the lookup table. If it encounters a new key value that does not exist in the cached table, it makes another request to the lookup table in the database to find it and then caches it too.

Run as a separate process can be encountered in many other transforms and object configuration options. It is useful when the transform is performing high-intensive operations consuming a lot of CPU and memory resources. If this option is checked, Data Services creates separate subdataflow processes that perform this operation. Potentially, this option can help parallelize object execution within a dataflow and speed up processing and transformations significantly. By default, the OS creates a single process for a dataflow, and if not parallelized, all processing is done within this single OS process. Run as separate process help to create multiple processes helping main dataflow OS process to perform all extracts, join and calculations as fast as possible.

Target table performance options

Click on a target table to open its configuration options in the workspace window:

Target	**Options**	Bulk Loader Options	Load Triggers	Pre-Load Commands	Post-Load Commands	

Rows per commit: `1000`

Delete data from table before loading: ☑

Advanced:

General	
Column comparison	Compare by name
Number of loaders	1
Error handling	
Use overflow file	No
File name	Not Applicable
File format	Not Applicable
Update control	

Rows per commit is similar to **Array fetch size** but defines how many rows are sent to a database within the same network packet. Do decrease amounts of packets with rows for insert sent to a database you can increase this number.

Number of loaders helps to parallelize the loading processes. Enable partitions on the table objects on the **Datastores** tab if the tables are partitioned at the database level. If they are not partitioned, set the same number of loaders as **Degree of parallelism**.

9

Advanced Design Techniques

The topics we will cover in this chapter include:

- ▸ Change Data Capture techniques
- ▸ Automatic job recovery in Data Services
- ▸ Simplifying ETL execution with system configurations
- ▸ Transforming data with the Pivot transform

Introduction

This chapter will guide you through the advanced ETL design methods. Most of them will utilize Data Services features and functionality already explained in the previous chapters. As you have probably noticed, there are many ways to do the same thing in Data Services. The methods and logic you apply to solve the specific problem often depend on environment characteristics and some other conditions, such as development resources and extract requirements applied to the source systems. On the contrary, some of the methods and techniques explained further do not depend on all these factors and could be considered as ETL development best practices.

In this chapter we will discuss a very popular method of populating slowly changing dimensions in data warehouse, which require the use of a combination of Data Services transforms and dataflow design techniques.

We will also review automatic recovery methods available in Data Services, which allow you to easily restart previously failed jobs without performing extra recovery steps for various components of ETL code and underlying target data structures.

Another topic discussed in this chapter is the usage of system configurations in Data Services. This feature allows you to simplify your ETL development and makes it easy to run the same jobs against various sources and target environments.

Finally, we will review one of the advanced Data Services transforms that enables you to implement the pivoting transformation method on the passing data converting rows into columns and vice versa.

Change Data Capture techniques

Change Data Capture (**CDC**) is the method of developing ETL processes to propagate changes in the source system into your data warehouse for dimension tables.

Getting ready

CDC is directly related to another DWH concept of **Slowly Changing Dimensions** (**SCD**), the dimension tables that data changes constantly throughout the life of data warehouse.

A good example would be the `Employee` dimension table, which holds data on the employees in your company. As you can imagine, this table is in constant flux: new employees are hired and some employees leave the company, change positions and roles, or even transfer between departments. All these changes have to be propagated to an `Employee` dimension table in DWH from the source systems, which always store only the latest state of the `Employee` data. In DWH, in most cases, for most of the dimension tables, you want to keep the historical data to be able to derive the state of the `Employee` data at a specific point of time in the past. That is why **SCD** tables have extra fields to accommodate historical data and can be populated using various methods, depending on their type.

There are many different types of SCD tables, but we will quickly discuss only the three main ones as the rest are just combinations of these three. We will refer to SCD type numbers according to Ralph Kimball's methodology in brackets.

As an example, let's take the case of the `Employee` dimension table when one employee John gets transferred from marketing to finance.

No history SCD (Type 1)

Yes, a no history SCD table is one that does not store historical data at all. Records are inserted (new records) and updated (changes). Take a look at the following example.

The original record for John looks like this:

ID	NAME	DEPARTMENT
1	John	Marketing

Here's what the new record looks like after the changes are applied:

ID	NAME	DEPARTMENT
1	John	Finance

This type of SCD does not keep historical records at all; as you can see, there is no information that John has ever worked in a different department.

Limited history SCD (Type 3)

A limited history table uses extra fields in the same record to keep the current value and a previous value, as shown here:

ID	NAME	DEP_PREV	DEP_CUR	EFFECTIVE_DATE
1	John	Marketing	Finance	27/02/2015

It is "limited" as you have to add extra columns for every new "historical state" of the row. In the preceding example, you can keep track of only the current and previous values of the record.

Unlimited history SCD (Type 2)

Unlimited history is possible if you create multiple records for each entity. Only one record represents the current value. One of the variations of an unlimited history SCD is shown in the following table:

KEY	ID	NAME	DEPARTMENT	START_DT	END_DT	CUR_FLAG
1	1	John	Marketing	1582/01/01	27/02/2015	N
2	1	John	Finance	27/02/2015	9999/12/31	Y

The ID is a natural key in the dimension table. For John, this is 1. This type of SCD requires the creation of a surrogate key to define the uniqueness of the record. The CUR_FLAG field defines current record. The START_DT and END_DT columns show the period of time when the record was valid/current. Note that these date fields do not represent any business value such as start employment date or date of birth. They just show the start and end dates of the period when the record was valid (or current) and are only used to accommodate preserving historical records. When populating initial records for the first time in an SCD table, you may often want to use dates from the distant past and future, such as *1582/01/01* and *9999/12/31*, called "low" and "high" date values. This allows users to run reports which retrieve more accurate historical information.

By using a low date in the START_DT field, we mark the record as an initial historical record in our dimension table. The same goes for using a high date in the END_DT column. It always has a CURR_IND flag set to Y and shows the latest (current) record in the history table.

Each time you make a change to the Employee table, in our case to the NAME or DEPARTMENT fields, you have to update the "current" record by changing the END_DT and CUR_FLAG field values with the date of change and N, respectively, and you also have to insert a new record with START_DT set to the date of change and CUR_FLAG set to Y.

In this recipe, we will build a dataflow that populates the SCD table of the unlimited history type (as shown in the Type 2 example). Data Services has a special transform object called **History_ Preserving**, which allows the automatic update/insert of the changed and new history records.

How to do it...

To build the CDC process—which will update our target SCD table in data warehouse—from a source OLTP table, we need to have two dataflows. The first will extract data from the source OLTP system into a staging table located in the STAGE database, and the second will use this STAGE table to compare data in it with the target table contents and will produce the history records (in for of INSERT and UPDATE SQL statements) to propagate the date changes into a target SCD table.

1. Create a new job and new extract dataflow, DF_OLTP_Extract_STAGE_Employee, that extracts the Employee table from the HumanResources schema into a staging table, STAGE_EMPLOYEE.

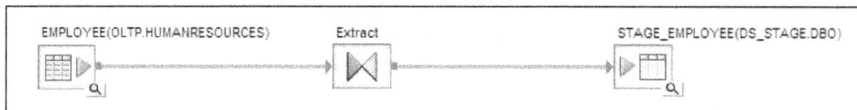

    For our future Employee SCD table, we will only be extracting the following list of fields from OLTP.EMPLOYEE:

Field	Description
BUSINESSENTITYID	Primary key for Employee records
NATIONALIDNUMBER	Unique national ID
LOGINID	Network logic
ORGANIZATIONLEVEL	The depth of the employee in the corporate hierarchy
JOBTITLE	Work title
BIRTHDATE	Date of birth
MARITALSTATUS	M=Married, S=Single
GENDER	M=Male, F=Female

Field	Description
HIREDATE	Employee hired on this date
SALARIEDFLAG	Job classification
VACATIOINHOURS	Number of available vacation hours
SICKLEAVEHOURS	Number of available sick leave hours

Map only these fields to the output schema of the **Extract** Query transform.

2. Create a new dataflow, DF_STAGE_Load_DWH_Employee, and link the first extract dataflow to it in the same job.

3. Create an empty target SCD table, EMPLOYEE, by using the CREATE TABLE statement in SQL Server Management Studio when connected to the AdventureWorks_DWH database.

```
CREATE TABLE [dbo].[EMPLOYEE] (
    [ID] [decimal](22, 0) NULL,
    [BUSINESSENTITYID] [int] NULL,
    [NATIONALIDNUMBER] [varchar](15) NULL,
    [LOGINID] [varchar](256) NULL,
    [ORGANIZATIONLEVEL] [int] NULL,
    [JOBTITLE] [varchar](50) NULL,
    [BIRTHDATE] [date] NULL,
    [MARITALSTATUS] [varchar](1) NULL,
    [GENDER] [varchar](1) NULL,
    [HIREDATE] [date] NULL,
    [SALARIEDFLAG] [int] NULL,
    [VACATIONHOURS] [int] NULL,
    [SICKLEAVEHOURS] [int] NULL,
    [START_DT] [date] NULL,
    [END_DT] [date] NULL,
    [CUR_FLAG] [varchar](1) NULL
) ON [PRIMARY]
```

4. Import the EMPLOYEE table created in the previous step into the DWH datastore.

5. Open the DF_STAGE_Load_DWH_Employee dataflow in the workspace window to edit it and add the required transformations, as shown in the following figure.

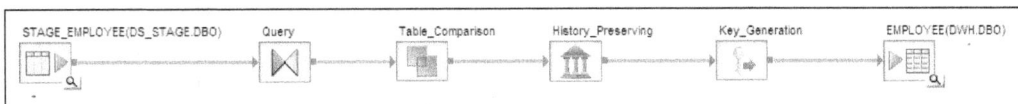

These steps explain the configuration of each of the DF objects we just used:

1. The **Query** transform is used to create an extra field, START_DT, of the date data type. It will be used by a **History_Preserving** transform to produce the start date of the history record in the target SCD table.

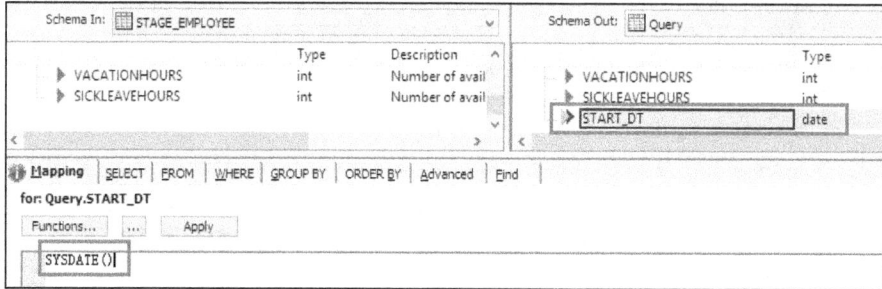

2. The **Table_Comparison** transform is used to compare the dataset from the STAGE_EMPLOYEE table to the target SCD table dataset in order to produce the rows of the INSERT type to create records which do not exist in the target but do exist in source according to specified key columns and rows of the UPDATE type. Source records of which the ID column exists in the target table will be used to provide new values for non-key fields. The input primary key column we specify for **Table_Comparison** to determine whether the record exists in the comparison table is BUSINESSENTITYID. The rest of the source columns go into the **Compare columns** section as we want to use all of them to determine if any value in any of these fields has changed.

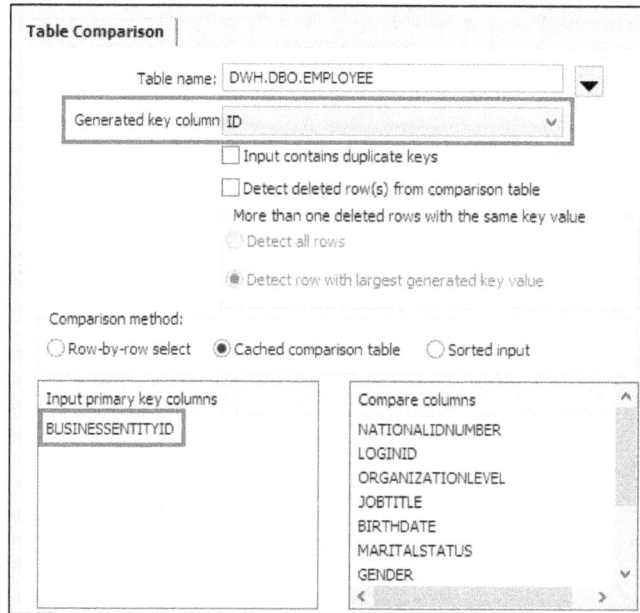

3. The **History_Preserving** transform works in tandem with **Table_Comparison** to produce "history" records updating the additional START_DT, END_DT, and CUR_IND fields, along with the rest of the non-key fields, or to create new history records for the INSERT type of rows defined by previous **Table_Comparison**.

History Preserving

Date columns

Valid from: START_DT

Valid to: END_DT

Valid to date value

New record: 9999.12.31 (yyyy.mm.dd or $name)

Old record: ◉ Use "valid from" date of new record

○ Use one day before "valid from" date of new record

Current flag

Column: CUR_FLAG

Set value: 'Y'

Reset value: 'N'

☐ Preserve delete row(s) as update row(s)

Compare columns

NATIONALIDNUMBER
LOGINID
ORGANIZATIONLEVEL
JOBTITLE
BIRTHDATE
MARITALSTATUS
GENDER
HIREDATE
SALARIEDFLAG
VACATIONHOURS
SICKLEAVEHOURS

The **Compare columns** section should have the same list of comparison columns as in the previous **Table_Comparison** transform. You can also control which format will be used as a high date (**9999.12.31**) and which values will be used in the **Current flag** field.

4. The **Key_Generation** transform generates surrogate unique keys in the ID field for our history SCD table EMPLOYEE as BUSINESSENTITYID will no longer represent the uniqueness of the record if multiple history rows are created for the same employee.

Key Generation

Table name: DWH.DBO.EMPLOYEE

Generated key column: ID

Increment value: 1

5. Save and execute the job initially to populate the target SCD table with the initial dataset. After running the job, if you check the contents of the target table, you will see that it represents the same dataset as in the OLTP.Employee table but with extra start/end date columns populated.

```sql
select
    ID, BUSINESSENTITYID, JOBTITLE, BIRTHDATE, GENDER, START_DT, END_DT, CUR_FLAG
from dbo.employee
```

100 %   ▾

☐ Results ☐ Messages

	ID	BUSINESSENTITYID	JOBTITLE	BIRTHDATE	GENDER	START_DT	END_DT	CUR_FLAG
22	76	145	Production Supervisor - WC30	1975-09-19	F	2015-09-04	9999-12-31	Y
23	77	146	Production Technician - WC30	1977-08-27	M	2015-09-04	9999-12-31	Y
24	78	148	Production Technician - WC30	1983-01-08	M	2015-09-04	9999-12-31	Y
25	79	149	Production Technician - WC30	1977-11-20	M	2015-09-04	9999-12-31	Y

> Note that, as this is the initial dataset, no history records have been created for any employee. Thus, the BUSINESSENTITYID column still has unique values in this dataset.

6. Let's generate some history records in our target SCD table. To do that, we have to make changes to the source OLTP table by executing the following statements in SQL Server Management Studio when connected to the AdventureWorks_OLTP database:

```sql
select * from HumanResources.Employee where
    BusinessEntityID in (1,999);


insert into HumanResources.Employee
(BusinessEntityID,NationalIDNumber,LoginID,OrganizationNode,
    JobTitle,BirthDate,MaritalStatus,Gender,
HireDate,SalariedFlag,VacationHours,SickLeaveHours)
values
(999,'999999999','domain\johnny',null,'Engineer','1982-01-
    01','S','M',SYSDATETIME(),1,99,10);


update HumanResources.Employee set JobTitle = 'CEO'
where BusinessEntityID = 1;
```

7. Now run the job a second time and check the contents of the target SCD table, `EMPLOYEE`, for employees with `BUSINESSENTITYID` set to 1 and 999.

```
select ID, BUSINESSENTITYID, JOBTITLE, BIRTHDATE, GENDER, START_DT, END_DT, CUR_FLAG
from dbo.employee where BUSINESSENTITYID in (1,999) order by BUSINESSENTITYID;
```

100 %

Results | Messages

	ID	BUSINESSENTITYID	JOBTITLE	BIRTHDATE	GENDER	START_DT	END_DT	CUR_FLAG
1	1	1	Chief Executive Officer	1963-03-02	M	2015-09-04	2015-09-04	N
2	2	1	CEO	1963-03-02	M	2015-09-04	9999-12-31	Y
3	292	999	Engineer	1982-01-01	M	2015-09-04	9999-12-31	Y

How it works...

Another important thing we have to discuss before we explain in detail how this CDC dataflow works is the difference between the different types of CDC architecture.

There are two basic types of CDC methods, or methods allowing you to populate SCD tables. They are usually called source-based CDC and target-based CDC. You can use either of them or even both of them simultaneously to populate any type of SCD table. They are different only in how changes in the source data are determined.

So, imagine that you have populated the `Employee` DWH dimension table (which has not been updated for a couple of days) on one hand and the source `Employee` OLTP table (which might or might not be different from the target DWH table's current snapshot of employee data).

Source-based ETL CDC

This method allows you to determine which employee records have had their values changed since the last time you updated the SCD dimension table in your data warehouse just by looking at the source `Employee` table. For this to work, the source table should have the `MODIFY_DATE` and `CREATE_DATE` fields in it, updated with the current date/time each time the record in the source `Employee` table gets updated or created (if it is a new employee record).

Another component required for source-based CDC is the date/time when the `Employee` table has been migrated to populate the DWH table for the last time (usually stored in an ETL log table and extracted into a variable, `$v_last_update_date`).

So, each time you perform an extraction of the source `Employee` table, you add a filtering condition, such as `SELECT * FROM EMPLOYEE WHERE MODIFY_DATE >= $v_last_update_date OR CREATE_DATE >= $v_last_update_date`. This allows you to extract significantly fewer records from the source system, increasing the ETL processing speed and decreasing your CPU, memory, and network resource consumption.

Then, in a dataflow that populates the target SCD table in DWH, you determine whether this is a new or updated record by checking the MODIFY_DATE and CREATE_DATE values. With the **Map_Operation** transform, change the record operation type to either INSERT or UPDATE to send them to the **History_Preserving** transform for history record generation.

Target-based ETL CDC

In target-based CDC, the whole source table is extracted and each extracted record is then compared with each target SCD table record. Data Services has an excellent transformation object, **Table_Comparison**, which performs this operation, producing INSERT/UPDATE/ DELETE records and sending them to the **History_Preserving** transform for history record generation.

There's no need to specify that pure target-based CDC is a resource- and time-consuming method, the main advantage of which is the simplicity of implementation. So, why not mix them together then to get the speed of source-based CDC when extracting fewer records and the simplicity of target-based CDC, using only two transforms, **Table_Comparison** and **History_Preserving**, to determine the rows for INSERT and UPDATE and for preparing history rows which will be sent to target SCD table.

In the steps of this recipe, we implemented a pure target-based CDC method. The following screenshot shows you one of the possible ways (in a very simplistic form) in which to update our target-based CDC to utilize the techniques of the source-based CDC method in order to determine the dataset for extraction with only the changed data:

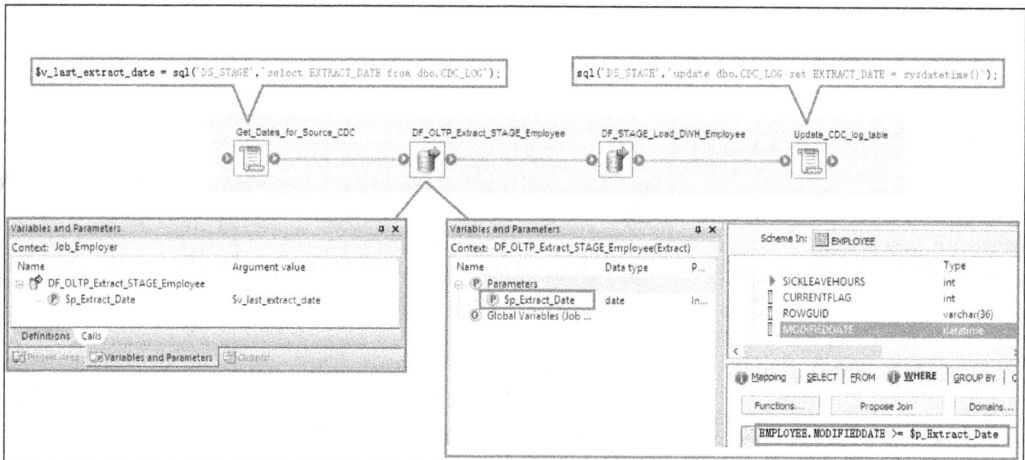

The initial script here uses the log table CDC_LOG to extract the date when the data was successfully extracted and applied to SCD target table the last time.

The CDC_LOG table has only one field, EXTRACT_DATE, and always has only one record showing when the CDC process was executed the last time. We extract this value from it before running our CDC dataflows and update it right after the successful execution of all CDC dataflows.

The final script updates the log table with the current time, so when the job is executed the next time, it will only extract records that have been modified since that date.

There are many variations of source-based CDC method implementation. They all depend on how often data is extracted, if there is a MODIFIED_DATE column on the source table, how intensively the source table is updated with new values, and so on.

The main idea here is to extract as few records as possible without losing the changes made to the source table.

Native CDC

Some databases, such as MS SQL Server and Oracle, have the **Native CDC** functionality, which can be enabled for specific tables. When any DML operations are performed on the table contents, the database updates the internal CDC structures logging when and how the table records were updated the last time. Data Services can utilize this native CDC functionality provided by the database. This configuration can be done at a datastore level by using datastore options when you create a datastore object.

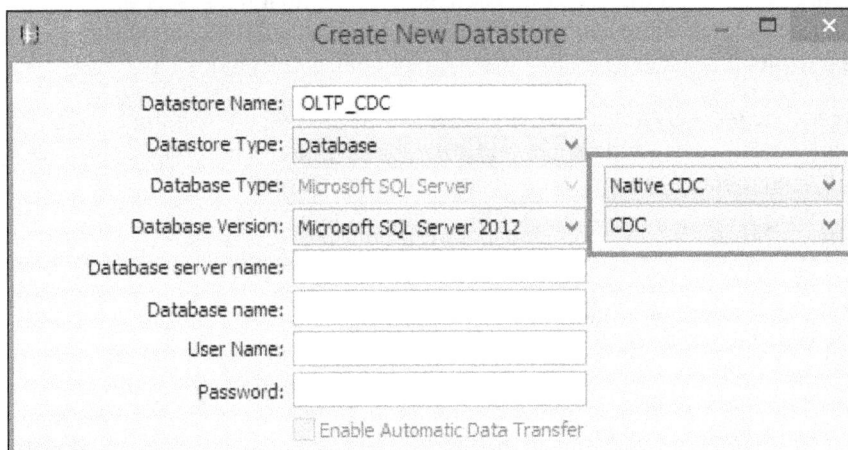

Create New Datastore	
Datastore Name:	OLTP_CDC
Datastore Type:	Database
Database Type:	Microsoft SQL Server
Database Version:	Microsoft SQL Server 2012
Database server name:	
Database name:	
User Name:	
Password:	

Native CDC / CDC options: Native CDC, CDC

☐ Enable Automatic Data Transfer

Using this functionality allows you to always select only changed records from the source database tables.

We will not discuss the details of using Native CDC in Data Services, but you can consider this task as a good homework practice and try to create your own CDC dataflows. Just do not forget that CDC has to first be enabled at the database level before you make any configuration changes on the Data Services side and start developing ETL.

Automatic job recovery in Data Services

The recovery process usually kicks in when Data Services jobs fail. A failed job, in most cases, means that some part of it has completed successfully and some part has not. The job which has failed right at the very beginning is rarely a problem and is of hardly any concern for recovery as all you have to do is to start it again.

Complications arise when the job fails in the middle of the insert, into a target table for example. Cases like that require you to either consider deleting already inserted records or even recovering a copy of the table from a backup using database recovery methods.

Recovery and error handling is an important part of robust ETL code. In this recipe, we will take a look at the methods used to develop ETL in Data Services and the functionality available in the software to make sure that the process of resuming failed processes goes as smoothly as possible.

The automatic job recovery feature available in Data Services does not fix the problems with the partially inserted data or missing keys problems (when an insert into a fact table cannot find the related key values in the referenced dimension tables because they have not been properly populated after the last job failure). Also, this feature does not protect you from poor ETL design or development errors when, for example, your ETL migration process does an automatic conversion of data between incompatible data types. In that case, it is your job to develop your ETL in such a way that you can cleanse the data if necessary and do manual conversions, making sure that you can either convert the value in the field between data types or set the row with this value aside to investigate or deal with it later.

The automatic job recovery feature simply tracks down the execution statuses of all dataflow and workflow objects from within a job, and if the job fails, it allows you to restart the job without the need to run successfully completed processes again.

Let's see how it works.

Getting ready

We will use the job from the previous recipe. This job contains two dataflows: an extract of the Employee table from the OLTP source database into the staging area and the load of the data from the staging table into the target data warehouse history table, Employee.

We have to emulate the failed process. To do that, we will drop the target dimension table populated by the second dataflow.

First of all, generate a CREATE TABLE statement from the table dbo.EMPLOYEE using SQL Server Management Studio. Do this by right-clicking on the table object and selecting **Script Table As | CREATE To | New Query Editor Window** on the context menu so that you can create a table with the same table definition without any difficulties. Save this code on your physical drive for later use to recreate the table:

```
CREATE TABLE [dbo].[EMPLOYEE](
    [ID] [decimal](22, 0) NULL,
    [BUSINESSENTITYID] [int] NULL,
    [NATIONALIDNUMBER] [varchar](15) NULL,
    [LOGINID] [varchar](256) NULL,
    [ORGANIZATIONLEVEL] [int] NULL,
    [JOBTITLE] [varchar](50) NULL,
    [BIRTHDATE] [date] NULL,
    [MARITALSTATUS] [varchar](1) NULL,
    [GENDER] [varchar](1) NULL,
    [HIREDATE] [date] NULL,
    [SALARIEDFLAG] [int] NULL,
    [VACATIONHOURS] [int] NULL,
    [SICKLEAVEHOURS] [int] NULL,
    [START_DT] [date] NULL,
    [END_DT] [date] NULL,
    [CUR_FLAG] [varchar](1) NULL
) ON [PRIMARY]
```

Then, execute the follow command to drop the table:

```
DROP TABLE [dbo].[EMPLOYEE]
```

How to do it...

1. Open `Job_Employee` in the workspace window and execute it.

2. On the **Execution Properties** window, check the option **Enable recovery**. This option will enable the execution status logging of the workflow and dataflow objects within the job.

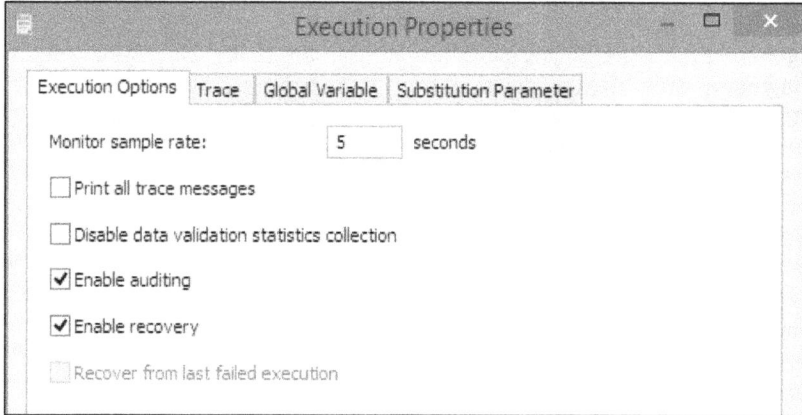

3. The first dataflow executes successfully, but the second one fails straightaway with an error message from the **Key_Generation** transform which sends the SQL statement `SELECT max(ID) FROM dbo.EMPLOYEE` in order to get the latest key value from the target table.

4. Now, return our missing table objects by executing the previously saved `CREATE TABLE` command in SQL Server Management Studio.

5. Execute the job again, but this time select the **Recover from last failed execution** option in the **Execution Properties** window.

6. The trace log states that `DF_OLTP_Extract_STAGE_Employee` is successfully recovered from the previous job execution.

```
Processing job <Job_Employer>.
Optimizing job <Job_Employer>.
Recovery enabled for job <Job_Employer>.
Running the job <Job_Employer> using the recovery information from previous run.
Job <Job_Employer> is started.
Data flow <DF_OLTP_Extract_STAGE_Employee> recovers successfully from previous run.
Process to execute data flow <DF_STAGE_Load_DWH_Employee> is started.
Data flow <DF_STAGE_Load_DWH_Employee> is started.
Cache statistics for data flow <DF_STAGE_Load_DWH_Employee> are not available to be used for optimization. You must collect
statistics before optimization can be done.
Data flow <DF_STAGE_Load_DWH_Employee> using PAGEABLE Cache with <3576 MB> buffer pool.
Data flow <DF_STAGE_Load_DWH_Employee> is completed successfully.
Process to execute data flow <DF_STAGE_Load_DWH_Employee> is completed.
Job <Job_Employer> is completed successfully.
```

How it works...

The automatic recovery feature works only if you enable the flag on the job execution options window to enable the object status logging mechanism. If you haven't enabled it before your job fails, you cannot use the automatic recovery feature.

A very important thing before running the job again in recovery mode is to check why the job has failed. If the job failed in the middle of populating of one of the tables (dimension of fact), you have to understand the impact of running the same load process again without cleaning up already inserted records first.

In our recipe, we simulated the failure of the load dataflow, which populates the target dimension table. As it has the **Table_Comparison** and **History_Preserving** transforms, it is not a problem to execute it again without any preparatory steps using the same data set. Records that have already been inserted simply will not be considered by **Table_Comparison** for either INSERT or UPDATE and will be ignored, so it is safe for us to just restart the job in recovery mode.

> Always consider the type of failure and the nature of your data and how it is populated by your ETL before restarting the job in recovery mode to prevent inserting duplicates into your target tables or to avoid referencing missing key values.

The workflow object can group several child objects placed inside it as a single recovery transactional unit by using Recover as a unit option. This is useful when several of your dataflow objects work as a single unit in order to populate the specific target table by preparing data at a specific point in time. In that case, if some of these dataflows fail, you want to execute all sequences of dataflow from the beginning. Otherwise, Data Services will execute the job in the default recovery mode, skipping all previously successfully completed dataflows and workflows.

To use this ability, place both dataflow objects into the single workflow. Open the workflow properties and check the option **Recover as a unit**.

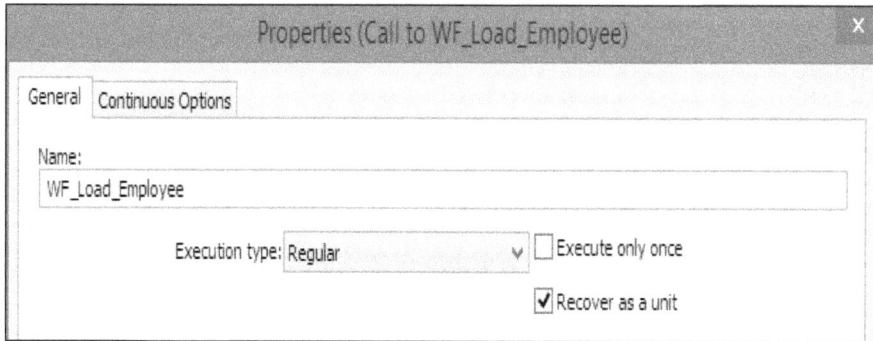

The workflow icon will be marked in the workspace window by a green arrow and small black cross so that you can visually differentiate which parts of your code behave as a transactional unit during the recovery process.

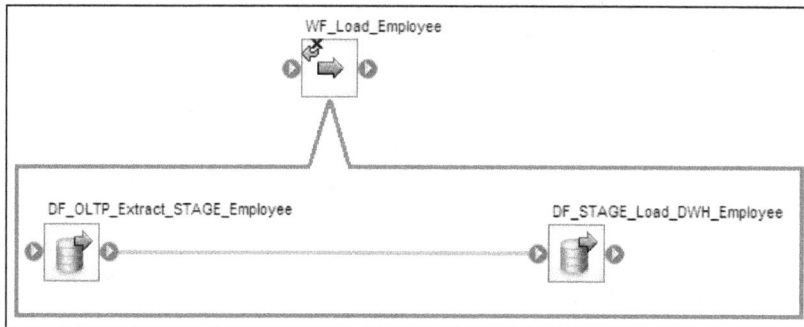

Note that script objects are not considered by recovery mode as they are part of the parent workflow object. You should keep that in mind before rerunning the job in recovery mode.

There's more...

Of course, the best way to make your life easier is to try to prevent the necessity of job recovery in the first place. One of the techniques that can be implemented to prevent possible problems with data recovery and job rerun complications is by putting extra code in the try-catch block. This code can be a set of scripts that will perform a table clean-up with a consequent "clean" failure so the job can simply be rerun without extra considerations and preparatory steps or so it could even be an alternative workflow that processes the data with a different method as compared to the original one that failed.

For example, if you use a dataflow that loads the flat file into a table, you can wrap it in a `try-catch` block. If it fails, execute another dataflow from a catch block to try to read the file again but from a different location or using different method.

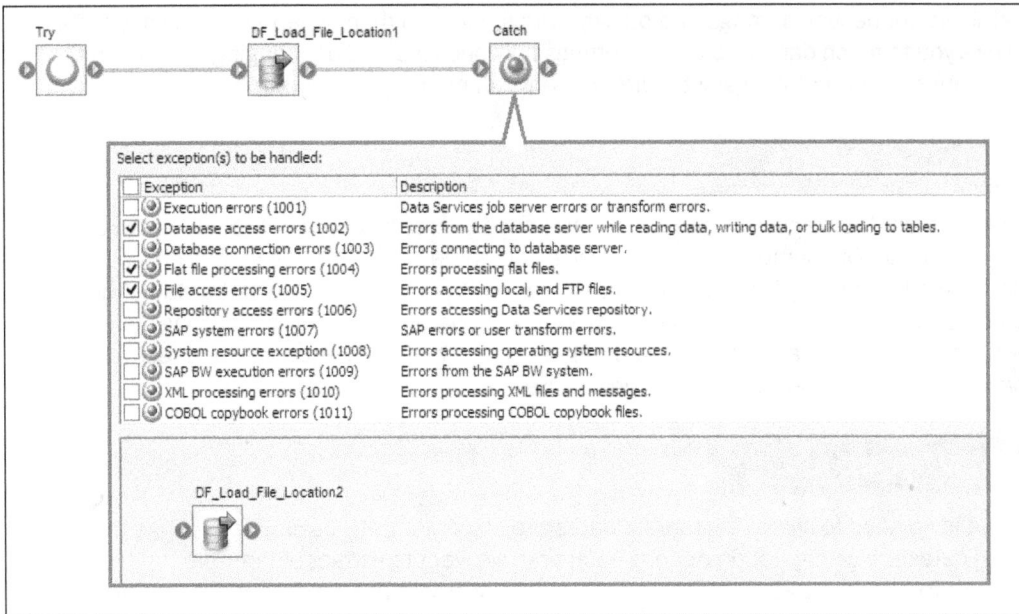

Simplifying ETL execution with system configurations

Working in multiple source and target environments is very common. The development of ETL processes by accessing data directly from the production system happens very rarely. Most of the time, multiple copies of the source system database are created to provide the working environment for ETL developers.

Basically, the development environment is an exact copy of the production environment with the only difference being that the development environment holds an old snapshot of the data or test data in smaller volumes for quick test job execution.

So, what happens after you create a datastore object, import all required tables from database into it, and finish developing your ETL? You have to switch to the production environment.

Data Services provides a very convenient way of storing multiple datastore configurations in the same datastore object, so you do not need to edit datastore object options each time you want to extract from either the production or development database environments. Instead, you can create multiple configurations that each use different credentials and different database connection settings and quickly switch between them when executing a job. This allows you to touch datastore object settings only once instead of changing them each time you want to run your job against a different environment.

Getting ready

To implement the steps in this recipe, we will need to create a copy of the AdventureWorks_ DWH database. Our sample database copy is named DWH_backup. Use any preferred SQL Server method to copy the contents of AdventureWorks_DWH into DWH_backup. The quickest way of performing this kind of backup is to back up the database using standard SQL Server methods available in the database object context menu, and then recovering this backup copy in the database with a new name.

How to do it...

There is no need to create a separate datastore object for DWH_backup or change the DWH datastore configuration options each time we want to extract either from AdventureWorks_DWH or DWH_backup. Let's just create two configurations for our DWH datastore.

1. Go to **Local Object Library | Datastores**.
2. Right-click on the DWH datastore and select **Edit...** from the context menu.
3. On the **Edit Datastore DWH** window, click on **Advanced<<** to open the advanced configuration part, and then click on the **Edit...** button against the **Configurations:** label.

4. In the top-left corner of the **Configurations for Datastore DWH** window, you can see four buttons that allow you to create a new configuration, duplicate the currently chosen one, and rename or delete configurations. Use them to rename the currently used configuration to DWH_Production and create a new configuration, DWH_Development.

5. Change the new DWH_Development configuration to be the default configuration by setting **Default configuration** to Yes. Note that this value changes automatically to **No** in other configurations.

6. Change the **Database name or SID or Service Name** option setting for
   DWH_Development to DWH_backup to point this configuration to another
   database. There is no need to change the other options as they will be identical
   for both configurations.

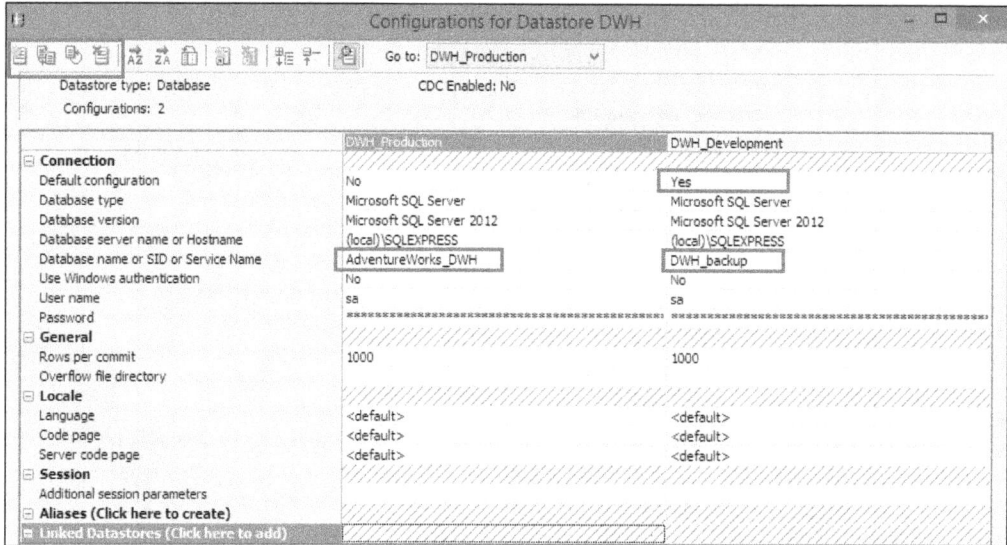

7. Now let's create system configurations so that we can choose the configuration setup
   when we run the job without the need to edit the datastore's **Default configuration**
   option. Go to **Tools | System Configurations...** and create two system configurations:
   Development and Production.

8. For the DWH record, set **Development** to DWH_Development and **Production** to
   DWH_Production.

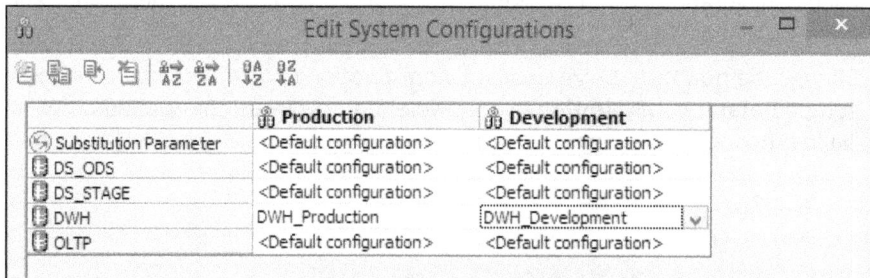

9. Click on **OK** to save the changes.

How it works...

Using configurations enables you to quickly switch between environments without the need to modify connectivity and configuration settings inside a datastore object.

System configurations extend the usability of datastore configurations even more by allowing you to select the combination of environments right at the job execution time.

> For the system configuration functionality to work, datastore configurations have to be created first.

Do you want to be able to extract from the production OLTP source but insert into the development DWH target within the same job without changing the ETL code or datastore settings? Just create a new system configuration that includes the required combination of various datastore configurations and execute the job with the system configuration specified.

Now, if you execute the `Job_Employee` job, just select the desired configuration in the job execution options:

System configuration:	Development ∨ Browse...
Job Server or Server Group:	JobServer_1 @ < Server Name >:3500 ∨
Distribution level:	Job

Use the **Browse...** button to review all system configurations created, if necessary.

Transforming data with the Pivot transform

The **Pivot** transform belongs to the Data Integrator group of transform objects, which are usually all about generation or transformation (changing the structure) of data. Simply put, the Pivot transform allows you to convert columns into rows. Pivoting transformation increases the number of rows in the dataset as for each column converted into a row, an extra row is created for every key (non-pivoted column) pair. Converted columns are called pivot columns.

Getting ready

Run the SQL following statements against the `AdventureWorks_OLTP` database to create a source table and populate it with data:

```
create table Sales.AccountBalance (
[AccountID] integer,
```

```
[AccountNumber] integer,
[Year] integer,
[Q1] decimal(10,2),
[Q2] decimal(10,2),
[Q3] decimal(10,2),
[Q4] decimal(10,2));

-- Row 1
insert into Sales.AccountBalance
    ([AccountID],[AccountNumber],[Year],[Q1],[Q2],[Q3],[Q4])
values  (1,100,2015,100.00,150.00,120.00,300.00);

-- Row 2
insert into Sales.AccountBalance
    ([AccountID],[AccountNumber],[Year],[Q1],[Q2],[Q3],[Q4])
values  (2,100,2015,50.00,350.00,620.00,180.00);

-- Row 3
insert into Sales.AccountBalance
    ([AccountID],[AccountNumber],[Year],[Q1],[Q2],[Q3],[Q4])
values  (3,200,2015,333.33,440.00,12.00,105.50);
```

The source table should look like the following figure:

	AccountID	AccountNumber	Year	Q1	Q2	Q3	Q4
1	1	100	2015	100.00	150.00	120.00	300.00
2	2	100	2015	50.00	350.00	620.00	180.00
3	3	200	2015	333.33	440.00	12.00	105.50

Do not forget to import it into the Data Services OLTP datastore.

How to do it...

1. Create a new dataflow and name it `DF_OLTP_Pivot_STAGE_AccountBalance`.

2. Open the dataflow in the workspace window to edit it and place the source table `ACCOUNTBALANCE` from the OLTP datastore created in the *Getting ready* section of this recipe.

3. Link the source table to the **Extract** Query transform, and propagate all source columns to the target schema.

4. Place the new **Pivot** transform object into a dataflow and link the **Extract** Query to it. The **Pivot** transform can be found in **Local Object Library | Transforms | Data Integrator**.

5. Open the **Pivot** transform in the workspace to edit and configure its parameters according to the following screenshot:

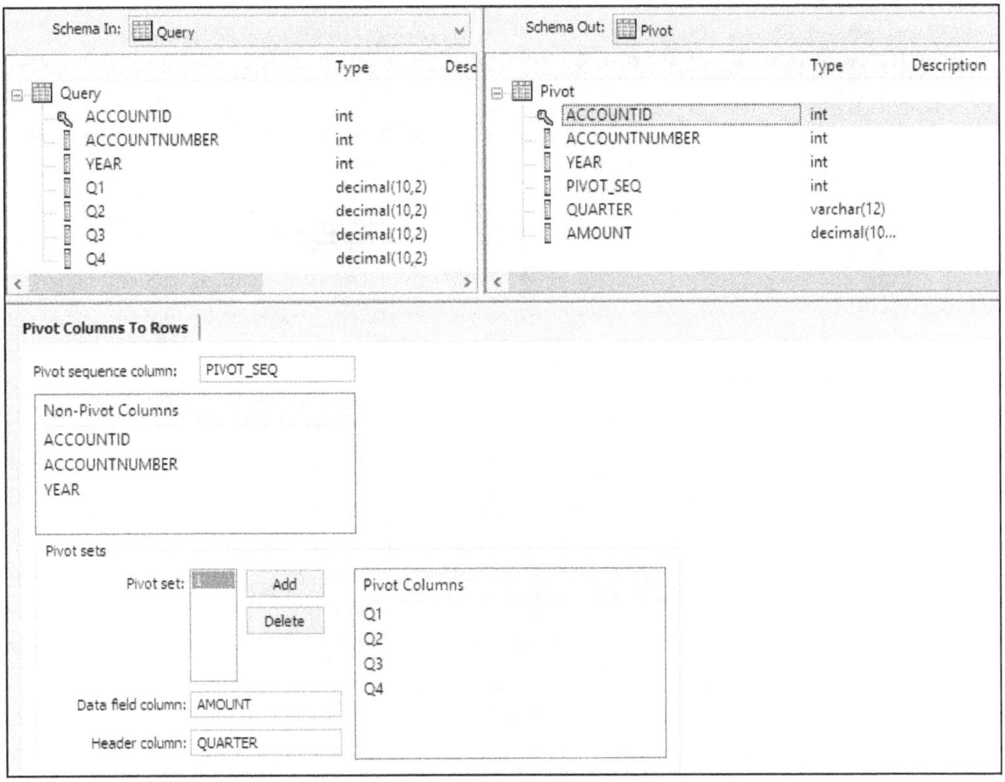

Schema In: Query			Schema Out: Pivot		
	Type	Desc		Type	Description
Query			Pivot		
ACCOUNTID	int		ACCOUNTID	int	
ACCOUNTNUMBER	int		ACCOUNTNUMBER	int	
YEAR	int		YEAR	int	
Q1	decimal(10,2)		PIVOT_SEQ	int	
Q2	decimal(10,2)		QUARTER	varchar(12)	
Q3	decimal(10,2)		AMOUNT	decimal(10...	
Q4	decimal(10,2)				

Pivot Columns To Rows

Pivot sequence column: PIVOT_SEQ

Non-Pivot Columns

ACCOUNTID
ACCOUNTNUMBER
YEAR

Pivot sets

Pivot set: [1]   Add   Delete

Pivot Columns
Q1
Q2
Q3
Q4

Data field column: AMOUNT

Header column: QUARTER

6. Close the **Pivot** transform and link it to another **Query** transform named Prepare_to_Load.

7. Propagate all source columns to the target schema of the Prepare_to_Load transform, and finally link it to the target ACCOUNTBALANCE template table created in the DS_STAGE datastore and STAGE database.

8. Before executing the job, open the Prepare_to_Load Query transform in the workspace window, double-click on the PIVOT_SEQ column, and check **Primary key** to specify an additional column as a primary key column for the migrated data set.

9. Save and run the job.

10. Open the dataflow again in the workspace window and import the target table by right-clicking on the target table and selecting **Import table** from the table context menu.

11. Open the target table in the workspace windows to edit its properties, and select the flag **Delete data from table before loading** on the **Options** tab.

12. Your dataflow and **Prepare_to_Load** Query transform mapping should now look like the following screenshot:

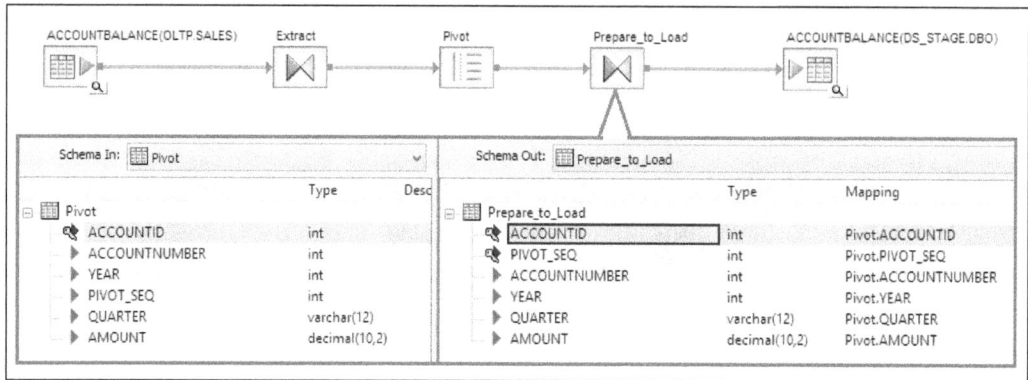

| | ACCOUNTBALANCE(OLTP.SALES) | Extract | | Pivot | | Prepare_to_Load | | ACCOUNTBALANCE(DS_STAGE.DBO) |

Schema In: Pivot				Schema Out: Prepare_to_Load		
	Type	Desc			Type	Mapping
⊟ Pivot			⊟ Prepare_to_Load			
⚷ ACCOUNTID	int		⚷ ACCOUNTID	int		Pivot.ACCOUNTID
▸ ACCOUNTNUMBER	int		⚷ PIVOT_SEQ	int		Pivot.PIVOT_SEQ
▸ YEAR	int		▸ ACCOUNTNUMBER	int		Pivot.ACCOUNTNUMBER
▸ PIVOT_SEQ	int		▸ YEAR	int		Pivot.YEAR
▸ QUARTER	varchar(12)		▸ QUARTER	varchar(12)		Pivot.QUARTER
▸ AMOUNT	decimal(10,2)		▸ AMOUNT	decimal(10,2)		Pivot.AMOUNT

How it works...

Pivot columns are the columns whose values will be merged into one column after the pivoting operation produces an extra row for each pivoted column. **Non-pivot columns** are the columns not affected by pivot operation. As you can see, pivoting operation denormalizes the dataset, generating more rows. This is why ACCOUNTID does not define the uniqueness of the record anymore and why we had to specify the extra key column PIVOT_SEQ.

	ACCOUNTID	PIVOT_SEQ	ACCOUNTNUMBER	YEAR	QUARTER	AMOUNT
1	1	1	100	2015	Q1	100.00
2	1	2	100	2015	Q2	150.00
3	1	3	100	2015	Q3	120.00
4	1	4	100	2015	Q4	300.00
5	2	1	100	2015	Q1	50.00
6	2	2	100	2015	Q2	350.00
7	2	3	100	2015	Q3	620.00
8	2	4	100	2015	Q4	180.00
9	3	1	200	2015	Q1	333.33
10	3	2	200	2015	Q2	440.00
11	3	3	200	2015	Q3	12.00
12	3	4	200	2015	Q4	105.50

You might ask *Why pivot? Why not just use the data as is and perform the required operation on the data from columns Q1-Q4?*

The answer in the given example is very simple. It is much more difficult to perform an aggregation when the amounts are spread across the different columns. Instead of summarizing by a single column with the sum(AMOUNT) function, we have to write the expression sum(Q1 + Q2 + Q3 + Q4) each time. Quarters is not the worst thing yet. Try to imagine the situation when the table has amounts stored in columns defining month periods or you have to filter by these time periods.

Of course, contrary cases exist as well—when storing data across multiple columns instead of just in one is justified. In these cases, if your data structure is not like that, you can use the **Reverse_Pivot** transform, which does exactly the opposite thing—converting rows into columns. Look at the example of the **Reverse_Pivot** configuration given here:

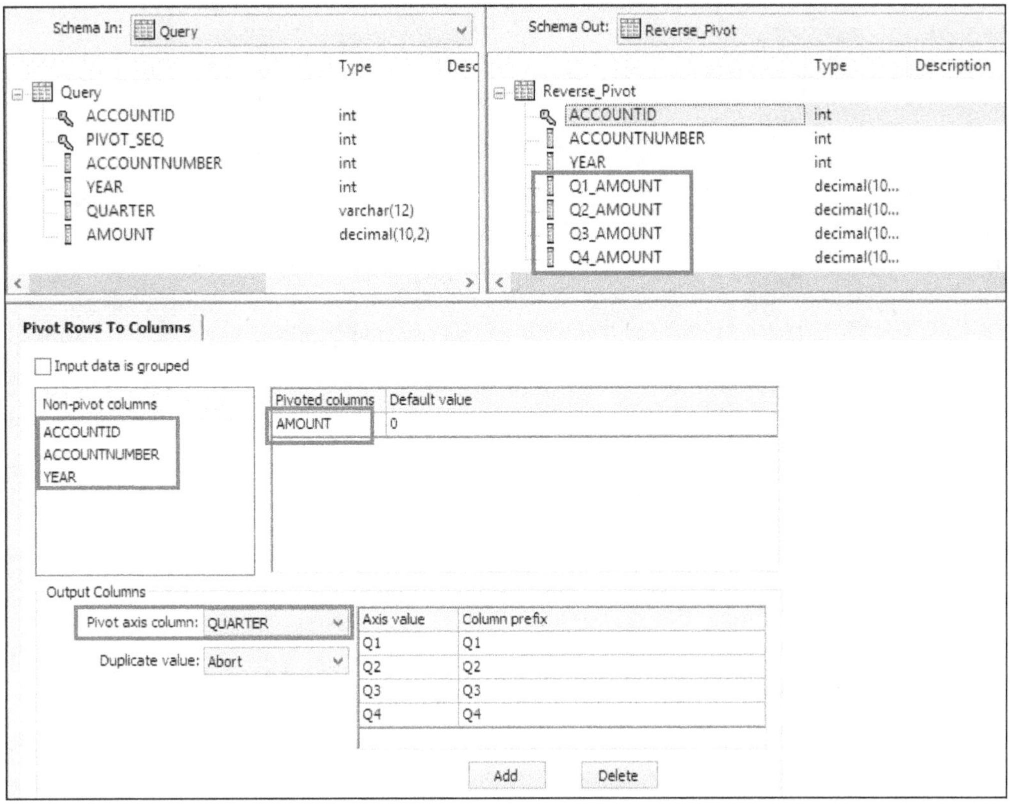

Reverse pivoting or the transformation of rows into columns has introduced another term: **Pivot axis column**. This is the column that holds the categories defining different columns after reverse pivot operation. It corresponds to the **Header column** option in the **Pivot** transform configuration.

10
Developing Real-time Jobs

The recipes and topics that will be discussed in this chapter are as follows:

- ▶ Working with nested structures
- ▶ The XML_Map transform
- ▶ The Hierarchy_Flattening transform
- ▶ Configuring Access Server
- ▶ Creating real-time jobs

Introduction

In all previous chapters, we have worked with batch-type job objects in Data Services. As we already know, a batch job in Data Services helps to organize ETL processes so that they can be started on demand or scheduled to be executed at a specific time either once or regularly.

The main difference between a real-time job and batch job is the way these two job objects are executed by Data Services engine. The purpose of a real-time job is to process requests providing response. So, technically, a real-time job could be running for hours, days, or even weeks without actually processing any data. Data Services engine actually executes the ETL code from within the real-time job object only when new request comes from an external service. Data Services uses this request message as the data source, processes this data, and sends the processed data back to external service in form of response message.

A new Data Services component called Access Server has come into the frame. Access Server plays the role of a messenger servicing real-time jobs. It is Access Server that accepts and sends back messages to be used as a source and target data for real-time jobs.

In this chapter, we will also review the concepts of nested structures—how and when they are commonly used. The main reason for this is that the real-time jobs often use XML technology to receive requests and send the responses back. The XML format is often used to exchange nested data structures.

We will also see how to create and configure Access Server to be able to use real-time job functionality and, finally, we will create a real-time job itself.

Working with nested structures

Earlier in this book, we worked solely with a flat structure—rows extracted from database tables and inserted back in a database table, or exported to a flat text file. In this recipe, we will take a look at how to prepare nested data structures inside a dataflow and then export it into an XML file as XML is a simple and very convenient way to store nested data and is most commonly used as a source and target objects in real-time jobs.

Getting ready

We will not need to have an XML file prepared for this recipe as we are going to generate them automatically with help of Data Services from datasets stored in our relational databases: OLTP and DWH.

We will construct the nested data structure of job title list, where each record (job title) will have a reference to a list of employees who have the same job title in the OLTP system.

Following is the visual presentation of this nested data structure:

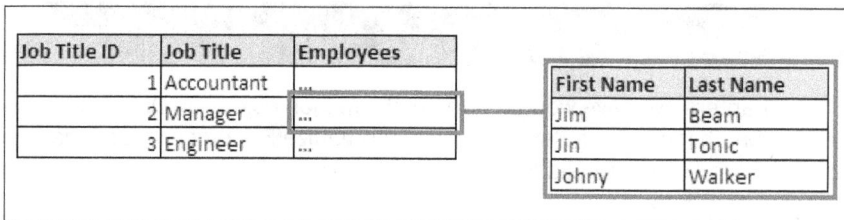

Job Title ID	Job Title	Employees		First Name	Last Name
1	Accountant	...			
2	Manager	...		Jim	Beam
3	Engineer	...		Jin	Tonic
				Johny	Walker

In the flat data structure, these would be two different tables and we would have to have reference key columns in both tables linking them together as a parent–child relationship.

A nested data structure allows you to avoid reference keys completely. In other words, we do not really need *Job Title ID* in order to link these two tables together. A list of employees will be literally stored in the same dataset in one of the fields for the specific job title.

We will source the list of job titles from the `HumanResources.Employee` table of our OLTP database. Person data such as first name and last name, will be sourced from the `Person.Person` table that is linked to the `Employee` table by the `BusinessEntityID` column.

How to do it...

1. Create a new dataflow, `DF_OLTP_XML`, and open it in the workspace window for editing.

2. Import, if necessary, two tables, `Person.Person` and `HumanResources.Employee`, into the OLTP datastore.

3. Place both tables in the dataflow `DF_OLTP_XML` as source table objects.

4. Place the `Get_Person` Query transform inside the workspace of `DF_OLTP_XML` and link it to the `Person` table object. Propagate three columns to the output schema of the Query—BUSINESSENTITYID, FIRSTNAME, LASTNAME—from the `Person` table.

5. Create two Query transforms to get the data from the `Employee` table: `Get_JobTitle_Person` and `Distinct_JobTitle`.

    `Get_JobTitle_Person` should select the dataset consisting of two columns BUSINESSENTITY_ID and JOBTITLE.

    `Distinct_JobTitle` should only select the JOBTITLE column.

6. In the `Distinct_JobTitle` Query Editor, tick the checkbox **Distinct rows...** on the **SELECT** tab and set up ascending sorting on the JOBTITLE column on ORDER BY tab.

7. Create the `Gen_JobTitle_ID` Query transform and link `Distinct_JobTitle` to it. This Query transform will be used to generate new unique identifiers for distinct values of job titles.

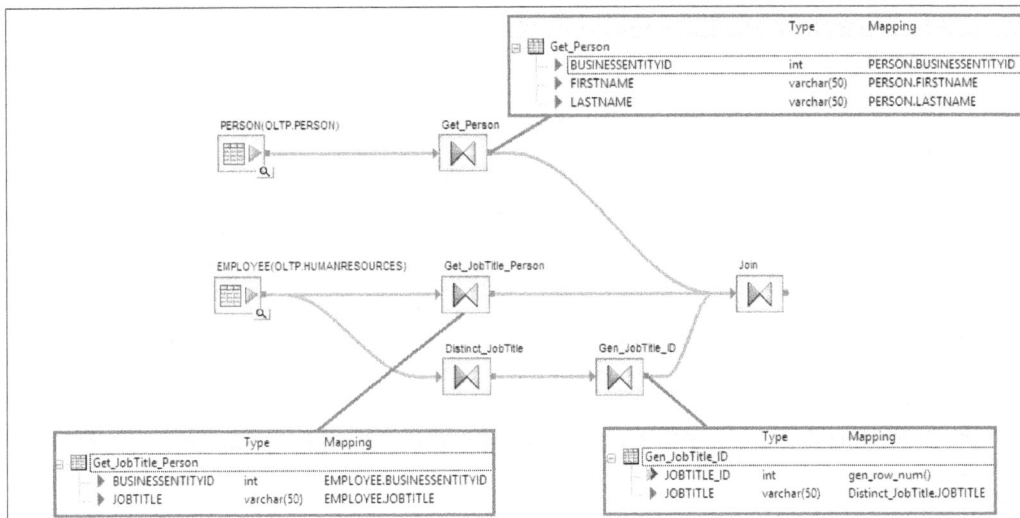

8. Finally, join all three Query transforms together using another `Join` Query and propagate four columns to the output schema: `JOBTITLE_ID`, `JOBTITLE`, `FIRSTNAME`, `LASTNAME`.

Join pairs:						
Left	Join Type	Right			Join Condition	
Get_Person	Inner join	Get_JobTitle_Person	...	◎	Get_Person.BUSINESSENTITYID = Get_JobTitle_Person.BUSINESSENTITYID	
↳	Inner join	Gen_JobTitle_ID	...	◎	Gen_JobTitle_ID.JOBTITLE = Get_JobTitle_Person.JOBTITLE	

9. Now that we have merged our data from multiple tables into one dataset, let's see what is required to convert this flat dataset to a nested one.

10. To do that, we have to split the flat data again, separating job titles from employee data. Both result datasets should have a reference key column, which will be used to define the relationships between the records.

   Create two Query transforms, `Q_JobTitle` and `Q_Person`, propagating `JOBTITLE_ID` in both Query objects:

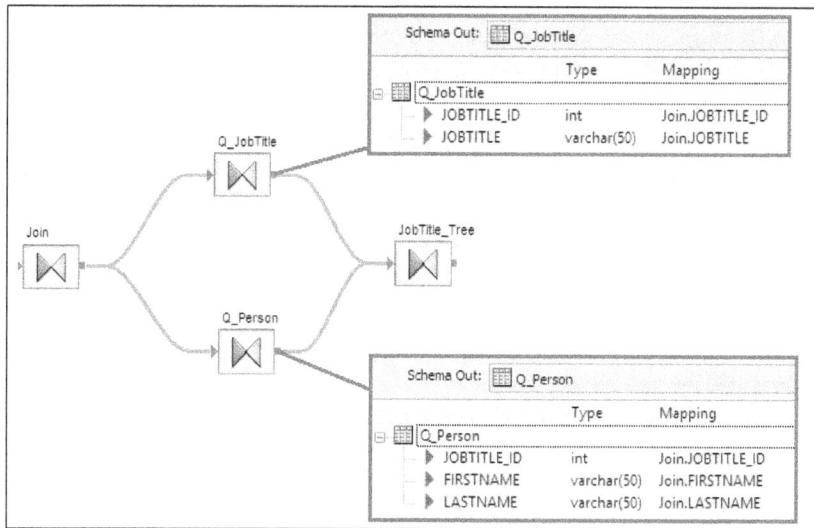

11. The nesting of the data happens in the Query transform object that is used to join the previously split datasets. Create the `JobTitle_Tree` Query transform and link it to both `Q_JobTitle` and `Q_Person`.

12. Open the `JobTitle_Tree` Query Editor in workspace window.

13. Drag and drop `JOBTITLE_ID` and `JOBTITLE` from `Q_JobTitle` input schema to the output schema.

14. Drag and drop the whole `Q_Person` input schema to the output schema. That will the place `Q_Person` table schema at the same level with the `JOBTITLE_ID` and `JOBTITLE` columns. `Q_Person` is now a nested segment inside the `JobTitle_Tree` schema.

15. Now, we can switch between output schemas by double-clicking on either `JobTitle_Tree` or `Q_Person`, or you can right-click on schema name and select **Make current...** from the context menu. That is necessary if you want to change settings on the Query transform tabs: **Mapping**, **SELECT**, **FROM**, **WHERE**, and so on. Those tabs are not shared by all nested output schemas and only "current" output schema values are displayed.

16. Make the `JobTitle_Tree` output schema current and select the **FROM** tab. Make sure that only one `Q_JobTitle` checkbox is selected.

17. Now, make the `Q_Person` output schema current.

18. On the **FROM** tab, tick only the **Q_Person** checkbox.

19. On the **WHERE** tab, put the following filtering condition:

```
(Q_Person.JOBTITLE_ID = Q_JobTitle.JOBTITLE_ID)
```

20. Finally, we have to output our nested dataset into a proper target object, which supports nested data. SQL Server does not support nested data, and that is why we will use an XML file as a target.

21. Select the **Nested Schemas Template** object from the right-side tool panel, 📄 , and place it as a target object linked to the last `JobTitle_Tree` Query transform.

22. Name the target object `XML_target` and open it in the workspace windows for editing. Specify the following options:

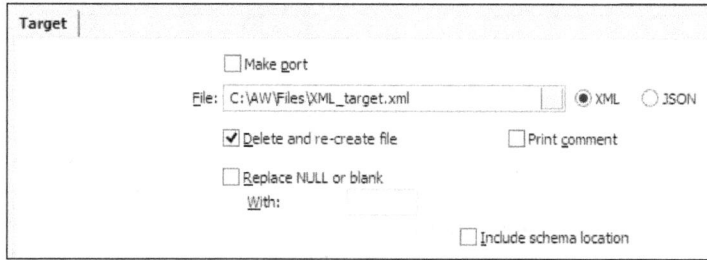

```
Target |
                          □ Make port
              File:  C:\AW\Files\XML_target.xml            ⦿ XML    ○ JSON
                     ☑ Delete and re-create file       □ Print comment
                     □ Replace NULL or blank
                        With:
                                               □ Include schema location
```

23. Your dataflow should now look like the following figure:

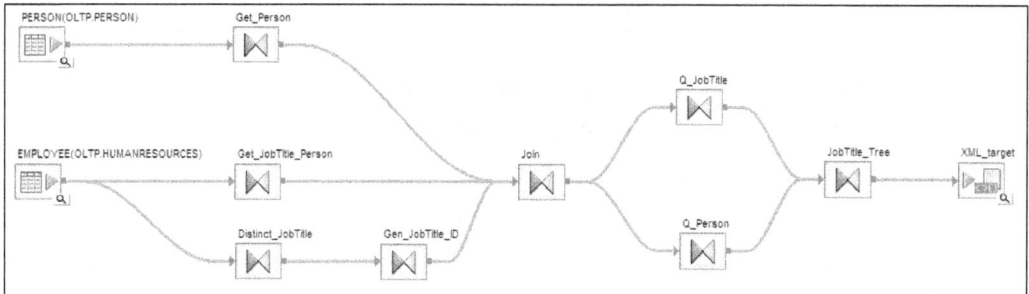

How it works...

Data Services allows you to view the target data loaded by the last job run from the XML target object in the same way as for target database table objects, as shown in the following screenshot:

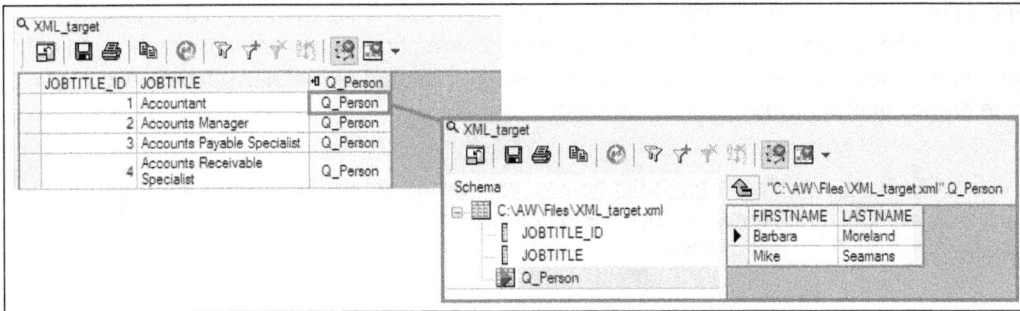

If you open the `XML_target.xml` file created in the `C:\AW\Files\` folder, you will see a common XML structure:

```xml
<?xml version="1.0" encoding="UTF-8"?>
<XML_target>
<JOBTITLE_ID>1</JOBTITLE_ID>
<JOBTITLE>Accountant</JOBTITLE>
<Q_Person>
<FIRSTNAME>Barbara</FIRSTNAME>
<LASTNAME>Moreland</LASTNAME>
</Q_Person>
<Q_Person>
<FIRSTNAME>Mike</FIRSTNAME>
<LASTNAME>Seamans</LASTNAME>
```

XML is just a convenient example of an object that can store nested data structure. Data Services has other target objects that can accept nested data such as BAPI functions and IDoc objects, both used to extract/load data from and into SAP systems. These methods and concepts will be introduced in the next chapter.

Data Services also supports the JSON format as another source or target for nested data structures.

Nested data is often called hierarchical data as it resembles the tree structure. If you imagine row fields to be leaves, then one of the leaves could be another tree (one row or multiple rows) stored inside a leaf section.

In other words, nested data simply means mapping source table as a column in the output object structure inside a dataflow.

In the previous chapters, we worked only with the flat table or file data when datasets consisted of multiple rows and each row consisted of multiple fields, each of which could only have one value (decimal, character, date, and so on.). Nested or hierarchical data allows you to reference another table inside a row field.

> Converting a flat dataset to a nested dataset normalizes it as you do not have to duplicate parent fields for every child set of rows.

You can see how a nested table segment is displayed among other parent columns. To define if a nested structure can have multiple records for every parent record, you can right-click on the nested table segment and select the **Repeatable** menu option. Unselecting this option will make the nested segment a one-record segment and will change the icon of the nested table segment from 田 to 匣.

There is more...

Data Services has full support of nested data structures. In the steps of this recipe, we used good old Query transform to generate it. In the next recipe, we will demonstrate how the same task can be implemented with the help of special Data Services transform—**XML_Map** transform.

The XML_Map transform

In the first recipe of this chapter, *Working with nested structures*, we built the nested structure with the help of the most universal transform in Data Services—**Query** transform. **Query** transform has the power to define column mapping, filter data, join datasets together, and merge data in nested segments. In fact, many transforms that you have used before, such as **History_Preserving**, **Table_Comparison**, **Pivot**, and others, can be substituted with the set of **Query** transforms. Of course, those would be complex ETL solutions requiring more development time, would be harder to maintain and read, and, most importantly, less efficient in terms of performance.

In this recipe, we will take a look at another transform **XML_Map**, which does exactly the same task as performed in the previous recipe—builds and transforms nested structures.

We will use the same source tables PERSON.PERSON and HUMANRESOURCES.EMPLOYEE to build a dataset of job titles with nested lists of employees.

Getting ready

We have everything we need for this recipe already: two source tables, PERSON.PERSON and HUMANRESOURCE.EMPLOYEE, imported in our OLTP datastore.

How to do it...

1. Create a new job and new dataflow and open it in the workspace.

2. Place the two tables PERSON and EMPLOYEE from the OLTP datastore inside a dataflow as source tables.

3. Drag and drop **XML_Map** transform from **Local Object Library | Transforms | Platform** into a dataflow workspace and link both source tables to it. When placing transform in the workspace, choose the **Normal mode** option.

4. Left-click on **XML_Map** to open it in workspace for editing.

5. First, build the parent data structure of job titles by mapping the JOBTITLE column from the EMPLOYEE source schema to the output **XML_Map** schema.

6. On the **Iteration Rule** tab, double-click on the iteration rule field and select the EMPLOYEE input schema.

7. On the **DISTINCT** tab, drag and drop the EMPLOYEE.JOBTITLE source column into the **Distinct columns** field.

8. On the **ORDER BY** tab, specify **Ascending** sorting by the EMPLOYEE.JOBTITLE source field, as shown in the following screenshot:

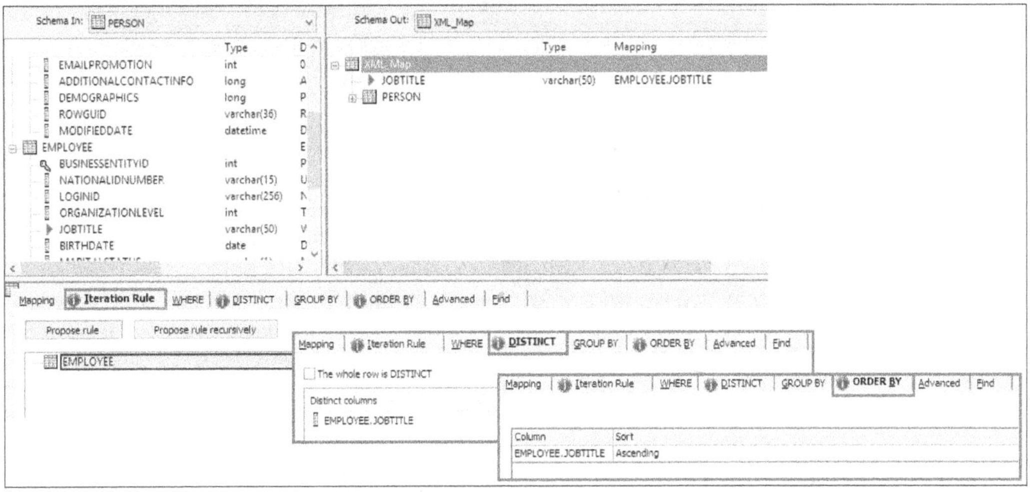

9. Now, add a nested dataset containing personal information. Drag the PERSON input schema to the output and make sure that it is added on the same level with the previously propagated JOBTITLE column.

10. Double-click on the output PERSON schema to make it current or use **Make current** from the context menu by right-clicking on the output PERSON schema.

11. On the **Iteration Rule** tab, select the INNER JOIN iteration rule and add both source input schemas underneath it.

12. On the same **Iteration Rule** tab, in the **On** field, specify the join condition:

```
PERSON.BUSINESSENTITYID = EMPLOYEE.BUSINESSENTITYID
```

13. On the **WHERE** tab, specify the join condition between parent and nested datasets in the output schema:

```
EMPLOYEE.JOBTITLE = XML_Map.JOBTITLE
```

14. Close **XML_Map Editor** and link **XML_Map** to **Query** transform object called `Gen_JobTitle_ID`, in which we will generate an ID column for the parent job title dataset.

Add the `JOBTITLE_ID` output column, as shown in the preceding screenshot, and put the mapping expression `gen_row_num()` for it on the **Mapping** tab.

15. After **Query** transform, add the **Nested Schemas Template** object as a target object. Configure it as an **XML** type with the file name: `C:\AW\Files\XML_map.xml`.

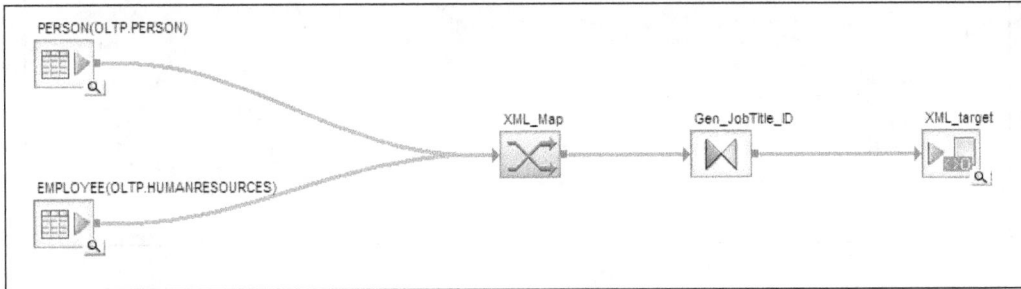

How it works...

The **XML_Map** transform properties are very similar to **Query** transform properties with a few exceptions where **XML_Map** has some extra functionality that can be used to build nested data structures.

What makes the **XML_Map** transform a really powerful tool is the ability to join any source input datasets (it does not matter if they come from flat data sources or nested data structures) and iterate on the combined dataset, producing required output results.

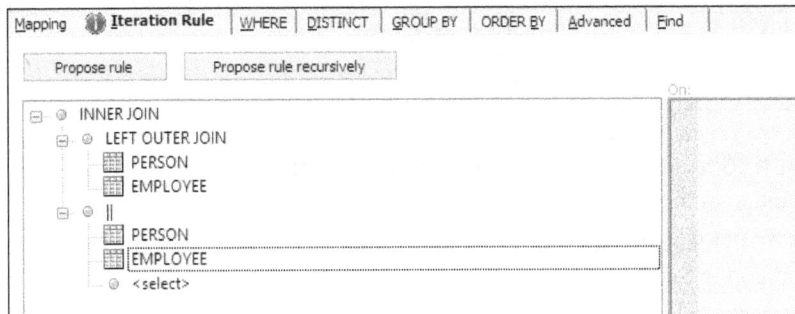

There are multiple types of join operations available:

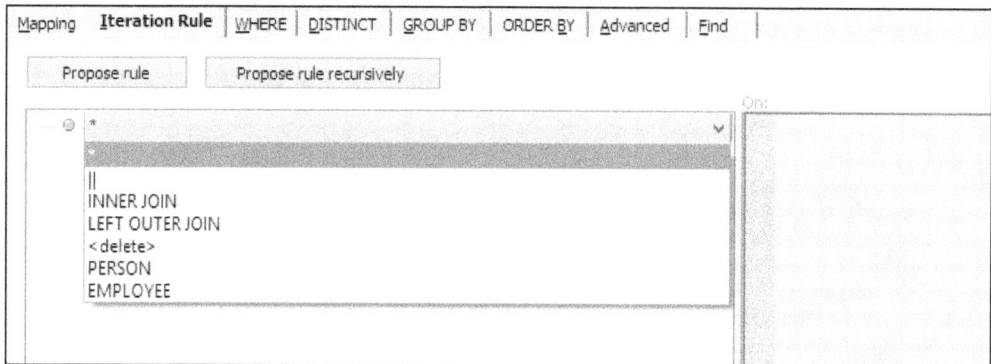

*   ▶ ***—cross-join operation**: This produces a Cartesian product of joined datasets. In SQL language, it is a normal INNER JOIN without the specified ON clause.

*   ▶ **||—parallel-join operation**: This is a non-standard SQL operation that basically concatenates the corresponding records from two joined datasets. See the example in the following figure:

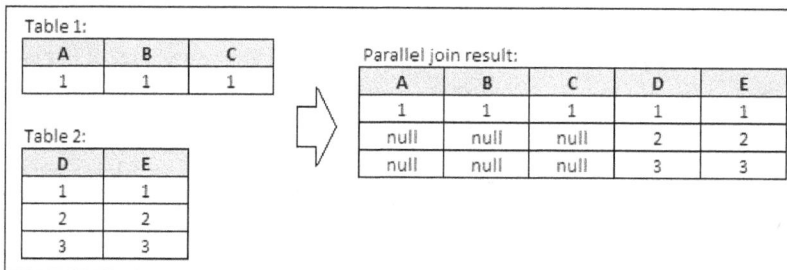

*   ▶ **INNER JOIN—standard SQL operation**: This is where you can specify the join condition in the **On** field.

*   ▶ **LEFT OUTER JOIN—standard SQL operation**: This is where you can specify the join condition in the **On** field.

In the previous steps of the recipe, we produced one hierarchical dataset with the help of **XML_Map**, which, in fact, has two datasets in it—a parent dataset of distinct job titles sourced from the EMPLOYEE table and a nested dataset of the employee's personal information which belongs to the specific job title.

If we just sourced personal information from only the PERSON table, we would not be able to specify which personal information (FIRSTNAME and LASTNAME) belongs to which job title.

By providing a joined dataset for personal information to iterate on, we could define the dependency for our nested structure by using the following expression in the **WHERE** tab, EMPLOYEE.JOBTITLE = XML_Map.JOBTITLE, which could be roughly translated to *build a dataset from the source tables, which contains the fields JOBTITLE, FIRSTNAME, LASTNAME, and nest the records with FIRSTNAME and LASTNAME fields inside the unique records of the output job title dataset by referencing the corresponding JOBTITLE column.*

The final Query transform, which is used to generate an extra output column with a unique ID for a parent job title dataset, is quite simple. We have already produced an alphabetically sorted and unique list of job titles in our parent data structure, and all that is left is to generate sequential numbers for each record, which can be easily done with help of the gen_row_num() function.

> Note how much more concise our ETL code has become with the use of the **XML_Map** transform as compared to the previous recipe where we built the same hierarchical dataset by only using **Query** transform objects.

The Hierarchy_Flattening transform

Sometimes, hierarchical data is not represented by nested (hierarchical) data structures but is actually stored within a simple flat structure in normal database tables or flat files. The simplest form of hierarchical relationships in data can be presented as a table that has two fields: parent and child.

Look at the example of folder hierarchy on the disk (as shown in the following figure). The structure on the left is visually simple to read and understand. You can easily see what is the root folder and what are the leaves, and can easily highlight the specific branch you are interested in.

Folder hierarchy on disk:

Level 0	Level 1	Level 2
Root	Folder 1	File 1
		File 2
	Folder 2	File 4
		File 5

Simplest presentation of folder hierarchy in a flat table:

Parent	Child
Root	Folder 1
Root	Folder 2
Folder 1	File 1
Folder 1	File 2
Folder 2	File 4
Folder 2	File 5

The table on the right is the simplest way to store the hierarchical relationships data in the flat format. This structure is extremely hard to query with the standard SQL language. Some databases like Oracle have special SQL clauses, which can help to query hierarchical data to be able to analyze it and present in an understandable and clear way. However, those hierarchical SQL statements can be quite complex and the majority of other databases do not support them at all, leaving you with the necessity to write stored procedures in order to parse this hierarchical data, answering even the simplest question like *select all "children" for specific "parent"*.

In this recipe, we will review the method that is available in Data Services to convert data from that simple flat hierarchical presentation of parent–child relationships into the more efficient and easy-to-use data structure that can be queried with a standard SQL language. This can be done with the **Hierarchy_Flattening** transform.

Getting ready

As we do not have multi-level parent–child relationship table, we should artificially create one. Let's build the hierarchy of locations using our three source tables from the OLTP database: ADDRESS (to source cities from), STATEPROVINCE (to source states from), and COUNTRYREGION (to source countries from)—all of them are from the same Person schema of the AdventureWorks_OLTP SQL Server database.

The resulting dataset will only have two columns—PARENT and CHILD—and each row in it will represent one link of the hierarchical dataset.

1. Create a new job and create a new dataflow in it named DF_Prepare_Hierarchy.

2. Open the dataflow in the workspace window for editing, and place three source tables in it from OLTP datastore: ADDRESS, STATEPROVINCE, and COUNTRYREGION.

3. Create Query transform State_City and join ADDRESS and STATEPROVINCE in it using the configuration settings, as shown in the following screenshot, propagating the STATEPROVINCE.NAME and ADDRESS.CITY source columns as output PARENT and CHILD columns respectively:

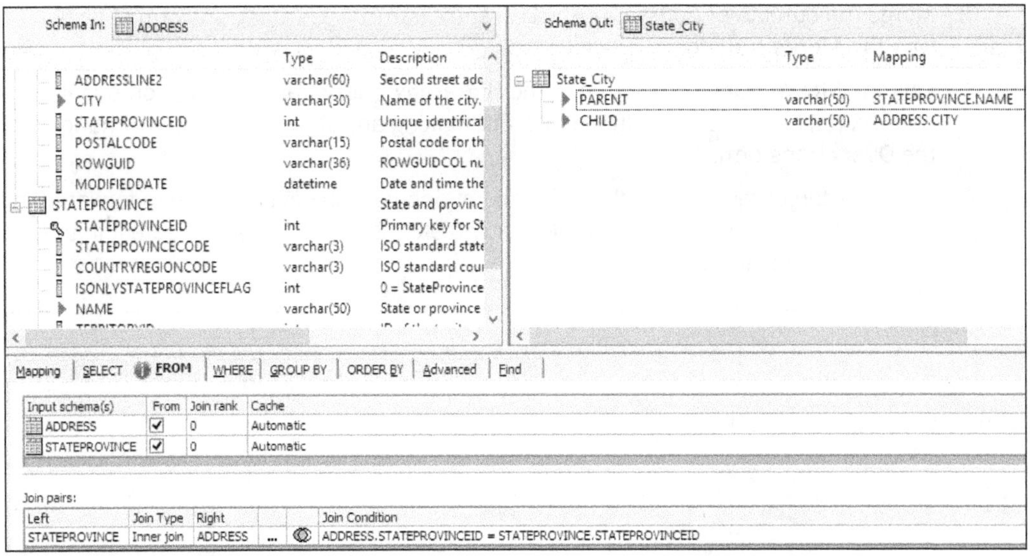

4. Create Query transform `Country_State` and join `COUNTRYREGION` and `STATEPROVINCE` in it using configuration settings, as shown in the following screenshot, propagating `COUNTRYREGION.NAME` and `STATEPROVINCE.NAME` source columns as output `PARENT` and `CHILD` columns respectively:

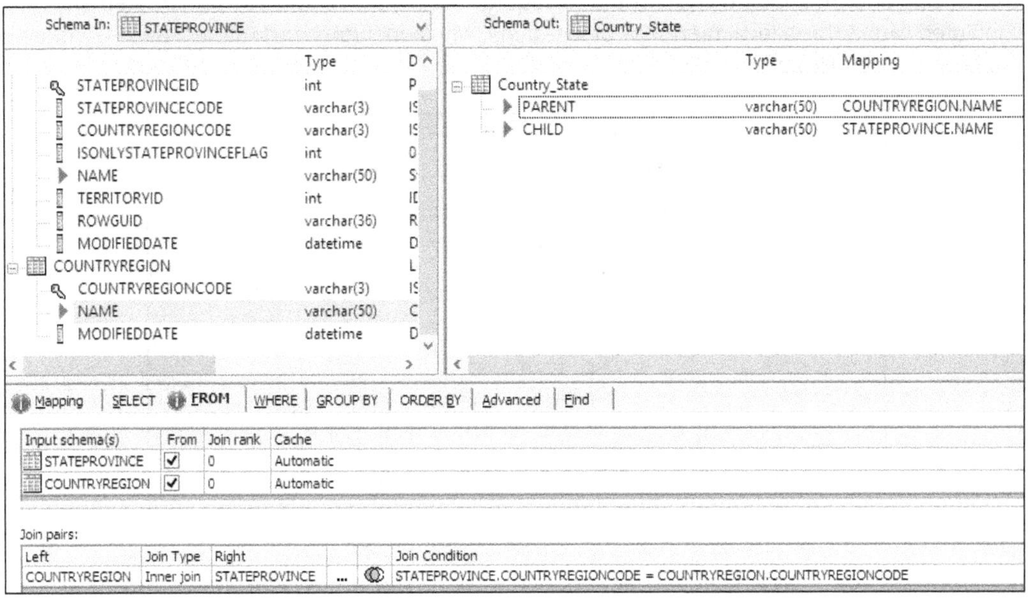

5. Merge the outputs of both `State_City` and `Country_State` transform objects with the **Merge** transform.

6. Link the **Merge** transform output to the **Hierarchy** Query transform and propagate both `PARENT` and `CHILD` columns without making any other configuration changes to the Query transform.

7. Place the target template table at the end of dataflow object sequence to forward the result data to. Name the target table `LOCATIONS_HIERARCHY` and create it in the `DS_STAGE` datastore.

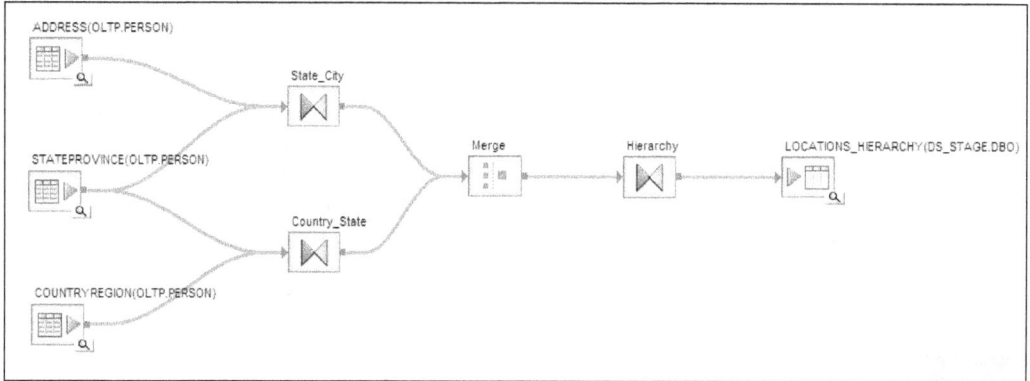

After saving and executing the job, the `LOCATIONS_HIERARCHY` table will be created and populated with a three-level hierarchy of locations, which include cities, states, and countries, as shown in the following screenshot:

Now, let's see how this dataset can be flattened with the **Hierarchy_Flattening** transform.

How to do it...

There are two different modes in which the **Hierarchy_Flattening** transform parses and restructures the source hierarchical data: **horizontal** and **vertical**. They produce different results, and we will build two different dataflows for each one of them in order to parse and flatten the source hierarchical data and compare the final result datasets.

Horizontal hierarchy flattening

The following are the steps to perform Horizontal hierarchy flattening.

1. Create a new dataflow, `DF_Hierarchy_Flattening_Horizontal`, and link it to the existing `DF_Prepare_Hierarchy` in the same job. Open it in the workspace for editing.

2. Put the `LOCATIONS_HIERARCHY` template table from the `DS_STAGE` datastore as a source table object.

3. Link the source table to the **Hierarchy_Flattening** transform object, which can be found in the **Local Object Library | Transforms | Data Integrator** section.

4. Open the **Hierarchy_Flattening** transform in the workspace window and choose the **horizontal** method of hierarchy flattening.

5. Specify the source `PARENT` and `CHILD` columns in the corresponding transform configuration settings:

6. Close the transform editor and link the **Hierarchy_Flattening** transform object to the target template table `LOCATIONS_TREE_HORIZONTAL` created in the `DS_STAGE` datastore.

Vertical hierarchy flattening

The following are the steps to perform vertical hierarchy flattening.

1. Create a new dataflow, `DF_Hierarchy_Flattening_Vertical`, and link it to the previously created `DF_Hierarchy_Flattening_Horizontal` dataflow in the same job. Open it in the workspace for editing.

2. Put the `LOCATIONS_HIERARCHY` template table from the `DS_STAGE` datastore as a source table object.

3. Link the source table to the **Hierarchy_Flattening** transform object, which can be found in the **Local Object Library | Transforms | Data Integrator** section.

4. Open the **Hierarchy_Flattening** transform in the workspace window and choose the **vertical** method of hierarchy flattening.

5. Specify the source `PARENT` and `CHILD` columns in the corresponding transform configuration settings:

6. Close the transform editor and link the **Hierarchy_Flattening** transform object to the target template table `LOCATIONS_TREE_VERTICAL` created in the `DS_STAGE` datastore.

7. Save and close the dataflow tab in the workspace. Your job should have three dataflows now: the first prepares the hierarchical dataset, the second flattens this dataset horizontally, and the third flattens the dataset vertically. Both result datasets are inserted in two different tables: `LOCATIONS_TREE_HORIZONTAL` and `LOCATIONS_TREE_VERTICAL`.

How it works...

The horizontal flattening result table looks like the following:

CURRENT_LEAF	LEAF_LEVEL	LEVEL0	LEVEL1	LEVEL2	LEVEL3
Palau	0	Palau	<Null>	<Null>	<Null>
France	0	France	<Null>	<Null>	<Null>
Rhône	1	France	Rhône	<Null>	<Null>
Côte d'Or	1	France	Côte d'Or	<Null>	<Null>
Loire Atlantique	1	France	Loire Atlantique	<Null>	<Null>
Aude	1	France	Aude	<Null>	<Null>
Hauts de Seine	1	France	Hauts de Seine	<Null>	<Null>
Boulogne-Billancourt	2	France	Hauts de Seine	Boulogne-Billancourt	<Null>
Paris La Defense	2	France	Hauts de Seine	Paris La Defense	<Null>
Courbevoie	2	France	Hauts de Seine	Courbevoie	<Null>

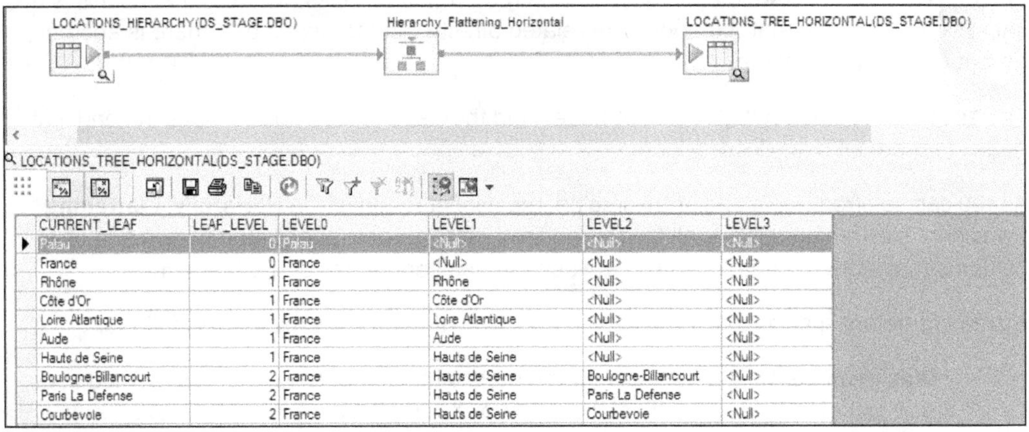

You can now see why it is called "horizontal". All levels of hierarchy are spread across different columns horizontally.

`CURRENT_LEAF` shows the name of the specific node and `LEAF_LEVEL` shows which column it can be found.

The convenience of this method is that you can see the full path to the node in one row, starting from the root node, and see the `LEVEL` columns where `LEVEL0` shows the root node.

Vertical flattening looks a bit different:

ANCESTOR	DESCENDENT	DEPTH	ROOT_FLAG	LEAF_FLAG
Kentucky	Somerset	1	0	1
Kentucky	Florence	1	0	1
Kentucky	Campbellsville	1	0	1
Kentucky	Saint Matthews	1	0	1
Kentucky	Newport	1	0	1
Kentucky	Kentucky	0	0	0
Quebec	Dorval	1	0	1
Quebec	Sainte-Foy	1	0	1
Quebec	Outremont	1	0	1
Quebec	Brossard	1	0	1

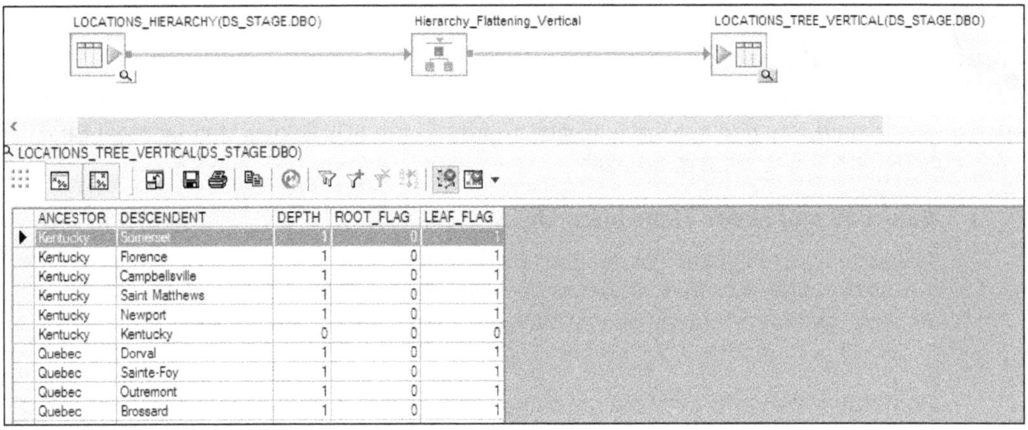

ANCESTOR and DESCENDENT are basically the same PARENT and CHILD entities, but output results set after hierarchy flattening have a lot more records as extra records showing the dependency were created between the two nodes even if they are not related directly.

The DEPTH column shows the distance between two related nodes, where 0 means this is the same node, 1 means that the nodes are related directly, and 2 means that there is another parent node between them.

The ROOT_FLAG column flags the root nodes and the LEAF_FLAG column flags the end leaf nodes that do not have descendants.

As you can see from the steps of this recipe, the configuration of the **Hierarchy_Flattening** transform is extremely simple. All that is required from you is to specify the parent and child columns that store the relationships between the neighbor nodes of the hierarchy.

Extra parameters specific to each type of hierarchy flattening are explained as follows.

> ▶ **Maximum depth**: It exists only for the horizontal method because this method uses new columns for new levels of hierarchy, and Data Services needs you to specify how many extra columns you want to create in your result target table. Imagine the situation when your hierarchical dataset stores an extremely deep hierarchy—100 levels or more—and you do not know about this after having looked at the unflattened hierarchy representation with only parent and child fields. In that case, a table with a few hundred columns for each hierarchy level may not be what you are looking for. So, this parameter allows you to control the flattening behavior of the transform.

> ▶ **Use maximum length paths**: This parameter is specific to only the vertical method of hierarchy flattening. It affects only the value of the DEPTH field in the result output schema. It works only in situations when there are multiple paths from the descendent to its ancestor and they are of a different length. Selecting this option will always pick the highest number for the DEPTH field out of these multiple paths.

Querying result tables

Now, let's try to query a result table so that you could see how easy it is to now perform the analysis of the data. You can run the following queries in the SQL Server Management Studio when connected to the STAGE database.

> ▶ **Select all root nodes of the hierarchy**:
> ```
> select CURRENT_LEAF from dbo.LOCATIONS_TREE_HORIZONTAL
>    where LEAF_LEVEL = 0 order by CURRENT_LEAF;
> select ANCESTOR from dbo.LOCATIONS_TREE_VERTICAL where
>    DEPTH = 0 and ROOT_FLAG = 1 order by ANCESTOR;
> ```

> Both SQL statements produce the same result—a list of 13 root nodes (we know that those are countries).

▶ **Check if "United States" node has a leaf node "Aurora" among its dependents:**

```
select * from dbo.LOCATIONS_TREE_HORIZONTAL where LEVEL0 =
   'United States' and CURRENT_LEAF = 'Aurora';
select * from dbo.LOCATIONS_TREE_VERTICAL where ANCESTOR =
   'United States' and DESCENDENT = 'Aurora';
```

The result returned by two queries looks different:

	CURRENT_LEAF	LEAF_LEVEL	LEVEL0	LEVEL1	LEVEL2	LEVEL3
1.	Carson	2	United States	California	Carson	NULL

	ANCESTOR	DESCENDENT	DEPTH	ROOT_FLAG	LEAF_FLAG
1	United States	Carson	2	1	1

You can see that the horizontal view is more convenient if you want to see the full path to the leaf node from the top root node.

The vertical view is more convenient to use in SQL queries as sometimes you do not have to figure out which column you have to use if you want to do a specific operation on a specific level of hierarchy. Result columns of vertical hierarchy flattening are always the same and static, whereas horizontal hierarchy flattening produces a number of columns that depends on the depth of the flattened hierarchy.

The decision of what type of hierarchy flattening to use should be made after taking into account the type of SQL queries that will be used to query this flattened data.

> If you have experimented with the hierarchy flattening result datasets, you would have probably noticed that some queries written against "horizontal" and "vertical" result tables produce different results and are not exactly what is expected. That happens because our parent and child columns are text fields (names of the countries, regions, and cities), and they do not represent the uniqueness of every node. For example, there is a state "Ontario" that belongs to Canada and a city "Ontario" that belongs to the state California. Data Services does not know about the fact that these two are different nodes and considers them to be the same node (as the name value matches). You should keep that in mind and use unique identifiers for the nodes in parent and child fields for hierarchy flattening to produce valid and consistent results.

Configuring Access Server

Access Server is required for real-time jobs to work. In this recipe, we will go through the steps of creating and configuring the Access Server component that will be required for our next recipe, where we are going to create our first real-time job.

Getting ready

Access Server can be created and configured with the help of two Data Services tools: Data Services Server Manager (   ) and Data Services Management Console (   ).

How to do it...

1. Start SAP Data Services Server Manager.

2. Go to the **Access Server** tab.

3. Click on the **Configuration Editor** button.

4. On the **Access Server Configuration Editor** window, click on the **Add** button.

5. Fill in the Access Server configuration fields, as shown in the following screenshot:

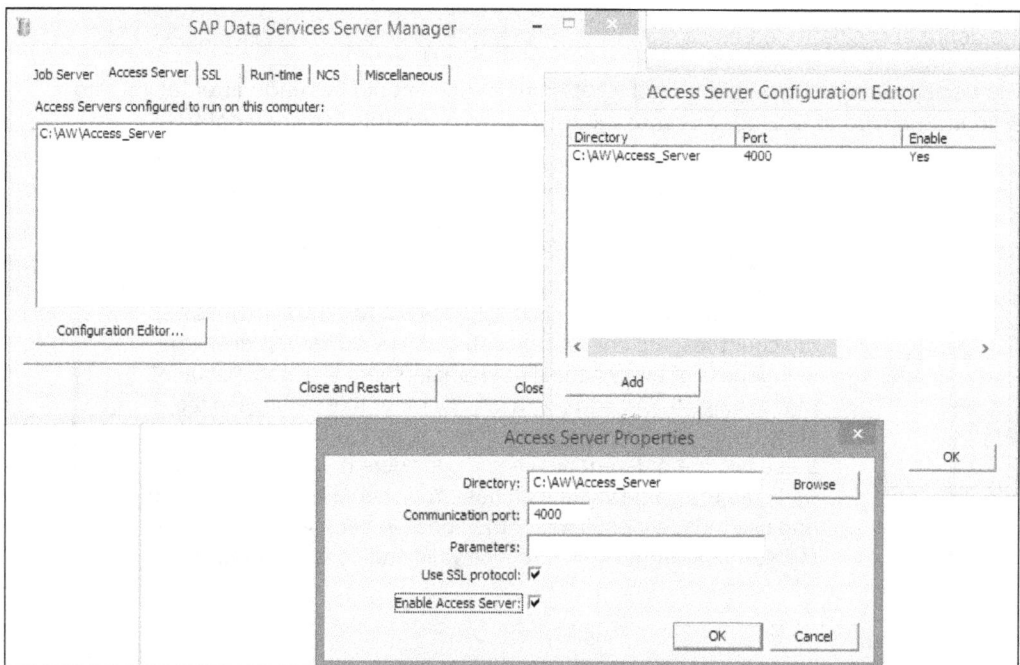

6. Do not forget to enable Access Server by ticking the corresponding option.

7. Click on **OK** to close and save the changes.

8. Start the SAP Data Services Management console in your browser and log in.

9. Go to the **Administrator | Management** section.

10. Click on the **Add** button to add the previously created Access Server.

11. Specify the host name and Access Server communication port, and click on **Apply** to add the Access Server.

Add/Edit Access Server		
Enter Access Server connection information		
	Machine Name:	IVANSHOMNIKOV
	Communication port:	4000
	Use SSL protocol:	Yes ▼
Ping Reset Apply		

How it works...

Access Server is a standard Data Services component that serves as a message broker accepting requests and messages from external systems, forwarding them to Data Services, real-time services for processing, and then passes the response back to the external system.

In other words, this is the key component required in order to feed real-time jobs with the source data and get output data from them.

We will create a real-time job in the next recipe and explain the design process of real-time jobs in detail. In the meantime, you should only know that the main source and target objects of real-time jobs are messages (most commonly in an XML structure) and that Access Server is responsible for delivering those messages.

With the preceding steps, the Access Server service was created and enabled in the Data Services environment and is now ready to accept the requests from external systems.

Creating real-time jobs

In this recipe, we will create real-time jobs and emulate the requests from the external system using the SoapUI testing tool in order to get the response with processed data back. We will go through all the steps required to configure all components required for real-time jobs to work.

Getting ready

In this section, we will install the open source SoapUI tool and create a new project that will be used to send and receive SOAP messages (XML-based format) to and from Data Services.

Installing SoapUI

You can download and install SoapUI using the URL `http://www.soapui.org/`.

The installation process is very straightforward. All you have to do is just follow the instructions on the screen.

After the installation is complete, start the SoapUI. Use the **SOAP** button in the top tool bar menu to create a new SOAP project. Specify the project name and initial WSDL address, as shown in the following screenshot:

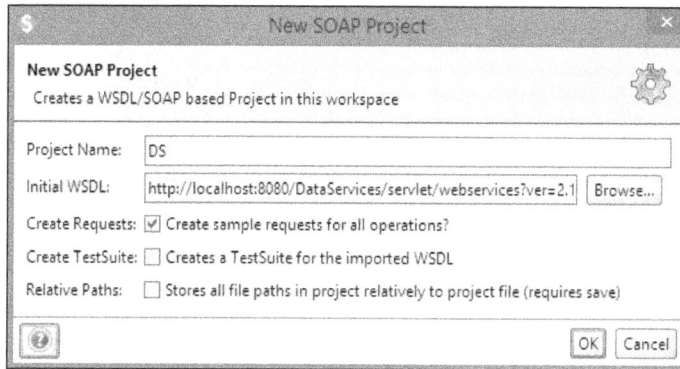

The initial WSDL address can be obtained from Data Services. To get it, log in to **Data Services Management Console**, go to the **Administrator** section, choose **Web Services**, and click on the **View WSDL** button at the bottom of the main window.

In the new opened window, select and copy the top URL address and paste it in the **New SOAP Project** configuration window, as shown in the following screenshot:

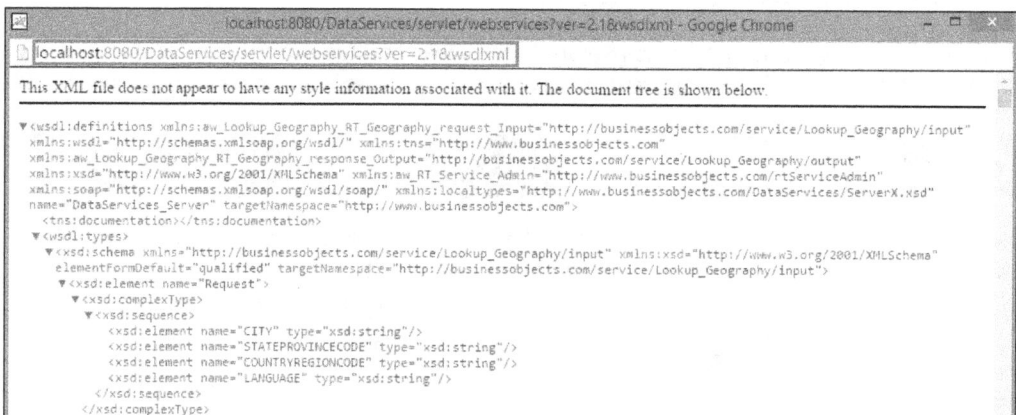

At this point, we have made an initial configuration and can proceed with actually creating real-time jobs at the Data Services side.

How to do it...

Now, we have an "external" system in place and configured in order to send us request messages. We remember that the Data Services component responsible for accepting these messages and sending them back is Access Server, and it was already configured by us in the previous recipe. Now, we need the last and most important component to be created and configured—Data Services real-time job, which will be processing these SOAP messages and returning the required result.

The goal of our real-time job will be to provide the full names of the location codes for a specific city and the postal code of the city.

1. Go to the **Local Object Library | Jobs** section, right-click on **Real-Time Jobs**, and choose **New** from the context menu.

2. Any real-time job is created with two default mandatory objects that define the borders of the real-time job processing section: **RT_Process_begins** and **Step_ends**.

3. Create two scripts, `Init_Script` and `Final_Script`, and place them correspondingly before and after real-time job processing section.

4. Inside the real-time job processing section, create a dataflow and name it `DF_RT_Lookup_Geography`, as shown in the following figure:

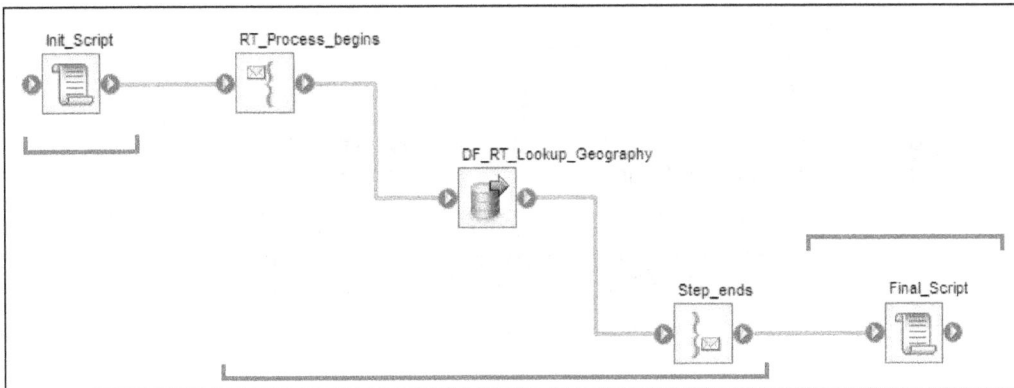

5. Now, open the dataflow `DF_RT_Lookup_Geography` for editing in the main workspace window. First we have, to create file formats for our request and response messages.

6. Create a request file in your `C:\AW\Files` folder named `RT_request.xsd`:

```
<?xml version="1.0" encoding="UTF-8"?>
<xsd:schema  xmlns:xsd="http://www.w3.org/2001/XMLSchema">
  <xsd:element name="Request" >
    <xsd:complexType>
      <xsd:sequence>
        <xsd:element name="CITY" type="xsd:string"/>
```

```
      <xsd:element name="STATEPROVINCECODE"
        type="xsd:string"/>
      <xsd:element name="COUNTRYREGIONCODE"
        type="xsd:string"/>
      <xsd:element name="LANGUAGE" type="xsd:string"/>
    </xsd:sequence>
  </xsd:complexType>
 </xsd:element>
</xsd:schema>
```

7. Create a response file in your `C:\AW\Files` folder named `RT_response.xsd`:

```
<?xml version="1.0" encoding="UTF-8"?>
<xsd:schema  xmlns:xsd="http://www.w3.org/2001/XMLSchema">
  <xsd:element name="Response" >
    <xsd:complexType>
      <xsd:sequence>
        <xsd:element name="CITY" type="xsd:string"/>
        <xsd:element name="POSTALCODE" type="xsd:string"/>
        <xsd:element name="STATEPROVINCENAME" type=
          "xsd:string"/>
        <xsd:element name="COUNTRYREGIONNAME" type=
          "xsd:string"/>
      </xsd:sequence>
    </xsd:complexType>
  </xsd:element>
</xsd:schema>
```

8. To create a request message file format, open **Local Object Library | Formats**, right-click on **Nested Schemas**, and choose **New | XML Schema...** from the context menu. Specify the following settings in the opened **Import XML Schema Format** window:

9. To create a response message file format, open **Local Object Library | Formats**, right-click on **Nested Schemas**, and choose **New | XML Schema...** from the context menu. Specify the following settings in the opened **Import XML Schema Format** window:

Import XML Schema Format	✕

Format name:	RT_Geography_response
File name / URL:	C:\AW\Files\RT_response.xsd Browse...
Namespace:	⌄
Root element name:	Response ⌄
	Abstract Type... Substitution Group...
Circular level:	0
Default varchar size:	1024
	☐ Automatically assign content type
	☐ Import base64 binary data types as blob
	OK Cancel

10. Import RT_Geography_request as a source object into the dataflow DF_RT_Lookup_Geography and link it to the **Request** Query transform, propagating all columns to the output schema. Choose the **Make Message Source** option when importing the object into a dataflow.

11. Import RT_Geography_response as a target object into the dataflow DF_RT_Lookup_Geography. Choose the **Make Message Target** option when importing the object into a dataflow.

12. Import the `DIMGEOGRAPHY` table object from DWH datastore and join it with the **Request** Query transform using the `Lookup_DimGeography` Query transform. Configure the mapping settings according to the following screenshots:

Schema In: Request			Schema Out: Lookup_DimGeography		
	Type	Description		Type	Mapping
⊟ DIMGEOGRAPHY			⊟ Lookup_DimGeography		
⚷ GEOGRAPHYKEY	int		▶ CITY	varchar(30)	DIMGEOGR...
▶ CITY	varchar(30)		▶ POSTALCODE	varchar(15)	DIMGEOGR...
▯ STATEPROVINCECODE	varchar(3)		▶ STATEPROVINCENAME	varchar(50)	DIMGEOGR...
▶ STATEPROVINCENAME	varchar(50)		▶ COUNTRYREGIONNAME	varchar(50)	decode(Req...
▯ COUNTRYREGIONCODE	varchar(3)				
▶ ENGLISHCOUNTRYREGIONNAME	varchar(50)				
▶ SPANISHCOUNTRYREGIONNAME	varchar(50)				
▶ FRENCHCOUNTRYREGIONNAME	varchar(50)				
▶ POSTALCODE	varchar(15)				
▯ SALESTERRITORYKEY	int				
▯ IPADDRESSLOCATOR	varchar(15)				
⊟ Request					
▯ CITY	varchar(1024)				
▯ STATEPROVINCECODE	varchar(1024)				
▯ COUNTRYREGIONCODE	varchar(1024)				
▶ LANGUAGE	varchar(1024)				

Mapping | SELECT | FROM | WHERE | GROUP BY | ORDER BY | Advanced | Find

for: Lookup_DimGeography.COUNTRYREGIONNAME

Functions... | ... | Apply

```
decode (
Request.LANGUAGE = 'EN',DIMGEOGRAPHY.ENGLISHCOUNTRYREGIONNAME,
Request.LANGUAGE = 'SP',DIMGEOGRAPHY.SPANISHCOUNTRYREGIONNAME,
Request.LANGUAGE = 'FR',DIMGEOGRAPHY.FRENCHCOUNTRYREGIONNAME,
DIMGEOGRAPHY.ENGLISHCOUNTRYREGIONNAME
)
```

13. Go to the **FROM** tab and configure the join conditions for `LEFT OUTER JOIN` between the **Request** Query transform and `DIMGEOGRAPHY` source table:

Join pairs:

Left	Join Type	Right			Join Condition
Request	Left outer join	DIMGEOGRAPHY	...	◎	Request.CITY = DIMGEOGRAPHY.CITY and Request.STATEPROVINCECODE = DIMGEOGRAPHY.STATEPROVINCECODE and Request.COUNTRYREGIONCODE = DIMGEOGRAPHY.COUNTRYREGIONCODE

14. Link the `Lookup_DimGeography` Query transform to the target `RT_Geography_response` XML schema object.

15. Your dataflow should look like the following figure:

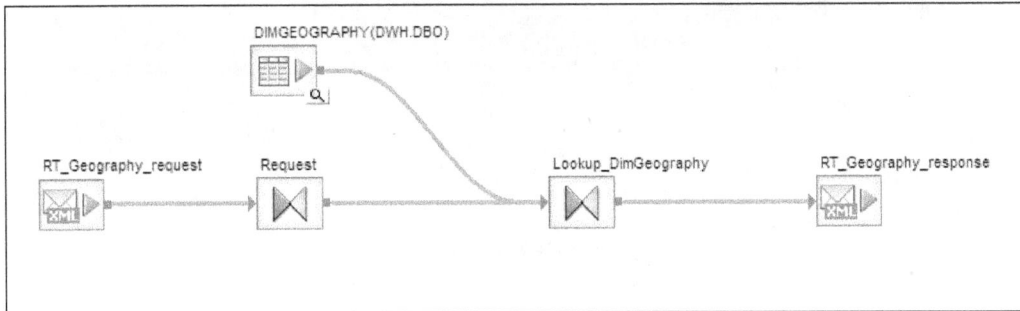

16. Save and validate the job.

How it works...

The dataflow we created in our real-time job accepts XML messages (requests) as an input and produces XML messages (responses) as an output.

We use the `DIMGEOGRAPHY` table from our data warehouse to fetch the postal code, full state/province name, and country name in either French, English, or Spanish, depending on which city and language code were received in the request message.

Basically, our real-time job serves as a lookup mechanism against data warehouse data.

Let's publish our real-time job as a web service and do our first test run to see how the exchanging messages mechanism works.

1. Open the **Data Services Management Console | Administrator | Real-Time | <Your Server Name>:4000 | Real-Time Services | Real-Time Service Configuration** tab.

2. Click on **Add** to add the real-time service `Lookup_Geography`; use the following settings to configure it, and click on **Apply** when you have finished:

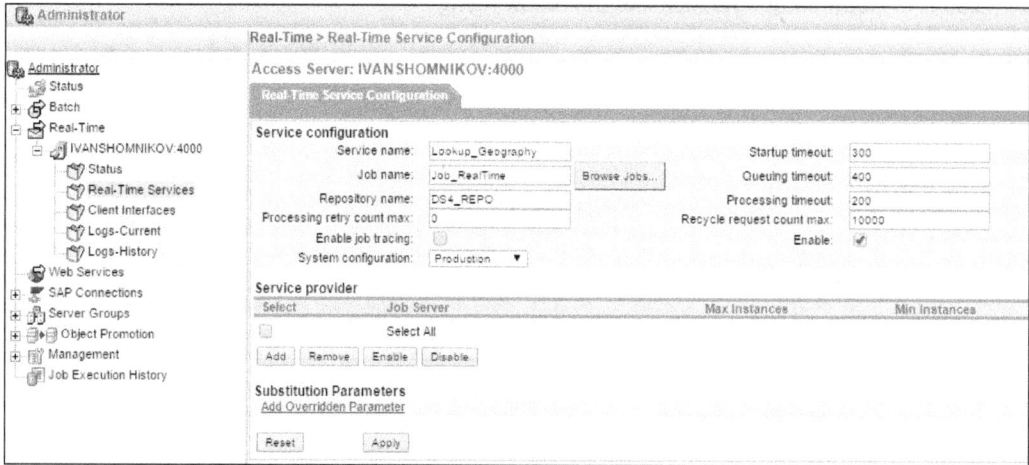

3. Go to the next **Real-Time Services Status** tab and start the service just created by selecting it and clicking on the **Start** button:

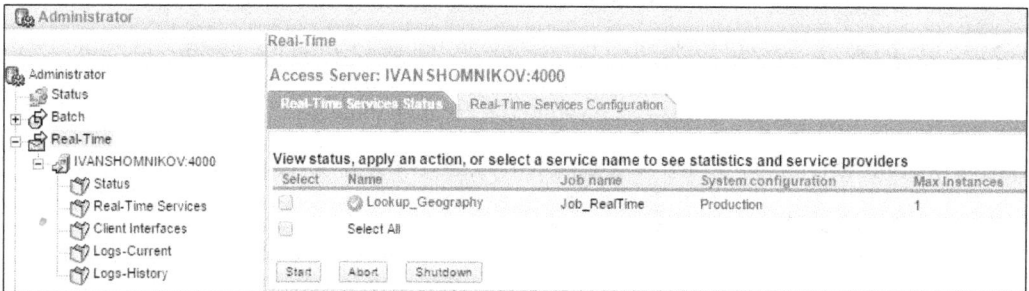

The icon of the real-time service should become green.

1. Go to the **Administrator | Web Services | Web Services Configuration** tab.

2. Select **Add Real-Time Services** in the below combobox and click on the **Apply** button on the right.

3. Select `Lookup_Geography` from the list and click on **Add**:

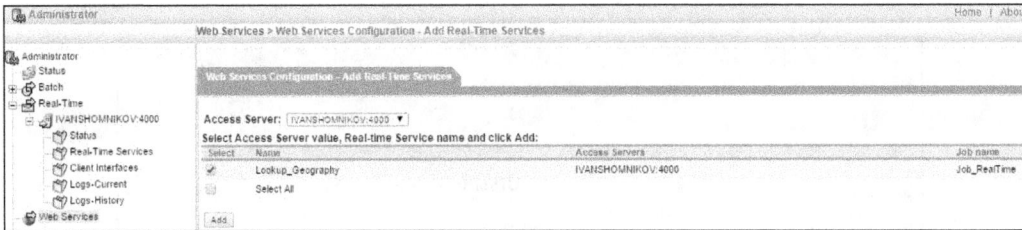

4. The `Lookup_Geography` real-time service should appear on the **Web Services Status** tab, as shown in the following screenshot:

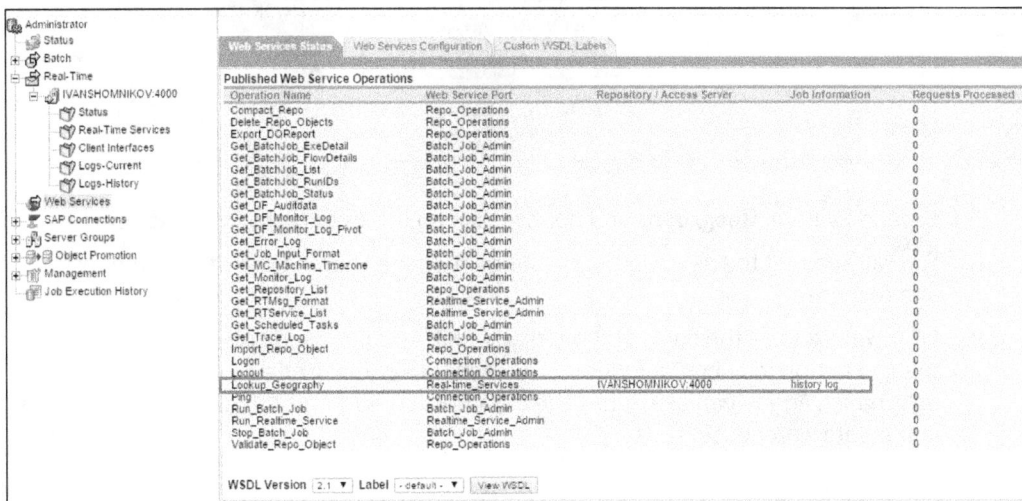

5. We have successfully published our created a real-time job as real-time web service. Now, open SoapUI and make sure that you can see the `Lookup_Geography` web service. To do that, start the SoapUI tool and expand the **DS Project | Real-time_ Services** tab in the project tree panel.

6. Right-click on the **Lookup_Geography** item and choose **New request** from the context menu.

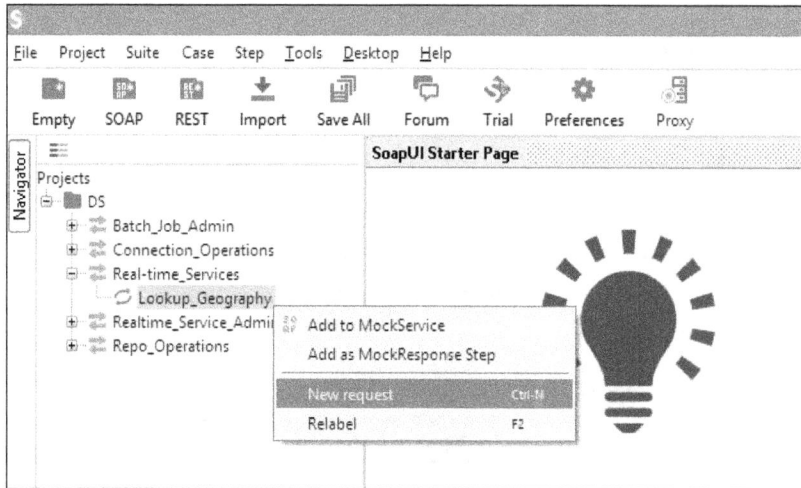

7. Expand **Lookup_Geography** and double-click on the **Geography_request** item.

8. You will see that the new window on the right opens showing two panels: request and response.

9. Fill in values in all the fields of the request XML structure and click on the green triangle button to submit a request. The response is received and displayed in the right panel. As you can see, it has the data from DIMGEOGRAPHY table, which resides in the data warehouse:

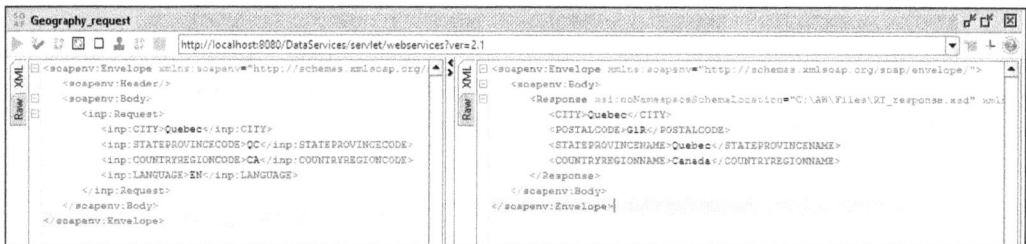

> One of the most popular cases of using real-time jobs is cleansing the data through web services requests. A real-time job receives the specific value and passes it through the Data Quality transforms available in Data Services in order to cleanse it and then returns the result in the response message.

11
Working with SAP Applications

Introduction

This chapter is dedicated to the topic of reading and loading data from SAP systems with the example of a SAP ERP system. Data Services provides quick and convenient methods of obtaining information from SAP applications. As this is a quite vast topic to discuss, there will be only one recipe but, nevertheless, it should cover all aspects of extracting and loading data into SAP ERP.

Loading data into SAP ERP

We will not discuss the topic of configuring the SAP system to communicate with the Data Services environment as it would require another few chapters on the subject and, most importantly, it is not the purpose of this book. All this information can be found in detailed SAP documentation available at `http://help.sap.com`.

We presume that you have exactly the same Data Services and staging environments configured and created in the previous chapters of this book and have also installed and configured the SAP ERP system, which can communicate with the Data Services job server.

In this recipe, we will go through the steps of loading information into the SAP ERP system by using Data Services. In one of our preparation processes, we will be generating data records for insertion right in the dataflow, when usually, you have the data ready to be loaded in the staging area extracted from another system.

We will also review the main SAP transactions involved in the process of manually creating data objects, monitoring the loading process on the SAP side, and the transaction, which might be used for the post-load validation of loaded data.

We will be using the example of creating/loading batch data, which is related to material data in SAP ERP. First, we will create the specific material required for the batch data to be loaded. Then, we will create the test batch manually to see how it is done on SAP side, and then we will develop ETL code in Data Services, which will prepare the batch record and send it to the SAP side.

Getting ready

The first thing we have to do is to create the material for which we will be creating batches in SAP.

1. Log in to the SAP ERP system and run the transaction **MM01** to create new material.

2. Specify **Material** as RAWMAT01, **Material Type**, and **Industry sector**:

Create Material (Initial Screen)

Select View(s)	Org. Levels Data

Material	RAWMAT01
Industry sector	Chemical industry ▾
Material Type	Raw materials ▾
Change Number	

Copy from...

Material	

3. Select the following views for the new material: **Basic data 1**, **Basic data 2**, **Classification**, and **General Plant Data \ Storage 1**:

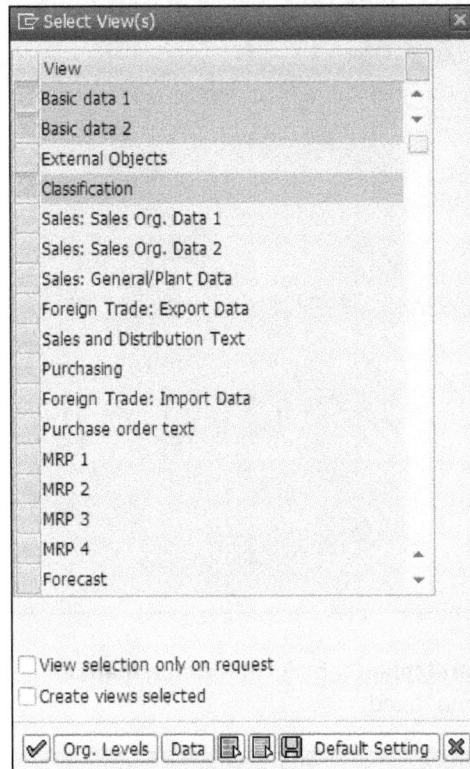

4. On the next window, specify **Organization Levels**:

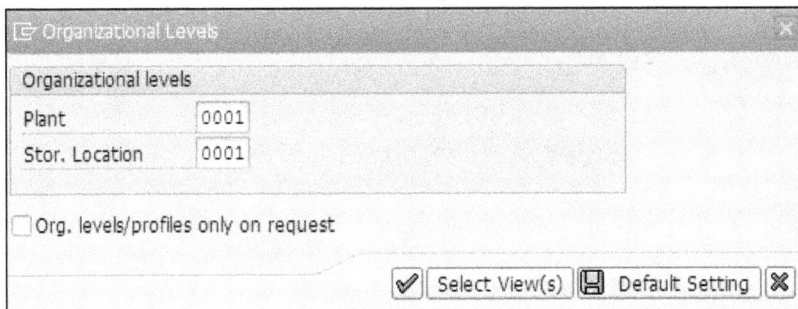

5. On the next screen, define **Base Unit of Measure** and material description:

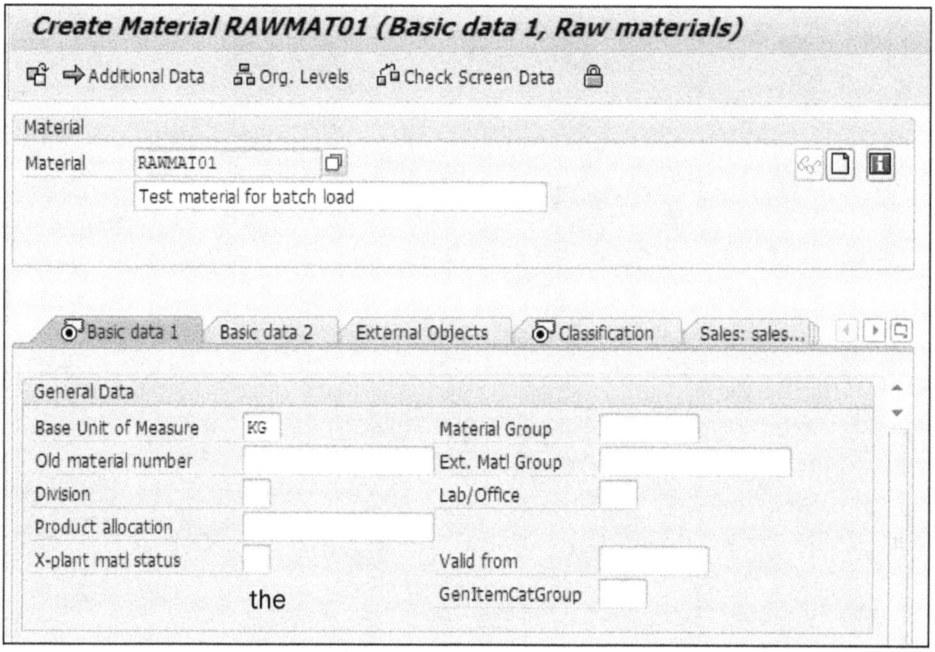

Create Material RAWMAT01 (Basic data 1, Raw materials)

⤷ ➡Additional Data   🔠Org. Levels   🔍Check Screen Data   🔒

Material

Material	RAWMAT01
	Test material for batch load

Basic data 1 | Basic data 2 | External Objects | Classification | Sales: sales...

General Data

Base Unit of Measure	KG		Material Group	
Old material number			Ext. Matl Group	
Division			Lab/Office	
Product allocation				
X-plant matl status			Valid from	
	the		GenItemCatGroup	

6. On the **Sales: general/plant** tab, tick the **Batch management** checkbox to define the material as batch managed:

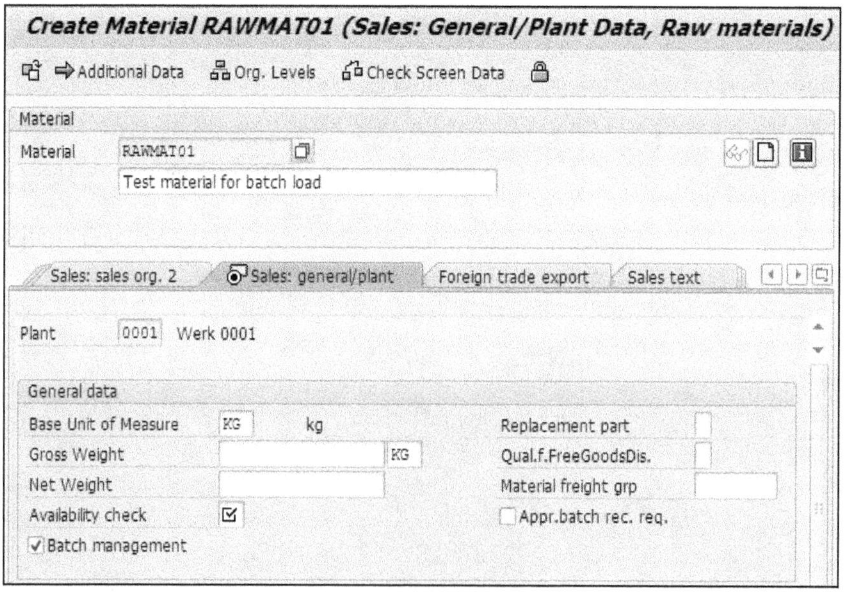

Create Material RAWMAT01 (Sales: General/Plant Data, Raw materials)

⤷ ➡Additional Data   🔠Org. Levels   🔍Check Screen Data   🔒

Material

Material	RAWMAT01
	Test material for batch load

Sales: sales org. 2 | Sales: general/plant | Foreign trade export | Sales text

| Plant | 0001 | Werk 0001 |

General data

Base Unit of Measure	KG	kg	Replacement part	
Gross Weight		KG	Qual.f.FreeGoodsDis.	
Net Weight			Material freight grp	
Availability check	☑		☐ Appr.batch rec. req.	
☑ Batch management				

7. Finally, on the **Classification** tab, classify the material as the raw material of class type 023:

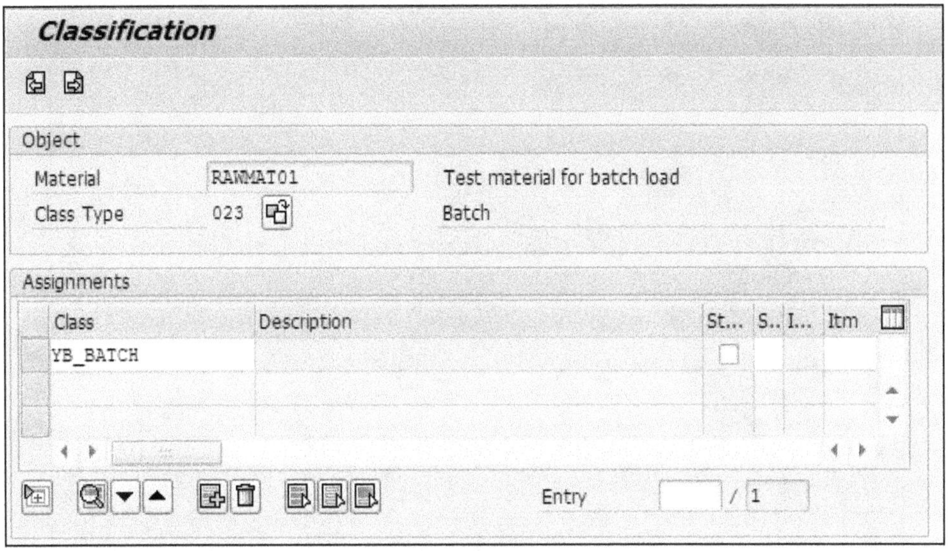

Classification

Object

Material	RAWMAT01	Test material for batch load
Class Type	023	Batch

Assignments

Class	Description	St...	S..	I...	Itm	
YB_BATCH		☐				

Entry ___ / 1

Click on the **Continue** (*Enter*) button in the top-left corner to save and create new material.

Now, we can manually create the first batch object for our new material so that we can later compare it to the batch object that will be generated and inserted by Data Services jobs automatically.

8. Run the transaction **MSC1N** to create a new batch, and specify the material number and batch name that you would like to create:

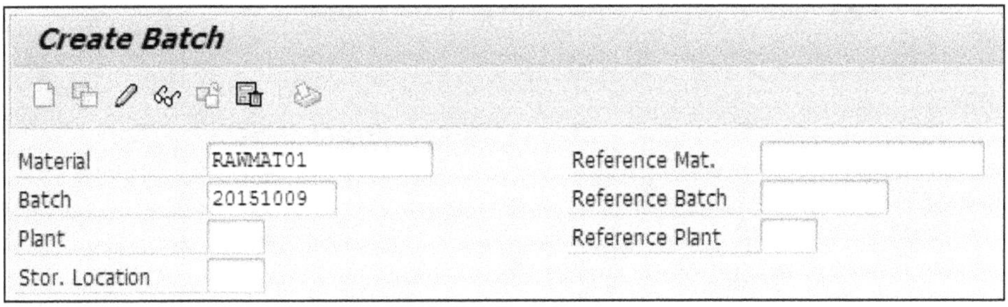

Create Batch

Material	RAWMAT01	Reference Mat.	
Batch	20151009	Reference Batch	
Plant		Reference Plant	
Stor. Location			

9. Click on **Continue**, and on the next screen, fill in the values for the following fields: the **Date of Manufacture** batch, the **Last Goods Receipt** date, and **Ctry of Origin**:

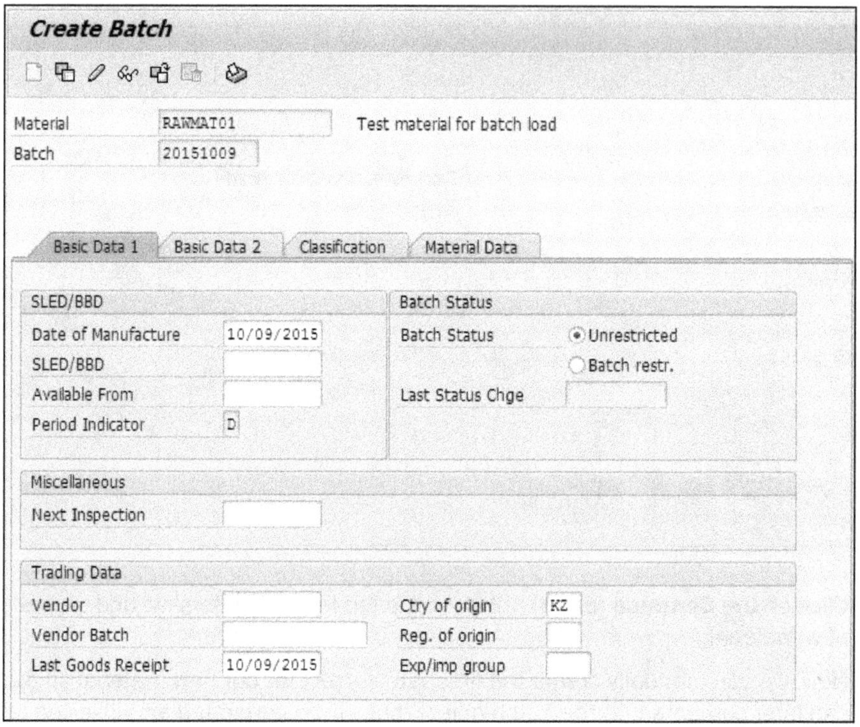

Create Batch

🗋 🖳 ✏ ⚙ 🖳 📄 ◈

Material	RAWMAT01	Test material for batch load
Batch	20151009	

Basic Data 1 \ Basic Data 2 \ Classification \ Material Data

SLED/BBD		Batch Status	
Date of Manufacture	10/09/2015	Batch Status	⦿ Unrestricted
SLED/BBD			○ Batch restr.
Available From		Last Status Chge	
Period Indicator	D		

Miscellaneous	
Next Inspection	

Trading Data			
Vendor		Ctry of origin	KZ
Vendor Batch		Reg. of origin	
Last Goods Receipt	10/09/2015	Exp/imp group	

---

10. Click on **Continue** to save and create a new batch, **20151009**.

    The last preparation step we have to complete is the configuration of a partner profile in our SAP ERP so that the system can accept the IDoc messages containing the batch data that will be sent to SAP ERP from Data Services.

11. Run the transaction **WE20** to configure the partner profile.

12. On the **Partner profiles** window, select the **Partner Type LS** section and select the client you are currently using:

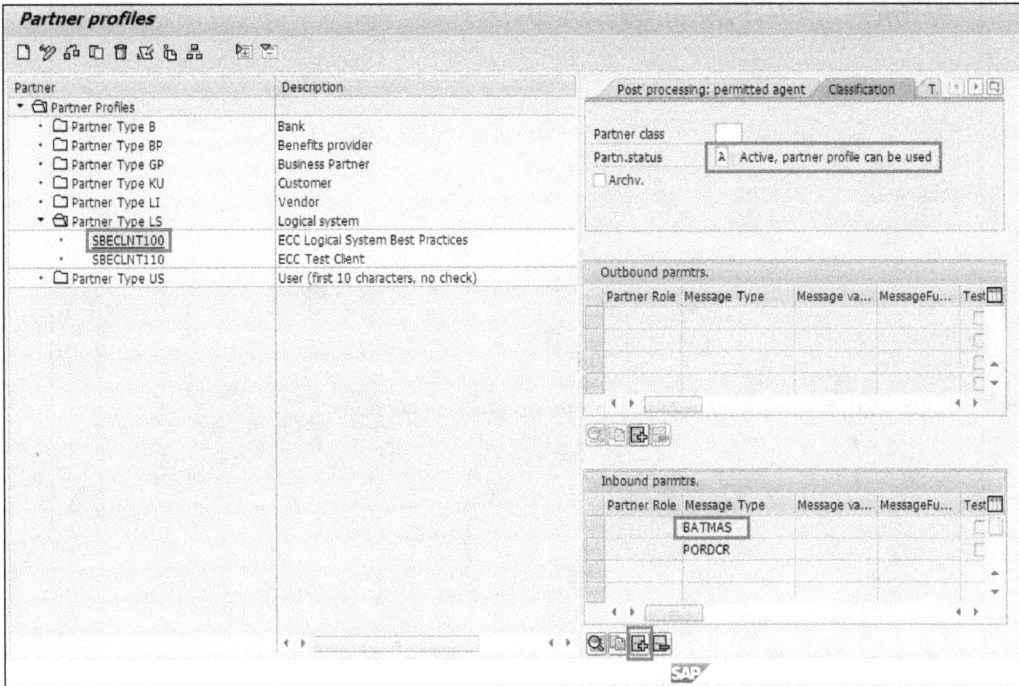

Partner profiles

Partner	Description
▼ 📁 Partner Profiles	
• 📁 Partner Type B	Bank
• 📁 Partner Type BP	Benefits provider
• 📁 Partner Type GP	Business Partner
• 📁 Partner Type KU	Customer
• 📁 Partner Type LI	Vendor
▼ 📁 Partner Type LS	Logical system
• SBECLNT100	ECC Logical System Best Practices
• SBECLNT110	ECC Test Client
• 📁 Partner Type US	User (first 10 characters, no check)

Post processing: permitted agent   Classification

Partner class

Partn.status   A Active, partner profile can be used

☐ Archv.

Outbound parmtrs.

Partner Role	Message Type	Message va...	MessageFu...	Test

Inbound parmtrs.

Partner Role	Message Type	Message va...	MessageFu...	Test
	BATMAS			
	PORDCR			

Make sure that your **Partn.status** is **Active** on the **Classification** tab and that you have **BATMAS** specified in the **Inbound parmtrs** list. If not, then click on the **Create inbound parameter** button under the **Inbound parmtrs** tab and define the BATMAS inbound parameter:

```
Partner profiles: Inbound parameters

Partner No.        SBECLNT100   ECC Logical System Best Practices
Partn.Type         LS
Partner Role       [    ]


Message type       BATMAS
Message code       [    ]
Message function   [    ]            Test

┌─ Inbound options ─┐ Post processing: permitted agent   Telephony

Process code        BAPI
✓ Cancel Processing After Syntax Error

Processing by Function Module
○ Trigger by background program
◉ Trigger Immediately                    ⇨   Options
```

Now, everything is ready on the SAP ERP side and all we have to do is create the Data Services job that will generate and send the data into the SAP ERP system for insertion.

How to do it...

1. Start Data Services Designer and go to **Local Object Library | Datastores**.

2. Right-click on the empty space of the **Datastores** tab and choose **New** from the context menu in order to create new datastore object.

3. Create a new datastore, SAP_ERP, by specifying the datastore type **SAP Applications** and database server name along with your SAP credentials.

4. Click on the **Advanced** button and specify the additional settings required for setting up the connection to the SAP ERP system, such as **Client number** and **System number**. See the following screenshot for the full list of configuration settings:

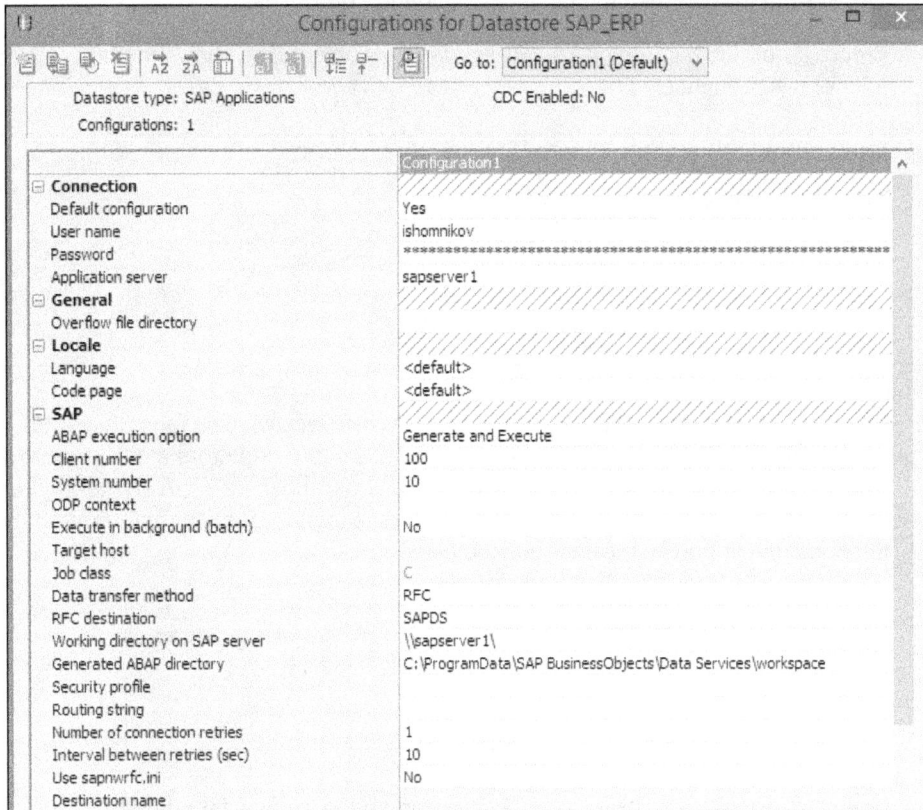

Click on **OK** to create the datastore object.

5. Import the following objects in your datastore by right-clicking on the required section of the object you want to import and choosing the **Import By Name...** option from the context menu:

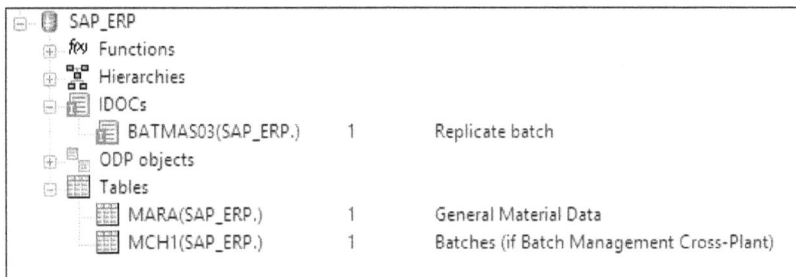

The IDoc object BATMAS03 will be used as a target object to transfer batch data to the SAP system.

The MARA and MCH1 tables will be used as source objects to extract data from the SAP system for pre-load and post-load validation purposes.

6. Create a new job containing four linked dataflow objects, as shown in the following screenshot:

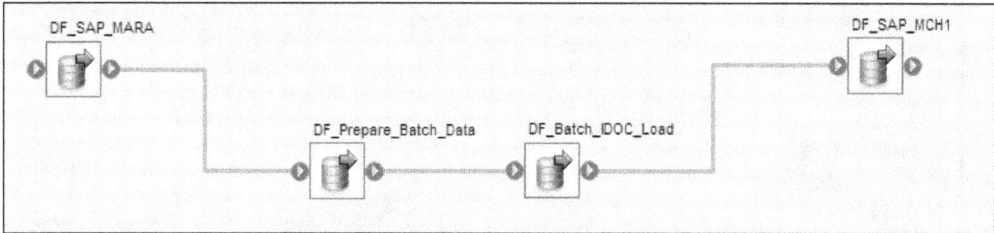

7. Open the first DF_SAP_MARA dataflow in the workspace window for editing and specify the MARA table object imported in the SAP_ERP datastore as a source and the new SAP_MARA template table in the STAGE database as a target. Propagate all columns from the source MARA table to SAP_MARA using Query transform. Run the job once and import the target table object:

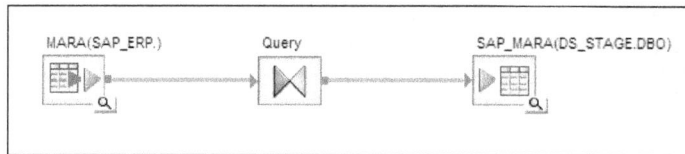

8. Open DF_Prepare_Batch_Data in the workspace window for editing.

9. Add the **Row_Generation** transform as a source. Set it up to generate only one record with the row number starting at 1.

10. Link it to the Create_Batch_Record Query transform, which will be used to define the fields of the created record. Use the following screenshot as a reference for column names and mappings:

11. Add another Query transform named `Validate_Material`, link `Create_Batch_Record` to it, and propagate all columns from the input schema to the output schema.

12. Add an extra column as a new function call of the `lookup_ext` function and configure it as shown in the following screenshot, looking up the `MATNR` field from the `SAP_MARA` table by the `MATERIAL` field value from the input schema:

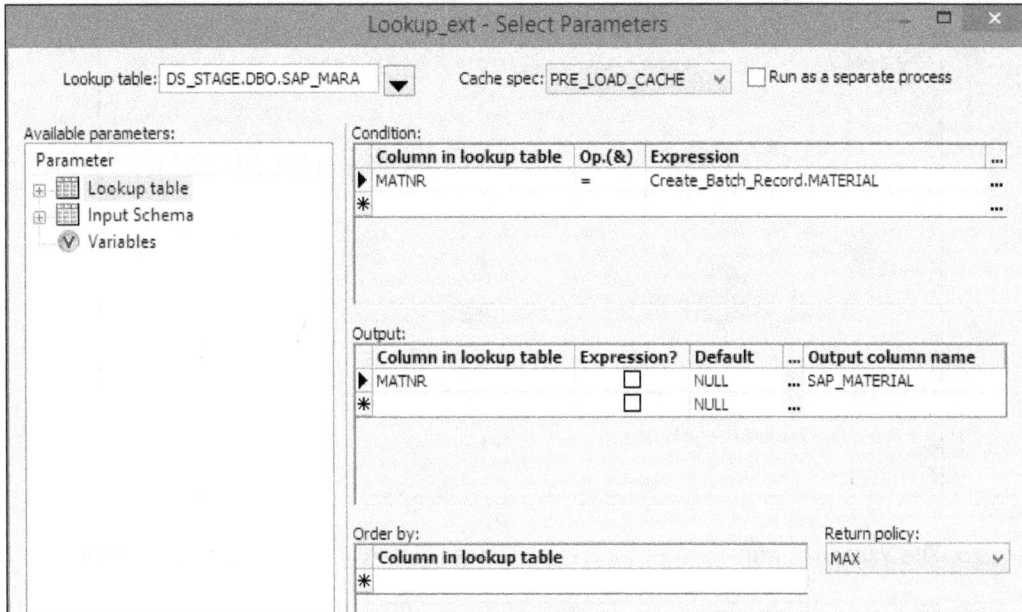

13. Add the **Validation** transform, forking the dataset into three categories—**Rule**, **Pass**, and **Fail**, sending the outputs to three target tables: `BATCH`, `BATCH_REJECT`, and `BATCH_REJECT_RULE`, as shown in the following screenshot:

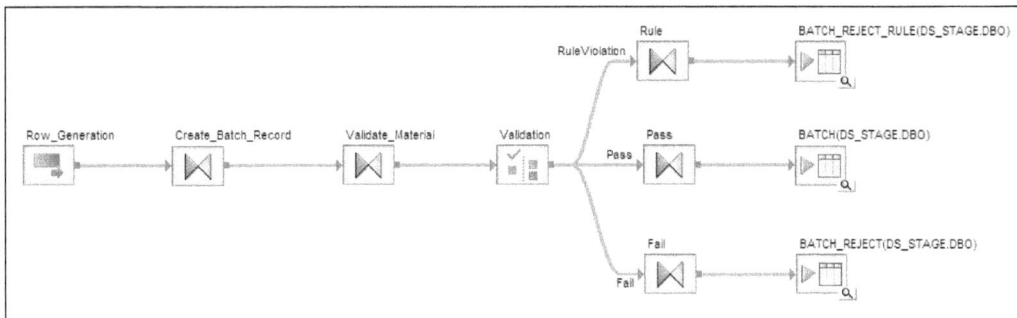

14. Open the **Validation** transform in the workspace window for editing and adding a new validation rule:

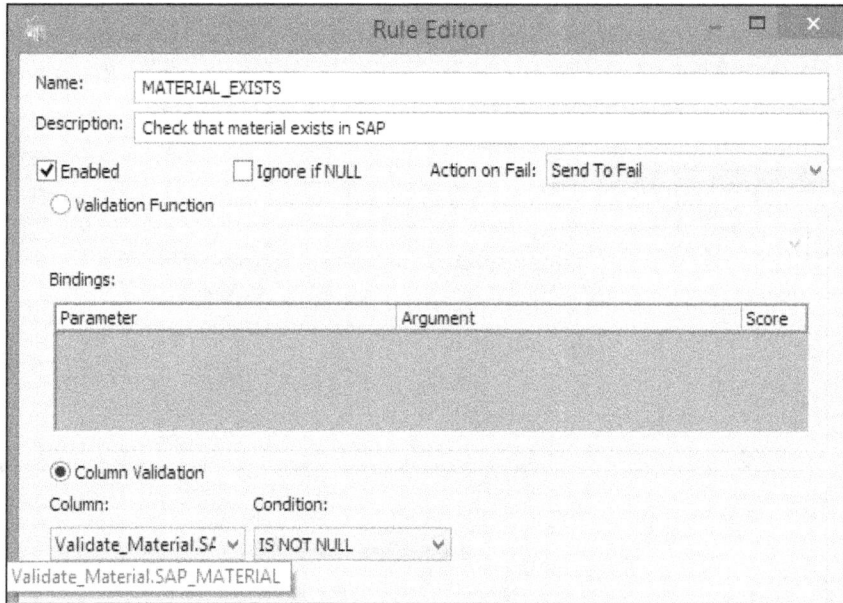

15. The Validation transform editor should look as shown in the following screenshot:

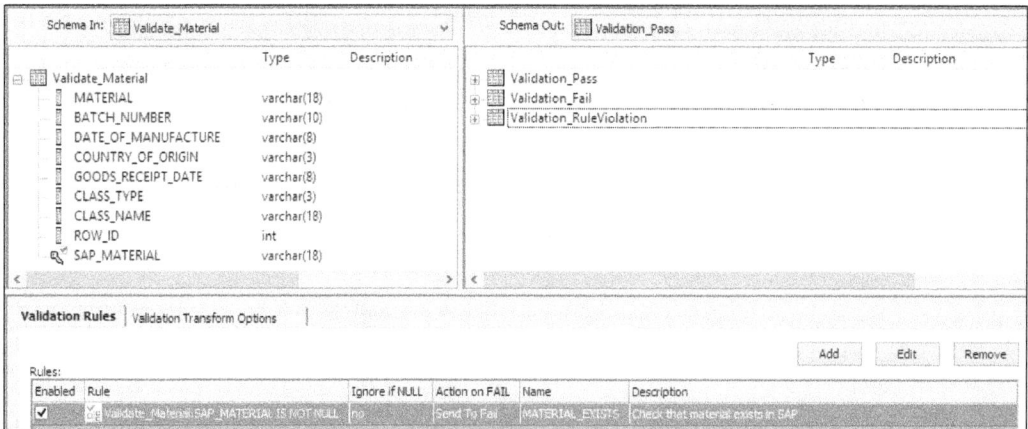

Close the dataflow and save the job.

16. Open the third dataflow, DF_Batch_IDOC_Load, in the workspace window for editing.

17. Build the structure of the dataflow, as shown in the following screenshot. The steps to configure each of the dataflow components will be provided further.

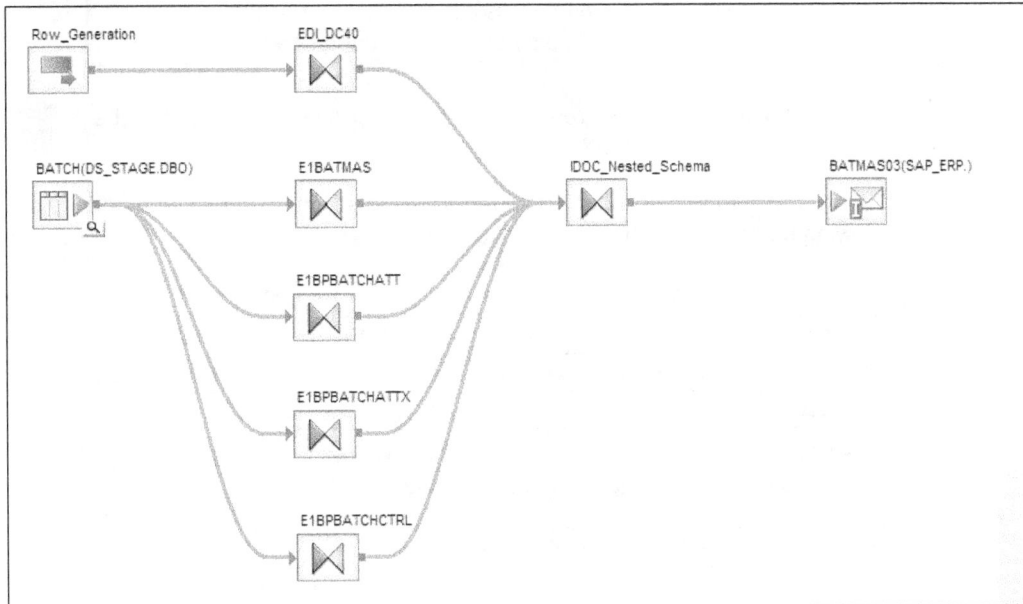

18. The **Row_Generation** transform should be configured to generate one record. Use the following table to define output schema mappings in the EDI_DC40 Query transform. The following table has the records only for the mandatory columns of the EDI_DC40 IDoc segment. Populate the rest of them with NULL values.

Column name	Data type	Mapping expression
TABNAM	varchar(10)	'EDI_DC40'
MANDT	varchar(3)	'100'
DOCREL	varchar(4)	'740'
DIRECT	varchar(1)	'2'
IDOCTYP	varchar(30)	'BATMAS03'
MESTYP	varchar(30)	'BATMAS'
SNDPOR	varchar(10)	'TRFC'
SNDPRT	varchar(2)	'LS'
SNDPRN	varchar(10)	'SBECLNT100'
CREDAT	date	sysdate()
CRETIM	time	systime()
ARCKEY	varchar(70)	'1'

> Please keep in mind that some of the values in mapping expressions for this specific segment, EDI_DC40, are specific to your own SAP environment. Some of them are MANDT and SNDPRN, which should be obtained from your SAP administrator.

To obtain the full list of columns required for the specific segment, refer to the BATMAS03 object structure itself.

19. Open the E1BATMAS Query transform in the workspace window for editing and define the following mappings for the output schema columns:

Column name	Data type	Mapping expression
MATERIAL	varchar(18)	BATCH.MATERIAL
BATCH	varchar(10)	BATCH.BATCH_NUMBER
ROW_ID	int	BATCH.ROW_ID

20. Open the E1BPBATCHATT Query transform in the workspace window for editing and define the following mappings for the output schema columns:

Column name	Data type	Mapping expression
LASTGRDATE	date	to_date(BATCH.GOODS_RECEIPT_DATE, 'YYYYMMDD')
COUNTRYORI	varchar(3)	BATCH.COUNTRY_OF_ORIGIN
PROD_DATE	date	to_date(BATCH.DATE_OF_MANUFACTURE, 'YYYYMMDD')
ROW_ID	int	BATCH.ROW_ID

21. Open the E1BPBATCHATTX Query transform in the workspace window for editing and define the following mappings for the output schema columns:

Column name	Data type	Mapping expression
LASTGRDATE	varchar(1)	'X'
COUNTRYORI	varchar(1)	'X'
PROD_DATE	varchar(1)	'X'
ROW_ID	int	BATCH.ROW_ID

22. Open the E1BPBATCHCTRL Query transform in the workspace window for editing and define the following mappings for the output schema columns:

Column name	Data type	Mapping expression
DOCLASSIFY	varchar(1)	'X'
ROW_ID	Int	BATCH.ROW_ID

23. Open the IDOC_Nested_Schema Query transform in the workspace window for editing.

24. Drag and drop EDI_DC40 and E1BATMAS segments from the input schema into the output schema of the IDOC_Nested_Schema Query transform.

25. Double-click on output schema IDOC_Nested_Schema to make its status to "current", open the **FROM** tab, and select only the E1BATMAS input schema. Mark the EDI_DC40 segment in the output nested schema as repeatable (the full table icon). If the segment schema is created as repeatable by default then do not change it. Mark the E1BATMAS output schema segment as non-repeatable. To do that, make it current by double-clicking on it, and then right-click on it, unselecting the **Repeatable** option from the context menu. See the difference between the output schema icons for EDI_DC40 and E1BATMAS as for repeatable and non-repeatable segments.

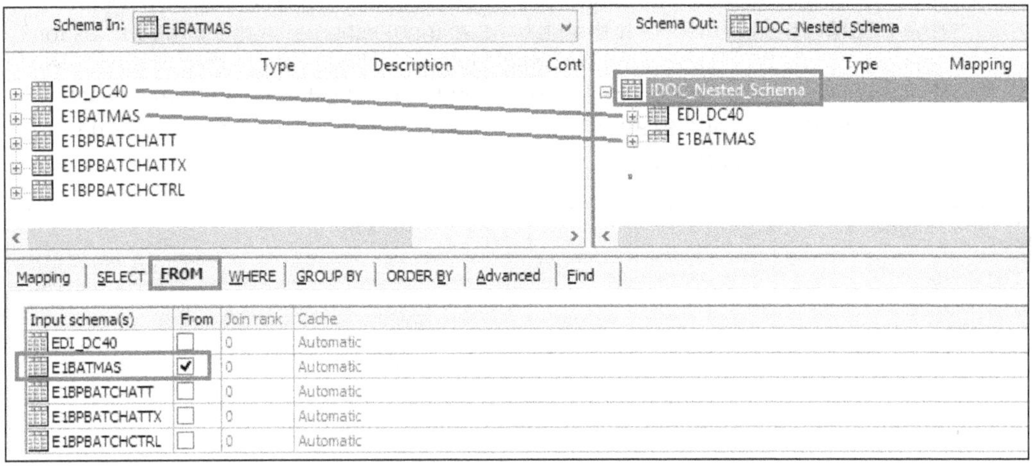

26. Double-click on the first `EDI_DC40` output segment to make its status "current". Open the **FROM** tab and select only the `EDI_DC40` input schema:

27. Double-click on the second `E1BATMAS` output segment to make it current. Open the **FROM** tab and select only the `EDI_DC40` input schema, in the same way as for the previous `EDI_DC40` output schema. Also, delete the `ROW_ID` column from the output schema and drag and drop the rest of the input schemas `E1BPBATCHATT`, `E1BPBATCHATTX`, and `E1BPBATCHCTRL` inside the `E1BATMAS` output schema creating nesting structure:

28. Double-click on the nested `E1BPBATCHATT` output schema to make it current. Delete the `ROW_ID` column from the output schema. On the **FROM** tab, select the `E1BPBATCHATT` input schema. On the **WHERE** tab, specify the filtering condition: `(E1BPBATCHATT.ROW_ID = E1BATMAS.ROW_ID)`.

29. Perform the preceding same step for the next output segment. Double-click on the nested `E1BPBATCHATTX` output schema to make it current. Delete the `ROW_ID` column from the output schema. On the **FROM** tab, select the `E1BPBATCHATTX` input schema. On the **WHERE** tab, specify the filtering condition: `(E1BPBATCHATTX.ROW_ID = E1BATMAS.ROW_ID)`.

30. Perform the same preceding step for the next output segment. Double-click on the nested `E1BPBATCHCTRL` output schema to make it current. Delete the `ROW_ID` column from the output schema. On the **FROM** tab, select the `E1BPBATCHCTRL` input schema. On the **WHERE** tab, specify the filtering condition: `(E1BPBATCHCTRL.ROW_ID = E1BATMAS.ROW_ID)`.

31. The target object `BATMAS03` imported into the `SAP_ERP` datastore should be configured using the values shown in the following screenshot. Open the `BATMAS03` target object in the dataflow in the main workspace for editing to configure it.

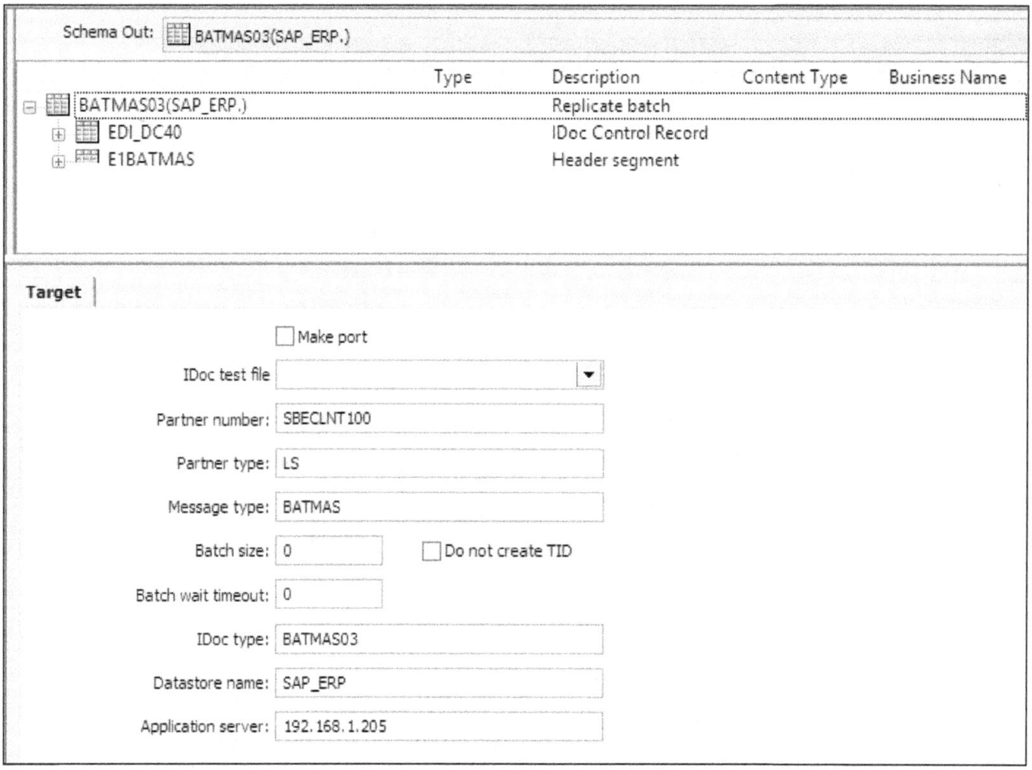

Schema Out: BATMAS03(SAP_ERP.)					
	Type	Description	Content Type	Business Name	
BATMAS03(SAP_ERP.)		Replicate batch			
EDI_DC40		IDoc Control Record			
E1BATMAS		Header segment			

Target

☐ Make port

IDoc test file [▼]

Partner number: SBECLNT100

Partner type: LS

Message type: BATMAS

Batch size: 0   ☐ Do not create TID

Batch wait timeout: 0

IDoc type: BATMAS03

Datastore name: SAP_ERP

Application server: 192.168.1.205

Close the dataflow object. Save and validate the job to make sure that you have not made any syntax errors in your dataflow design.

32. Open the last dataflow, `DF_SAP_MCH1`, for editing in the workspace window.

33. Add the `MCH1` table from the `SAP_ERP` datastore as a source object.

34. Propagate all the columns from the `MCH1` table to the output schema using the linked Query transform.

35. Add a new template table,-`SAP_MCH1`, from the `STAGE` datastore as a target table object.

36. Save, validate, and run the job.

How it works...

The preceding steps show the common process of loading data into the SAP system using the IDoc mechanism. The load process usually consists of few steps:

- ▶ Extract master data from the SAP system to make sure that we are referencing the correct objects existing in the target system
- ▶ Process of building/preparing dataset for load
- ▶ Process of loading the data into SAP
- ▶ The post-validation process of extracting data loaded in SAP back into the staging area for validation

Let's review all these processes built in the form of a dataflow in more detail.

The first dataflow, DF_SAP_MARA, will be extracting material data from SAP ERP for validation purposes to make sure that we do not try to create a batch for material that does not exist in the target SAP system.

The second dataflow, DF_Prepare_Batch_Data, prepares the batch record to be loaded in SAP. As you can see from the output schema mapping of one of the Query transforms, we prepare the batch 2015100901 to be created for material RAWMAT01. As you might remember, we have already manually created batch 20151009. The rest of the mappings show that we have also populated the **Ctry of origin**, **Last Goods Receipt**, and **Date of Manufacture** fields.

The third dataflow, DF_Batch_IDOC_Load, transforms the prepared batch record into the nested format of an IDoc message and sends this IDoc message to SAP. Further more, we will take a look at how you can monitor the process of receiving and loading IDocs on the SAP side.

Finally, the fourth dataflow, DF_SAP_MCH1, extracts the SAP table MCH1, which contains information about batches created in SAP for post-load validation purposes. That allows us to see which batches were actually loaded in SAP and run the SQL queries in our staging area to validate field values.

IDoc

IDoc is a format and transfer mechanism that SAP systems use to exchange data. Data Services utilizes this mechanism in order to send and receive information from SAP systems. IDocs that the SAP system receives are called **inbound** and IDocs sent by SAP are called **outbound**. You saw that transaction WE20 was used to configure Inbound IDoc parameters so that SAP could successfully accept BATMAS IDoc messages sent to it from Data Services.

BATMAS IDoc used to load batch data has a nested structure, and that is why we had to nest multiple datasets with the help of Query transform. We used artificial ID key ROW_ID to link all the nested segments together.

Keep in mind that Data Services does not load data in SAP tables directly itself. All Data Services does is prepares the data in the IDoc format so that it can be received by SAP and loaded into SAP tables using internal mechanisms/programs.

Monitoring IDoc load on the SAP side

Data Services sends IDoc messages to SAP synchronously. An IDoc message is received by SAP and then processed. Only after that does Data Services sends the next IDoc message. Sometimes, this process can take quite a long time. All you will see in trace log on the Data Services side is one record indicating that the dataflow loading data is still running.

To see what is going on the SAP side—how many IDocs fail and how many of them are processed successfully by SAP—you can use transaction BD87:

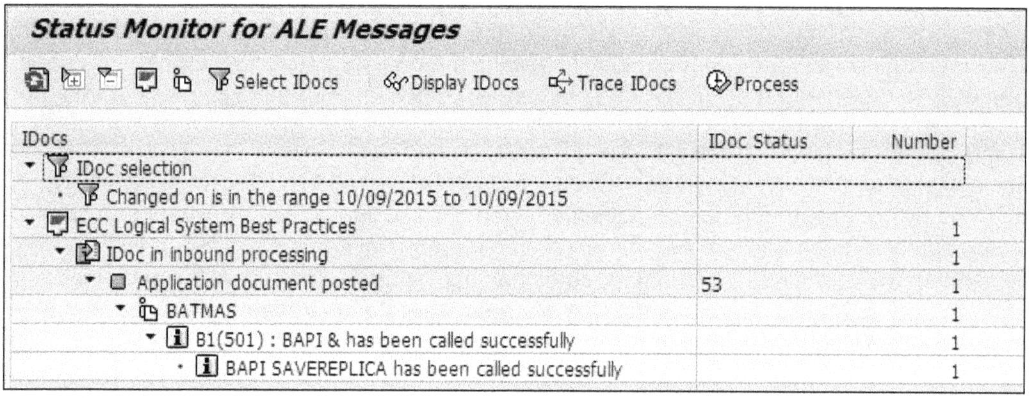

By expanding the BATMAS section and double-clicking on the actual IDoc record that you are interested in, you can see the data in the IDoc nested segments:

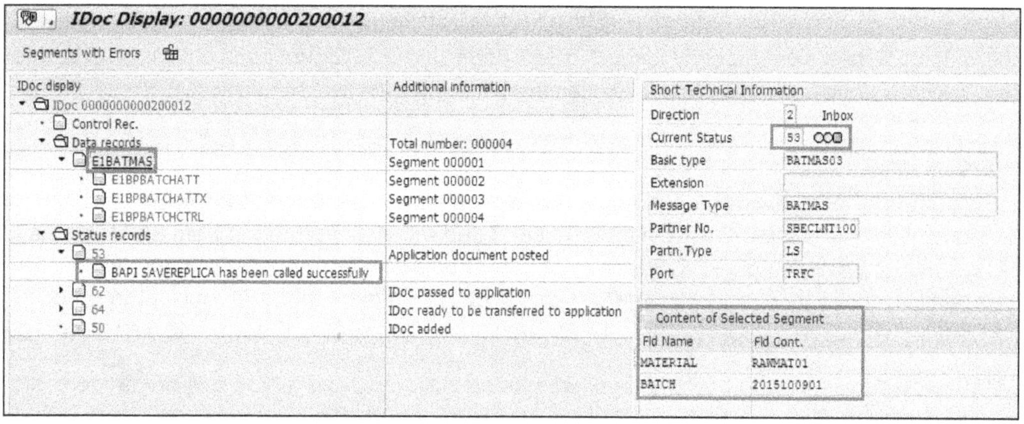

Other useful information available on this screen includes:

▸ The status of the IDoc (processed successfully or failed)

▸ Error messages (if failed)

▸ Data records stored in IDoc message (E1BATMAS, E1BPBATCHATT, E1BPBATCHATTX, and E1BATCHCTRL segments)

As you can see, the EDI_DC40 segment is not visible as it is an IDoc header itself. Information we have provided in this segment is available in the **Short Technical Information** panel and defines the behavior of IDoc processing.

By clicking on the **Refresh** button on the **Status Monitor for ALE Messages** screen, you can see in real time how the IDocs received by SAP are processed.

Post-load validation of loaded data

We know that one of the tables in SAP where batch master data is stored is MCH1. Knowing which physical tables are actually populated with data when you enter data manually via transactional screens, or loading data coming from external systems via an IDoc mechanism, is useful as you can always extract the contents of these tables to perform post-validation tasks.

To view our newly created batch 2015100901, we can use transaction MSC3N (**Display Batch**):

Or, we can see the contents of the MCH1 table directly using the SE16 transaction (**Data Browser**):

Data Browser: Table MCH1 Select Entries   2

Check Table...

Table: MCH1
Displayed Fields: 22 of 35   Fixed Columns: 3   List Width 0250

MANDT	MATNR	CHARG	LVORM	ERSDA	ERNAM	AENAM	LAEDA
100	RAWMAT01	20151009		10/09/2015			00/00/0000
100	RAWMAT01	2015100901		10/09/2015			00/00/0000

You can see both batches here: the one created manually and the one loaded with the help of Data Services.

Do you remember that we developed a dataflow to extract the MCH1 table to validate loaded data? Let's check the actual records extracted right after the loading process has been completed by browsing the contents of the SAP_MCH1 table in our staging area:

A SAP_MCH1(DS_STAGE.DBO)

MANDT	MATNR	CHARG	LVORM	ERSDA	ERNAM	AENAM	LAEDA	VERAB	VFDAT	ZUSCH
100	RAWMAT01	20151009	" "	2015.10.09	ISHOMNIKOV	" "	1900.01.01	1900.01.01	1900.01.01	" "
100	RAWMAT01	2015100901	" "	2015.10.09	ISHOMNIKOV	" "	1900.01.01	1900.01.01	1900.01.01	" "

The CHARG column in the MCH1 table stores the batch number values.

> As technical names in SAP tables can be quite difficult to understand, you can use transaction SE11 to see the descriptions of the columns for the specific table.

There is more...

We have just scratched the surface of one of the possible methods of reading/loading data from the SAP system.

There are many other methods that can be used to communicate with SAP systems: ABAP dataflows, BAPI calls, direct RFC calls, Open Hub Tables, and many others.

Choosing between these methods usually depends on the type of tasks that have to be implemented, the amount of transferred data, and the type of SAP environment used.

12

Introduction to Information Steward

In this chapter, we will see the following recipes:

▸ Exploring Data Insight capabilities

▸ Performing Metadata Management tasks

▸ Working with the Metapedia functionality

▸ Creating a custom cleansing package with Cleansing Package Builder

Introduction

SAP Information Steward is a separate product that is installed alongside SAP Data Services and SAP Business Intelligence and provides additional capabilities for business and IT users in order to analyze data quality and create cleansing packages that can increase data cleansing processes ran by Data Services.

To cover all functionalities of Information Steward, we would have to write another book. In this chapter, we will explore the main functions of Information Steward that proved themselves to be the most valuable to users of the product.

All these activities relate to specific areas within the SAP Information Steward application.

> Log in to the SAP Information Steward application at
> `http://localhost:8080/BOE/InfoStewardApp`.

On the main page, you can see five tabs that represent the four main areas of the Information Steward product functionality, as shown in the following screenshot:

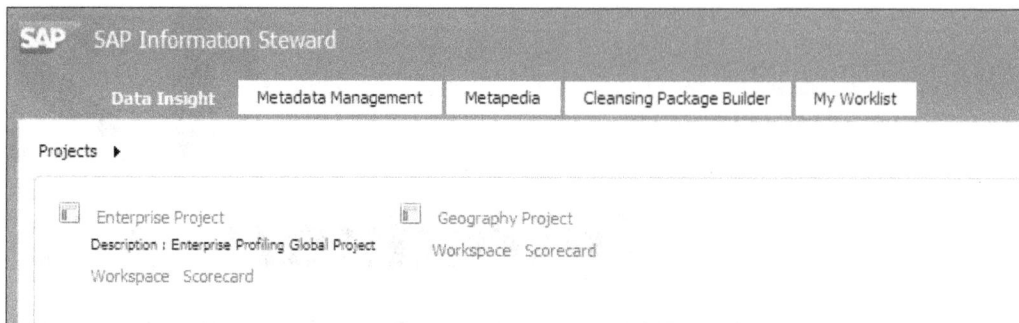

Exploring Data Insight capabilities

The **Data Insight** tab is the first tab, and it enables you to profile the data available from different sources, build validation rules for the data, and design a scorecard in order to see a visual representation of the quality of your data.

Getting ready

Before we log in to the SAP Information Steward application, we have to create couple of Information Steward objects in a standard **Central Management Console** (**CMC**). The goal of this preparation step is to define the sources of data that Information Steward can connect to in order to perform data quality and analysis tasks. You can define some data sources directly in the Information Steward application like a flat file, but some of them should first be created as connections in the CMC Information Steward area.

1. Log in to **CMC** at `http://localhost:8080/BOE/CMC`.
2. Go to the **Information Steward** section.
3. Click on **Connections** and click on the **Create connection** button in the top menu.

4. Fill in all the required fields, as shown in the following screenshot, in order to create a connection object to the `AdventureWorks_DWH` SQL Server database:

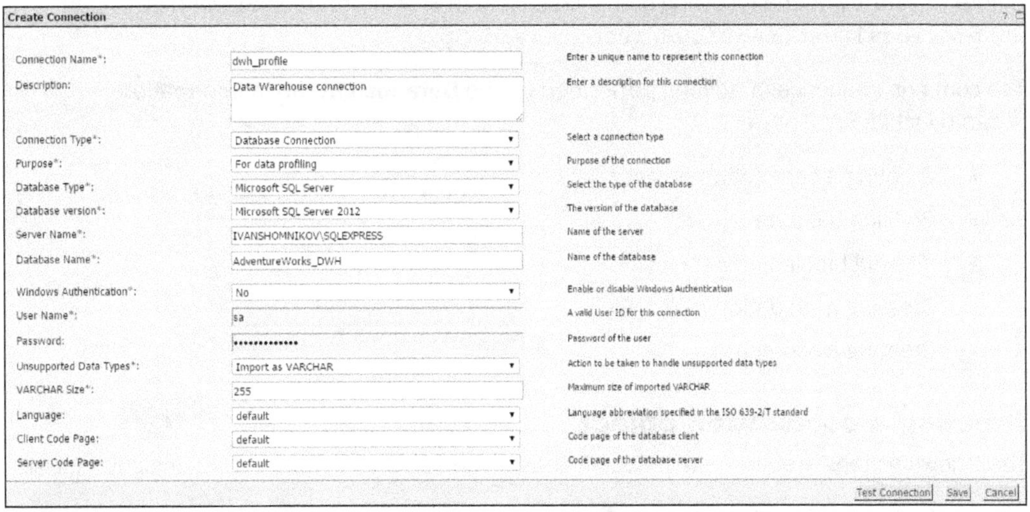

5. Click on the **Test Connection** button to validate the information entered, and then click on the **Save** button to save the connection and exit the **Create Connection** screen.

6. The `dwh_profile` connection should appear in the list of connections that can be used in Information Steward.

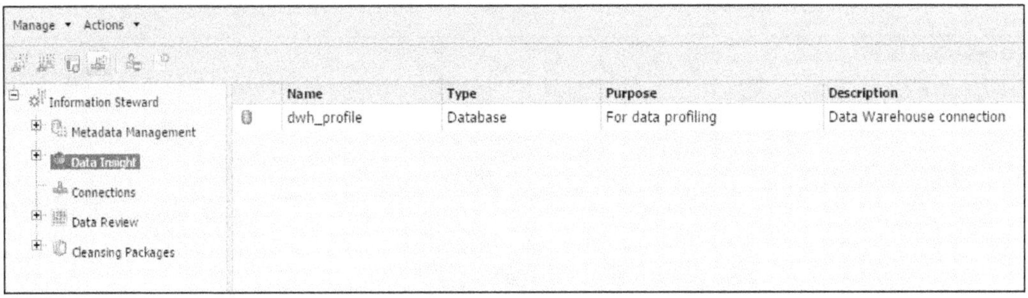

7. Finally, let's create a new Data Insight project called **Geography**. To do that, go to the **Data Insight** section and click on the **Create a Data Insight project** button.

How to do it...

Before you start with the following steps, first log in to SAP Information Steward at `http://localhost:8080/BOE/InfoStewardApp`.

The common sequence of actions performed on the **Data Insight** tab in Information Steward includes:

 ▶ Creating a connection object

 ▶ Profiling the data

 ▶ Viewing profiling results

 ▶ Creating a validation rule

 ▶ Creating a scorecard

Creating a connection object

The following steps are required to specify the source of our data for our Data Insight analysis.

1. Go to **Data Insight | Geography Project**.

2. Select the **Workspace Home** tab and click on the **Add | Tables...** button in the top-left corner.

3. In the opened window, select the `dwh_profile` connection object, then expand it, select the `dbo.DimGeography` table, and then click on the **Add to Project** button, as shown in the following screenshot:

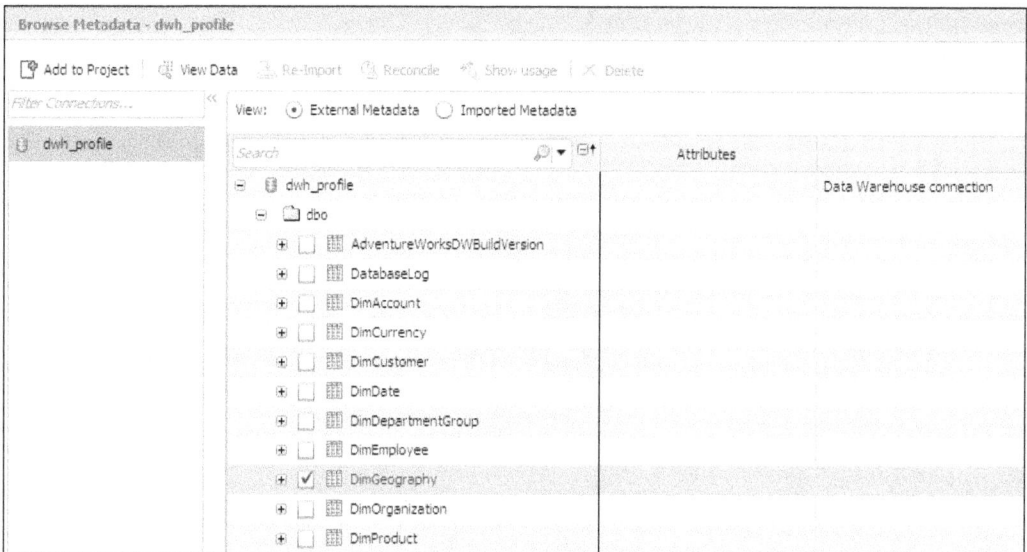

Profiling the data

Profiling or gathering various kinds of information about the data can be used for data analysis.

1. To profile the data in the added `DimGeography` table, you can use various profiling options. Let's collect uniqueness profiling data. On the **Workspace Home** tab, select the `DimGeography` table in the `dwh_profile` connection and click on the **Profile | Uniqueness** button in the **Profile Results** toolbar menu.

2. In the **Define Tasks: Uniqueness** window, specify which columns you want to gather a uniqueness profile information for. Select **City** and **CountryRegionCode** and click on the **Save and Run Now** button, as shown in the following screenshot:

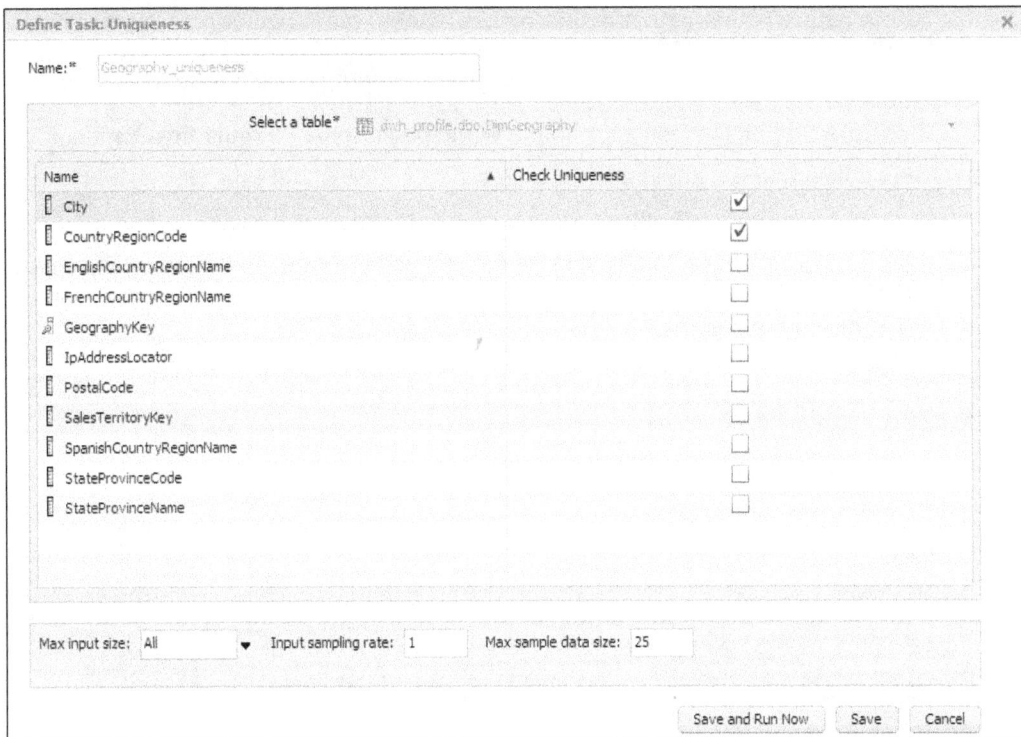

Define Task: Uniqueness		×

Name:*	Geography_uniqueness	

Select a table*   dwh_profile.dbo.DimGeography

Name	▲	Check Uniqueness
City		☑
CountryRegionCode		☑
EnglishCountryRegionName		☐
FrenchCountryRegionName		☐
GeographyKey		☐
IpAddressLocator		☐
PostalCode		☐
SalesTerritoryKey		☐
SpanishCountryRegionName		☐
StateProvinceCode		☐
StateProvinceName		☐

Max input size:	All	Input sampling rate:	1	Max sample data size:	25

Save and Run Now   Save   Cancel

3. To gather column profiling information, select the `DimGeography` table and click on the **Profile | Columns** button in the toolbar menu of the **Workspace Home | Profile Results** tab. Specify a name for the column profiling task, `Geography_column_profiling`, and select all profiling options: **Simple**, **Median & Distribution**, and **Word Distribution**. Then, click on the **Save and Run Now** button to create and execute the column profiling task.

4. Select the **Tasks** section on the left-side panel to see both the profiling tasks created in the previous steps. You can run them any time from this tab to refresh the profiling data according to the parameters specified.

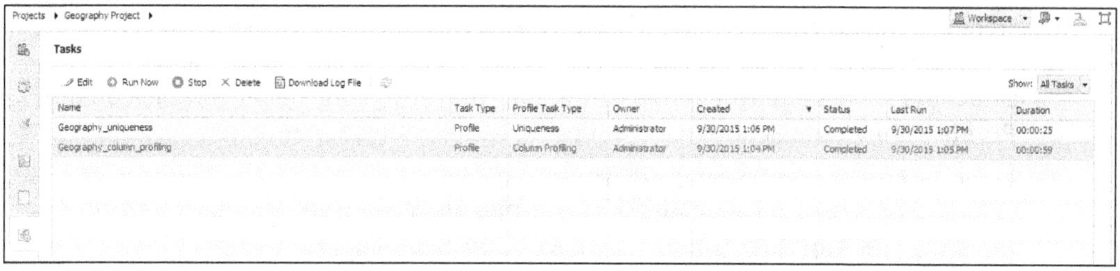

Name	Task Type	Profile Task Type	Owner	Created	Status	Last Run	Duration
Geography_uniqueness	Profile	Uniqueness	Administrator	9/30/2015 1:06 PM	Completed	9/30/2015 1:07 PM	00:00:25
Geography_column_profiling	Profile	Column Profiling	Administrator	9/30/2015 1:04 PM	Completed	9/30/2015 1:05 PM	00:00:59

Viewing profiling results

The following steps show you how to view the previously gathered profiling results.

1. To see the data profile results, go to the **Workspace Home | Profile Results** tab.

2. Expand the table you are interested in to see its columns and select it.

3. Click on the **Refresh | Profile Results** button in the toolbar menu.

4. Then, by clicking on the field or specific number you are interested in, you can see the detailed result for this field in the extra windows on the right-hand side of the screen, and at the bottom, as shown in the following screenshot:

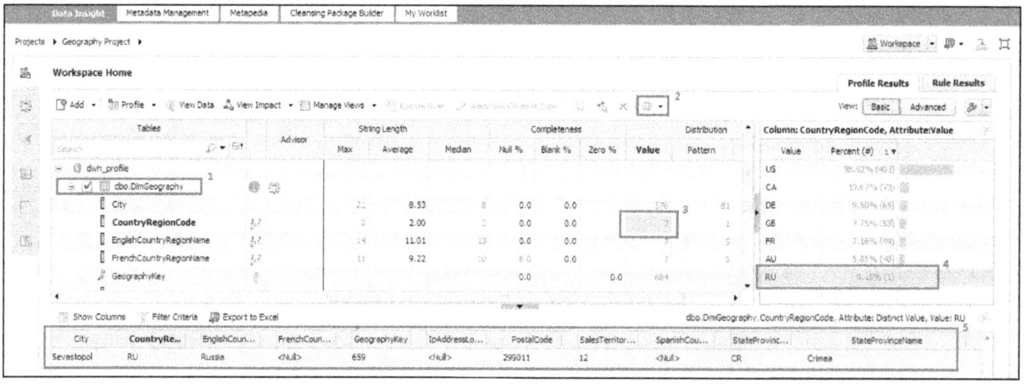

5. To see the results of the uniqueness profile information collected, select the **Advanced** view mode under the **Profile Results** tab.

6. In the opened window, click on the green icon in the **Uniqueness** column and select the key combination you have gathered information on. In our case, we have gathered uniqueness profiling information for two columns of the DimGeography table, **City** and **CountryRegionCode**, as shown in the following screenshot:

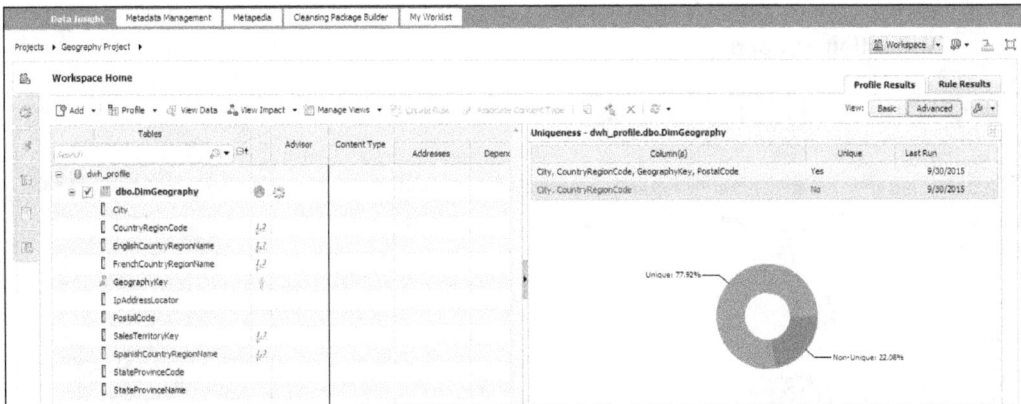

By hovering your cursor over the red zone showing the percentage of non-unique records the for selected combination of columns, you can see detailed information such as the percentage of non-unique rows and number of non-unique rows. In our case, it is *22.08%* and *151*. By clicking on the red zone, you can display non-unique rows at the bottom of the screen.

So far, we have gathered two types of profiling information: column profile data and uniqueness profile data for the DimGeography table located in our data warehouse.

Creating a validation rule

Now, let's see how you can create a validation rule in Information Steward and display the result of applying it to the dataset in a graphical form by using scorecards.

1. On the **Workspace Home | Profile Results** tab, you can find a yellow icon in the **Advisor** column against the dbo.DimGeography table, as shown in the following screenshot:

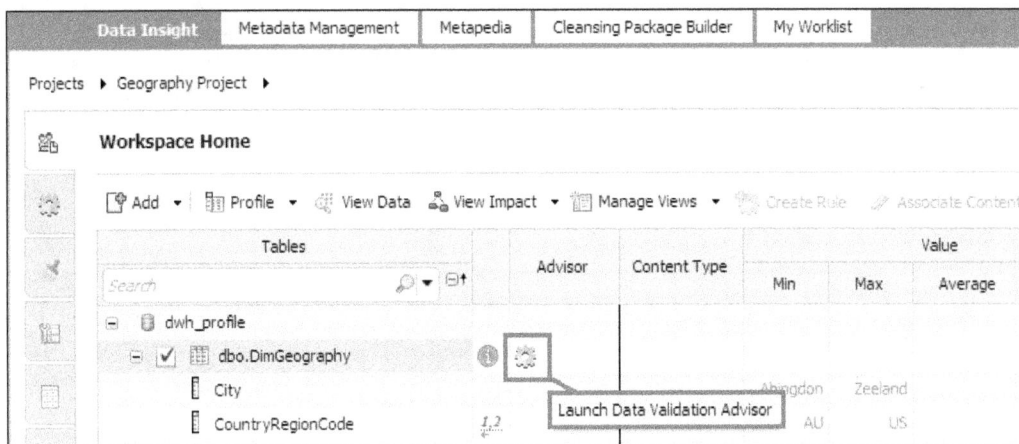

2. Click on the yellow icon shown in the preceding screenshot to launch **Data Validation Advisor**:

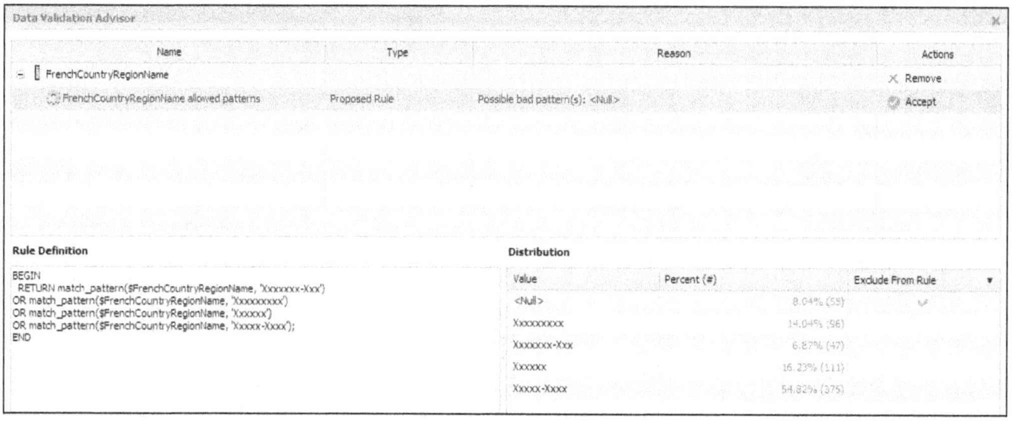

3. We are not going to accept the validation rule suggested by **Data Validation Advisor** and will create our own custom validation rule.

    Our custom rule will check if the `DimGeography` table record has translated values in both the columns, `FrenchCountryRegionName` and `SpanishCountryRegionName`. To create a new rule, open the second vertical table **Rules**, which is next to the **Workspace Home** tab, and click on the **New** button from the toolbar menu to create a new rule.

4. Fill in all the configuration fields of the new `French_Spanish_CountryRegionName` rule, as shown in the following screenshot:

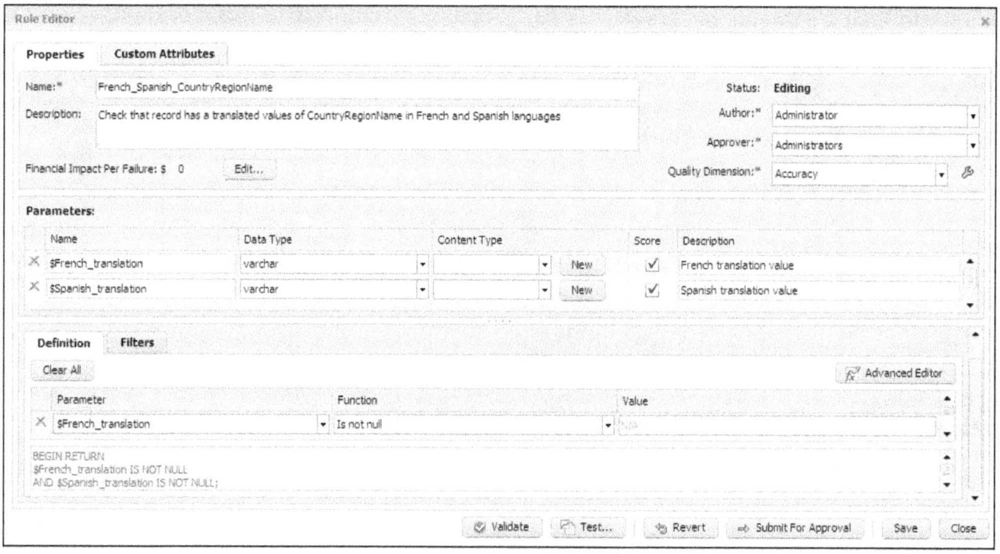

We have created two parameters, $French_translation and $Spanish_translation, of the varchar data type. Each parameter checks the value in each of the two columns, and in the **Definition** tab, we have specified the condition to be applied to the values.

5. Click on the **Submit for Approval** button. The rule will be sent to the **Tasks** tab for approval by a category of users specified in the **Approver** field on the **Rule Editor** window.

6. The rule can be approved from the **My Worklist** section, as shown in the following screenshot:

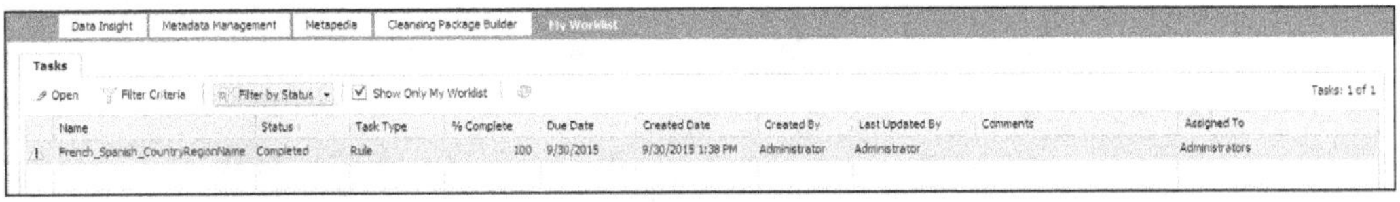

7. Go to the **Workspace Home | Rule Results** tab and click on the **Bind to Rule** button.

8. Bind the rule parameters to the dwh_profile.dbo.DimGeography fields, as shown in the following screenshot, and click on the **Save and Close** button:

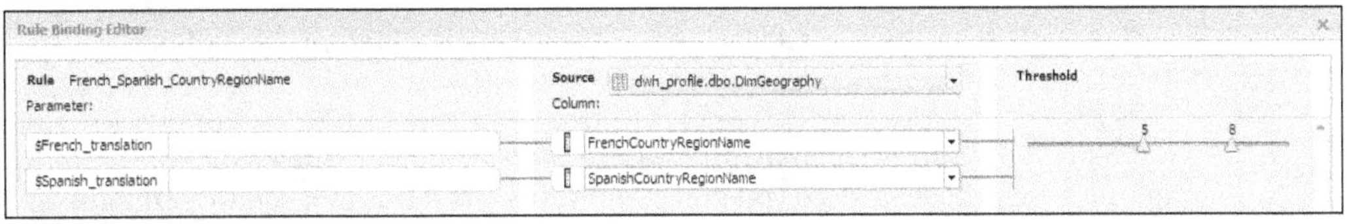

9. Click on **Refresh | Rule Results** to see the results of applying the rule to the columns of the table specified, as shown in the following screenshot:

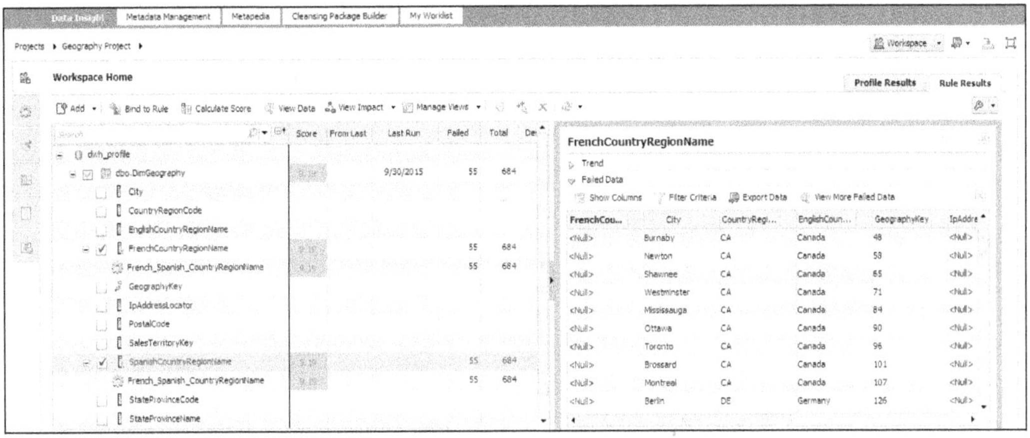

The left side of the screen shows the rule scores for the specified fields and the number of records that passed/failed the rule. In our example, 55 rows do not have either a French or Spanish translation in the `FrenchCountryRegionName` and `SpanishCountryRegionName` fields.

You can see the actual records in the right-side panel.

10. You can see the rule result on the **Rules** tab directly. All you need to do is select the rule and click on the **Bind** button. The rule result appears on the right side of the screen, as shown in the following screenshot:

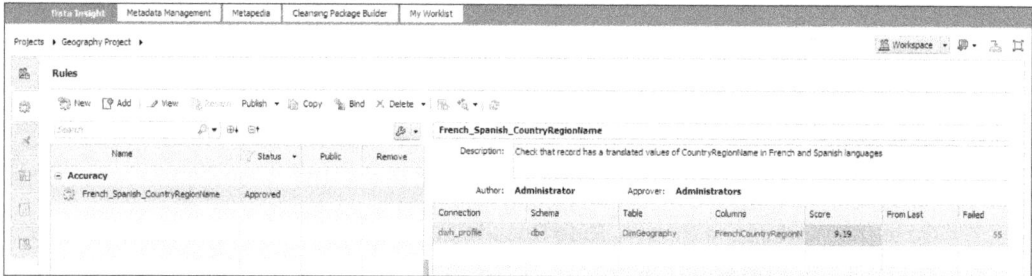

Creating a scorecard

Scorecards are a convenient way to visualize and present historical information about validation rule results.

1. A scorecard can be created on the **Scorecard Setup** tab. This is a very straightforward process where you first specify **Key Data Domain**, **Quality Dimension**, then the rule you want to include in the scorecard output, and, finally, perform rule binding to link the rule to the actual dataset, as shown in the following screenshot:

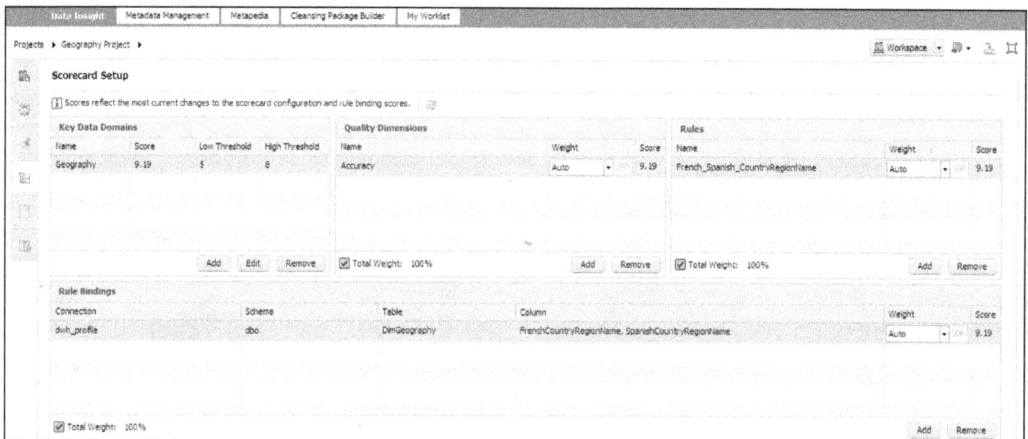

2. To view the scorecard results, go to **Workspace Home** and select the **Scorecard** view mode instead of **Workspace** in the combobox location in the top-right corner, as shown in the following screenshot:

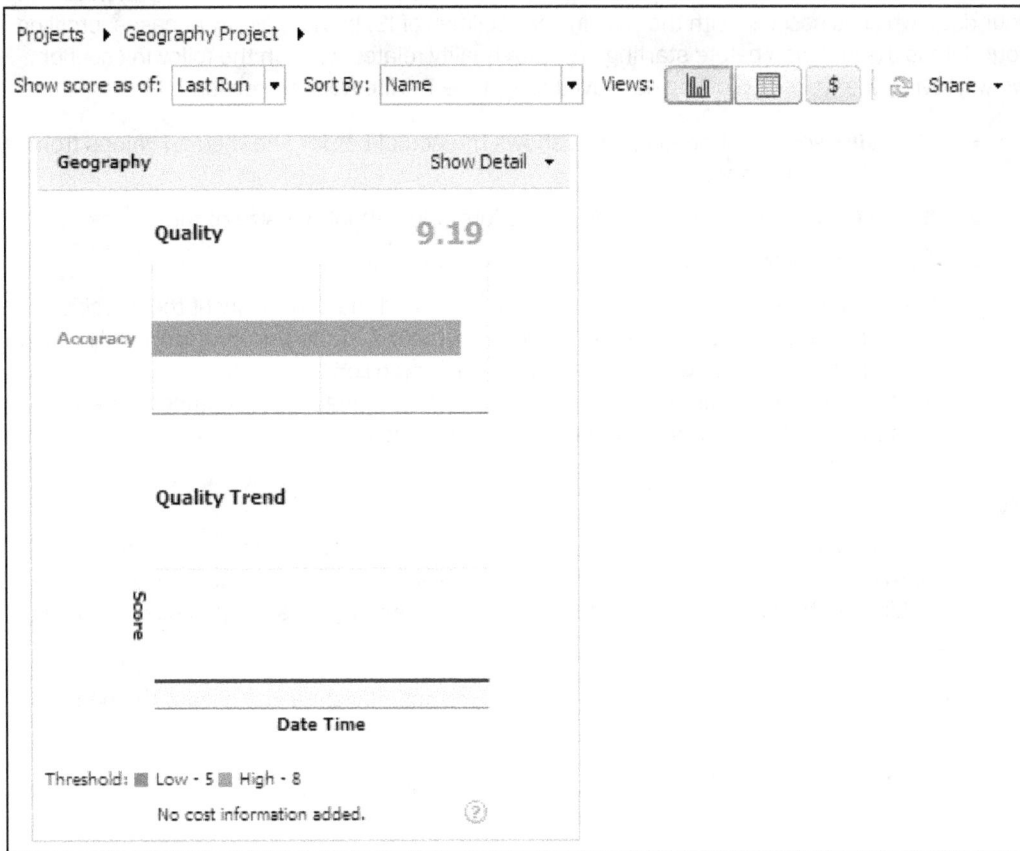

```
Projects  ▶  Geography Project  ▶

Show score as of:  Last Run ▼    Sort By:  Name        ▼    Views:  [▮▮]  [▤]  [$]    ⟳ Share ▼

  Geography                              Show Detail ▼

          Quality                    9.19

  Accuracy  [████████████████████]


          Quality Trend



  Score



                    Date Time

  Threshold: ▮ Low - 5 ▮ High - 8
           No cost information added.    ⑦
```

How it works...

Now, after we have created our connection object, gathered the profiling data, applied the validation rule, and even created the scorecard to see its results, let's see in more detail the various aspects of the steps performed.

Profiling

As you can see, working in Information Steward is a very intuitive process.

As mentioned earlier, the **Data Insight** section of Information Steward is all about understanding your data, which is possible with the profiling capabilities of IS. In the majority of cases, profiling your data is the first step before starting any data quality related work. In the following section, we will review the types of profiling data available in the **Profile Results** section.

> ▶ The **value** section of profiling data shows the actual border and median values from the dataset for a specific field.

> ▶ **String Length** profiling values provide information about the size of the values.

> ▶ The **completeness** section helps you to see any gaps in the data.

> ▶ **Distribution** can be extremely useful to understand the cardinality of the specific fields in your dataset. For example, seeing number 7 in the **Distribution | Value** field of the profiling result data against the `CountryRegionCode` field, we will know that we have only seven different values in that field. Clicking on that number shows us those values and their distribution in the right-hand side panel.

Rules

Rules allow you to analyze the data according to custom conditions. Rules are created for general rule parameters so that you can apply the same rule to different datasets, if necessary. Linking the rule to a specific dataset is called **binding**. It is the process of linking rule parameters to actual table fields.

Rules are usually defined by business users to understand how data complies with specific business requirements.

Information Steward offers a **Data Validation Advisor** feature that proposes the preconfigured rules depending on the profiling results of your data.

Scorecards

Scorecards allow you to group your rules and help you to see trends in data scores calculated by specific rules.

There is more...

There is much more to the Data Insight functionality than presented in this recipe. We have just scratched the surface of the basic functions available in this area of Information Steward.

It is possible to specify file formats directly in Information Steward in order to source data from flat files and from Excel spreadsheets.

Another great thing about Information Steward Data Insight is that it allows you to build data views that are based on multiple sources of information.

The intuitive and well-documented interface allows you to easily experiment and play with your data on your own. This is always a very fascinating process that does not require any deep technical knowledge of the underlying product.

Performing Metadata Management tasks

The second tool available in Information Steward after Data Insight is Metadata Management.

The **Metadata Management** tool is used to collect metadata information from various systems in order to get a comprehensive view of it and to analyze the relationships between metadata objects.

In this recipe, we will take a look at the example of using **Metadata Management** on our Data Service repository, which stores the ETL code developed for recipes of this book.

Getting ready

As with Data Insight, we have to first establish connectivity to the Data Services repository. This is usually an administration task that can be done in CMC in the **Information Steward | Metadata Management** section. Click on **Create an integrator source** and fill in all the required fields, as shown in the following screenshot, to define a connection to Data Services repository for the Metadata Management tool:

After creating an integrator source object, you have to run it by using the **Run Now** option in the object's context menu. That operation will perform the collection of metadata or information about all the objects in the Data Services repository. Remember that any recent changes made to the repository after this operation will not be propagated to the collected Metadata Management snapshot, so you would need to either run it manually or schedule it to run regularly according to your requirements.

The following screenshot shows you how to use the **Run Now** option:

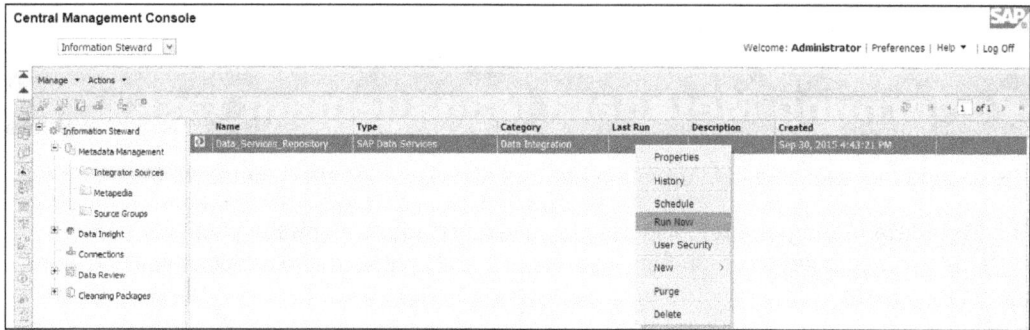

The **Last Run** column shows you when the integrator source data was last updated.

To see the history of runs, just select **History** from the integrator source objects context menu, as shown in the following screenshot:

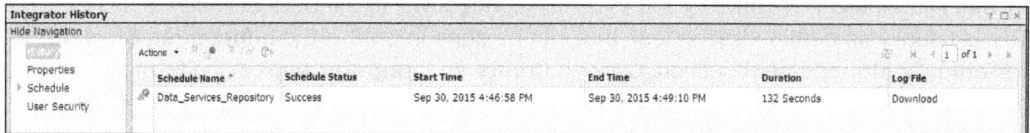

This screen can show you how long it took to collect metadata information from the repository and even provides access to the database log of the metadata collection process, which can be used for troubleshooting any potential problems.

How to do it...

Now that we have defined the connection to our Data Services repository and collected the metadata snapshot using this connection in CMC, we can launch the Information Steward application to use the **Metadata Management** functionality.

1. Log in to Information Steward and go to the **Metadata Management** section, as shown in the following screenshot:

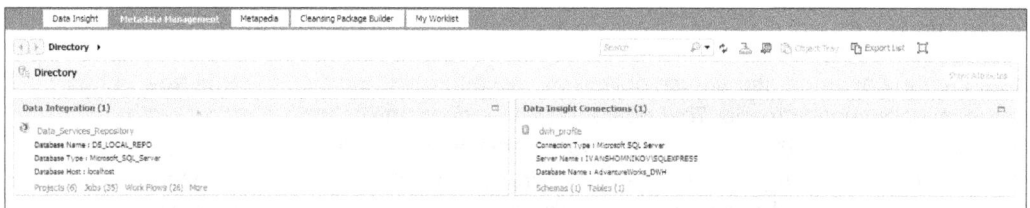

2. Click on the `Data_Services_Repository` source in the **Data Integration** category and on the opened screen, look for the `DimGeography` table using the **Search** field. The **Search Results** section at the very bottom shows you all the possible matches, so all you have to do is select the object you need—table from the `STAGE` database under the `Transform` schema:

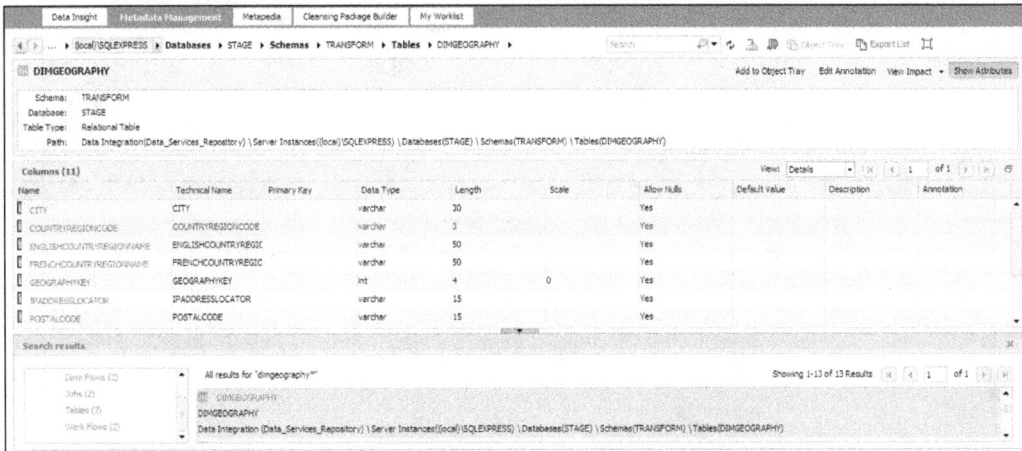

3. To see the impact the table has on another object in ETL repository, click on the **View Impact** button. You should see something like the following screenshot:

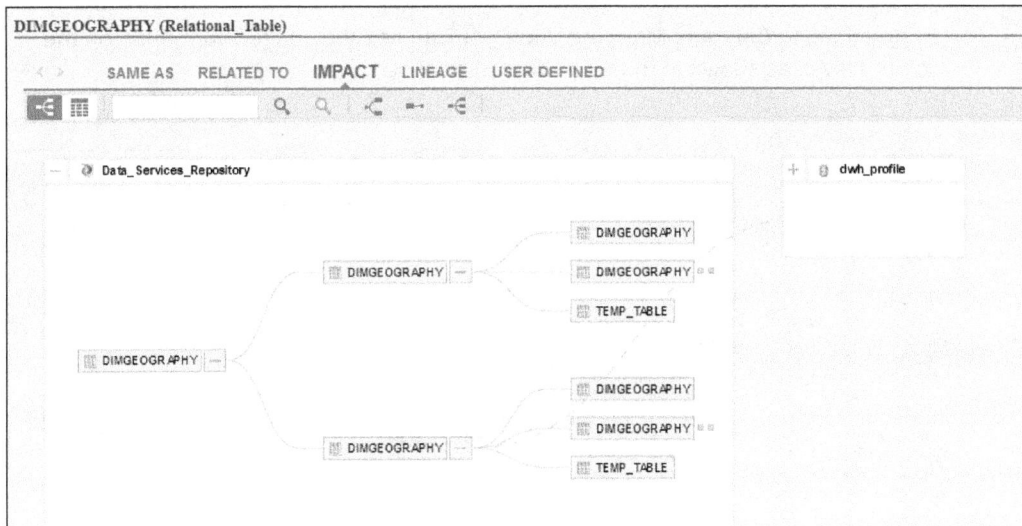

You can see that the `DimGeography` table is used as a source to populate the other `DimGeography` tables (from `AdventureWorks_DWH` and `DWH_backup databases`).

4. Click on the **LINAGE** section in the same window to see the source object for the `DimGeography` table of the `STAGE` database `Transform` schema, as shown in the following screenshot:

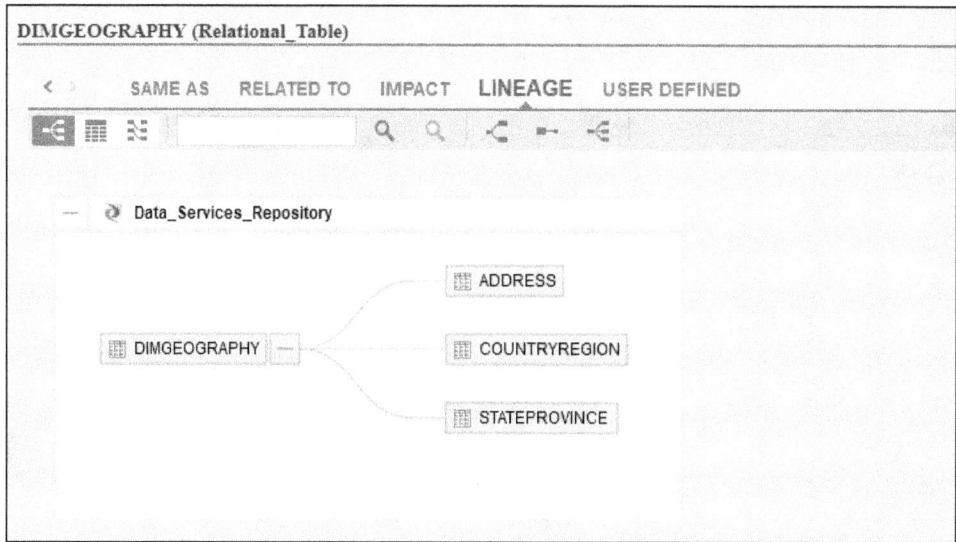

You can see that the data came from three tables: `ADDRESS`, `COUNTRYREGION`, and `STATEPROVINCE`.

5. By switching to **Columns Mapping View**, you can see the linage information on the column level, as shown in the following screenshot:

6. Close this window to go back to the main **Metadata Management** working area. Now, let's define the relationship between the two tables from the Data Services repository are not directly related to each other in ETL code: STAGE.Transform.DIMGEOGRAPHY and STAGE.Transform.DIMSALESTERRITORY. To do that, you have to select each table in the **Search results** section at the bottom and click on the **Add to Object Tray** button.

7. When both tables are added into **Object Tray**, click on the **Object Tray (2)** link at the top of the screen (right to the **Search** field).

8. In the opened window, select both objects, as shown in the following screenshot:

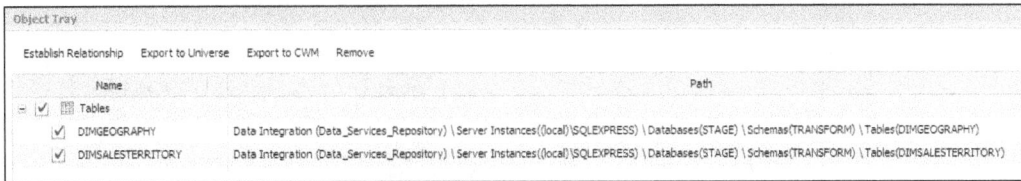

	Name	Path
	Tables	
	DIMGEOGRAPHY	Data Integration (Data_Services_Repository) \ Server Instances((local)\SQLEXPRESS) \ Databases(STAGE) \ Schemas(TRANSFORM) \ Tables(DIMGEOGRAPHY)
	DIMSALESTERRITORY	Data Integration (Data_Services_Repository) \ Server Instances((local)\SQLEXPRESS) \ Databases(STAGE) \ Schemas(TRANSFORM) \ Tables(DIMSALESTERRITORY)

9. Click on **Establish Relationship** and configure the desirable relationship between these two objects, as shown in the following screenshot:

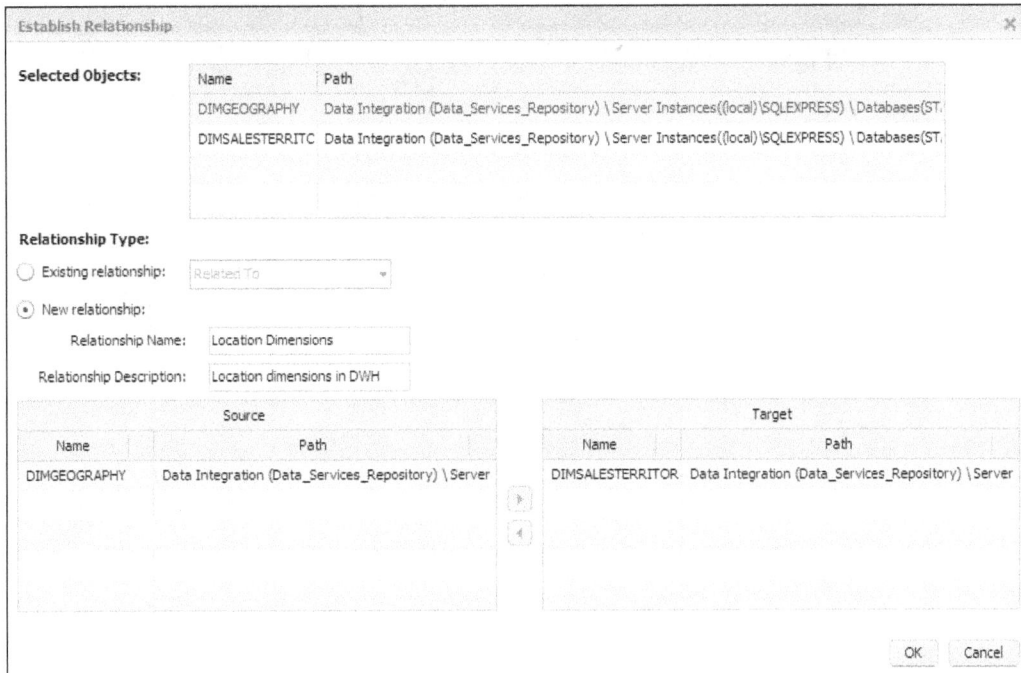

10. Now, if you click on the **View Related To** button, you can see that the relationship information appears on the screen, as shown in the following screenshot:

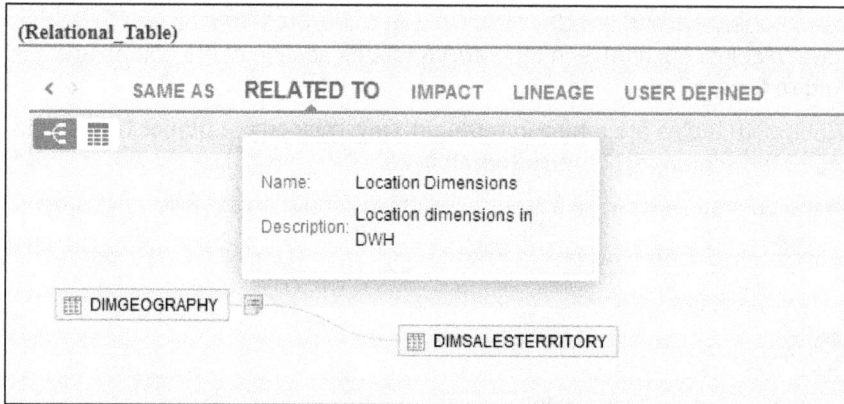

11. To export the information from this screen into an Excel spreadsheet, click on the **Export the tabular view to an Excel file** button in the top-right corner.

12. Choose the **Open with Microsoft Excel** option, as shown in the following screenshot:

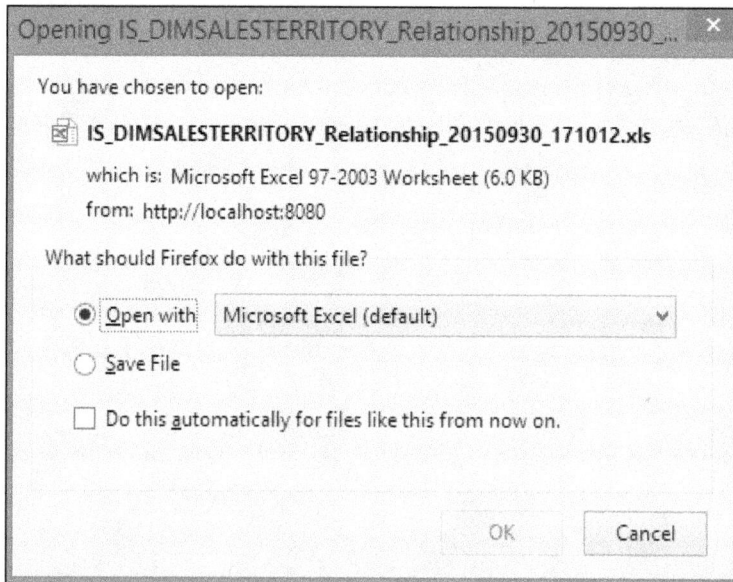

13. The generated Excel spreadsheet could be sent to other business users, used in further analysis, or simply used as a piece of documentation for ETL metadata.

Version	Date Created			
14.2.4 630	2015-09-30 17:10:14			

Version | Object | Relationships | ⊕

Name	Value
Root Object	DIMSALESTERRITORY
Full Path	Data Integration (Data_Services_Repository) \ Server Instances((local)\SQLEXPRESS) \ Databases(STAGE) \ Schemas(TRANSFORM) \ Tables(DIMSALESTERRITORY)
Relationship Type	Related To

Version | Object | Relationships | ⊕

Source Objects	Target Objects	Type	Relationship Attributes
DIMGEOGRAPHY	DIMSALESTERRITORY	Location Dimensions (User Defined)	Type: Location Dimensions (User Defined)
Type: Tables	Type: Tables		Description: Location dimensions in DWH
Schema: TRANSFORM	Schema: TRANSFORM		
Database: STAGE	Database: STAGE		
System: Data_Services_Repository	System: Data_Services_Repository		

Version | Object | Relationships | ⊕

How it works...

Metadata management can link information provided by multiple sources in order to perform lineage and impact analysis on objects. In our example, we used only the Data Services repository, but multiple sources, such as Business Intelligence metadata are often imported along with source database objects and the Data Services metadata. That allows you to see the full picture of what is happening to a specific dataset, starting from its extraction from the database, which ETL transformations are applied to it, which target table the transformed data is loaded to, and, finally, which BI universes and BI reports use it.

On top of that you can create user–customer relationships between objects that are not related to each other either directly or indirectly.

Working with the Metapedia functionality

Think of Metapedia as Wikipedia for your data. Metapedia is used to build a hierarchy of business terms and descriptions for your data, group them into categories, and even associate actual technical objects like pieces of ETL code and database tables with these terms.

In this recipe, we will create a small glossary of business terms in Information Steward and learn how it can be distributed outside of the system to be updated by business users and imported back into Information Steward.

How to do it...

1. Log in to Information Steward and go to the **Metapedia** section.

2. Click on the **New Category** button to create a new category, Geography, as shown in the following screenshot:

Metapedia Category				✕
Properties	**Custom Attributes**			
Name:*	Geography	Keywords:	Location, Geography, City, Country, State, Region	
Author:	Administrators ▾			
			(Use commas(,) to separate entries)	
Description:	Category for location terms			
			Save	Save and Close

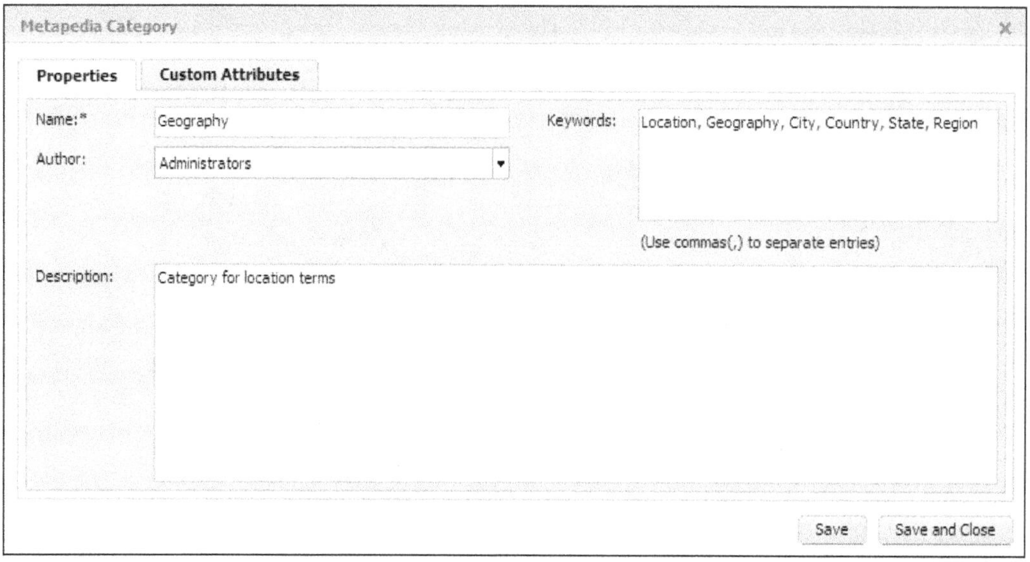

Specify the keywords to be associated with the category for an easy search and click on the **Save** button to create the category.

3. Choose **All Terms** and click on the **New** button to create a new term, Post code, as shown in the following screenshot:

Metapedia Term			
Properties	**Custom Attributes**		
Name:*	Post code	Status:	New
Description*		Author:*	Administrator ▾
Post code information		Approver:	▾
		Synonyms:	
			(Use commas(,) to separate entries)
Tahoma ▾ B I U ■		Keywords:	
http://			(Use commas(,) to separate entries)

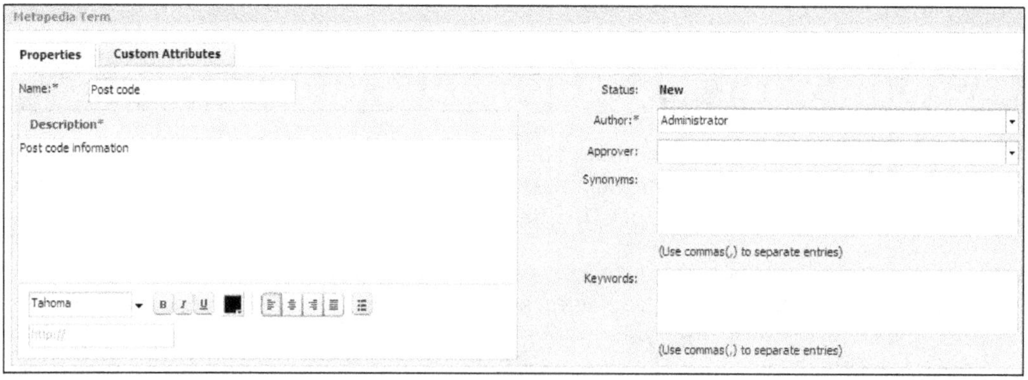

Click on **Save** to create it and close the window.

4. Now, select the created term in the list of terms and click on **Category Actions | Add to Category**.

5. On the opened category list screen, select the `Geography` category and click on **OK**, as shown in the following screenshot:

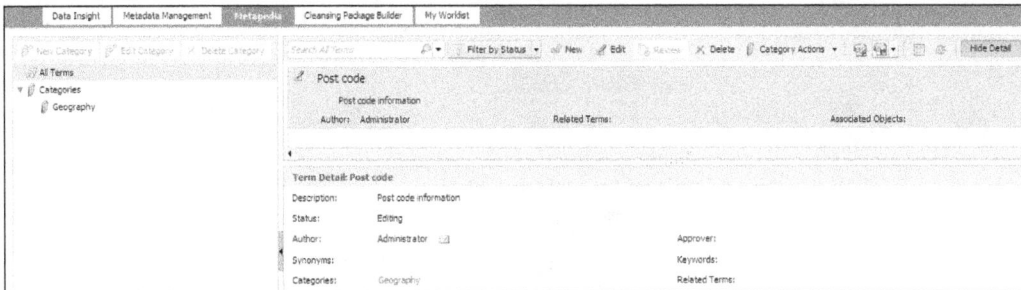

6. Click on the **Export Metapedia to MS Excel file** button and select the **All Terms** option.

7. In the prompt window, select **Export term description in plain text format**.

8. Save the file on the disk. Now, let's perform some modifications to the file as if we are business users who have been told to create a glossary of terms and categories using this Excel spreadsheet.

9. Add the new terms on the **Business Terms** tab of the spreadsheet, as shown in the following screenshot:

	A	B	C	D	E	F	G	H
1	**Name**	**Categories**	**Description**	**Keywords**	**Synonyms**	**Author**	**Approver**	**Status**
2	Post code	Geography	Post code information	PO, box		Administrator		Editing
3	City	Geography	City names	City, Town, Village, Location		Administrator		Editing
4	Person	Human Resources	Person information	Employee, HR, Person				
5								
6								
7								

Version | **Business Terms** | Business Categories | (+)

10. Add the new categories on the **Business Categories** tab of the spreadsheet, as shown in the following screenshot:

	A	B	C	D
1	**Name**	**Description**	**Keywords**	**Author**
2	Geography	Category for location terms	Location,Geography,City,Country,State,Region	Administrators
3	Human Resources	Category for HR terms	Person, Employee, Salary, Vacation, DOB	Administrators
4				
5				
6				
7				

Version | Business Terms | **Business Categories** | (+)

11. Go back to **Information Steward | Metapedia** and click on **Import Metapedia from MS Excel file**. Specify the file modified in the previous step, as shown in the following screenshot:

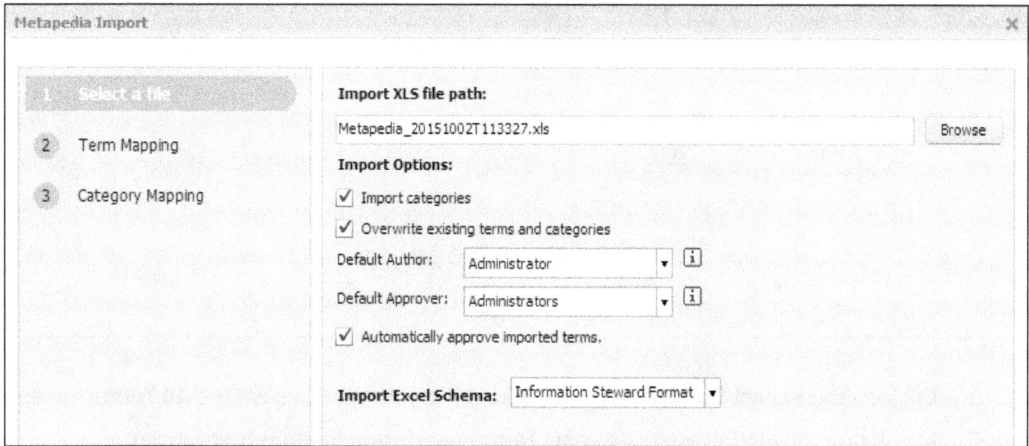

Note that importing information from this spreadsheet will automatically approve all terms and will change their statuses from **Editing** to **Approved**.

12. To associate a term with actual technical objects, double-click on the specific term and click on the **Actions | Associate with objects** button on the term editor screen. Select the objects you want to associate with the term one by one by clicking on the **Associate with term** button. Click on **Done** after you have finished.

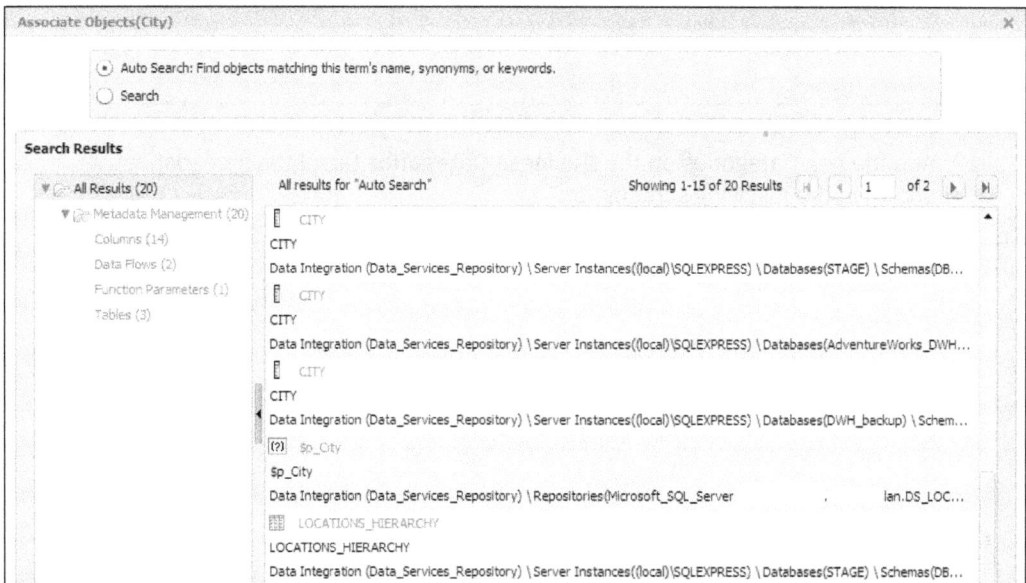

13. We have associated two objects, table `CITY` and parameter `$p_City`, from our Data Services repository with the term `City`, as shown in the following screenshot:

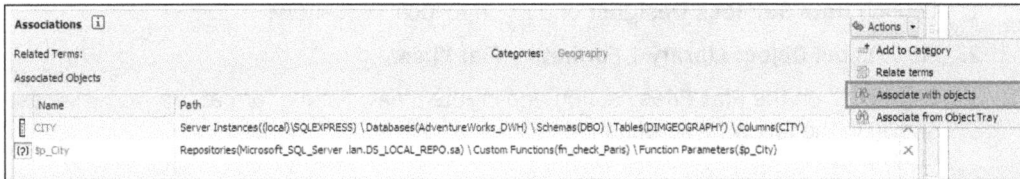

How it works...

The main function of Metapedia is to provide a glossary to browse and understand the data presented and categorized in clear business terms. In other words, the purpose of Metapedia is to provide a clear translation of technical terms into terms that could be understood by business.

It is a simple but very efficient solution, and in this recipe, we demonstrated how a simple glossary can be created in Information Steward Metapedia, and then exported into a spreadsheet for distribution and imported back with updated information.

This is very useful if you need to gather this kind of information from users who do not have knowledge or access to Information Steward and create terms and categories directly in the system.

Creating a custom cleansing package with Cleansing Package Builder

In *Chapter 7, Validating and Cleansing Data* (see the recipe *Data Quality transforms – cleansing your data*), we already used the default cleansing package `PERSON_FIRM` available in Data Services for data cleansing tasks.

In this recipe, we will create a new cleansing package from scratch with the help of Information Steward and publish it so that it can be used in Data Services transforms.

Our new custom cleansing package will be used to determine the type of street used in the address field of the `Address` table from the OLTP database.

Getting ready

The Information Steward **Cleansing Package Builder** tool requires a sample flat file with data that is used to define cleansing rules. The following steps describe how to prepare such a flat file with sample data.

As we are going to use our custom cleansing package to cleanse the OLTP.Address table data, we will generate our sample dataset from the same table.

1. Launch **Data Services Designer** and log in to local repository.

2. Go to **Local Object Library | Formats | Flat Files**.

3. Right-click on the **Flat Files** section and create a new flat file format, PB_sample, as shown in the following screenshot:

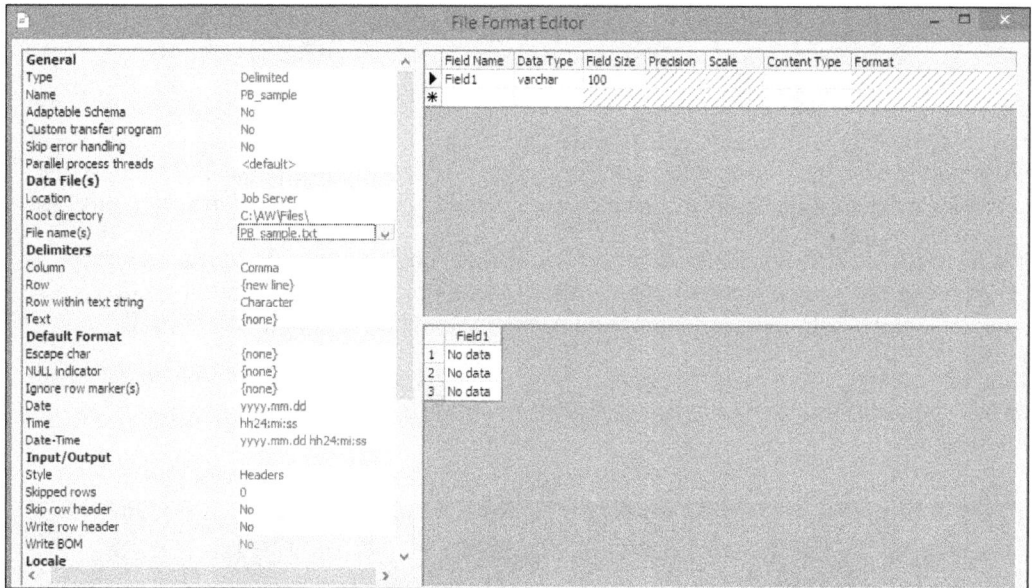

4. Create a new job and new dataflow. Inside a dataflow, put the OLTP.ADDRESS table as a source table.

5. Link the source table to Query transform and propagate only the ADDRESSLINE1 column to the output schema.

6. Link the output of a Query transform object to the target file based on the PB_sample file format created earlier.

7. Save and run the job. The PB_sample.txt file should appear in the C:\AW\Files\ folder.

How to do it...

Now, after we have created a sample file, we can finally start the Information Steward application and use **Cleansing Package Builder** to create our new custom cleansing package.

1. Launch the Information Steward application and go to the **Cleansing Package Builder** area.

2. Click on **New Cleansing Package | Custom Cleansing Package** and specify the package name and sample data file in the first step of package builder:

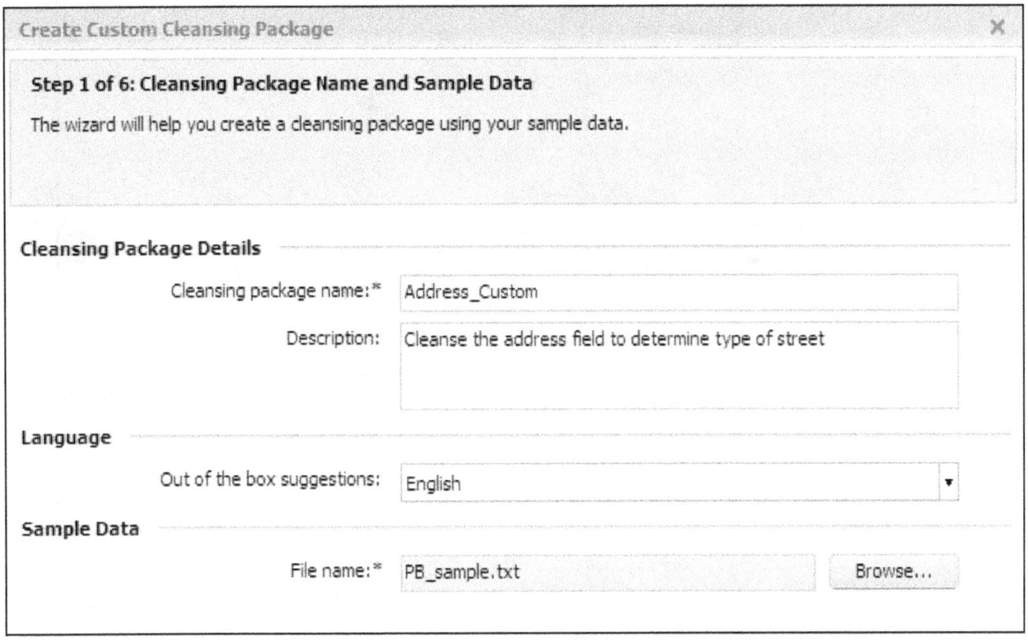

Create Custom Cleansing Package ✕

Step 1 of 6: Cleansing Package Name and Sample Data

The wizard will help you create a cleansing package using your sample data.

Cleansing Package Details

Cleansing package name:* `Address_Custom`

Description: `Cleanse the address field to determine type of street`

Language

Out of the box suggestions: `English` ▼

Sample Data

File name:* `PB_sample.txt`   Browse...

---

3. Step 2 of package builder contains information which helps to parse the sample data correctly:

4. At step 3 of the package builder, you should define the number of records taken from the sample file to be used in the package design process. The maximum number of rows is 3,000. Specify the random mechanism of obtaining rows from the sample file, and number of rows to get is 3,000.

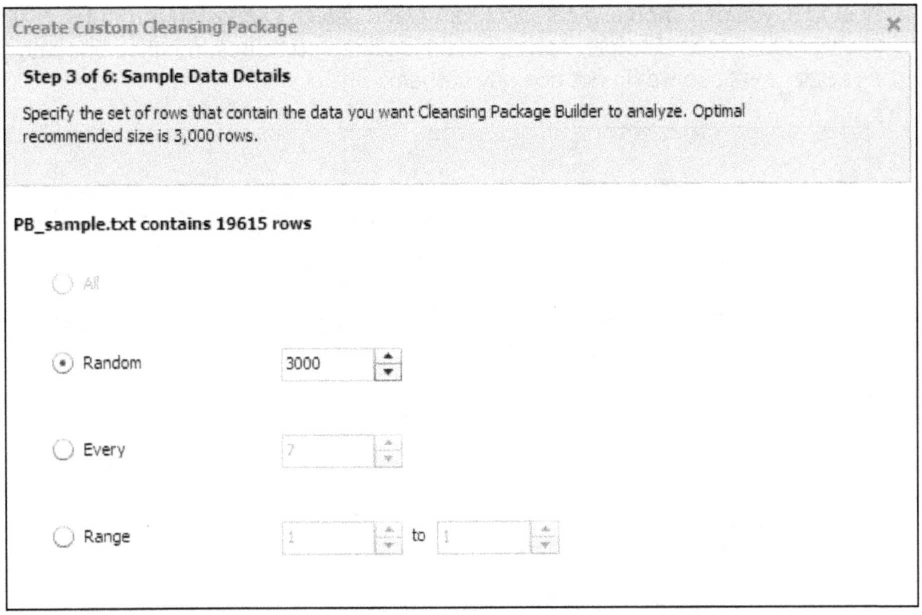

Create Custom Cleansing Package   ✕

Step 3 of 6: Sample Data Details

Specify the set of rows that contain the data you want Cleansing Package Builder to analyze. Optimal recommended size is 3,000 rows.

PB_sample.txt contains 19615 rows

○ All

⦿ Random   3000 ⏶⏷

○ Every   7 ⏶⏷

○ Range   1 ⏶⏷ to 1 ⏶⏷

5. Step 4 defines the parsing strategy:

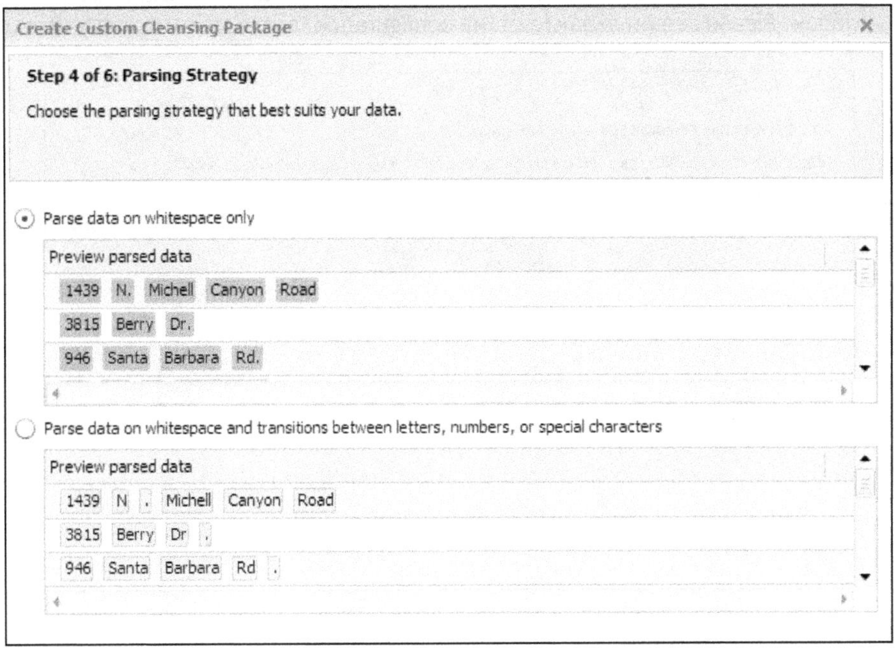

Create Custom Cleansing Package   ✕

Step 4 of 6: Parsing Strategy

Choose the parsing strategy that best suits your data.

⦿ Parse data on whitespace only

Preview parsed data

1439	N.	Michell	Canyon	Road
3815	Berry	Dr.
946	Santa	Barbara	Rd.

○ Parse data on whitespace and transitions between letters, numbers, or special characters

Preview parsed data

1439	N	.	Michell	Canyon	Road
3815	Berry	Dr	.
946	Santa	Barbara	Rd	.

6. At step 5, you can choose a category name and assign suggested attributes to it if you want to. In our example, none of the suggested attributes matches our category STREET_TYPE, so we do not tick any of them:

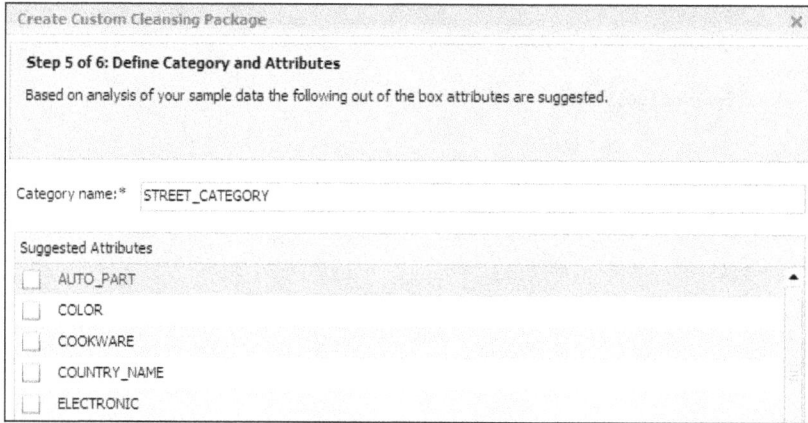

7. At step 6, we create attributes for our STREET_CATEGORY category and categorize the values found in the sample file against the attributes. The **Standard Forms** column defines the standardized form of the parsed value and the **Variations** column defines what variations will be standardized to the value specified in the Standard Forms window. Please see an example of the configuration for the DRIVE_ATTR attribute:

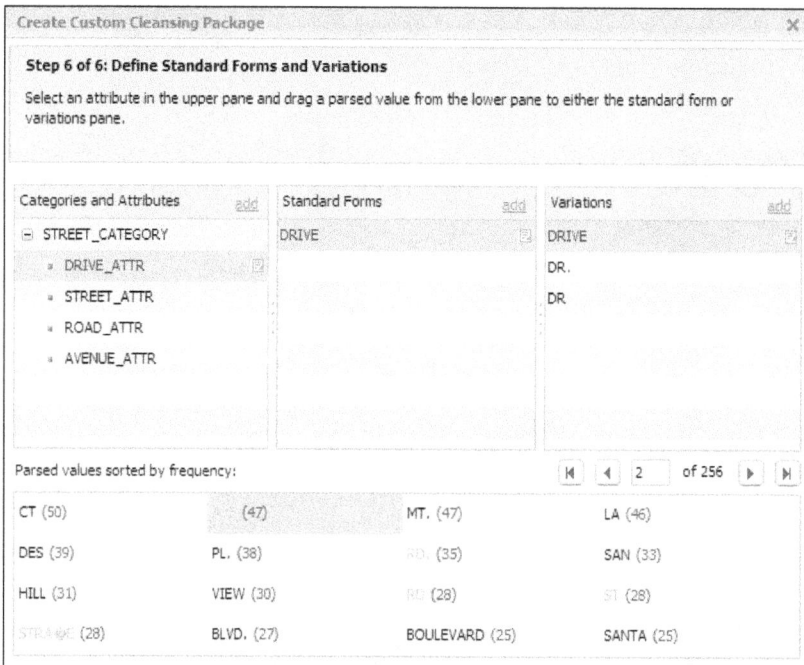

8. Another example is the STREET_ATTR attribute:

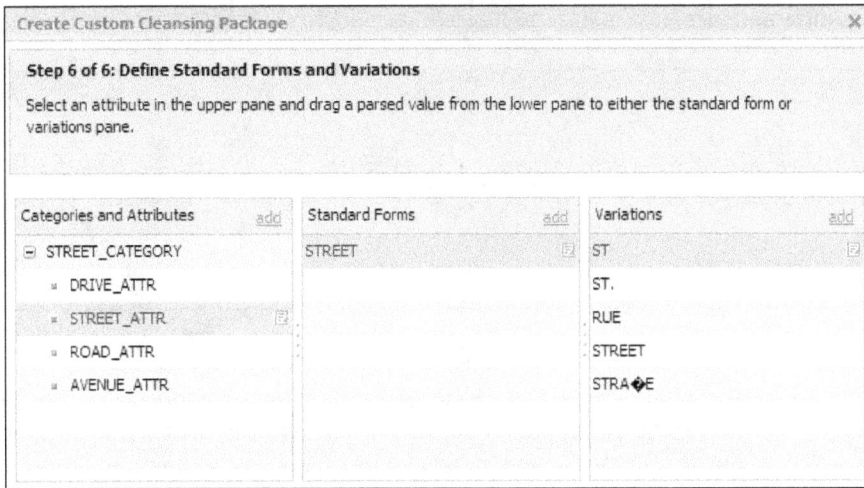

You can see how we have assigned STREET values to the standard form that are visually and syntactically very different, like *Strase* and *Rue*.

9. After step 6, you might think you have created your package and that the job is done. This is almost true. We have just passed the basic cleansing package builder wizard steps in order to create the canvas for our new package. The real work starts when you double-click on the package in the Cleansing Package Builder area and the package editor opens. It has two main editing modes: **Design** and **Advanced**. We are not going to work with the advanced design mode as it would take another book to cover all the aspects of fine-tuning your cleansing package in this mode.

10. In the meantime, you have probably noticed that our custom package was created with the lock icon:

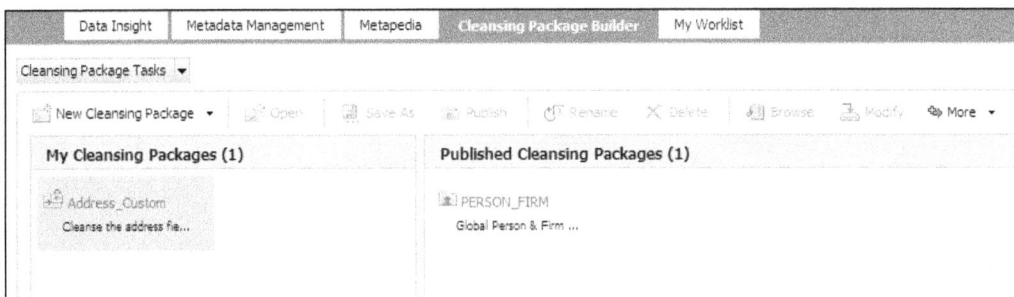

11. Information Steward needs some time to finish its background processes of the package creation, so you have to wait for couple of minutes until the icon changes to different one:

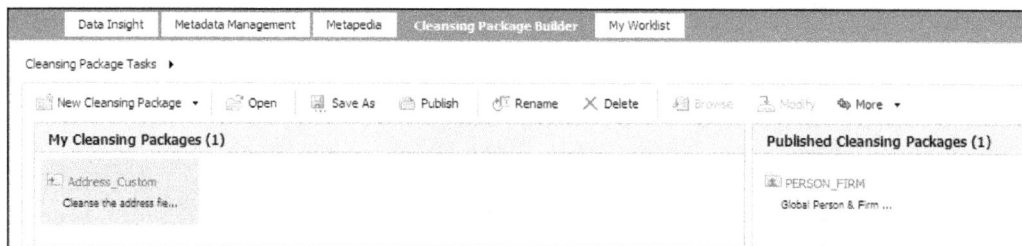

| Data Insight | Metadata Management | Metapedia | **Cleansing Package Builder** | My Worklist |

Cleansing Package Tasks ▸

New Cleansing Package ▾ | Open | Save As | Publish | Rename | ✕ Delete | Browse | Modify | More ▾

My Cleansing Packages (1)

Address_Custom
Cleanse the address fie...

Published Cleansing Packages (1)

PERSON_FIRM
Global Person & Firm ...

12. Now the package is ready to be published. Select the package on the left and click on the **Publish** button in the toolbar menu. The clock icon on the package in the right-side panel means that Information Steward is still performing background operations in order to publish the package and make it available for usage in Data Services:

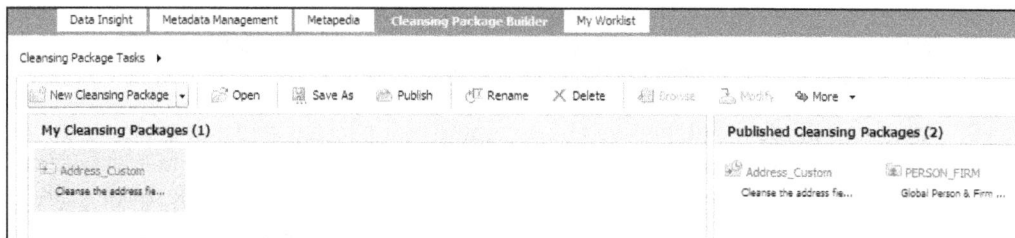

| Data Insight | Metadata Management | Metapedia | **Cleansing Package Builder** | My Worklist |

Cleansing Package Tasks ▸

New Cleansing Package ▾ | Open | Save As | Publish | Rename | ✕ Delete | Browse | Modify | More ▾

My Cleansing Packages (1)

Address_Custom
Cleanse the address fie...

Published Cleansing Packages (2)

Address_Custom
Cleanse the address fie...

PERSON_FIRM
Global Person & Firm ...

13. When the package publication is finished, the icon changes again:

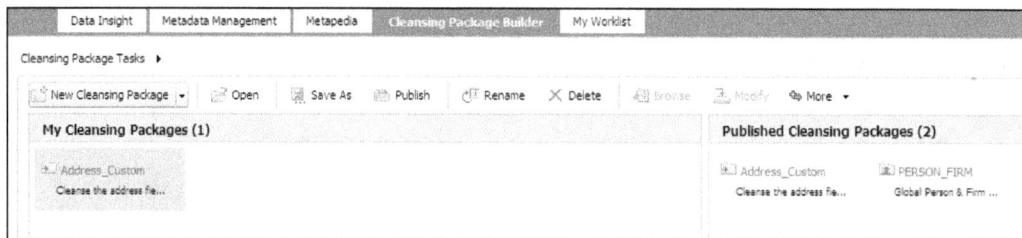

| Data Insight | Metadata Management | Metapedia | **Cleansing Package Builder** | My Worklist |

Cleansing Package Tasks ▸

New Cleansing Package ▾ | Open | Save As | Publish | Rename | ✕ Delete | Browse | Modify | More ▾

My Cleansing Packages (1)

Address_Custom
Cleanse the address fie...

Published Cleansing Packages (2)

Address_Custom
Cleanse the address fie...

PERSON_FIRM
Global Person & Firm ...

14. You can continue fine-tuning your package by entering package **Design** mode. This mode shows you the result of your actions immediately in the table at the bottom:

How it works...

Let's see how the cleansing package we created could actually be used in Data Services to perform data cleansing tasks.

1. Start **Data Services Designer**.

2. Create a new job and new dataflow.

3. Import the OLTP.ADDRESS table as a source table object.

4. Link the source table to the **Query** transform and propagate only the ADDRESSLINE1 column to the output schema as we are going to perform cleansing only on this column.

5. Link the **Query** transform object to the **Data_Cleanse** transform, which can be found in **Local Object Library | Transforms | Data Quality | Data_Cleanse**.

6. Open the imported **Data_Cleanse** object for editing in the main workspace window and go to the first tab, **Input**.

7. Map the input ADDRESSLINE1 field to the MULTILINE1 transform input field name:

8. Go to the second **Options** tab and configure the following options specifying our new created `Address_Custom` as the cleansing package:

Input	Options	Output		

Filter: ○ Best practice   ● All

Option Name	Option Value
⊞ Common	
⊞ Report And Analysis	
⊟ ⚠ **Cleansing Package**	
⚠ **Cleansing Package Name**	Address_Custom
Content Domain Sequence	GLOBAL
⚠ **Output Format**	ADDRESS_CUSTOM
⊟ ⚠ **Options**	
⊟ ⚠ **Input Word Breaker**	
⚠ **Break On Whitespace Only**	YES
⊞ Standardization Options	
⊞ Date Options	
⊞ Phone Options	
⊟ ⚠ **Parser Configuration**	
⚠ **Parser Sequence Multiline1**	STREET_CATEGORY
Parser Sequence Multiline2	
Parser Sequence Multiline3	
Parser Sequence Multiline4	
Parser Sequence Multiline5	
Parser Sequence Multiline6	
Parser Sequence Multiline7	
Parser Sequence Multiline8	
Parser Sequence Multiline9	
Parser Sequence Multiline 10	
Parser Sequence Multiline 11	
Parser Sequence Multiline 12	
⚠ **Filter Output Fields**	SHOW_ALL_FIELDS
Memory in KB for Cache	0

9. Finally, open the third tab **Output** and define the following output columns that will be produced by **Data_Cleanse** transform:

Input	Options	Output		

Filter: ○ Best practice   ● In use   ○ All

PARENT_COMPONENT	FIELD_NAME	FIELD_CLASS	Type	Content Type
☑ ▶ EXTRA1	EXTRA	PARSED	varchar(255)	None
☑ ▶ STREET_CATEGORY1	AVENUE_ATTR	STANDARDIZED	varchar(255)	None
☑ ▶ STREET_CATEGORY1	DRIVE_ATTR	STANDARDIZED	varchar(255)	None
☑ ▶ STREET_CATEGORY1	IGNORED	STANDARDIZED	varchar(255)	None
☑ ▶ STREET_CATEGORY1	ROAD_ATTR	STANDARDIZED	varchar(255)	None
☑ ▶ STREET_CATEGORY1	STREET_ATTR	STANDARDIZED	varchar(255)	None

10. Close the **Data_Cleanse** transform object and link it to newly imported template table, `ADDRESS_CLEANSE_STREET_TYPE`, created in the `DS_STAGE` datastore.

11. Your dataflow should look like that in the following figure:

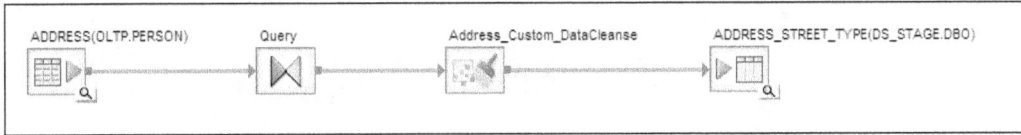

After you have saved and ran the job, you can see that the cleansing package "categorized" and populated columns have been created for each attribute of STREET_CATEGORY:

ADDRESS_STREET_TYPE(DS_STAGE.DBO)

ADDRESSLINE	AVENUE	DRIVE	ROAD	STREET	IGNORED	EXTRA
1050 Creed Ave	AVENUE	<Null>	<Null>	<Null>	<Null>	1050 Creed
1050 Creed Ave	AVENUE	<Null>	<Null>	<Null>	<Null>	1050 Creed
1050 Greenhills Circle	<Null>	<Null>	<Null>	<Null>	<Null>	1050 Greenhills Circle
1050 Greenhills Circle	<Null>	<Null>	<Null>	<Null>	<Null>	1050 Greenhills Circle
1050 Oak Street	<Null>	<Null>	<Null>	STREET	<Null>	1050 Oak
1052 Stanford Street	<Null>	<Null>	<Null>	STREET	<Null>	1052 Stanford
1053 Rain Drop Circle	<Null>	<Null>	<Null>	<Null>	<Null>	1053 Rain Drop Circle
1054 Vine Circle	<Null>	<Null>	<Null>	<Null>	<Null>	1054 Vine Circle
1054 Vloching Circle	<Null>	<Null>	<Null>	<Null>	<Null>	1054 Vloching Circle
1055 Horseshoe Road	<Null>	<Null>	ROAD	<Null>	<Null>	1055 Horseshoe
1055, rue Basse-du-Rocher	<Null>	<Null>	<Null>	STREET	<Null>	1055, Basse-du-Rocher

How well a cleansing package does its job solely depends on your ability to define rules and configure it to accommodate all possible scenarios that can be seen in your data.

For example, "Circle" has not been categorized as we simply did not define any rule regarding the "Circle" value.

This is one of the simplest cases of the cleansing task but it should give you an idea of the Information Steward capabilities in this area.

There is more...

Open a cleansing package by double-clicking and going to the **Advanced** mode to see how many options exist for creating and tuning cleansing rules and algorithms. You can define new rules and change the already created ones to make your cleansing process behave differently. The complexity of a cleansing package is restricted only by your fantasy and the complexity of the accommodated cleansing process requirements.

Index

[PACKT] PUBLISHING enterprise ⌘
professional expertise distilled

Thank you for buying
SAP Data Services 4.x Cookbook

About Packt Publishing

Packt, pronounced 'packed', published its first book, *Mastering phpMyAdmin for Effective MySQL Management*, in April 2004, and subsequently continued to specialize in publishing highly focused books on specific technologies and solutions.

Our books and publications share the experiences of your fellow IT professionals in adapting and customizing today's systems, applications, and frameworks. Our solution-based books give you the knowledge and power to customize the software and technologies you're using to get the job done. Packt books are more specific and less general than the IT books you have seen in the past. Our unique business model allows us to bring you more focused information, giving you more of what you need to know, and less of what you don't.

Packt is a modern yet unique publishing company that focuses on producing quality, cutting-edge books for communities of developers, administrators, and newbies alike. For more information, please visit our website at www.PacktPub.com.

About Packt Enterprise

In 2010, Packt launched two new brands, Packt Enterprise and Packt Open Source, in order to continue its focus on specialization. This book is part of the Packt Enterprise brand, home to books published on enterprise software – software created by major vendors, including (but not limited to) IBM, Microsoft, and Oracle, often for use in other corporations. Its titles will offer information relevant to a range of users of this software, including administrators, developers, architects, and end users.

Writing for Packt

We welcome all inquiries from people who are interested in authoring. Book proposals should be sent to author@packtpub.com. If your book idea is still at an early stage and you would like to discuss it first before writing a formal book proposal, then please contact us; one of our commissioning editors will get in touch with you.

We're not just looking for published authors; if you have strong technical skills but no writing experience, our experienced editors can help you develop a writing career, or simply get some additional reward for your expertise.

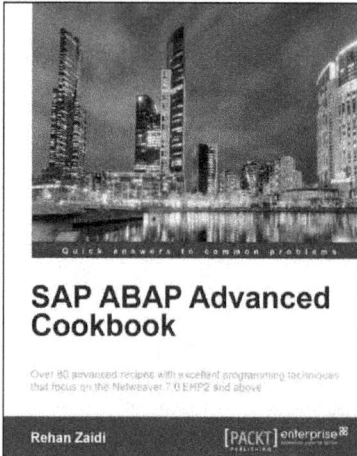

SAP ABAP Advanced Cookbook

ISBN: 978-1-84968-488-0   Paperback: 316 pages

Over 80 advanced recipes with excellent programming techniques that focus on the Netweaver 7.0 EHP2 and above

1. Full of illustrations, diagrams, and tips with clear step-by-step instructions and real time examples.

2. Get to grips with solving complicated problems using Regular Expressions in ABAP.

3. Master the creation of common Design Patterns using ABAP Objects.

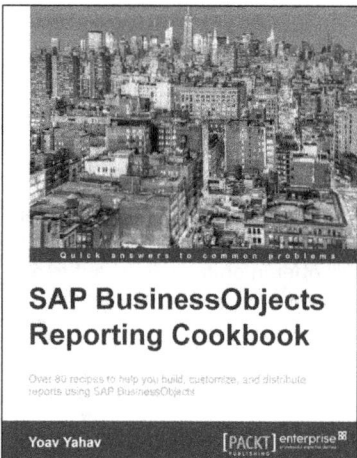

SAP BusinessObjects Reporting Cookbook

ISBN: 978-1-78217-243-7   Paperback: 380 pages

Over 80 recipes to help you build, customize, and distribute reports using SAP BusinessObjects

1. Discover how to master different business solutions which will help you deliver high quality reports to your organization and clients.

2. Work efficiently in a BI environment while keeping your data accurate, secured, and easily shared.

3. Learn how to build and format reports that will enable you to get the most useful insights from your data.

Please check **www.PacktPub.com** for information on our titles

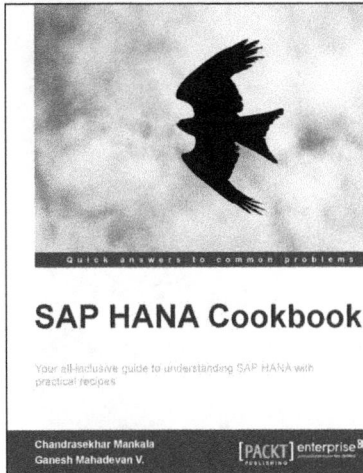

SAP HANA Cookbook

ISBN: 978-1-78217-762-3   Paperback: 284 pages

Your all-inclusive guide to understanding SAP HANA with practical recipes

1. Understand the architecture of SAP HANA, effectively transforming your business with the modeler and in-memory computing engine.

2. Learn about Business Intelligence, Analytics, and Predictive analytics on top of SAP HANA Models.

3. Gain knowledge on the process of transforming your data to insightful information using the Modeler.

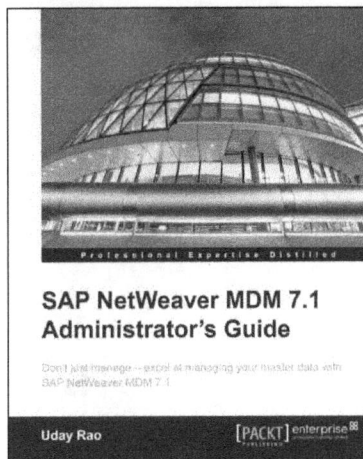

SAP NetWeaver MDM 7.1 Administrator's Guide

ISBN: 978-1-84968-214-5   Paperback: 336 pages

Don't just manage – excel at managing your master data with SAP NetWeaver MDM 7.1

1. Written in an easy-to-follow manner, and in simple language.

2. Step-by-step procedures that take you from basic to advanced administration of SAP MDM in no time.

3. Learn various techniques for effectively managing master data using SAP MDM 7.1 with illustrative screenshots.

www.ingramcontent.com/pod-product-compliance
Lightning Source LLC
Chambersburg PA
CBHW080140220326
41598CB00032B/5125